Double Ghosts

Sources and Studies in World History

Kevin Reilly, Series Editor

Double Ghosts

OCEANIAN VOYAGERS ON EUROAMERICAN SHIPS

DAVID A. CHAPPELL

M.E. Sharpe
Armonk, New York
London, England

Library of Congress Cataloging-in-Publication Data

Chappell, David A., 1946–
Double ghosts : Oceanian voyagers on Euroamerican ships / David A. Chappell.
p.   cm.
Includes bibliographical references and index.
ISBN 1–56324–998–7 (hardcover : alk. paper).
ISBN 1-56324-999-5 (paperback : alk. paper)
1. Merchant mariners—Oceania.
2. Merchant marine—Oceania.
3. Oceanians.
I. Title.
VK221.C47   1997
387.5'0995—dc21
96–48629
CIP

Printed in the United States of America

The paper used in this publication meets the minimum requirements of
American National Standard for Information Sciences—
Permanence of Paper for Printed Library Materials,
ANSI Z 39.48-1984.

BM (c)   10   9   8   7   6   5   4   3   2   1
BM (p)   10   9   8   7   6   5   4   3   2   1

To my parents, and to Uschi

~ *Contents* ~

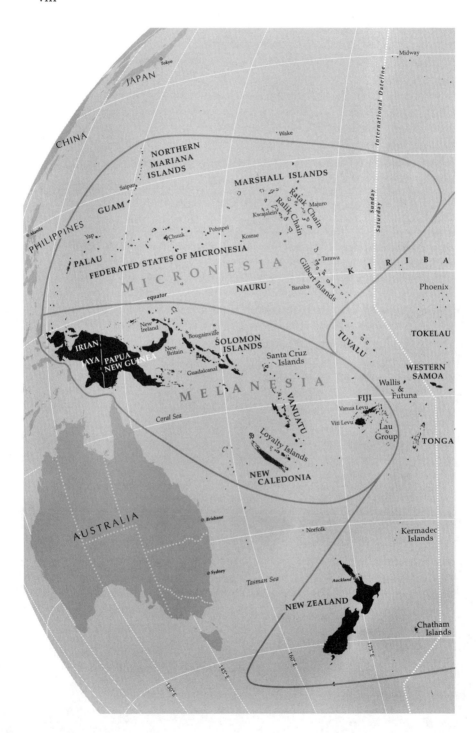

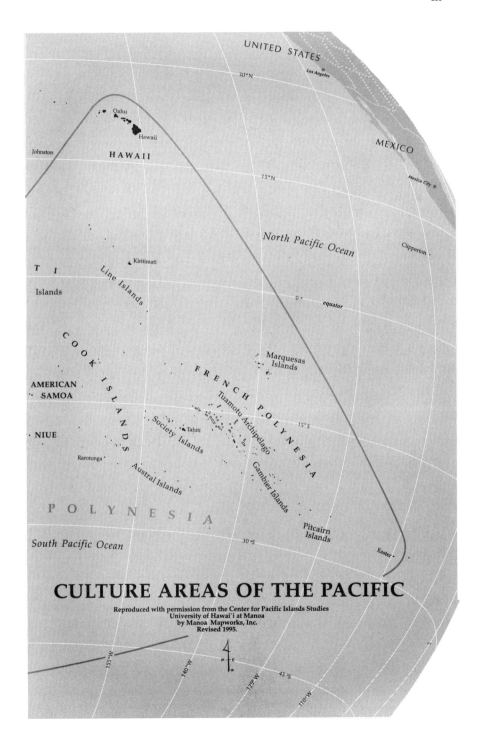

CULTURE AREAS OF THE PACIFIC

Reproduced with permission from the Center for Pacific Islands Studies
University of Hawai'i at Manoa
by Manoa Mapworks, Inc.
Revised 1995.

~ *Series Foreword* ~

Modern world history, like anthropology, has roots in Western exploration and expansion. The formative vantage point of both fields is the bow of the sailing ship. Perhaps there is no part of the world for which this viewpoint has remained more enshrined in Western culture than the Pacific Islands. Islands like Tahiti, Bora Bora, Maui, Samoa, and Fiji in Western imagination are "feminine," passive places to travel *to:* to see, paint, describe, or act upon.

In *Double Ghosts,* David Chappell reminds us that the beach has two sides, and that in any case "the border of a seafaring people does not begin on the beach but beyond it, in the waters they have fished, sailed across, and memorized for generations." For over a thousand years, the peoples of Oceania colonized the islands of the Pacific with their double-hulled canoes. The age of European and American sailing ships began a "second diaspora" for many Pacific Islanders. Chappell takes us onto these ships. We see how important these islanders were to Western sailing, whaling, charting, communication, and trade. We see the variety of roles that Pacific Islanders played: initially more often abducted guides, interpreters, and scientific "specimens," but increasingly voluntary workers, pilots, adventurers, and diplomats. By the mid-nineteenth century, Chappell tells us, perhaps a fifth of the sailors on American whaling ships alone were Pacific Islanders. Fully a fifth of Hawaiian young adult males went overseas. Many sailed the Pacific rim, some travelled to India, and some sailed the three oceans to Europe. More than half never returned, but some returned to sail again.

For the historian, these travelers were "double ghosts." Not only were their memories largely lost to the oral cultures they left behind, but only pieces of their stories were written by the Western chroniclers (and these in numerous Western languages). Their memories had been dismembered, some floating like pieces of flotsam on the largest ocean in the world, others scribbled in memoirs, histories, and novels, published in the capitals of European commerce, half a world away.

We are, therefore, doubly grateful to David Chappell for his efforts at retrieving the stories that sailed and settled on waves from New Zealand to New England, and for reorganizing them into the language of the islands, the beaches, and the seas, so that we can understand the experiences of the people as vividly as they lived their lives. He has given double ghosts redoubled life by his meticulous gathering and by his eloquent presentation.

Kevin Reilly

~ *Preface* ~

Beaches are beginnings and endings. They are the frontiers and boundaries of islands. . . . On land, behind the beach, life is lived with some fullness and with some establishment. On the sea, beyond the beach, life is partial and dependent. Ships are distorted segments living. . . .[1]

In Manu'a, the ancient sacred district of Samoa, I sat listening to a *matai* (titled chief) share stories from the mythic past. I especially enjoyed the accounts of sailing voyages between Samoa, Tonga, and Fiji. At one point I suggested that he try to write down his vast knowledge for others to study. He laughed and said he had started to do just that and wrote about thirty pages. But then hurricane Tusi came along and blew it all away! He decided his namesake, Tagaloa (the Creator), was trying to tell him something: The best place to keep history is in your head, and not everyone should have equal access to it. Before writing reached Oceania (the Pacific archipelagoes of Polynesia, Micronesia, and Melanesia), traditional orators had passed on chants, genealogies, and stories from generation to generation, like living encyclopedias.

Then in the sixteenth century, waves of European explorers, missionaries, traders, and colonial administrators began to produce written records of the region. Their accounts were often one-sided, however, and the beach of contact was really two-way: both indigenous and foreign actors played key roles. Only in the 1950s did modern historians attempt to write Oceanians more fully into their "culture contact" stories, by combining various kinds of evidence, both oral and written.[2] This book will take that process of rediscovery a step further and pursue the Pacific Islanders who crossed the beach to counter-explore Euroamerican shipping.

As early as 1522, just after Ferdinand Magellan's first contact with Guam, Oceanians began to travel aboard European ships. At first, they were kidnapped as guides or workers, but by 1767 Pacific Islanders began to volunteer to voyage on the strange vessels. By the mid-nineteenth century, perhaps as many as one-fifth of the sailors in the American whaling fleet were so-called *kanakas*—a term meaning "person" in Hawaiian, which referred to native laborers in Pacific trade pidgin. These daring travelers provided the basis for Queequeg, Herman Melville's harpooner in *Moby Dick*. They were heirs of the epic voyages of their ancestors, and also precursors of the thousands of Oceanians seeking jobs and education in industrial countries today. Like the native missionaries and migrant plantation laborers of their era, *kanaka* seamen helped to mediate between indigenous custom and the encroaching world economy. Some traveled as "ennobled tourists"—as guides for explorers and pampered specimens for naturalists—and visited Europe or New England. James Cook tried to set up "Omai," his protégé in England, like a country squire back on Huahine, and modern biographies keep Omai's memory alive.[3]

Yet recovering the stories of most other Oceanian travelers is more difficult, because the oral traditions about their journeys are scattered across a vast sea of islands, and the written data are fragmentary and dispersed through hundreds of journals, logs, and memoirs. The subjects of this study are thus double ghosts, fleeting shadows in the tombs of time. First, they are deceased physically and survive textually mainly through the biased, selective recollections of their white shipmates. Even the custom of giving *kanaka* crewmen nicknames—or just listing them as "natives"—confuses their identities. Thus disguised, they nevertheless left a dynamic impression on their chroniclers, whose caricaturish portraits reveal their own naiveté and vulnerability as they tried to depict unfamiliar "others" in their midst. Their quoted words should not be taken as literal truths but rather as glimpses of the mentalities that *kanaka*s had to endure. Consider this comment of mixed disdain and awe by a captain's son, after a 300-pound Hawaiian called Big Man fell twenty feet into a cargo hold, headfirst: "Now, in the name of common sense, of what was the skull composed that withstood such a shock? If of common material, how thick was it? In what way would a mere thirty-two pound cannon ball, dashed by a human hand, harm the head of a Kanaka?"[4] What we can conclude is that Big Man fell and fortunately survived. The rest is condescending sarcasm.

Fortunately, a score of oral traditions help us to test that tone against indigenous perspectives. For example, on the atoll of Ebon in the Marshall Islands, a young man called Lojeik once paddled his canoe out beyond the reef to test the intentions of a visiting ship. The evil strangers kidnapped Lojeik, however, and after many years, his family gave him up for dead. In revenge, the villagers plotted to kill some sailors who came ashore from a later ship. As they discussed among themselves which warrior would take out each stranger, one visitor surprised them by speaking in their own language: he warned them not to attack because the white men had powerful weapons. The Ebonese scoffed at this threat, but the interpreter told his crewmates to demonstrate their guns by firing at a coconut tree. They did so, shooting off fronds and nuts with loud noises in a cloud of smoke. Finally, the speaker opened up his sailor shirt and revealed his warrior tattoo—it was Lojeik![5]

This tale clearly recalls how much ship life had changed Lojeik, to the point where his own family supposedly did not recognize him at first. Perhaps even his story identity comes from a nickname like Jake. Moreover, despite his unhappy departure and dramatic homecoming, his *kanaka* life beckoned him on. The tradition goes on to say that Lojeik chose to remain at sea for many years before finally returning home for good. Why? Whoever he was before shipping out had been reborn at sea, by undergoing rites of passage, cross-cultural initiations into the global maritime circuit. This was the second way our subjects became ghosts: many actually perished overseas or stayed abroad, but even those who survived to come home were recrossing a *limen,* or threshold, between worlds. Anthropologist Victor Turner once described three stages in initiation rituals, which will provide a format for this book. First, the neophyte separates from his previous identity in society, sometimes through symbolic forms of death. Then he enters a liminal state "betwixt and between" what he has been and will become. In that phase, he is "structurally invisible," like an embryo taking shape out of sight, or a student learning new skills and roles. According to Turner, "novel configurations and ideas may arise" because transitional beings have no rank or property of their own. They must submit to the authority of their instructors, even during testing ordeals, and they tend to relate to fellow initiates as equals, who are also becoming. It is a time to reflect, to shed old habits and try out new things. Ideally, the last stage involves returning to society with "more alert faculties . . . to become once more subject to custom and law." The implication is that the graduate of liminality will contribute more fully to the community because of what he has learned during the rite of passage.[6]

Yet the story of Lojeik suggests that liminality itself could become a way of life for some voyagers. As we shall see, they might never readjust to their homeland, if they even come back to try. Others did return, as Lojeik finally did, and contributed linguistic and technical knowledge to their chiefs. On Euroamerican vessels, ennobled tourists usually lived like the ship's officers in aft cabins, while *kanaka* crewmen shared the crowded forecastle with fellow workers. Once they infiltrated foreign shipping, Pacific Islanders learned to play roles in a theatrical drama with many stage sets and costume changes. Collectively, they came to resemble Joseph Conrad's "secret sharer of my cabin and my thoughts, as though he were my second self . . . striking out for a new destiny."[7] The first two chapters of this book will describe the historical context and process of shipping out. The next two will examine the initiations and ordeals of *kanakas* aboard ship, and the next three their cross-cultural adventures as sailors in Oceania, around the Pacific rim, and farther afield in Europe and the United States. After undergoing all those rites of passage, survivors returned home as prodigal "ghosts," changed beings. The last two chapters are reflections on their collective legacy and its significance.

Such voyagers, whether privileged or proletarian, took grave risks, but they show that Pacific Islanders did not simply wait for the outside world to overwhelm them. The border of a seafaring people does not begin on the beach but beyond it, in the waters they have fished, sailed across, and memorized for generations. When James Cook explored the Society Islands in 1769, he was guided by a local navigator, Tupaia, who could even translate for Cook with New Zealand Maori—distant "relatives" for a Ra'iatean like Tupaia. *Kanakas* thus exchanged their own maritime heritage for new firsthand skills and transacted nautical adventures in strange vessels, leaving a legacy of innovation. Whether they wound up as beachcombers on other islands, after being dropped on a generic reef before their ship left the Pacific, or managed to return home, they could often parlay their exotic travels into service to chiefs as interpreters, trade negotiators, war leaders, or gunsmiths. Foreign ships in the Pacific also wanted native seamen who knew the region. One nineteenth-century captain wrote, "No one ought to attempt a voyage through the South Sea Islands without carrying an extra crew of this kind."[8]

Herman Melville, Joseph Conrad, Richard Henry Dana, and Louis Becke, among others, all turned their seafaring into maritime literature, where the difference between fiction and memoirs can get murky. Their *kanakas* are both projections from Euroamerican imaginings onto darker-skinned peoples and archetypes for the roles assigned to Oceanian seamen. Melville, for example, lionized Queequeg in a playful way that he no doubt expected would sell to his American audience:

> In Queequeg's ambitious soul, lurked a strong desire to see something more of Christendom than a specimen whaler or two. His father was a high Chief, a king; his uncle a High Priest; and on the maternal side he boasted aunts who were the wives of unconquerable warriors. There was excellent blood in his veins—royal stuff; though sadly vitiated, I fear, by the cannibal propensity he nourished in his untutored youth.[9]

Conrad does the opposite in *Lord Jim,* in which he describes a dark Solomon Islander kidnapped in his youth, whose captain ordered him to murder people in the night "as you send a spaniel after a stick in the water."[10]

Embedded in these characters are Euroamerican notions of "noble and ignoble savages." After all, Robinson Crusoe's "Friday" had already set the
standard for servile propriety—he was even escaping from cannibals.[11]
High-born Queequeg rose to harpooner, a typical promotion on whalers, yet
Conrad's unnamed Solomon Islander showed the dependent behavior of
hostages to fate: he had to play another game to survive. Chiefly voyagers
like Tupaia sometimes enjoyed proper respect, but in the early days even
low-born Islanders like Omai might masquerade in the *limen*.

*Kanaka*s also worked on land in the Pacific basin, from the fur trade in the
American Northwest to sandalwood trading in Melanesia, and in the second
half of the nineteenth century, ships recruited 120,000 indentured laborers for
plantations in Queensland, Australia, or in Fiji or Samoa. This labor trade has
so far attracted more research and writing, because its *kanaka*s tend to be better
documented than native seamen. A relevant issue that arises from that
historiography, however, is voluntarism versus coercion: To what degree were
the recruits choosing to embark, or were they "blackbirded" (kidnapped), and
how harsh was their work environment? In short, should they be portrayed as
exploited victims or as opportunists? Clive Moore argues that coercion and
exploitation did occur, but after British regulation began in the 1870s the main
form of kidnapping was cultural: the recruiters knew better than the Islanders
what signing a three-year contract really meant.[12] Recent studies of plantation
labor resistance reveal that *kanaka*s had a spectrum of options, from accommodation (to survive under harsh conditions) to overt rebellion. One tactic was
what James Scott calls the "weapons of the weak"—acts of noncooperation,
such as sabotage or malingering, that renegotiated power relations.[13]

The evidence on maritime *kanaka*s is primarily anecdotal but suggests
varying combinations of accommodation and resistance. This study will
draw on the experiences of 250 individuals, following them off their islands, onto ships and other beaches and, if they survived, home again. The
reader is advised not to worry about remembering the names of all the
characters in the story that follows, though some will become memorable as
recurring motifs, but instead to focus on the collective experience that their
fragmentary adventures bring to life. As frustratingly incomplete and superficial as the data are, these *kanaka*s clamor (in my thoughts) to be resur-
rected, and perhaps doing so will inspire more searches by local specialists
for oral traditions, which probably exist on every island. This book, then,
attempts to open up a neglected but significant topic. Meanwhile, the plantation labor trade, Polynesian missions to the western Pacific, and ongoing
interisland canoe contacts are parallel historical phenomena that overlapped
with *kanaka* voyaging, as we shall see.

To a certain extent, I can empathize with the Pacific Islanders who boarded foreign ships to see the world. I still remember August 1971, when I rode a launch out into Singapore harbor at six in the morning to find a ship, any ship, that would take me anywhere in the world. I was too young to be truly afraid, only curious—we all think we are immortal in our twenties. Experiential travel is a form of heroism, when you look back on it, but at the time it simply seems necessary, a personal rite of passage we seek out to learn more about the world and ourselves. Every new thing we touch, every communicative gesture, strange vowel, or initiative food we try adds another degree of difference, of "otherness," to whomever we might have been if we had stayed home. On one ship, the noise of the engine room made it hard for my supervisor to hear my name clearly, so he called me "Bill." We were too busy for me to correct him, so I kept that name to the end of the voyage, partly out of convenience and partly out of curiosity: Who might this Bill be? As we shall see, this liminal renaming was a common experience for ennobled tourists and *kanaka*s alike, because Euroamericans found it hard to pronounce their real names correctly.

On another ship, off the cape of southern India, I saw converging ocean currents bring together a cross-section of sea life—bewildered turtles, colorful snakes, playful dolphins, schools of wayward fish, even a long trail of debris, perhaps from some river flash flood, that stretched from horizon to horizon. Like a fragile message across time and space, the flotsam held its scroll-like form only until new currents and winds muddled the record. Doing history is a bit like that: gathering textual artifacts, sifting and arranging them into an interpretation before the weather changes. Like all stories, this one will be revised by future tellers, perhaps with new insights or details, because each generation interprets the past with fresh priorities. What we produce, like that trail of former lives across the sea, is ultimately as subjective as a sailor's tale in which "truth" is less important than persuasion, enlightenment, or simply entertainment.

I would like to thank people who have helped to guide me on my own literary journey, most notably Brij Lal, David Hanlon, Jerry Bentley, John Stephan, Robert Kiste, Harry Maude, Greg Dening, Francis Hezel, Alan Howard, Jan Rensel, Rhys Richards, Jerry Knight, Lenn Lenja, Jane Moulin, the University of Hawai'i History Department faculty and staff, the Hamilton Library staff, and the East-West Center, which financed the research and writing of my Ph.D. dissertation. I would also like to thank Stephen Dalphin and Esther Clark of M.E. Sharpe, Paul Finkelman, Philip Curtin, Clive Moore, Ron Crocombe, Ian Campbell, and Kevin Reilly for their help in getting the manuscript into published form. Any failings are my own.

Note

I have tried, when feasible, to use the modern names of Pacific Island groups (e.g., Kiribati, not Gilbert Islands) and the indigenous forms of individual Islander names. If, however, no "authentic" equivalent was readily available for the sometimes odd spellings of native names by outsiders, I have used the form most common in the written records rather than create even more "Bills." Finally, in Fijian, "c" is pronounced as "th," "d" as "nd," and "b" as "mb"; Samoan has an understood "n" before a "g"; and "ti" is pronounced "s" in i-Kiribati.

Double Ghosts

～ 1 ～

A Second Diaspora

Close to the sky-eyes of the night,
Dancing with the souls of dead warriors,
You shall sail away in the canoe of the Sky-God—
In Taua's canoe, to the home of the trade-wind.

—Pukapukan chant[1]

The Pacific covers one-third of the earth's surface, more than all the land masses combined, and its maximum width reaches halfway around the world. For millennia, sheer distance created an equilibrium of disinterest that divided the region into local networks. Oceania, the inner Pacific, was a galaxy of volcanic archipelagoes hovering just out of reach of the Pacific rim civilizations. Yet thousands of years ago, daring sailors began to navigate eastward from Southeast Asia to discover almost every inhabitable island. This epic series of small-scale migrations was a diaspora, or dispersal, across a vast "sea of islands," a holistic circuit nurtured and expanded by ongoing voyages.[2] For example, oral tradition says that Hawai'i Loa found the islands that bear his name on a fishing expedition and later returned with his family. He broke off contact with Tahiti when his relatives there began to offer human sacrifices to a war god. But later the priest Pa'ao traveled north to Hawai'i, after a dispute with his own brother that took the lives of both their sons. Pa'ao introduced sacrificial temples to the war god Ku and purified the chiefly bloodline by bringing high-born Pili from Tahiti.[3] Oceania's geographic isolation was thus more relative than absolute.

In the sixteenth century, European ships began to arrive in the Pacific—so (mis)named by Ferdinand Magellan after surviving stormy Cape Horn. Apart from Guam, on the galleon route between Manila and Mexico, the Spanish impact was fleeting. Yet by the eighteenth century, scientific explorers and China traders had begun to integrate Oceania into global commerce. Gradually, many indigenous seafarers transferred their maritime heritage to the new vessels, in what became a second diaspora. By the 1840s, thousands of Hawaiians sailed on whaling ships as far as New England. Others joined the Tahitian royal guard, trapped for furs in Northwest America, or preached Christianity in Micronesia. Perhaps thirty thousand Oceanians worked and traveled on foreign ships during the first century of regular contact.[4] From "Joseph Freewill," a Mapian who climbed the mast of a ship in 1767 and refused to let go, to King Kalakaua of Hawai'i, the first monarch to travel around the world in 1881, Oceanians used the new vessels to launch another era of voyaging. This chapter examines the historical context for that second diaspora. Today, a third diaspora has taken half a million Oceanians from resource-poor islands to industrial countries in the anglophone Pacific rim.[5]

Ancient Maritime Frontiers

Before European contact, interaction between Oceanians and Pacific rim peoples was negligible. Native Americans like the Aleuts of Alaska were audacious seafarers, fishing and seal-hunting in cold northern waters, but they lacked sails and the westerly *kuroshio* current was most likely to carry them southeast along the American coast. Pacific Northwest peoples built large sea-going canoes and hunted whales, but they believed that the ocean had a distant fog-bound edge over which no human could return.[6] Peru was a more likely source of visitors, as Thor Heyerdahl's *Kon Tiki* voyage proved in 1947 by sailing before the prevailing easterlies to the Tuamotus. Native Peruvian merchants had once plied their coast in balsa rafts; according to legend, Inca Tupac Yupanqui sailed west and returned with "black people, gold, a chair of brass and a skin and jawbone of a horse."[7] Yet lasting cultural exchange between Oceania and Native America was perhaps limited to trading the South American sweet potato for the Asian coconut.[8]

Nor did the superpowers of East Asia explore the inner Pacific, despite some speculation about ancient contact with America. Japan's seafaring was directed primarily at Asia, though *kuroshio* castaways could have arrived in the Americas and Hawai'i. China's seagoing junks sailed as far south and west as Africa, but a strong current was thought to drag ships down into a whirlpool in the middle of the "eastern ocean." Another belief was that three islands rich in gold, silver, and an herb that conferred immortality lay hidden in mists far to the east. Early Chinese emperors sent a series of expeditions, one of them supposedly carrying three thousand male and female virgins, to find the magic isles, without success. Yet when the Chinese first moved seaward down the Huang He valley, they encountered tattooed maritime peoples who ranged as far as Taiwan and beyond.[9] In fact, insular Southeast Asia was the ancestral home of today's Oceanians.

Austronesian-speakers carried neolithic tools, root crops, livestock, and navigation skills eastward, and Malay or Bugis traders later followed, nurturing a sporadic, indirect link between their Chinese and Japanese customers and Melanesia, the gateway to Oceania.[10] Unlike other peoples, Pacific Islanders regarded the open ocean as a road map, not a barrier. Their navigators worshipped nature and used currents, stars, and other signs to sail routes that mythic heroes had pioneered in double-hulled canoes. Since 1976, reenactments by canoe replicas such as the *Hokule'a* have demonstrated that Oceanians were capable of long-distance navigation as far as two thousand miles. Ancient chants record such deeds in detail: "The handle of my steering paddle thrills to action, my paddle named Kautu-ki-te-rangi. It guides to the horizon but dimly discerned . . . the untraced path our ship must go."[11] Oral tradition claims that on one of his journeys north, Hawai'i Loa encountered and recruited "people with slanting eyes"—the lost Chinese virgins? Hotu Matua's Marquesans followed a dream upwind into the rising sun to Easter Island. Sacred Ra'iatea, northwest of Tahiti, sent out many voyagers, such as Kupe, who reportedly chased a supernatural octopus to Aotearoa (New Zealand). The theatrical *arioi* of Ra'iatea made offerings to 'Oro before setting out on missionary journeys: "Give us a breeze, to encompass us from behind, that we may sail as smoothly as upon a bed."[12]

Even after colonizing uninhabited islands, seamen of the first diaspora continued to voyage, founding Polynesian outliers in Micronesia and Melanesia and establishing exchange networks that linked communities. The large, populous, and culturally diverse islands of Melanesia, in particular, developed intricate trade systems based on silent barter, pidgin languages, and shell money. In the Trobriand Islands of eastern New Guinea, voyagers exchanged shell necklaces for armbands in the Kula ring circuit to build personal bonds and facilitate peaceful trading. The nearby Siassi became professional middlemen who traded mats for pottery, for wooden bowls, and, ultimately, for the pigs they needed in rituals. Known as congenial, smooth-talking con men, the Siassi say, "People pay us for our sweat."[13] In the Micronesian *sawei* system, canoes from a dozen atolls sailed west as far as seven hundred miles to the high island of Yap, where they exchanged gifts with fictive "kin" as insurance against natural disasters. The chiefly families of Fiji, Tonga, and Samoa exchanged prestige goods and spouses in an intricate political arena, and a Rarotongan author, studying his own family genealogy, argues that interisland voyaging helped to spread pan-Polynesian customs.[14]

So much circulation demanded a protocol for receiving visitors. On Ulithi atoll in the Carolines, even returning travelers were expected to announce themselves formally at the men's meeting house: "To violate this
necessary gesture is considered to be an outrageous breach . . . punishable
in drastic ways."[15] Castaways in Oceania often had their canoes and possessions confiscated by their hosts in return for being accepted into the community. In Palau, the world beyond the horizon was regarded as a source of
potential danger, so visitors were conducted to a chief, who assessed their
possible impact. If not killed outright, they might become servile "drift-
wood," but over time their descendants could move up in rank to become
"new sails" with some access to land, then "old sails" with eligibility to
hold lesser offices, and finally "trees" who could earn high titles. In Fiji,
newcomers had to show proper respect as guests for generations. Chiefs
might receive better treatment, as in Aotearoa, where later Maori migrants
intermarried with their predecessors but assumed commanding rank. In
northern Vanuatu, ambitious leaders monopolized trade and took titles com-
memorating their journeys to "the end of the earth."[16]

Euroamerican Contact

From first contact with Magellan off Guam in 1521, indigenous canoes
approached and surrounded the new vessels, intimidating ship crews who
were extremely far from home. Magellan had not only crossed the Pacific
but also missed every inhabited island, so his men were starving and sick.
Antonio Pigafetta complained that Chamorros "boarded the ships and stole
one thing after another, to such an extent that our men could not protect
their belongings." In the ensuing violence, the Spaniards destroyed most of
the huts and boats in a village and may have fed the intestines of dead
natives to vitamin-starved shipmates. In 1595, four hundred Marquesans in
seventy canoes greeted their first Spanish visitors. They swarmed over Alvaro de Mendaña's ship and boldly handled whatever was within reach.
They studied the Spaniards' beards and faces, danced and clowned with
foreign shirts around their necks, cut off slices of meat in the cook's galley,
and tried to haul the ship to the beach with a rope. Mendaña's conquistadores began shooting and by their pilot's own estimate killed two hundred
Marquesans.[17]

Such extroverted greetings were not as common in the xenophobic
Tuamotus or the parts of New Guinea that had been exposed to slave
raiding,[18] but it seems clear that many Oceanians preferred to learn the
strangers' intentions before they reached the beach. This testing process
might include racing foreign vessels with swift local sailing craft or cling-

ing to the gunwales of boats going ashore. When Samuel Wallis "discovered" Tahiti for England in 1767, more than a hundred canoes carrying eight hundred Tahitians came out to explore his ship. By 1789, Tahitians had "encompassed" European ships. An Englishman lamented,

> we were so crowded by the natives that we could scarce move, or hear each other speak; which occasioned our officers some trouble in working the ship. . . . Our guests took up their abode with us without the least ceremony, asked for combs and scissors, and cut and dressed each other's hair, admiring themselves at the same time in the looking-glass. At dinner, they made no scruple of helping themselves the instant the victuals were placed on the table; one seizing the head of a large pig, and another a whole quarter. . . . Our visitors, not content with pestering us with their company in the daytime, took it into their heads to stay on board all night; and talked so much, and so loud, that it was impossible for us to get any sleep . . . we never went on shore without being followed by a crowd of people of both sexes, and all ages, who strove to get near and touch us, some of them stroking their hands down our backs and sides, and others admiring our clothes.[19]

Evidence suggests that, at first, some Oceanians may have regarded the newcomers as more than mere curiosities, because humans with "sparkling eyes" could be spirits in disguise. Tahitian canoers hovered around Wallis's vessel "and lookt at our ship with great astonishment." After debating among themselves, they made a lengthy speech, holding up leaves as peace offerings. Finally, "one fine brisk young man" climbed up the side and into the rigging, laughing and staring. He would not come down or accept gifts, however, until "several of the Indians allong side made Long talks and throwd in several Branches of plantain Trees."[20] In Hawai'i, ruling chiefs were believed to have divine *mana* (power), so Captain James Cook was welcomed as royalty by commoners falling "flat on their faces . . . till I made signs to them to rise." Two men holding pigs circled him a dozen times, while others chanted prayers. His arrival coincided with the Makahiki festival, and some priests seemed to have greeted him as the returning god Lono.[21] Some Maoris were also unsure about Europeans in the beginning. One remembered running away as a child from Cook's crew,

> but, as the goblins stayed some time, and did not do any harm to our braves, we came back one by one, and gazed at them, and we stroked their garments with our hands, and we were pleased with the whiteness of their skins and the blue of the eyes of some of them.[22]

Whatever their first impressions, Pacific Islanders soon decided that white men were human, because they physically consumed (and passed) food, yielded to the temptations of women, angered over petty property loss (after receiving offerings), and felt pain.[23] Once the mystique wore off,

Oceanians wanted the exotic material goods that foreign ships carried, from metal to ornaments. Accounts of native "theft" and consequent violence pervade the early records, because European explorers were only passing through and defended their notions of private property against Oceanian customs of communal sharing. Moreover, what were the rules in a *limen* between cultures, a no man's land that challenged assumptions and bred innovations? Communication was a basic problem, since neither side knew the other's language. The Marquesans greeted the Spaniards as friends, but the pilot wrote, "it was not understood why they gave us a welcome, or what was their intention. . . . The evil things that happened might have been avoided if there had been someone to make us understand each other." Instead of responding kindly, the Spanish shot the natives for sport and even stole the offerings they had left at their temples.[24]

Clearly, not only Oceanians tested property rights. John Marra, a member of Cook's crew in Tahiti, excused theft because it also existed in England: "Is it not very natural, when a people see a company of strangers come among them, and without ceremony cut down their trees, gather their fruits, seize their animals, and, in short, take whatever they want, that such a people should use as little ceremony with the strangers, as the strangers do with them?"[25] Yet Cook was brutal on his last voyage, destroying canoes and houses on Mo'orea because of a stolen goat, and flogging, cutting off the ears, and shaving the head of a Boraboran who stole a sextant. In Hawai'i, oral tradition records that canoers saw on Cook's ship a wealth of iron, something they knew, perhaps from flotsam, and regarded as sacred. A warrior named Kapupu'u declared, "I'll go and gather that treasure because that's how I make my living, merely scooping up whatever I can." The British said the first native who boarded Cook's ship quickly overcame his awe and "without asking any questions" began to take the ship's lead and line, saying, "I am only going to put it into my boat." He was shot and killed, but ashore other warriors tried to confiscate the ship's boat until the British killed another man. Only then did priests warn people not to anger the whites. At Kealakekua Bay, trying to seize a Hawaiian ruler to recover a stolen boat cost Cook his life.[26]

Some early visitors claimed that native theft from foreigners normally occurred on shipboard, not on shore, where fear of supernatural recourse usually kept Hawaiians, Tahitians, and Maoris from stealing among themselves. Sea captains tried to protect their limited capital by creating borders with tents, ropes, bayonets, or fixed visiting hours and by demonstrating their firearms.[27] Even so, their ships became places to break the rules, as Oceanians knew them. In first encounters on deck, they seemed to find things so unusual that they felt released and expressed themselves in playful ways. Cook described it best in Hawai'i: "their eyes were continually flying from object to object, the wildness of their looks and actions fully express'd their astonishment. . . ." When a chief could not resist the temptation to steal some iron, "he was exceedingly abash'd and frighten'd at being detected, and offer'd a very fine red Cloak he had on as a ransom for his pardon." Ship visits gradually undermined the traditional Hawaiian *kapu* (law) system until it was abolished in 1819.[28]

Oceanians coped with foreign shipping in various ways, from giving the vessels new names in their own language to capturing and looting ships in revenge for mistreatment. They also learned to get exotic trophies by exchanging gifts, island-style. Wallis turned his cannons on crowds of "impudent" Tahitians who tried to take iron from his ship, but he later befriended their chiefess Purea, who wept when he left. In fact, local elders quickly saw how longingly Wallis's sailors looked at Tahitian women and ordered young dependents to line up on the beach. In sign language, they told the visitors to choose as many girls as they liked for sex, and to give iron nails in return. When a French ship arrived the next year, Tahitian canoes greeted it with naked women crying "tayo" (friend). In addition, local men exchanged names with white seamen and were helpful in return for gifts. By 1797, the missionary ship *Duff* found that if each Englishman chose a native friend to carry his knife and other valuables, thefts stopped. In 1824, a Russian captain noted, "in less than an hour these friendly allies were soon walking in couples, arm in arm, about the deck, as though they had been acquainted for years."[29] Such personal interchanges spread around the Pacific like a liminal frontier, and peaceful trade began.

Whether swimming or in canoes, salesmen climbed aboard even before ships anchored, carrying their wares on their backs and turning the deck into a lively marketplace: "Each one more eager than the last, they endeavoured to barter their oranges, lemons, cocoa-nuts, bananas, pine-apples, hens and eggs."[30] One visitor was amazed by the amount of food and handicrafts brought to his cabin: "The audacious islander advanced toward us as far as four sea leagues; choppy waves, storms don't frighten him from his adventurous course: he seemed, from his fragile boat, to defy peril."[31] By 1824, even the Tahitian royal family had difficulty boarding a ship through the throngs of "bummers" (vendors). Like the Siassi, Oceanian traders quickly learned to drive a hard bargain. As early as 1565, the Chamorros of Guam used sign language to barter baskets of provisions for Spanish iron. But the bottoms of their baskets of food were filled with sand and stones and their gourds of coconut oil concealed seawater; later, bales of rice purchased by ships contained sand and rocks.[32]

In 1767, Wallis's shipmaster wrote of Tahitians, "the people of this

Country deale very cunningly, if they bring down three or four different things to sell, they always indeavour to sell the worst first, and if they get what they want for any trifeling thing that they can easily Spear [spare] they carry back their Hogs pigs and fowls." Women were soon asking for iron spikes, not just nails.[33] Another captain claimed that Tahitians "subtlely tricked" their first Spanish visitors with "old and worn mats and scraps of native cloth, which they sold as new, but were often full of perfectly disguised mends and patches." Tahitians bought a jacket from a Russian officer with "a pearl which had been ingeniously made out of an oyster-shell." Foreign beads and trinkets soon lost their appeal, as Marquesans showed in 1798: "the small looking-glasses, and bright buttons, when handed to them they would turn over and over, examining every part very carefully before they gave up their articles, then after pondering the pros and cons, they would return the glasses, and point to the pieces of iron hoop."[34]

Ship captains soon called Hawaiians the "Jews of the South Seas" and likened Maoris to "the most crafty Jews on the Royal Exchange."[35] Fijians and New Caledonians received similar grudging tribute by the 1840s. If their first price was agreed to, they often raised it even higher. Pacific Islanders might sell half-finished mats rolled up to look whole and quickly paddle off, or sell woven hats, steal them back, and resell them to the next (or same) ship.[36] Systems developed in which Oceanians used white flags as signals for trade, exchanged goods with ships via ropes or baskets, waited their turn to bargain, arranged precise terms, and kept careful accounts. The "curios" they sold to sailors were the beginnings of tourist art, and visitors bemoaned the natives' knowledge of Spanish dollar values. Islanders also added the new imports to traditional exchange networks, sending steel tools to outer islands, and they used foreign ships to acquire prestige items of Pacific origin, such as fine *tapa* (bark cloth), red bird feathers, *tabua* (whales' teeth), or stone currency. In Fiji, Euroamerican whaling caused inflation in *tabua*, gifts that sealed alliances.[37]

Maritime Transformations

The detailed data collected by naval explorers enticed Euroamerican traders into the Pacific. The Spanish galleons had bypassed most of Oceania and used Mexican silver to buy Asian luxuries in Manila, but after the 1780s Anglo-American merchants catered to the China market with furs from the American Northwest (via Hawai'i) and island products like sandalwood and bêche-de-mer (sea slug). Whalers, sealers, and the British convict colony in Australia also purchased provisions from Oceania. Increasingly, Pacific Islanders became dependent on imports they could not replicate: Europe sold manufactured goods so cheaply that it became easier to buy an ax than to make an adze. By 1839, Hawai'i imported four times as much as it exported, and many Maoris and Tahitians had begun to regard imports as necessities. The traders were joined by missionaries in vessels of their own, who taught not only Christianity but also "civilizing" manual skills to produce, among other things, exports.[38]

Frequently visited ports adapted to foreign needs: ferrying or swimming out water casks; providing recreation; doing laundry; raising potatoes, wheat, corn, cabbages, and melons; and selling as many as four hundred hogs at a time. Young men learned to amuse ship crews by diving for nails, pins, buttons, coins, tobacco, or bits of iron hoop—using the trick that such items often zigzagged through the water more slowly than a man could swim. They also worked as commercial divers to repair ship hulls, untangle cables, or retrieve lost anchors and pulleys. Oceanians served as pilots and interpreters, hauled ships into port, worked the docks, and learned shipbuilding and maintenance skills. Grass huts around quiet bays yielded to mercenary-minded towns with busy wharves and streets of coral buildings. Unfortunately, these ports also became conduits for epidemics such as venereal disease, smallpox, and tuberculosis that devastated vulnerable island populations.[39]

Ambitious chiefs promoted trade by protecting ships and punishing thieves, guided visitors through familiar waters, and sailed as honored passengers, often exchanging names with sea captains and sleeping on mats in their aft cabins. Curious, they rang ships' bells, listened to Euroamerican music, tried using rapiers, witnessed cannon and rocket displays, and studied magnets and compasses. Covetous, they wheedled gifts, donned foreign clothes, ate and drank at captains' tables, and began to hoard their new acquisitions. The price such rulers paid was mounting debts to foreigners, who shrewdly sold on credit and could call in naval warships to enforce payment, perhaps in land for plantations. But until the 1840s, chiefs managed to protect their sovereignty by adding firearms and Western-style ships to strategies to expand their power. By 1800, three main hubs anchored the commerce of Oceania: Papeete in Tahiti, Honolulu and Lahaina in Hawai'i, and Bay of Islands in New Zealand (in tandem with Sydney, Australia).[40]

In 1767, Tahiti became the first regular provisioning station for European ships in the South Pacific. Before then, explorers had raced across the world's largest ocean to avoid starvation or scurvy. Instead of searching for the Northwest Passage between the Pacific and Atlantic, John Byron set a record for circumnavigating the globe—just under two years (1764–66). Beginning with Wallis's visit, however, Tahiti earned a reputation for hospitality. Thanks to the diplomacy of the Pomare family, Tahiti profited not only from pork sales to Australia but as a regional hub for sandalwood trading in the Marquesas and Australs, pearling in the Tuamotus, and whaling off Peru. A London Missionary Society (LMS) ship, the *Duff,* arrived in 1797, bringing not only preachers and hardware to Pomare II but also an arsenal of cannons and muskets to support a Christian monarch. By 1815 he had converted and conquered Tahiti from 'Oro. With the help of mission carpentry and trade profits, Pomare and other chiefs began to acquire Western-style vessels and whaleboats. A chief of Mo'orea even exchanged his double-hulled canoe for a missionary-built schooner. Ra'iatea acquired its own fleet of seven sloops and schooners and helped to build missionary John Williams's *Messenger of Peace* in order to expand its contacts.[41]

The LMS had come equipped with a Tahitian vocabulary compiled by *Bounty* mutineers and hoped "to extend the use of that dialect as far as possible." Thus, Tahitian Christian teachers helped Pomare II to spread his authority over the Society Islands, the Tuamotus, and Australs, where he wanted a royal monopoly over pork, pearls, and sandalwood exports. Sailing to convert Raivavae in a sandalwood vessel in 1819, he wrote: "We went forth and neared the Southern parts ... carrying guns." Pomare II, however, was only a nominal Christian, and at times his drive for power clashed wills with his missionary advisers. Once, he angrily instructed one of his ship captains: "You are to seek out Polynesians in Port Jackson [Australia] ... we will not sell pigs to those preachers." Yet the Pomares' net did not always catch its prey. They nurtured familial and patron-client bonds with chiefs in the Tuamotus and Australs, but local divers worked independently on foreign vessels to buy weapons and exotica. In 1826, Pomare II's queen ordered loyal warriors from Ana'a to seize unlicensed (i.e., untaxed) pearling ships in the Tuamotus. Te'ao of Ra'iatea traveled with the king on that ship to Raivavae, but he later became a "heretical" prophet opposed by both Pomare and the LMS.[42]

The new maritime diaspora would not be easy to control. Ever since Cook's visit, Tahitians had ridden passing ships like taxis from island to island, saying "Me ship, captain; me go Tahiti." A few wanted to go to Pretane. In fact, Pomare I himself had asked at least three times to be taken to England to meet King George but had always been refused. The *Duff* engaged several Tahitians as intermediaries to other islands, and Captain James Wilson wrote, "The natives were now crowding the ship more than ever, and many of them were very importunate to go to Pretane." As Australian pork buyers and Anglo-American whalers frequented the Society Islands, young men heard wondrous tales about England and began shipping out as sailors. A captain said of them, "they speedily perform the duties of ordinary seamen with steadiness and ability." France conquered the islands in the 1840s, despite generations of British contact, but Tahitians continued to ship out on anglophone vessels.[43]

In late 1778, as Cook's *Resolution* passed by Hawai'i on its return journey south, a young chief named Kamehameha came out from Maui and spent the night on board. According to oral tradition, "The people thought Kamehameha had been taken to Kahiki," beyond the horizon. They wept at his loss, but the next morning he returned in a canoe, with apparent insight into the future. Three months later, just before Cook's death at Kealakekua Bay, Kamehameha went out to the ship again and bartered his feather cloak for iron daggers. He was not awestruck by the whites; he used them for his own purposes. Cook's crew had purchased furs from Northwest American Indians, so in 1786 British and American tradeships began passing through Hawai'i on their way to China. Kamehameha monopolized sales of hogs, sandalwood, pearls, and salt and used spies to learn exactly what cargoes ships carried and their current world market values. He stored his treasures in a well-guarded stone warehouse. He also acquired the firepower to expand his realm. In the "Battle of the Red-Mouthed Gun," he reinforced his fleet of double-hulled war canoes with a captured schooner manned by kidnapped white beachcombers who knew how to use cannons.[44]

In 1794, Kamehameha broke Makahiki *kapu* by riding a short distance on George Vancouver's HMS *Discovery*. He was able to persuade the English carpenters to construct him an armed schooner, the *Beretane* (Britannia). Kamehameha continued to study foreign ship designs and equipment and to build or acquire Western-style vessels until he had forty by 1811. These he maintained well, crewed with Hawaiians instructed by beachcombers, and used to help him unite the Hawaiian Islands for the first time. In order to train a pool of capable seamen, now-King Kamehameha I encouraged Hawaiians to work on the foreign ships going between America and China. Archibald Campbell, his sailmaker, concurred with other foreigners when he said of the trainees, "In a short time they become useful hands."[45] Kamehameha sent his own sandalwood shipments to China in ships manned by Hawaiians, but Canton charged him such ruinous harbor fees that he instituted port dues at Honolulu. His son Liholiho sent brigs manned by Hawaiians to Kamchatka and Northwest America with salt for the Russian fur trade. Although the ships were received cordially by Russian officials, the main rewards they brought back were gifts of deer and bears. By 1820, the new Japan grounds were bringing whalers through Hawai'i, and foreigners soon wanted land for plantations.[46]

After Hawaiian unification in 1810, the former war fleet declined, and several of its best brigs were pirated away by Spanish, British, or French warships. Examining an up-to-date Russian ship in 1824, Admiral Kalanimoku was said to have lamented the passing of Kamehameha I five years earlier: "Thou wast taken from us too soon!" The remaining vessels served mainly as royal pleasure craft or interisland carriers. Hawaiian royalty and chiefs often bought yachts on credit, like the eighty-thousand-dollar *Cleopatra's Barge* in 1821, and celebrated on their voyages between pleasure stops. Such vessels may have cost their size in sandalwood and been built of short-lived wood or wound up on a reef, but they had "showy cabins with looking glasses, sofas with red morocco cushions" for the royal entourages. In contrast, a typical interisland vessel carried livestock, cargo, and nearly five hundred people, "occupying the hold, the steerage, the cabin, the deck, the rigging and the tops." Native Hawaiian captains, supercargoes, and sailors operated this so-called mosquito fleet, which provided employment to an increasing number of local men.[47]

Some were colorful, such as "Admiral" John Hall, "a native of uncommonly good nature" who enjoyed recalling the Royal Hawaiian Navy court-martial that had stripped him of his epaulets and banished him to a long career in the interisland service. Hawaiian crews handled dangerous surf with enthusiasm, dexterity, and discipline: a second mate named Kauhane knocked out a disobedient crewman's eye, but he was acquitted in court. They also began playing ukeleles and singing for hula dancers to earn tips from travelers. Local passengers took along dried fish and poi and regarded a slow trip as more for their money. Inexpensive and maneuverable Hawaiian cargo schooners would continue to serve the islands even after the introduction of steamers in the 1850s. The hard-working steamer *Kilauea* connected the islands with ten-day circuits for two decades and inspired an appreciative chant:

> Beloved ship, sea-roving steed . . .
> Now Kilauea's prow heads into the wind,
> smoke breaks from stack, ripples over the sea,
> paddle wheel slowly revolves . . .
> given with a King's love.[48]

Cook's explorations brought the large, forested islands of Aotearoa to the attention of the British, who made "New Zealand" a maritime frontier of their colony in Australia after 1788. Sydney enveloped the Maori in a web of trade that ranged from China to the Americas. Whalers, sealers, traders, missionaries, and convict runaways came to Bay of Islands, where Ngapuhi Maoris adapted to the new commerce by selling timber, flax, potatoes, and wheat to acquire metal tools and other manufactured goods. They never united politically, but their chiefs gained *mana* (power) through warfare, so they used firearms and beachcombers to defeat old enemies. In 1814, Samuel Marsden established a mission station at Bay of Islands, and Maoris regularly visited his church farm at Parramatta outside Sydney. Australian-based British whalers also began taking Maoris as crew. As early as 1796, the *England's Glory* transferred to the arriving *Mermaid* a Maori harpooner-pilot who worked for pay.[49]

In 1805 the governor of New South Wales criticized whalers for taking "incredulous" Maoris away from their islands and leaving them in Sydney. He forbade the hiring of Oceanians without official permission; he also outlawed their being physically abused, abandoned without pay, or taken east of Cape Horn. Such rules were not easily enforced, however, because almost a decade later, Governor Lachlan Macquarie had to reissue similar decrees. In 1823, a Royal Marine commander in Sydney condemned the destructive warfare caused by selling muskets to Maoris and asked to be put in charge of colonizing New Zealand. His request was backed by a letter from three Australian-based whaling firms that argued, "we shall soon have great numbers of the natives who will be very glad to be taken on board our ships and in a very short time become most valuable seamen, being very powerful, brave, and with strong natural abilities. There are a very few New Zealanders at this time in British whalers, and their conduct is such as to merit the best treatment." Three years later, another memorial from Sydney whalers said that "there are no less than 12 New Zealand men on board one single whale-ship" and that their islands would prove as effective a base for the China trade as Hawai'i and Tahiti were.[50]

Maoris adapted foreign nautical technology to their own needs. In 1810, Chief Tara of the Bay of Islands received a small, flat-bottomed boat and several gallons of whale oil as a reward for testifying (falsely) to vengeful whalers against the accused perpetrators of the *Boyd* massacre. In 1823, Chief Hongi Hika bought a ship's longboat for use in his wars, and by 1838 many chiefs regarded whaleboats or skiffs as more desirable transport than elaborately carved canoes. In 1840, Bay of Islands chiefs signed the Treaty of Waitangi with England, without realizing they were giving up their sovereignty. Many died or lost lands in ensuing wars of resistance. Nevertheless, Maoris continued to acquire Western-style vessels until they had a "mosquito fleet" of forty-five cutters and schooners. The small coastal vessels relied primarily on Maori seamen, of whom it was said, "They adapt themselves readily to European navigation and boating . . . and in Cook's Straits many boats are manned by them alone."[51]

Whaleships like the *Governor* and the *Chance* were Maori-operated and competed effectively with foreign vessels, as did Maori schooners trading for sandalwood, tortoise shell, and bêche-de-mer as far north as Wallis Island. Bay whaling drastically depleted right whale calves and breeding cows, but local Maoris continued to hunt them with either wooden or explosive harpoons into the twentieth century. Maoris sold whales they caught on their own, but they also adopted foreign seamen's clothing, boiled blubber in the tryworks, and accepted payment in slops (dry goods). Right whaling stations at Cloudy Bay enabled Maoris to break into the industry, as when four shipped as ordinary seamen aboard the British whaler *Australian.* By the 1830s, captains regularly hired Maori crew, though exact numbers are unavailable. The anecdotal evidence suggests that Maoris may have been second only to Hawaiians in shipping out. According to Benjamin Morrell, "They make excellent sailors, too, after a short course of training." Morrell regarded Bay of Islands Maoris as "civilized, rational business people." He turned down a Ngapuhi chief's request to take him to America, but he had no qualms about kidnapping a Micronesian and a Melanesian as curiosities to display in New York.[52]

Guam, which had become the first foreign colony in Oceania in 1668, was never a fourth shipping hub to balance Hawai'i, Tahiti, and Sydney–New Zealand. Spanish conquest, relocation to Guam, and disease devastated the Chamorros of the Marianas, though over time the survivors recovered in numbers and indigenized many aspects of Spanish culture, including Catholicism. Despite Spanish dreams of denying other powers access to Micronesia, a pro-Spanish Chamorro, Don Alonso Soon, failed in his attempt to reconnoiter the Carolines in 1689. Corrupt governors, ill-disciplined Mexican and Filipino garrisons, and declining population made Guam a burden on Spain. By the eighteenth century, the Manila-Mexico galleons began bypassing Guam, which also lost its regular shipping ties with Manila. After the Nootka Incident of 1790, when Spain could not defend its Northwest American claims from Anglo-American fur trading ships, the Manila-Mexico galleons ceased altogether. It would be interlopers who developed regular trade contacts with Micronesia on their voyages to China or on whale hunts, just as British privateers had raided the Spanish treasure galleons by hiding in the Carolines.[53]

Ironically, Carolinian atoll-dwellers would connect the Spanish Marianas to the rest of Micronesia. In 1788, Luito of Lamotrek used navigational chants to reopen the ancient sailing route between the Carolines and Guam. Vice-Governor Don Luís de Torres welcomed the overture, but Luito's death temporarily closed the opportunity. In 1804, now-Governor Torres visited Woleai and persuaded the Islanders to make their Guam visits an annual event; he even broke precedent and allowed them to settle on Guam or Saipan. After his diplomacy, regular fleets of Carolinian canoes traded for iron at Guam. They also gathered pigs, yams, and arrowroot from Saipan, Tinian, and Rota and thus provided interisland shipping for the Marianas. To compensate for the demise of Chamorro canoe building, the Spaniards actually began to buy Carolinian sailing craft—just when the use of Western-style vessels was spreading to the atolls. By 1828, Chief Oralitau of Elato was operating his own sailing ship, whose crew dived for and marketed bêche-de-mer.[54]

Meanwhile, in the southwestern quarter of Oceania, Melanesia lagged behind in participation in the foreign maritime circuit. Malaria, recurrent hostility among its many small polities, extreme linguistic diversity (over one thousand languages), and European prejudice toward its dark-skinned "cannibals" long deterred outside penetration. But the sandalwood rush of the 1840s would open even this relative backwater to commerce and missionization.[55] Given their seafaring heritage and growing interaction with foreign shipping, it would be surprising if Oceanians had *not* begun to voyage on the new vessels. Moreover, the emerging global economy needed not only Pacific products and consumers but local land and labor. By the 1820s, Hawaiian children were drawing European ship designs in the sand and playing with carefully crafted models in coastal ponds. Within a generation, one-fifth of the kingdom's young men sailed off on whaleships every year.[56] Around the Pacific, a second diaspora was underway, but the process of shipping out would go through historical phases, as we shall see, from early kidnapping to regulated voluntarism, and from ennobled tourism to colonial humiliation.

Wahine

The circulation of Oceanians on Euroamerican vessels was for the most part socially incomplete, because it was a male enterprise. Yet women did enter the maritime *limen,* especially in port. *Wahine* (native women)[57] traded sex and other services for gifts or payment, which they shared with their families and chiefs. In Hawai'i, Cook tried to ban sexual contact with his crew to avoid spreading venereal disease, but he failed, and according to indigenous oral tradition, accepted a high-ranking consort himself. She was Lelemahoalani, the daughter of a Kaua'i chief, and she reported back to her people that white men groaned in pain when she stuck her fingernails into them, so they could not be gods as the Lono priests claimed. Just as they had once sought higher status and gifts in relationships with chiefs, women now looked to foreign explorers, fur traders, and whalers. Some chiefs tried to control the ship trade, even sending *wahine* out as "gifts," but sexual exchanges enabled commoners to acquire valuable imports. By the 1820s, busy Honolulu harbor greeted visiting ships with "propositions shouted at us by all the women round about and by all the men in the name of all the women."[58]

The voluntarism of *wahine* varied, ranging from self-assertion to exploitation by both indigenous and foreign men. Euroamerican accounts often employ military imagery to describe their aggressiveness. In 1786, La Pérouse claimed his line of marines could not prevent Hawaiian women from boarding his ship: "Their manners were gentle, sprightly, and engaging: against such attacks, an European who has sailed round the globe, a Frenchman in particular, has no weapons of defence." Women sang, danced, and pushed their way below deck, from Polynesia to ports west. Yet it was Tahitian male elders, as we have seen, who first offered young women to foreign seamen. Between Cook's second and third expeditions, Maori women at Queen Charlotte Sound changed from being jealously guarded kin to barter for iron nails. As ship calls at Bay of Islands increased, Maoris began to offer even chiefs' daughters as consorts, and muskets could buy the favors of not only slaves but also married females. Chiefly pimps squabbled over the territories their women worked, accompanied them to the ship to see that they had sex with as many sailors as possible, and collected their earnings. In Micronesia, women helped their families with earnings, but they often had to swim out to ships, where native canoers pulled them up by the hair and demanded "tobak" (tobacco) for their services.[59]

Yet *wahine* seem to have extracted some sense of self-worth from their role in the *limen*. Tahitian and Hawaiian women proudly displayed the calico dresses and other gifts they received from sailors. A notorious Maori woman named Mary was banned from a missionary vessel but retorted that "the New Zealand women were quite as handsome as those of Europee." She took an Englishman halfway to shore in her canoe and then told him he would have to swim the rest of the way unless he gave her some fishhooks. Aware of the terms of trade, he had brought a few along. A young Maori consort, nicknamed Mrs. Goshore from her previous sailor affairs, married a Captain Jones and "picked up a good deal of our language." Maori women stayed with their "husbands" as long as the ship was in their islands, sometimes for months, cooking and washing clothes. Some remained so loyal to their men that they had to be evicted by force, whereupon they cut themselves with shells and followed in canoes as far as they could. Wives of bay whalers negotiated marriage agreements and used family connections to acquire land. One saved her lover's life after he had insulted some Maoris.[60]

Oceanian women thus spent so much time on ships that they helped in trading and cross-cultural mediation. Soon after the early sex-for-nails trade began in Tahiti, "Young Girls … hade now rose their price … from a twenty or thirty penny nail, to a forty penny, and some was so Extravagant as to demand a Seven or nine Inch Spick [spike]." In 1772, South Island Maori females came aboard Cook's ship and established friendly trade relations between their people and the strangers. When the *Bounty* arrived at Tahiti in 1788, a sailor wrote, "some of the Weomen who came on board became very Intiligent in a short time and soon brought their quondum husbands into a method of discourse by which evry thing was transacted." *Wahine* seemed at times to maintain the upper hand in such trading, as Cook reported rather ruefully at Tahiti in 1773,

> Oreo at this time introduced into the ship two very pretty young women, these two beauties attracted the notice of most of the officers and gentlemen who made love to them in their turns, the ladies very obligingly received their addresses, to one they gave a kind look to another a smile, thus they distributed their favours to all, received presents from all and at last jilted them all.[61]

The shipboard *limen* bred innovations, and women who spent so much time among strangers were in the frontline of cultural change. Richard Cruise claimed that Maori women on English ships experimented with Western dress and customs, because "the mild treatment of the Europeans, when compared with that of their own countrymen, had gained their esteem and admiration." Hawaiian women paid less attention to *kapu* on board ships and began eating forbidden foods in the company of white sailors. By 1810, the same year that Kamehameha I united Hawai'i, Queen Ka'ahumanu was breaking custom by eating pork and shark with male ship officers. She swore her hosts to secrecy, but nine years later, she intimidated Kamehameha II into eating with her, in effect abolishing *kapu*. In 1820, American missionaries arrived with their own rules, which the Queen enforced. They banned prostitution, but New England whalers still tried to buy or kidnap Hawaiian women. Even a U.S. warship forced the government to send out prostitutes, as a missionary lamented, "In the dusk of the evening of the next day a boat with females passed from the harbor and a shout arose among the shipping at the glorious victory."[62]

Wahine also traveled on foreign ships. In 1774, an attractive Boraboran woman journeyed with Cook from Tahiti to Ra'iatea, and after his death at Hawai'i in 1779, seven women sailed with his ships as far as O'ahu, helping the British to provision. But at every stop, they also danced a hula describing Cook's mortality, so surgeon David Samwell wrote, "They would willingly have accompanied us further, but at last we came to think that they had spread the news of our Misfortune far enough." The first indigenous woman to leave Hawai'i was "Winee," who was hired as a maidservant for the wife of an English fur trading captain in 1787. According to John Meares, Winee "possessed virtues that are seldom to be found in the class of her countrywomen to which she belonged; and a portion of understanding that was not to be expected in a rude and uncultivated mind." Winee died after visiting China, but five years later, two high-born Hawaiian *wahine,* Raheina and Timaro, survived a voyage and returned home. They had been kidnapped from Ni'ihau by a fur trader and taken to Northwest America, but explorer George Vancouver brought them home again, treating them as ladies on his ship. Petite, fifteen-year-old Raheina seemed to fulfill the crew's male fantasies, by wearing the riding habit they gave her with elegance, even taking care not to expose her ankles when climbing the ship's ladders.[63]

Some women left their islands with white husbands. Tano Manu of Tahiti traveled as a language instructor with her Swedish beachcomber husband on the mission ship *Duff.* According to the approving captain, "by conducting herself in a modest, affable, and obliging manner, [she] was kindly treated by all on board: she was also of a good natural understanding, evidently susceptible of improvement, and always ready to communicate." As a reward, she received "a warm week-day dress, and a shewy morning gown and petticoat for the Sundays; and as she always kept herself clean, when dressed she made a very decent appearance; taking more pains to cover her breasts, and even to keep her feet from being seen, than most of the ladies of England have of late done."[64] In 1803, the Marquesan chiefess Enaoaeata married English beachcomber Edward Robarts. She bore him a daughter and left with him as his "royal consort," saying, "There's the land that gave me breath. There's my friends and relations. I forsake them all for your sake." Ena went to Tahiti, the Tuamotus, New Zealand, and, finally, Calcutta, where she died. In 1845, Mary Lucatt of Ra'iatea visited Valparaiso and crossed a plain to see Santiago, where her husband wrote, "She was delighted with the scenery, gardens, birds, cattle, flocks, etc., and all the novelties that met her eye; and I enjoyed, beyond measure, witnessing her delight, and listening to the naiveté of the expressions which her admiration called forth."[65]

By the nineteenth century, female royals traveled on foreign ships. In 1823, Queen Kamamalu of Hawai'i went with her husband, Kamehameha II, on a diplomatic mission to England, along with other high chiefs and chiefesses. Reluctant to go, she chanted mournfully on the beach before boarding a whaleship, and tragically she died of measles while with the king in London. Her companion, Chiefess Liliha, survived to return home on HMS *Blonde,* whose officers were impressed with her table manners and modesty. In 1865–66, Queen Emma, widow of Kamehameha IV, visited

Europe. In England, she visited her favorite correspondent, Queen Victoria, partly to win support for the Anglican Church in Hawai'i. King Kalakaua's sister, Lili'uokalani, accompanied his queen, Kapiolani, to London to attend Queen Victoria's Golden Jubilee in 1887. Lili'uokalani used her time on the ship from New York to London to compose songs, including one for Queen Victoria. While in England, however, Kapiolani learned that Kalakaua had been stripped of his powers in a constitution imposed by armed foreigners in Honolulu, a sad precedent for Lili'uokalani's own over-throw in 1893.[66]

Like their male counterparts, *wahine* sometimes suffered on ships. In 1815, convicts en route to Australia seized their vessel, the *Venus,* kid-napped three Maori women from the North Cape of New Zealand, and sailed into oblivion. Similarly, five Marquesan women of high rank were abducted from Hiva Oa in 1850 by the captain and mate of an American whaler. After jumping overboard in California, they were finally freed by a court in San Francisco, where a newspaper reported, "During the voyage, the females were treated with great cruelty." Caught between male domina-tion on shore and aboard ship, women found it difficult to escape gender roles, especially if they were of low status. Yet sometimes they could parlay their monopoly of femininity into respectable positions as informants and diplomats. In 1791, two Palauan women helped a British captain befriend New Guineans by paddling around confidently in local canoes, and entre-preneur Peter Dillon used Maori and Tongan women to allay suspicions among Solomon Islanders. At Vanikoro, a chiefess aboard offered local women beads from the rail.[67]

The struggle of Oceanian women on the liminal deck was a microcosm of the second diaspora. Most never traveled as far as male seamen did, but their portion of the maritime frontier was as intense as it could get. Within the gender roles open to them, *wahine* explored new possibilities for them-selves and their societies. Even transient encounters in busy seaports could leave lasting impressions, as this Hawaiian chant about crowded Honolulu harbor in the whaling era reveals:

> I have seen in my heart
> that sea of forest trees
> of tall-masted ships returning . . .
> Love's gaze is keen and long.
> Perhaps I should show my love by asking his:
> Come back, dear love, bring ease to me,
> comfort of mind.[68]

~ 2 ~

Shipping Out

The thought came to me in Tahiti:
"I shall sail away like the white man,
I shall paddle to some distant country,
I shall hunt in some amorous land." [1]

Oceanians' entry into foreign shipping did not go smoothly at first, despite their ancient maritime heritage. The earliest who sailed on European ships were "blackbirded" (kidnapped) by conquistadores or predatory freebooters. There was sad precedent for this inhumanity in the slave raiding of eastern Indonesia. In the tenth century, black Papuan captives from New Guinea were known to be on Java, and Papuan war canoes took Malay prisoners in return. As late as 1816, a ten-year-old slave boy called "Dick Papua" was brought from Java to London, examined like a specimen, and later returned to what was then the Dutch East Indies. By that time, however, a countertrend of more voluntary recruitment had begun. In 1763, the Peace of Paris between England and France permitted scientific naval exploration of the Pacific. Contemporary Enlightenment philosophers sought "noble savages" uncorrupted by "civilization," and merchants wanted regular trade contacts, so opportunities arose for shipping out as local guides or as crew replacements. With more familiarity and growing demand, Oceanian voyagers found niches ranging from proletarian kanaka to ennobled tourist. [2]

Blackbirding Conquistadores

Europeans began to abduct Oceanians in 1522, one year after the first Spanish visit to Guam. When Magellan lost his life in the Philippines, the *Victoria* sailed westward to Spain, but the *Trinidad* had to undergo repairs in the Spice Islands (Moluccas) of Indonesia. Six months later, the *Trinidad* tried to make it to Panama with a small cargo of valuable cloves, but northeasterly trade winds drove the ship to the Marianas. Chamorro boatmen off Agrihan were so aggressive that the ship could not anchor, so the captain seized a man to obtain information. The Chamorro could only tell his captors the names of the Marianas Islands in his language, so he was released at Maug. Three members of the crew also deserted there, including Gonzalo de Vigo, who survived to be the first European beachcomber in Oceania. The *Trinidad* finally gave in to prevailing winds and limped back to the Moluccas, where a storm destroyed it.[3] Capturing Oceanians as informants became common for early European explorers in the Pacific. They lacked interpreters, so captains hoped to transform their prisoners into religious converts and good-will ambassadors.

Foreign vessels also needed native labor when illness or desertion depleted crews so far from home. In 1526, the *Victoria* sailed from Mexico to fight Portugal for control of the Moluccas and found de Vigo at Guam. Before leaving, according to Andrés de Urdaneta's account, "we took eleven natives to work at the pumps, because there were many sick on board." The Chamorros were apparently abducted after being lured aboard to trade. We might expect de Vigo to have persuaded young seafarers to join the expedition, but perhaps the memory of their bloody conflict with Magellan made the Chamorros distrust the Spaniards, or else the scurvy-ridden crew was too desperate to risk a refusal. The "Guam eleven" made it to Mindanao in the Philippines, but local hostility prevented the Spaniards from provisioning. If they survived hunger and the illnesses killing many of the Spanish crew and commanders, the unfortunate Chamorros may have become embroiled in the war over the Moluccas.[4] As sparse as the facts about this journey are—one phrase in a journal—it reveals what *kanaka*s often experienced. The Chamorro pumpers are mentioned only once, and not by name, because their fate, like their identities, was not deemed worthy of record despite the valuable service they provided.

The Spanish records are remarkably candid about their mistreatment of "Indians," perhaps demonstrating a conquest mentality they had transferred from their long wars against the Moors to their new empires in the Americas.[5] Yet Iberians were also capable of more tolerant opinions about Oceanians. Pigafetta, Magellan's chronicler, said of the Chamorros, "They are of our stature, and are well-formed." He admired their outrigger canoes, which he noted "can sail in either direction, without having to be turned about," and "are like dolphins, leaping from wave to wave." In 1525, Portuguese visitors to the Carolines wrote, "Both men and women were quite pleasant in appearance ... without any malice, fear, or cautiousness ... they were amidst the simplicity of the First Age."[6] Overall, these Europeans seemed to regard Pacific Islanders, like the ocean itself, as secondary to their designs in the Americas and Asia. The struggle between Spain and Portugal over Moluccan cloves led only indirectly to the first attempt to enlist an Oceanian as a cross-cultural mediator.

In 1528, the hard-pressed Spanish contingent at Tidore sent Alvaro de Saavedra back to Mexico for reinforcements. He faced the same problem as the *Trinidad* and spent a month waiting for favorable winds off the coast of New Guinea. After "black, ugly and naked" Papuans shot arrows at his men from their canoes, he captured three natives. Two jumped into the sea, but the third traveled with Saavedra (who never did make it to Mexico) to Guam, the Philippines, the Moluccas, and finally back to New Guinea on May 3, 1529:

> We landed him on the same island whence we had taken him. He had be-
> come a Christian and had acquired our language. He had been taught that he
> might tell the natives what people we were, and that if they would bring us
> provisions we would pay for them. That we might not have to get the boat
> out, and as he was ready to swim, the Captain let him swim of his own
> accord. But the natives of the island killed him in the water, and he cried out
> to us, but nevertheless they killed him. So we made sail. . . ."[7]

What went through the mind of this quasi-Hispanicized Papuan as he stood in the shallows off his own island, unrecognized and unwelcome after a year's absence? Was he perhaps killed in revenge for his own kidnapping? Had he landed on the wrong beach, or perhaps returned to a changed context? We only know that his new mentors offered him no assistance on his lonely mission, so that his adventures and explanations never reached the ears of his people. It was a clumsy, tragic homecoming, the only attempt of its kind in the Spanish records until the early eighteenth century. Spain lost the Moluccas to Portugal by treaty in 1529, but Manila became the Spanish entrepôt for Asian luxuries. In 1565, Miguél López de Legazpi claimed the Marianas and the Philippines for Spain. In defiance, the Chamorros resisted annexation. Legazpi hanged three wounded warriors and was ready to execute a captive when Spanish friars intervened to save the man's life. Legazpi took the Chamorro to the Philippines, where the prisoner sailed to Mexico in the first treasure galleon from Manila. Meanwhile, a vessel had separated from Legazpi's expedition and passed through the Caroline Islands on its way to the Philippines. After a violent encounter at Chuuk (Truk), the Spanish tempted some fishermen off Sorol by dropping a red jacket in the sea as bait. When a canoe came close enough, a conquistador leaned over, grabbed a boy by the hair and pulled him onto the ship. The young captive received a haircut, a shirt and trousers, and a new name: Vincent, the saint on whose feast day he lost his freedom. Apparently only a trophy, he lived to witness the Spanish annexation of the Philippines. His rechristening and new appearance were typical for Oceanians on foreign ships.[8]

Inspired by the legend of Inca Tupac Yupanqui, the Spanish also sent three expeditions from Peru to Melanesia, hoping to find the mines of ancient Israel's King Solomon. On the final expedition in 1606, Pedro de Quiros had four Santa Cruz Islanders seized and bound in their own chief's hut. Chief Tumai of Taumaco had befriended Quiros, but the Spanish diverted his attention, and by the time he heard the captives crying for help from the ship, it was too late. Three prisoners escaped by jumping into the sea. Despite entreaties from the Spaniards about divine grace and riches, one escaping swimmer "with great effrontery . . . took off a shirt he had on." Quiros gave the remaining captive his own patron saint's name, Pedro. The young man explained that he had already been a prisoner on Tumai; hence he chose to cast his fate with the Spaniards. He dutifully attended Catholic mass and, according to Quiros, "went about dressed in silk with a cross on his breast, and bow and arrows, so astonished and pleased at all he saw, and at his cross, that he looked about and showed it, putting his hand on it, and named it many times." Quiros apparently believed he was rescuing Pedro from heathenism. "The cross," he wrote, "elevated the mind, even of a barbarian who did not know its significance."

Quiros also wanted native intermediaries, because his was a mission of colonization. In 1595, when he had been chief pilot for Mendaña, Quiros had attributed the violence between Spaniards and Marquesans to a lack of communication, so at Gaua in Vanuatu, he captured two more men and had them padlocked to prevent escape. One man was of obvious high rank and fearless; he asked many questions and was "put in the stocks, but on a bed where he could sleep." The second prisoner jumped overboard and swam around the ship in the dark with a heavy padlock and chain on his foot. For four hours, the swimmer and the imprisoned chief cried out to each other "in such doleful tones that it caused grief to all." Finally the swimmer was rescued, fed well and given wine, and put into the stocks for the night: "There both remained all night, talking sadly and in confusion." The next day the Spaniards cut their hair and beards, trimmed their nails "with scissors, the uses of which they admired," and dressed them in bright silks and plumed hats. They also received gifts of knives, and mirrors "into which they looked with caution." Dressed in "coloured taffeta," they won their freedom by helping their captors buy provisions.

On an island he called Espíritu Santo (Holy Spirit), Quiros established a doomed colony: New Jerusalem. When the Spanish became a burden on local food supplies, however, the natives cut off provisions, so Quiros attacked a village and captured three boys, the oldest of whom was seven years old. Quiros wrote that saving the souls of the three hostages was "predestined." He would "send them back clothed and kindly treated." In reality, he used them as decoys to obtain food and water and ignored their begging—and that of their fathers—for freedom. In Spanish, Quiros scolded a boy, "Silence, child! You know not what you ask. Greater good awaits you than the sight and the communion with heathen parents and friends." Pedro, the earlier captive from Taumaco, joined the Spanish on forays. "He took his bow and arrows," Quiros wrote, "to fight against the blacks of this bay who seemed to be enemies of his, because although left at large, he never once wanted to go with them. He had a good disposition." Quiros described the local Islanders, because they opposed the Spanish invasion and the kidnapping of their children, as untrustworthy and "vile."

Quiros failed to find Solomon's gold or to create a viable Spanish colony on Santo, but he took Pedro and a boy he called Pablo to Mexico, as "small fruit" for his labors. Pablo outlived his two younger compatriots en route to Acapulco, but he died at the tender age of eight on Ascension Day in 1607. Quiros mourned the loss of his "very beautiful eyes, very good form of body" and "docile and pleasant" nature. Pedro, a twenty-five-year-old weaver and archer with a wife and son back home, was really named Luca. He tried so desperately to speak Spanish, "he was sometimes angry, and at other times with the utmost strenuousness laboured to make himself understood." Pedro claimed "with great action and ecstacy" that his islands had abundant pearls. He "showed a great desire to return to his country, to tell the Lord of Taumaco all the good we had done to him . . . and to bring his son, and come and live with us." Both "Indians" said their prayers obediently and perished within a year of their arrival in America. Ironically, Pablo had witnessed the burial at sea of an aged priest and had been puzzled when the corpse was tossed overboard. He had wondered aloud how the good father could get to heaven with weights on his feet.[9] Metaphorically, the gloomy event presaged his own fate.

The "blackbirding" continued when Luís Vaez de Torres parted from the increasingly irrational Quiros in mid-1606 and headed for the Philippines by way of southern New Guinea. Two Papuans ventured out to the ship in a canoe, only to be seized and ransomed for "a fine big pig." After a bloody battle with villagers, Don Diego de Prado y Tovar was moved by the "many dead children they were carrying in their arms." He rescued a teenaged girl "with the most lovely face and eyes that could be imagined" from sailors who began to fight over her. But he chose fourteen boys and girls from six to ten years of age to be baptized in Manila. On another island, the Spaniards took three young women "for the service of the crew of the ship," one of whom later gave birth on a gun carriage. Her baby died in Manila, but the mother lived and "learned to speak." Torres also seized six men in a canoe and chose for conversion "a fine big youth, who after he learned to speak told us in Manila how in that country there were plenty of brilliant red stones like those worn by Spaniards in their finger-rings. . . ."[10]

"Learning to speak" was, so far, a rather one-sided process. It required learning the kidnapper's language and adopting his customs. The Spanish accounts admit frankly that the Oceanians aboard their ships were prisoners and praise them only if they were docile and obedient. Those who reached foreign lands such as the Philippines or Mexico tried various survival techniques, from conforming to rules to tantalizing their captors with tales of riches in their homelands. Yet travel outside Oceania was a serious health risk for Pacific Islanders, even if they played their roles properly. Early Spanish contact with Oceania was thus fleeting and incompetent. Passing conquistadores were unlikely to be culturally sensitive, because as Greg Dening has said, "The future did not bind them. . . . They had no tomorrows in the places they visited." Not even the annual galleon route between Manila and Acapulco had significant impact on the inner Pacific, apart from the colonization and near-depopulation of Guam. By the late eighteenth century, the Pacific would cease to be what it never really was, a "Spanish Lake."[11]

The most colorful tale of involuntary Oceanian travel derives from a voyage by one of the freebooters who preyed on Spanish treasure galleons. In the late 1680s, William Dampier met "Jeoly," also known as the "Painted Prince" because of his tattoos, on Mindanao. Jeoly and his mother were castaways from Miangas atoll who had been blown by a storm to the Philippines, kidnapped by fishermen, robbed of their chiefly ornaments, and sold as slaves to the sultan's interpreter. Dampier next saw Jeoly in Madras, India. An English supercargo had bought him and his mother for sixty dollars and was willing to sell half ownership of both. The "Prince" remembered Dampier fondly, having been well treated on his ship at Mindanao; he hoped that the Englishmen would not beat him as his Filipino master had. Typically, Jeoly insisted that Miangas abounded in gold and spices, saying they were more numerous there than the hairs on his head. He also promised Dampier plenty of women if he would return them home, but the mother died in Sumatra. "I did what I could to comfort Jeoly," Dampier wrote, "but he took extremely, insomuch that I feared for him also." They set sail for England on a ship whose chief mate had bought the supercargo's share in Jeoly. In 1691, the "Prince" reached London, where Dampier sold his own share. Jeoly became a carnival chattel and died of smallpox in Oxford. His tragic career was summed up by Dampier:

> In the little printed Relation that was made of him when he was shown for a Sight in England, there was a romantick Story of a beautiful Sister of his [who was] a Slave with them at Mindanao; and of the Sultan's falling in Love with her; but these were Stories indeed. They reported also that this Paint was of such Virtue, that Serpents, and venomous Creatures would flee from him, for which reason, I suppose, they represented so many Serpents scampering about in the printed Picture that was made of him. But I never knew any Paint of such Virtue: and as for Jeoly, I have seen him as much afraid of Snakes, Scorpions, or Centapees, as my self.[12]

Ennobled Tourists

Peace between France and England transformed Pacific exploration, because it freed the navies of the two most powerful colonial powers to undertake systematic, scientific surveys of the seas. Would they discover a time-saving Northwest Passage between the Atlantic and Pacific, or a Terra Australis Incognita (unknown southern continent) that balanced the Eurasian landmass and kept the globe from falling off its axis? Geographic curiosity coincided with Enlightenment philosophy, which worshipped Reason but also indulged in romantic polemics—were there living specimens of "noble savages" who offered a glimpse into Europe's past before, as Jean-Jacques Rousseau claimed, "iron and wheat . . . ruined Mankind"? Rousseau praised uncorrupted "children of nature," like the American Indian chief who visited London and rejected everything before him except a warm blanket, which he rated "almost as good as an animal skin," and the African who had been raised as a white man, only to renounce Christianity and European dress when he went home, saying in Rousseau's words, "my resolution is to live and die in the Religion, the ways, and the customs of my Ancestors."[13]

As if to symbolize the new era, circumnavigator Philip Carteret picked up a voyager in the Mapia Islands, northwest of New Guinea in 1767. Handsome natives came out in canoes to trade coconuts for iron, he said, and a few climbed up the ship's masts: "One of their People would need stay with us notwithstanding all we & his Cammarades could persuede him to the Contrary, I therefor kept him as it was a free Act of his & called him Joseph Freewill." Joseph enlisted as an able-bodied seaman and traveled as far as Bonthain in the Dutch Celebes, where he recognized breadfruit and cooked some right away. But the familiar food came all too late: "he afterwards grue sickly from being so long at sea and died."[14] Free will apparently had its price. Wallis, who was separated from his colleague

Carteret by storms in the Strait of Magellan, came upon Tahiti. There he met a "Sensable and well behaved" young chief the English dubbed Jonathan:

> He took very particular notice of every thing which we showd him, and seemd greatly surprized at the construction of our ship ... but the thing which pleasd and Astonishd Jonathan the most of all, was the picture of a very handsome well drest young Lady, in Miniature, which the Docter Showd him, we made him understand that this was the picture of the women in our country and if he went with us he should have one of them always to Sleep with, this put him in such raptures of Joy that its imposible for me to describe he hugd the picture in his breast and kist it twenty times, and made several other odd motions, to show us how happy he would be with so fine a woman.... I realy belive he would have come to England for her hade we been willing to take him with us, and his friends contented to let him go.[15]

"Jonathan," however, did not go to England. The first Tahitian visitor to Europe sailed with French explorer Louis Antoine de Bougainville in 1768. When *L'Etoile* dropped anchor off Tahiti, not only naked women greeted the French. A young man named Ahutoru spent the night aboard "without being the least uneasy." Bougainville wrote, "The zeal of this islander to follow us was unfeigned ... he manifested it to us in the most expressive manner." Ahutoru was smaller and darker than other Tahitian men, which he explained by saying that he was the offspring of a chief by a captive woman. He told his hosts of Wallis's visit six months earlier, of interisland wars, and native names for plants. Like Jonathan, he seemed to be an aficionado of females, for he shocked the French by cheerfully detecting a disguised woman in their crew. The naturalist's assistant had been on board for half a year without anyone's noticing her gender, except the naturalist. Bougainville wrote of Ahutoru, "he possesses in understanding what he wants in beauty."

Just before the two French ships left, Ahutoru came on board again with his chief: "Ereti took him by the hand, and, presenting him to me, gave me to understand, that this man ... desired to go with us, and begged that I would consent to it. He then presented him to each of the officers in particular; telling them that it was one of his friends, whom he entrusted with those who were likewise his friends, and recommending him to us with the greatest signs of concern." After Bougainville accepted the offer, Ahutoru gave three of his pearl earrings to a pretty young woman in one of the canoes, embraced her, and pulled away despite her tears. If he really was the offspring of a war captive, he may have been regarded as expendable as an ambassador—and excited about a change of scene. As for Bougainville, he had fought a losing battle for France in Canada and failed in his attempt to annex the Falklands. He wanted Ahutoru, if he could be "converted" in Paris and returned alive, to become a pro-French agent in Tahiti.

Since both European visits to Tahiti had distinguished themselves with sexual debauchery, Ahutoru eagerly promised to guide the French to islands plentiful with "complaisant" women. Like Jonathan, he proposed to reciprocate later by "marrying for a time some white women." Yet once at sea, the Tahitian was surprised at how long the voyage became, which casts some doubt on his free will. He attempted to guide the French toward islands he knew, at one point even seizing the helm to get his way. Frustrated, he angrily pointed out a directional star, but his hosts treated his navigational knowledge as a mere curiosity:

> The next morning, by break of day, he climbed up to the top of the mast, and stayed there all the morning, always looking towards that part where the land lay, whither he intended to conduct us, as if he had any hopes of getting sight of it. He had likewise told us that night, without any hesitation, all the names which the bright stars that we pointed at, bear in his language. We have since been assured with certainty, that he knows the phases of the moon perfectly well, and is well acquainted with different prognosticks, which often give notice to navigators of the changes of weather that are to happen at sea some time after. One of the opinions of these people, which Aotourou made very intelligible to us is, that they positively believe that the sun and moon are inhabited.[16]

In Samoa, Ahutoru thought he was home again. He took off his French clothes and spoke to canoers in Tahitian, but they did not understand. Nor could he communicate with dark Solomon Islanders, whose appearance he disliked. He would survive his long journey to Europe, but he died of smallpox in the Indian Ocean on his way home, a human sacrifice to European romanticism. Bougainville's glowing account of Tahiti portrayed it as a "Land of Love" in a primeval Golden Age—an enduring tourist myth that Tahitians themselves helped to inspire with their sexual strategy for taming foreign warships.[17] Yet encyclopedist Denis Diderot wrote a critical supplement to Bougainville's published journal, musing, "for all our striving, we do ourselves as much harm as good ... men become more wicked and unhappy the more civilized they become." Diderot invented an old Tahitian who cursed the French for corrupting his island with disease and greed: "May the guilty sea, that spared your lives when you came here, now absolve itself and avenge [your] wrongs by swallowing you up on your homeward way!"[18]

Cook also took volunteers from the Society Islands as guides and curiosities. Tupaia, a priestly navigator, was the first and most respected. He was already a beachcomber, because Boraborans had invaded his native Ra'iatea and driven him to Tahiti, where he became adviser to Chiefess Purea in time for Wallis's visit. When the political tide turned against him, Tupaia attached himself to the Cook's *Endeavour* almost as soon as it arrived in 1769. He helped to provision the ship and volunteered to be a hostage so Cook could recover two deserters. He watched over scientist Joseph Banks's musket, cooked him a tasty meal of dog meat, and "got most enormously drunk" celebrating King George's birthday. Purea had just lost a local war, so Tupaia asked Banks to take him away to England. Cook had already noted, "several of the natives were daily offering them-selves to go away with us," but he refused to take responsibility for any on the part of the British government.

Banks volunteered to keep Tupaia "as a curiosity, as well as some of my neighbors do lions and tygers at a larger expence than he will probably ever put me to." Tupaia took along a twelve-year-old servant boy, Tayeto, and gave gifts to his former mentors. As the ship sailed away, he waved good-bye from the topmast, "after which," Banks wrote, "he came down and shewd no farther signs of seriousness or concern." Cook and other members of the crew praised Tupaia for his intelligence, breeding, and utility as a guide. He knew the resources of islands as far off as Tonga; he piloted Cook's ship through reefs and told his hosts about daily and seasonal wind changes. Cook called him "very intelligent" and "the likeliest person to answer our purpose."[19] Unlike the French, Banks wanted to learn from Tupaia about native navigation:

> In their longer Voyages they steer in the day by the Sun and in the night by the Stars. Of these they know a very large part by their Names and the clever ones among them will tell in what part of the heavens they are to be seen in any month when they are above the horizon; they know also the time of their annual appearing and disappearing to a great nicety, far greater than would be easily believed by an European astronomer.[20]

Tupaia proved his diplomatic skills to Cook many times. At Huahine, he led the British officers ashore, where he stripped himself to the waist and paid his respects at the local temple. "As soon as we landed," Banks wrote, "Tupia squatted down on the ground and ranging us on one side and the Indians on the other began to pray." At Ra'iatea, his home island, Tupaia piloted the *Endeavour* into port, bought provisions, and even helped Cook to raise the British flag. Cook credited Tupaia with eliminating thefts at Ra'iatea, but the guide could also manipulate the British: he warned against visiting Borabora, which he said was barren and inhabited by criminals (who had chased him away from home). At Rurutu in the Australs, Tupaia warned the British that the natives on the beach were not friends, but in Aotearoa (New Zealand) he was able to translate fluently with the Maoris. Sadly, "tygerhood" could be fatal. Tupaia and his Tahitian servant boy both died of disease in Indonesia, like Joseph Freewill.[21]

In 1773, on his second expedition, Cook sought guides for his two ships but found no Tupaia. A seventeen-year-old commoner named Poreo, "having a curiosity to know a little more of the World than he could experience in Otahite, came on board and desir'd to be admitted as a Volunteer." Cook gave the young man's father a hatchet and other gifts, but canoers still came out to ask for the boy's return and to warn Poreo he would die overseas like Ahutoru and Tupaia. Poreo wept, but Cook and scientist Johann Forster took him into a cabin and "adopted" him as their son; he embraced them and later ate and slept in their cabin. Cook thought Poreo "might be of service to us on some occasion" and turned down many more who wanted to go. He claimed that both Poreo's father and the canoers cared less about the boy than they did about getting more gifts, but Poreo wept as Tahiti receded. He jumped ship at Taha'a, reportedly for a woman he had met.

At Huahine, meanwhile, Omai joined Cook's companion ship as a refugee. Boraboran imperialism had driven him, like Tupaia, away from his native Ra'iatea. The Boraborans had killed his father in battle and taken Omai as a captive to their island. But Omai claimed he had escaped one night, by stealing a canoe and imitating the Boraboran accent in the dark. In Tahiti, one of Wallis's musket balls had wounded him in the side, but now on Huahine, he was in danger of being sacrificed to the gods for committing "blasphemy." Desperate, he had planned to interfere with the provisioning of the ship if they did not rescue him. He asked Cook to take him to Britain, and Cook agreed despite a protest from the local chief. Omai enlisted as able-bodied seaman Tetuby Homy, aged twenty-two, but he was nicknamed Jack and seemed to have had no work duty other than dispensing grog. It quickly became clear that Omai was no Tupaia. On his home island of Ra'iatea, Omai not only failed to deter theft, as Tupaia had, but he had to flee to the ship in the middle of the night because he heard that Boraborans were plotting to kill him. Omai claimed to be the second son of a chief, an apprentice to a priest, and "a great traveller, having been at most of the Islands within their knowledge."

In reality, Omai was a commoner and, like Ahutoru, darker than most Tahitians. He hoped people would no longer laugh at his color and flat nose when he returned with "many fine things" from England.[22] Cook became reluctant to take away another Society Islander, so he tried to dissuade a young Boraboran on Ra'iatea who offered to replace Poreo:

> Frankly I told him that if he went to England it was highly probable he would never return, but if after all he choosed to go I would take care of him and he must look upon me as his Father, he threw his arms about me and wept saying many people persuaded him to stay at the isle. I told him to go a Shore and speak with his friends and then come to me in the morning. He was very

well beloved in the Ship for which reason every one was persuading him to go with us, telling what great things he wou'd see in England and return with immence riches, according to his Idea of riches, but I thought it proper to undeceive him, thinking it an Act of the highest injustice to take away a person from these isles against his own free inclination under any promise whatever much more that of bringing them back again.[23]

Hitihiti's real name was Mahine, but he had exchanged names earlier with a chief of Mo'orea. He urged naturalist George Forster to take him to England, so Cook took him onto the *Resolution* and sent less qualified Omai to the companion vessel, the *Adventure*. Both young men traveled around the Pacific in an unsuccessful search for the southern continent for several months before returning to the Society Islands. Hitihiti disembarked at Ra'iatea, but Omai, his quest for status as yet unfulfilled, went on to London.

Their value as linguists was uneven, but ambassadorial life had its rewards: both drank *kava* and ate heartily, and they joined the British in enjoying local women. Hitihiti bought Easter Island wood carvings as souvenirs because he found them better than Tahiti's, but he acted superior to both Marquesans and Maoris. Despite New Zealand's forests and wild fowl, Hitihiti pitied Maoris for their poverty and was horrified when they offered him cooked human flesh. Forster wrote, "he hardly could see the cruel Scene, & went immediately into the Cabbin & shed a flood of tears." His experience near Antarctica may have convinced him not to go to England. Hitihiti paced the deck, warmed himself by a fire in the captain's cabin, and showed his disgust with the cold climate and salted meat rations. He called snow "white rain" and icebergs "white land" when he returned home, but no one believed that water could turn as solid as stone. In 1777, on his return voyage, Omai flaunted his wealth in New Zealand and hired two Maori servant boys. In Tonga, he was no longer afraid to enter a temple. Cook agreed only to remove his hat and untie his pigtail, but Omai stripped down to a loincloth and walked inside, a fellow explorer.[24]

Because Hitihiti and Omai survived their voyages, at least five other Society Islanders used Cook's ships for local transportation, and many volunteered to go farther. Cook opposed enlisting Oceanians as servants, unless they were chosen by his own guides as retainers, but that rule would be broken by William Bligh. In 1788-89, Bligh spent six months collecting Tahitian breadfruit seedlings to help feed African slaves in Jamaica. Having sailed with Cook, he at first refused to take any natives with him, though Pomare I himself asked to go. Then half the crew of the *Bounty* mutinied and set Bligh adrift. Hitihiti had been serving as an adviser to Pomare I, but he seemed ready to leave again and joined the mutineers. Reputedly an excellent marksman, Hitihiti was the only Tahitian that Fletcher Christian allowed to carry a musket. After failing to found a colony on Tubuai, the mutineers split into two factions. One group sailed with Christian, six local men and a dozen women, to Pitcairn Island. The rest stayed on Tahiti to serve Pomare in wars. Hitihiti helped Pomare to conquer Mo'orea, and he warned the mutineers when the *Pandora* came to arrest them in 1791.

As for Bligh, he survived the long journey back to England and actually returned to Tahiti in 1792 to complete his mission. For the second time, he turned down aged Pomare I's request to go to England, but he found that "our friendship hinged on my complying with his request to take one of his Men, who he said would be of great service to him when I sent him out again, from the many things he could learn and see in England." Hence he accepted Maititi, an "active" twenty-two year old who was "above the common run of Men"—yet Bligh also described Maititi as a servant: "Such a Towtow is more likely to benefit his Country than a Chief who would be only led into Idleness and Dissipation as soon as he arrived in Europe, as was the Case with Omai." Maititi left Tahiti "without shedding a Tear," along with a stowaway nicknamed Jacket, who had been helpful to the botanists. Jacket would die prematurely in Jamaica, and Maititi in London, but the servant category was now open.[25]

Between 1772 and 1775, the jealous viceroy of Peru sent three expeditions to recruit Tahitians, "in order that the Indians over there should witness in the persons of their countrymen the good treatment that had been meted out . . . and the advantages of which they had been made sensible." After bestowing gifts, the first expedition "brought away" four males "of suitable ages and good intelligence, so that the experiment should not go amiss as we know from other accounts has happened with several travellers." Although the Spanish described all four Tahitians as volunteers, the eldest later warned his countrymen they too would be taken away if they came aboard the Spanish ship, and only the youngest seem to have traveled by their own or parental consent. The commander of the second expedition claimed, "An infinite number of Indians wanted to take ship with us for Lima, and tried every means they could by which to gain their wish: even stowing themselves away in the most out-of-the-way places." Yet five out of eight Society Islanders taken to Peru died, and despite viceroyal hospitality, only one survivor wanted to stay in Peru. The last expedition allowed no more travelers, not even Pomare's first cousin.[26]

The so-called Enlightenment did not end "blackbirding." In 1769, French explorer Jean-François de Surville decided to kidnap a Maori, "to try and obtain from him later what information I could about this country." North Cape Maoris treated the French scurvy-ridden crew hospitably, but Surville lost a boat in a gale and then saw "several blacks" around it on shore. He pursued them and asked one to come forward. A chief named Ranginui, who had provided the French with food and shelter, held up a leafy branch in friendship, only to be bound and taken to the ship. Ranginui wept and sighed a great deal but was put in irons. Surville had already kidnapped three Filipinos to replace deserters, and in the Solomon Islands he kept getting into fights with natives when he searched for drinking water. He decided to put two black Malagasy slaves into a captured canoe as bait: "We powdered their Kaffir hair as the people of this country do with lime and in this state they began to imitate the local people, circling the ship and making the same gestures we had seen them make."

A canoe approached, but the natives soon saw the ruse and tried to flee. French pursuers shot one man and dragged the other, kicking and biting, from the water. The next day, they tied thirteen-year-old Lova Saregua to a leash and forced him to lead them to water. Lova stalled for time and tried to cut the rope with some shells but was caught. Then he began to wail loudly and roll in the sand, but Surville beat him with the rope and put him in irons. Ironically, Lova shared a quarterdeck cabin with Ranginui and ate at table with him and Surville, whereas the Filipinos were treated as ordinary seamen. Ranginui died of despair in the Juan Fernandez Islands off Chile, and Surville drowned in heavy surf trying to go ashore in Peru. Lova survived to be presented "as a rarity" to the French Navy Minister Praslin, after whom Surville had renamed his home bay.[27] Cook too kidnapped Maoris in 1769, using Tupaia to lure their canoes close to the ship. The Maoris tried to escape, but the British killed several and captured three boys. Though well fed, dressed, and given gifts, they at first refused to go ashore and make friends where the British wanted them to, probably because it was hostile territory. They helped to make peace with some Maori warriors but begged to remain with the British until a friendly canoe rescued them.[28]

Another ennobled tourist, "Lee Boo" of Palau, survives only in a romanticized account written by George Keate, a friend of Voltaire's who never saw the Pacific. In 1783, a British East India Company vessel shipwrecked off Koror and the *ibedul* (chief) helped the crew build a new schooner. Captain Henry Wilson helped the *ibedul* win a few battles during his stay, and the chief wanted to learn more about British ways. "Raa Kook," the *ibedul*'s brother, had often worked alongside the British and wanted to go, but the chief said no, because Raa Kook was his heir. A young nephew of the *ibedul* had eagerly copied the manners of the British and also asked to go, but the chief scolded him for having "a rambling disposition" and neglecting his family. Instead, the chief had Lee Boo brought "from a distant place, where he had been under the care of an old man," and described his purported second son as amiable and sensible. The *ibedul* told Lee Boo to look upon Wilson "as another father" and asked the captain not to let Lee Boo "run after novelty" but "to make him an Englishman." Lee Boo died of smallpox in London, so Keate put these words into the *ibedul*'s mouth: "I know that death is to all men inevitable, and whether my son meets this event at PELEW, or elsewhere, is immaterial."[29]

From Carteret through Keate runs a compulsion in the journals to show the voluntarism of their passengers. Even the up-to-date Peruvian Spaniards claimed their Tahitians were recruited, like Cook's first Maori captives, for "good treatment" and eventual release. In fact, Tupaia and Omai were fleeing difficult situations, while Ahutoru and Lee Boo may have been expendable agents for chiefs seeking foreign ties and knowledge. Those who chose to ship out usually slept and ate in officers' cabins as specimens of otherness. Taking a "noble savage" out of his environment and putting a fork in his hands was almost a controlled experiment, a look at cultural assumptions and psychological projections in a distorted mirror. In 1787 Chief Ka'iana of Kaua'i boarded John Meares's *Nootka* amid a crowd of Hawaiians clamoring to go to "Britanee, Britanee." Ka'iana "was alone received to embark with us, amid the envy of all his countrymen." He joined a select club of Hawaiians that fur traders took to China and Northwest America "as objects of curiosity."[30]

Aotearoa had its share of ennobled tourists as well. In 1793, Lieutenant Governor Phillip King of Norfolk Island ordered HMS *Daedalus* to capture some Maoris from Bay of Islands to teach his female convicts how to weave flax into linen. Tuki and Huru, both of high rank, hesitated at first to board the ship, but they were enticed below deck with iron and other "curious things" and abducted. They actually disdained weaving as women's work, but they taught what they knew in about an hour and were sent home with gifts. They are credited with introducing potato cultivation to New Zealand, a new provision that Maoris sold to whalers. As early as 1796, Australian-based whalers began taking Maoris as crew, and within a decade Ngapuhi chiefs were shipping out on whalers to see in person what they had heard about Norfolk Island from Tuki and Huru. In 1805, Te Pahi, a Bay of Islands chief, took his five sons to Norfolk Island and Sydney, where they stayed with now-Governor King. Two of Te Pahi's sons worked on British ships; one vanished, but the other lived to meet the king of England. Missionary Samuel Marsden brought Maori chiefs back and forth between his farm near Sydney and his mission station at Bay of Islands with his own vessel, the *Active*.[31]

Such missionary ships opened an alternative circuit of diplomatic travel. The *Duff* took several Tahitians on its cruise in 1797, including Tano Manu, who taught the Tahitian language; a former *Bounty* associate called "Tom" who helped to provision the ship; and a man named Harraweia, who ran away in the Marquesas and stirred opposition to the English missionary instead of helping him. Opukahaia and Hopu of Hawai'i served on fur ships in Northwest America and reached New England, where they inspired the first missionaries to sail to their islands. The *Thaddeus* arrived from Boston in 1820 with four Hawaiians aboard, including George Kaumuali'i of Kaua'i, whose father had sent him to New England to be educated. That same year, Maori chief Hongi Hika visited Australia and England with a missionary and met King George IV. LMS preacher John Williams took native teachers and Christian chiefs from Ra'iatea to as far as Tonga and Samoa; he even kidnapped two Niueans, in spite of "their incessant howlings," to convert them. King George Tupou I of Tonga sailed to Sydney in a Methodist vessel in 1853.[32] The mystique of "tygerhood" would thus persist, even as working *kanaka*s increasingly assumed more proletarian roles.

Kanaka Recruitment

Crew replacements were sometimes kidnapped, as when whalers selected the fittest among Marquesan men who came out to sell provisions and forced the rest to jump overboard far from shore. Blackbirding would continue as an unsavory undercurrent, but economic demand stimulated a rising trend of voluntary recruitment. Shipping out might be formal or informal, depending on where and when the *kanaka* started his voyage. Some insinuated their way into crews by their good cheer and willingness to lend a hand. In 1789, Tahitians helped with an English ship's rigging in port, "though they in general were repaid for their kindness by abuse from the seamen." One persuaded the captain to give him passage to Tetiaroa, despite his brother's warnings that the ship might take him to England. In Hawai'i, the same vessel had to force eager volunteers off the ship. Hawaiians who helped to load and unload cargoes sometimes earned employment in a crew. One boy studied what sailors did on deck and cut fodder to feed a ship's goats. So "quick and cheerfully ready" was he that he talked the first mate into hiring him, despite his mother's tearful protests. Kokako, a Bay of Islands Maori slave, worked hard on a French vessel in port until the captain agreed to hire him. Delighted, he quickly assumed the haughty airs of a *uropi*. E Ware, or "Jim Crow," won his ship job by clowning as well as steering.[33]

Oceanians also developed personal bonds with foreigners in order to voyage. Moehanga of Aotearoa was "determined to see the world" and charmed a ship's surgeon, John Savage, who wrote, "several offered to accompany me to Europe, and I selected one, whose countenance pleased me." Standing in his canoe, Moehanga's father pressed his right eye against his son's left for twenty minutes and, as the ship sailed, prayed open-armed to heaven. Orphaned Henry Opukahaia dined at a captain's table, spent the night, and came to regard his host as a father figure. He escaped from his uncle's house through a hole in the wall, but the old priest followed him and collected a hog in "payment" for the boy's departure from Hawai'i. On another occasion, a mate from an American whaler befriended two Hawaiians in port, and that night they swam out to the ship and vowed to sail with him wherever he went. As early as the 1790s, Hawaiians were showing written letters of recommendation from previous ships. Other volunteers were vouched for by missionaries, won acceptance as shipboard vendors, or simply stowed away. In 1834, the *Arabella* hired Marquesan sailors on a deck crowded with chiefs, women, and potato salesmen.[34]

Growing familiarity with piloting foreign ships enabled Oceanians to compete with white beachcombers, especially in Hawai'i and the Society Islands. Jack Naihekukui was Kamehameha I's royal pilot, and Ra'iatea had its own pilot by 1829. A Tahitian named English Jim served on foreign vessels and piloted them into Matavai Bay from at least 1826 to 1842. "He handled the schooner quite masterly," a captain wrote, "and we reached our anchorage safely." Takai of Fiji could produce letters of recommendation; other Fijian pilots were reimbursed by naval expeditions with "many presents." Yet such written documents could backfire, as when a Hawaiian boarded a Russian vessel, "opened several rag bundles and produced some papers containing testimonials [which] described him as an able pilot, good swimmer and diver, and an expert swindler." The risk went both ways. A one-eyed man named Yanekari piloted a British ship through New Caledonia, but he had to find his own way home. In a sense, piloting meant reclaiming control of local waters. In 1843, Chief Tu'ungahala of Wallis (Uvea) insisted on becoming a pilot himself to replace an Englishman, saying, "If the chiefs of Uvea don't watch out, [foreigners] will soon be the masters here and they themselves slaves."[35]

The traditional diving ability of Pacific Islanders won them jobs with pearlers or bêche-de-mer traders. In 1813, an Australian captain hired Ra'iateans to dive for pearls in the Tuamotus, but by the 1820s, ships were hiring locally, particularly Chain (Ana'a) Islanders. They dived several fathoms in atoll lagoons for oyster shells, detaching them with one hand and holding them in the crook of their left arm until they arose with four or five; one old worm-eaten shell produced thirteen pearls. Hao and Rapa also provided pearl divers who, for payment in cloth, rum, and tobacco, might collectively bring up a ton of shell per six-hour day. One, nicknamed Ofai (stone), could stay down over a minute at a time, but deep dives caused earaches and nosebleeds. Another diver, Tiemu, learned enough English to serve as an interpreter. For payment in iron pots, flint, or cutlery, Yapese gathered bêche-de-mer (sea slugs), tossed them into boats, and cured them in smoking huts ashore. By the 1880s, two hundred Rotumans worked as pearl divers and boatmen in the Torres Straits between New Guinea and Australia, earning as much as two hundred pounds sterling a year.[36]

Regulation of *kanaka* recruiting first took the form of agreements between individual captains and chiefs. Powerful rulers could order commoners to ship out, prohibit them from doing so, or confiscate their earnings. Christian monarchs codified restrictions, as did colonial regimes. In 1841, for example, Hawai'i began to require ships to post a bond to encourage the safe return of recruits. While in Tahiti, one captain had his Hawaiian crewmen locked in jail to avoid forfeiting three hundred dollars if one deserted. Another captain, during a manpower shortage caused by the California gold rush, had to post a five-hundred-dollar bond for each recruit and pay one month's wages in advance. Hawaiian seamen could legally enlist only with official approval. In 1844, a whaler tried to take away a Maui boy who had signed the ship's papers without his father's consent, but it was forced to give him up at Honolulu.[37] Once the king granted permission to recruit, word was sent out and as many as five hundred men might assemble. The captain usually selected the fittest, but experienced older men like "Boatswain Tom" were hired as supervisors. Fur companies depended on hiring Hawaiian boat handlers on three-year contracts, for ten dollars a month plus food and clothing. Over a hundred potential cabin boys presented themselves to Amasa Delano in 1801, but he chose a lad attending the queen: "He lay down his fan of feathers and took his station at the back of my chair, or seat, and did not leave me one minute after, till I went on board."[38]

The trade in furs, sandalwood, and Tahitian pork, as well as whaling and sealing, brought so many *kanaka*s to Sydney that as early as 1805, New South Wales ordered sea captains to provide for the welfare of Oceanian seamen and to return them home. It also banned their mistreatment, or use along Australian coasts. Further orders in the 1810s required that they be paid fairly and recruited only with a chief's permission. Yet regulation did not always please recruiters. When New Zealand became a British colony in 1840, American whalers turned more toward Papeete, but then French annexation of Tahiti and its neighbors led to a rule that no seaman could embark without a police permit. Two Marquesans had to swim out to a whaleship, with the help of a third mate, and became harpooners. Fewer whalers called at Wallis and Futuna after French missionization in 1838–42, due to bans on prostitution. By the 1870s, Britain passed laws to protect Oceanian recruits with government agents and roving men-of-war. Both plantation laborers and sailors could ship out only if their chief gave permission, and if the captain had a license.[39]

Euroamerican vessels in the Pacific came to rely on Oceanian seamen by the nineteenth century, for their boat handling, endurance under the tropical sun, and insight into local customs and waters. *Kanaka*s voyaged for many reasons, from escaping from a bad situation to being "volunteered" by chiefs to personal adventure and material gain. Melville's fictional Queequeg foisted himself on a whaler that needed no additional crew. Despite the captain's initial refusal, Queequeg intercepted the departing ship, "with one backward dash of his foot capsized and sank his canoe; climbed up the chains; and throwing himself at full length upon the deck, grappled a ring-bolt there, and swore not to let it go, though hacked to pieces." In a real life case, the Mapias furnished another "Freewill" to a sandalwood trader in 1809: "Several wished to go with us. . . . One of them found his way into the cabin, and could not be persuaded to leave the vessel, so we took him with us and named him David Freewill. . . . We cut off his hair, which was three feet long, and hung over his shoulders before and behind, and dressed him in a jacket and trousers, which made him very proud."[40]

3

Rites of Passage

*Those who would go to sea for pleasure would go to hell
for a pastime.*

—European sailor's proverb[1]

Oceanians who worked or traveled on foreign ships entered a "wooden
world," which, despite resemblances to the Euroamerican societies that
produced the vessels, had its own distinctive customs.[2] *Kanaka*s would
undergo initiations by shipmates who had themselves once been inducted into the "fraternity." As global shipping developed, crews became increasingly cosmopolitan, because Euroamericans relied on
regional pools of nonwhite helpers or replacements. As early as the
seventeenth century, Spanish galleons brought Filipinos and Chinese
from Manila to Acapulco, where they mingled with Native American
and African sailors. Along the west coast of Africa, work gangs of native
"Kru-men" enabled foreign ships to function in humid, tropical climates
where white seamen had no immunities to local diseases. Bengali "lascars" provided a similar service for the British East India Company and,
along with quasi-Malay "Manila-men," found their way from Asian waters into the Pacific. United States vessels brought still more sailors of
African and Native American descent into the Pacific. The former were
often stereotyped as cooks and the latter as harpooners.[3]

American crews, which figured so prominently in the China trade and
Pacific whaling, were sometimes half to three-quarters foreign-born. The
crew of Melville's ill-fated *Pequod* was a realistic hodgepodge of ethnici-
ties, from Sicilian to Tahitian. Its three harpooners were Queequeg the Oceanian, Tashtego the Native American, and Daggoo the African; Manila-men
manned Captain Ahab's own whaleboat. Melville hinted that the mystic

quest for Moby Dick, the white whale, was symbolic of all things to all men: "In essence whiteness is not so much a color as the visible absence of color, and at the same time the concrete of all colors."[4] That metaphor could apply to assimilative Euroamerican shipping itself. Like Queequeg, *kanaka*s would assume great importance in the new maritime frontier, to the extent that they comprised about one-fifth of the sailors in the American whaling fleet by the mid-1800s.[5] They joined a multiethnic brotherhood of seafarers, whose experiences ranged from routine merchant service to whaling, with its uncertain pay, risky hunt, oily tryworks, and "dirty blubber hunters" who took pride in "following the seas for life."[6]

The privileged lifestyle of ennobled diplomats was usually quite different from that of working *kanaka*s, but all Oceanian voyagers had to adapt to new surroundings. Melville said Queequeg was "a creature in the transition state—neither caterpillar nor butterfly. He was just enough civilized to show off his outlandishness in the strangest possible manner. His education was not yet completed."[7] Stripped of its condescension, that is not a bad description of liminality. Like Queequeg the harpooner, Pacific Islanders were often able to transfer traditional skills to their new endeavors, and they actively mediated between ship and shore, making acculturation more of a two-way process. But as international as the shipping circuit became, it remained in essence colonial, because Euroamericans controlled the capital, technology, command structure, and, consequently, most of the profits. Once at sea, all hands had to become "a different breed of men . . . because the prospect of drowning concentrates a man's mind wonderfully."[8]

Euroamerican Shipboard Life

Ships that came to Oceania from Europe or America could never entirely represent their home societies. Captains had varying goals, from naval exploration with scientists and artists on board, to commerce, including whaling. There were missionary vessels, some built in the islands by the hands of converts, and passenger ships carrying convicts, plantation laborers, or organized companies of settlers. Nor were maritime labor markets always economically efficient, as the recurring theme of conscription demonstrates.[9] Yet work on Euroamerican ships tended to share a few broad traits that enabled the system to function reliably enough to attract investors. These characteristics need to be kept in mind as we explore the experiences of Pacific Islanders.

First, life was generally hierarchical and regimented. Officers were usually lodged and fed better in aft cabins, while the crew were crowded into the forecastle or gun deck, from which bells and whistles called them to serve their assigned watches twice a day. The British navy, which first explored the Pacific so systematically, was almost a replica of the English class system, except that it was possible for men like James Cook to work their way up through the ranks to become a maritime monarch. A sea captain was, in John Masefield's words, "not only a commander, but a judge of the supreme court, and a kind of human parallel to Deity.... His word was absolute." Cruel masters "could single out and break the heart of any man whom they disliked." "Jack Tar" often risked his life between a devilish captain and the deep blue sea, because shipmasters had to maintain order in a cramped community in which lives depended on each other. Flogging around the fleet, running the gauntlet, and keelhauling were common punishments in the British navy. Cook actually disciplined more seamen than did the more notorious Bligh of the *Bounty*—without inspiring a mutiny.[10]

As Euroamerican countries went through the rite of industrialization in the late eighteenth and nineteenth centuries, seamen became transferable from one job title and wage category to another, almost like standardized parts. Press gangs often "crimped" (forcibly enlisted) sailors, but even voluntary recruits found themselves proletarianized and segregated into the lower deck. The market value of English sailors increased during wartime, when half died at sea. Benjamin Morrell recommended "treating seamen like men, instead of lording it over them as if they were slaves," but this attitude was exceptional. J. Ross Browne wrote, "There is no class of men in the world who are so unfairly dealt with, so oppressed, so degraded, as the seamen." Yet he also said of his own shipmates, "A more ignorant, heartless, treacherous, beastly set of men, I think, never existed.... They were all blustering and cowardly." Sailors were social marginals to begin with, ranging from hardened ex-convicts to poor, inexperienced "greenhands." Cook's historian, J.C. Beaglehole, described Cook's crew as "the ordinary British sailors of the time ... so savage, brutal, drunken, insensitive, and blasphemous that one wonders that even a kindly Deity permitted the ship to put to sea."[11] Hence the argument for a strong hand.

Second, Euroamerican shipping was capitalistic, that is, profit-oriented, which placed a premium on cost-efficiency and individual merit. A greenhand, or landsman, would make the lowest wage and enjoy the least status as one of

> the waisters, the men stationed in the waist, the men "without art or judgment," who hauled aft the fore and main sheets, and kept the decks white. They were the scavengers, swabbers, pumpers, the doers of the ship's dirty work, the pigsty keepers, and ship's sewer men. They were sometimes ordinary seamen who were strong enough but too stupid to be stationed aloft. Generally they were landsmen, unfit for other duties.[12]

English vessels going overseas recruited mariners from deep-sea fishing and coastal coal shipping. With experience, a man could rise to be ordinary seaman, able-bodied seaman, boatswain (bosun), or mate. On whaleships, sailors were paid a lay, or percentage of the final gross profit, according to their skill rating. A boatsteerer (harpooner) was paid well, because without his accuracy on the hunt, no whales would be caught. He would spear a whale from the bow of the boat, then trade places at the rudder (hence his title) with the mate, who would make the final kill. There were also specialists, like the carpenter or cook (whose only qualification, in the British navy, was to be a disabled pensioner). A purser managed the ship's supplies, including the "slop chest" from which sailors purchased dry goods. He received bonuses for unused supplies, a practice that did not always endear him to the crew. As Una Robertson says, "Where the purser was in league with the captain he could keep livestock such as hogs and cattle on oatmeal and pease charged to the accounts of dead sailors." Some shipmasters deliberately badgered crewmen into deserting to save the cost of their wages.

Third, Euroamerican shipping relied on a resident labor force that developed its own communal identity and language. Sailors formed friendships in the dank forecastle but more particularly on shared watches, usually one four-hour shift during the day and another at night. Half a dozen men might work together, eat from a common pot, exchange stories, and drink grog, a watered-down rum ration. Greenhands often had mentors, who in return for advice received choicer portions of food and bigger shares of grog from their messmates. "Youngsters," Robertson says, "were sometimes bullied and deprived of the best victuals by the older men." This prison-like system of mateship meant that forecastles on whaleships, in Samuel Morison's words, were "more efficient schools of vice than reformatories." Yet Samuel Johnson claimed, "No man will be a sailor who has the contrivance to get himself into a jail; for being in a ship is being in a jail with the chance of being drowned. ... A man in jail has more room, better food, and commonly better company."[13] Old hands taught neophytes nautical terms, sailor slang, and a trade pidgin that ranged from the Americas to Canton. They bestowed nicknames "that arose from personal peculiarities, or from some whim of the sailors with whom they messed: and they were consequently seldom called by their real names, except at muster."[14]

Seamen who crossed the Line (equator) for the first time went through the rite of Neptune, which inducted them into the Realm of the Deep. On the eve of that fateful passage over an invisible world demarcation, King Neptune might call from under the bow, "Ship ahoy!" After the ship identified itself, Neptune would ask if any of his children on board had never seen his dominions? The captain would say aye, so the Sea King made an appointment for noon the following day. The great crossing could be cele-brated, under the gaze of Neptune's royally garbed retinue, by shaving the neophyte in a chair built to tip backwards and dunk its occupant into a water-filled canvas: "Two sailors immediately seize the victim and dip and splash him around until he is greatly exhausted and nearly drowned." This ceremony crushed egos into collegial unity. To forego the shaving and dunk-ing, greenhands were sometimes allowed to pay a fine, by buying grog for Neptune and his entourage. Too many fines paid, however, made one "god" so merry that, "tired of being out of his element," he jumped overboard and had to be rescued. Jacques Arago wrote that his ship's cook defended him-self from his would-be initiators with an iron spit: "In vain did the pipes of the pumps drench the unruly cook with salt water, which mingled with the sauces he had prepared, without making them any the worse."[15]

Life on a Euroamerican ship, whether whaler, man-of-war, or merchant-man, could thus be harsh, even for seamen who supposedly shared the dominant value system. Long voyages, bad food, brutal working conditions, poor sanitation, narrow living space, and low pay caused desertions, espe-cially in the palmy Pacific. Why, then, would men go to sea? Perhaps wanderlust, if they came from fishing ports with rugged hinterlands, but poverty of choice usually underlay such dreaming. As pearl trader Louis Kornitzer wrote, "The sheer need for cash starts more men off on adven-tures than your romantic would allow. I was in sore straits for money. It seemed to me then that I needed it more than any man in England." In the words of Melville's Ishmael, the "everlasting itch for things remote" was rendered more inspirational by empty pockets and, "a damp, drizzly No-vember in my soul." As for the tyranny of life aboard ship, he asked, "Who aint a slave?" Seaports were havens for semiskilled misfits and proletarian refugees who gained the odd freedom of "almost nomadic mobility." Sail-ors could be fired from one ship and hired on another almost the very next day, because their life was so hard that recruits were not always readily available.[16]

Seamen also developed a well-deserved reputation for irresponsible "binges" in port and for shipping out again when they were broke. Once at sea, their pay advances and purchases from the ship's slop chest sometimes put them into debt before they returned to port. In Oceania, sailors were not renowned for their morality, as missionary Sheldon Dibble lamented: "When they pass Cape Horn they hang up their consciences there till they return." Dillon called his crew, "without exception the most abandoned set I ever met with; they were all deserters from other ships, not one of them going by his proper name." Some ships themselves bore false names and recruited crew illegally. Euroamerican vessels, then, would expose *kanakas* to a special kind of "civilization," the negative imprint of which was be-moaned by some observers. Young Hawaiians who shipped out, for example, were unlikely to learn frugality. They tended to squander their pay advances before the ship sailed, or refuse to reenlist until their money was gone. In 1827, the log of the *Owhyhee,* which was trading for furs on the Columbia River, recorded, "Sweetened a Conacher [*kanaka*] for stealing run, 2 dozen [lashes]."[17]

Initiations

A somewhat ironic adjustment that some Oceanians endured on foreign ships was seasickness, a common rite of passage for continental recruits. Apparently, the movement of larger hulls on the waves was significantly different from what canoe travelers were used to, as numerous accounts testify. Until he acquired his "sea legs," Lee Boo often had to lie down, and he dreamt that his parents knew he was sick. It was customary for "old salts" to taunt greenhands about their seasickness; Captain Dumont d'Urville ridiculed a Maori chief who was his guest: "It was indeed curious to see this savage, who would have faced death without flinching on a battlefield, so downcast and griefstricken that he abandoned himself to his sorrow and whined plaintively like a sulky child who cannot get his own way." Raymond Davis wrote just as unsympathetically of his whaleship's newly hired *kanaka*s, as they rolled back and forth between the rails whenever the ship moved, groaning in their own spilled food and vomit. In 1795, the fur traders *Lee Boo* and *Jackall* escaped captivity, in part, because the Hawaiian warriors on board became seasick.[18]

Less surprising a test of fortitude was homesickness. Tupaia, already exiled from his own island, was said to show no regret about leaving Tahiti, and J.C. Mullett said that two Hawaiians who volunteered to ship out were "strangers to fear [and] always ready to brave any danger, at the word given." But other Oceanians wept or sang sadly as the ship sailed far from home; some tried to steer the ship toward a familiar star, or voiced despair during a storm. Captives, of course, had special reasons to lament their plight and would search the horizon for a known landmark. When John Williams kidnapped two Niueans to convert them, he recorded their unhappiness: "As the youths perceived that we were losing sight of their island, they became most frantic in the expressions of their grief, tearing their hair and howling in the most affecting manner. . . . For the first three or four days . . . we could induce them neither to eat, to drink nor to sleep." Dumont d'Urville kidnapped five men from Tikopia and wrote, "These poor wretches at first wanted to throw themselves into the sea to get back to their island, and they asked for pieces of wood, indicating by signs that these would be sufficient to keep them afloat."[19]

Yet even willing voyagers could experience "cultural kidnapping." Omai barely escaped from being sacrificed on Huahine and murdered on Ra'iatea, so he was afraid that the first shipboard church service he saw was another attempt on his life. Other Islanders feared that their white hosts were cannibals because of the peculiar foods they ate, such as salted ribs and hard brown biscuits. Kadu of Woleai was relieved when he saw cattle for the first time in Alaska and was told that the meat came from them. Williams's captive Niueans at first refused cooked flesh in disgust, thinking they too would be cannibalized, until they saw the sailors preparing and eating a pig. Such ignorance could reverse itself, as when Euroamericans were unaware of Oceanian territoriality. Dumont's Maori guides were embarrassed because approaching canoers were old enemies; they hid their faces and "begged, nay, implored me to kill the newcomers. They went so far as to demand guns so that they could fire on them themselves."[20] Bougainville claimed that Ahutoru was so impressed by French medical techniques that he "would often fall into an ecstatic fit, and blush for his own country, saying with grief, *aouaou Taiti*." The Tahitian might only have been flattering his hosts, but Nena of Kosrae, uncertain about a Russian ship's forge, bell, and telescope, clung to the captain's arm. Nevertheless, familiarity could demystify alien technology. Morrell's Melanesian captive studied foreign tools and machinery to master "the use and principle of every operation."[21]

Many island cultures had intoxicants, from kava to ti root, and alcohol abuse was a Euroamerican sailor tradition, especially in port. Temoana of Nukuhiva learned to drink wine from a shipmaster who urged him, despite his initial dislike of the first taste, "Drink a little, and by and by you will love it."[22] By 1877, a labor recruiter boarded the *Bobtail Nag* in Sydney to find "a mixed crew of white men and Kanakas sprawling about the deck in various stages of inebriation, and in positions and attitudes which may be described as the sentimental, the pegged out, pugilistic." Bay of Islands, where sailors often found lodging in grog shops, witnessed fights between drunken *kanaka*s and local men, usually over women. Tamana Jack of Kiribati frequently squabbled with Maoris and once lost his clothes in a bar fight. Whaling captain Frank Bullen wrote about seeing his crew, "including the Kanakas, emerge from a grog-shop plentifully supplied with bottles, and seating themselves on the beach, commence their carouse. The natives evinced the greatest eagerness to get drunk, swallowing down the horrible 'square gin' as if it were water. They passed with the utmost rapidity through all the stages of drunkness. Before they had been ashore an hour, most of them were lying like logs, in the full blaze of the sun, on the beach."[23]

Another initiation that Oceanian recruits experienced, often with delight, was adopting new clothing. Although they might not always be uniformed, Euroamerican seamen did their own tailoring and had a certain kit, walk, and look, as if they belonged to "another country." As Richard Henry Dana explained in 1840,

> A sailor has a peculiar cut to this clothes, and a way of wearing them which a green hand can never get. The trousers, tight round the hips, and thence hanging long and loose about the feet, a superabundance of checked shirt, a low-crowned, well-varnished black hat, worn on the back of the head, with half a fathom of black ribbon hanging over the left eye, and a slip-tie to the black silk neckerchief, with sundry other minutiae, are signs, the want of which betrays the beginner at once.[24]

In 1829, the crew of a U.S. warship dressed up visiting Marquesans: "They had been but a few minutes with us, before they were metamorphosed, from bare savages, into sturdy tars, in frocks, trowsers, and tarpaulin." After a whaler recruited a Hope (Arorae) Islander in 1854, "The old man sent him forward and told us to use him well and learn him something. One gave him a shirt, another a hat, pants, etc. We then cut his hair, put a knife in his pocket, Christened him Hope and had him metamorphosed into a Yankee sailor." [25]

Hawaiian historian John Papa I'i wrote that foreign clothing was a primary incentive for *kanaka*s to enlist, since payment was often in the form of slops. One Hawaiian became quite a dandy, "curled and perfumed like his white shipmate, and wearing Congress boots on his feet, and gloves on his hands, and smiles on his dusky face."[26] Gifts of apparel were not only a form of assimilation but also a means of pacification when a common language was lacking, especially if the voyager's voluntarism was questionable. Quiros and Cook, as we have seen, tried to befriend their captives with Western-style clothes. Even castaways had to conform to the dress, hairstyle, and cleanliness standards of their foreign rescuers, though shoes could be difficult to enforce. Foreign clothing became an acquired taste for Lee Boo of Palau. At first, he took off the shirt and waistcoat he received, but he always wore his trousers. Keate wrote of him, "when he had been a little time accustomed, his new-taught sense of propriety was so great, that he would never change his dress, or any part of it, in the presence of another person, always retiring for that purpose to some dark corner where no one could see him."[27]

Ennobled tourists were likely to receive finer clothing than what was available in the ship's slop chest, but status is by definition relative. *Kanaka* "haves" might show off their acquisitions ostentatiously to "have-nots," or even express embarrassment at other Oceanians' nakedness. Omai flaunted his London souvenirs to Maoris to arouse envy, and that display helped him to recruit two servant boys. Kadu so enjoyed his new finery that he disdained even to look at his Marshallese friends:

> Kadu, who had been presented with a yellow cloak, and red apron, walked proudly in his ludicrous finery, without condescending to notice his companions, who gazed on him with astonishment from their boats, and could not conceive the metaphorphosis. In vain they cried "Kadu! Kadu!" He did not deign them a look, but walked proudly about on the deck, always taking care to turn himself in such a manner that they might be able to admire his finery.[28]

In 1824, Te Pehi Kupe of Aotearoa jumped onto the British whaler *Urania* leaving most of his traditional attire in a canoe, which he sent away. Wearing nothing but a mat, he insisted that the captain take him to see King George so that he could receive guns and clothing, like Hongi Hika. Three years later, the Maori commoner Moehanga, who had been to England, asked Peter Dillon to taken him to Calcutta, because he wanted a red soldier's jacket to complement his old cap. The Maori slave Kokako, who was escaping to become a *uropi,* put on his new French clothes "straight away as if he had been used to them all his life."[29]

Euroamericans projected their own imaginations onto *kanaka* costume changes. Charles Stewart, on a ship in the Marquesas, preferred natives attired in "the glittering buttons, epaulets, and laced hat of an officer thickly thronged, or the less expensive but gayer uniform of a marine" to "the wild islander, with his tataued skin, savage ornaments, unlanced spear, and war-club tufted with the hair of enemies, slain by him in battle." Yet as sailor clothing made its way onto Pacific Islands, visitors also mocked the "bohemian" trappings of local boatmen dressed in motley hand-me-downs. In 1840, Francis Olmstead laughed at seeing two Hawaiians in Honolulu lord it over their poorer compatriots. One wore a sailor's heavy pea jacket without pants, and the other wore big boots and a loincloth. Such comments were ironic, considering the flights of fancy that Euroamericans sometimes indulged in when they gave Oceanians clothes. One British crew hired a ni-Vanuatu interpreter and dressed him up "in a delightful Christy Minstrel dress."[30]

In fact, the Islanders had their own agendas. Poreo of Tahiti used his British costume as a disguise on unfamiliar Huahine, even muttering English-sounding nonsense words when he went ashore with Cook. Opai, a Hawaiian on the *Hope* in 1791, insisted on wearing his best American suit when going ashore for water in the Marquesas. "When he returned on board," his captain wrote, "I enquired of him what he had seen on shore, and his answer was many fine women. I asked him if he saw nothing else, but he said no, for the women crowded about him so as to shut away other objects from his sight."[31] Oceanian interpreters sometimes removed their foreign clothes in order to win the confidence of other Pacific Islanders, as Ahutoru did in Samoa, and chiefly ambassadors donned their traditional costumes when they deemed it appropriate. Maori chiefs wore their mats on shipboard and in Australia, but when they arrived back in New Zealand, they went ashore in red military uniforms, armed with swords, pistols, and muskets, to impress rivals.[32]

Another identity change was nicknaming. Such labels could be sarcastic at times, but the practice also resembled Oceanian customs of exchanging names or adopting new titles. Hitihiti, one of Cook's guides, had been Mahine before he exchanged names with a chief on Mo'orea. Ahutoru exchanged names with Bougainville and called himself Boutavery, but on his way home from France he changed his name to Mayoa. Not all nicknames could be chosen: indigenous names were often difficult for outsiders to pronounce, so *kanaka*s received monickers according to the time-honored whims of their messmates. Omai became "Jack" among his English crewmates and Able-Bodied Seaman Tetuby Homy in the ship's record.[33] Americans called *kanaka*s Jack or Tom, Ben Franklin or Andrew Jackson, nautical terms like Ropeyarn or Luff, and the names of their islands, such as Owhyhee (Hawai'i) or Oneehehow (Ni'ihau). In 1849, only two of ten Hawaiians hired by an English ship kept their real names. "Chance, or some peculiarity of the individual," Davis wrote, "soon fastened new appellations upon the [*kanaka*s], and they bore them thereafter, while with us." The origins of Big Man and Little Bill are obvious. Old John Gilpin apparently had the same posture as an English cartoon character.[34]

Morrell, in Robinson Crusoe style, called his New Guinean "Sunday," after the day he was captured. But he later told the American press that the dark-skinned man's real name was Tellum-by-by Darco! Oceanians sometimes borrowed names from men they admired or resembled, in a form of cross-cultural theater. Opai of Kaua'i sailed to the American Northwest, China, and Boston and took the name Jack Ingraham from his second shipmaster, but on the island of Hawai'i he was known as Kalehua. Another Hawaiian in the fur trade called himself George Washington. In 1834, a Fijian took the name Verani, having been on a French ship, but by 1850 he was a Christian convert named Elijah. Maori chiefs traveling with Dillon asked him for English names in order, they believed, to be treated better. He gave them outlandish titles, such as Admiral Thaki, King Charley Moyhanger, or Marquis Wyemattee; he named one after a Dr. Robert Tytler who had taken him to court in Tasmania, and others after Irish personalities, such as His Royal Highness Brian Boroo, a celebrated king who had died fighting the Danes.[35]

Every nation baptized Oceanian recruits its own way, adopting them into its "family" on the sea. Identities could even change from one ship to another, making it more difficult to keep track of *kanaka*s in the records. A Dutch trader hired a Hawaiian sailor who had already served on several American whalers and renamed him Kroon (Crown, after the coin). Spaniards and Russians named their recruits according to the saint's feast day when they came aboard. Alfred Tetens said he named Hermann Vesta after his ship, the *Vesta,* and the Euroamerican name for the islands, the Hermits. Because of their repetitious monarchy, British ships produced a fair number of Georges. The catch-all family name "Kanaka" is ubiquitous in ships' records, but it represented more a genealogy of category than of ancestry. For example, the whaler *Two Brothers* hired two "kanakas" in 1859, and almost exactly two years later, it discharged a Harry Kanaka and a Peter Kanaka and hired two other "kanakas" it called Bob and Dick. The Hawaiian word for person migrated around the Pacific in shipboard pidgin. Spanish explorers transferred Columbus's misnomer to the Pacific by calling Melanesians "Indians," and as late as 1827, Dillon, who interacted with Pacific Islanders as much as anyone, was still calling his Polynesian crewmen "Indians"—even those he took to India itself. Less officially, there were more pejorative racial epithets such as savage, blackboy, nigger, buck, or fuzzy-wuzzy, but *kanaka* grouped Oceanian sailors (and plantation workers) into a pan-Pacific brotherhood.[36]

The pidgin they learned to speak also became a multiethnic medium. Some Euroamerican explorers or traders made an effort to learn indigenous languages, which missionaries often transliterated (and standardized), but Oceanians on foreign ships normally had to adopt the language of their hosts or employers, at least in "broken" form. Ahutoru and Omai had trouble learning French or English and relied on translators who knew some Tahitian, but the Tahitians taken to Peru were interviewed in Spanish and reportedly described visits to their island by Wallis, Bougainville, and Cook. Surville's captive Solomon Islander was said to learn French with great facility, though staying in Peru mingled Spanish into his vocabulary and accent. In the nineteenth century, Anglo-American ships dominated Pacific commerce, so *kanaka*s learned more English, including swearing. "Whaler's Maori" evolved along the coasts of New Zealand; Te A'ara, a Maori chief who learned English on whalers, took the name George and greeted foreigners with an ironic "How do you do, my boy?"[37] Messmates taught greenhands work vocabulary, as when Jo Bob of Rarotonga passed on shipboard terms to a Black Portuguese recruit from the Cape Verde Islands on night watch. But every mate was responsible for the efficiency of his watch. In bad weather off the coast of Peru, one failed to communicate successfully with his Tahitian crew and caused the ship to wreck.[38]

The rite of Neptune was a more overt initiation into the family of the forecastle. An English crew warned its Tahitian recruits about "infernal spirits rising out of the water" whenever ships reached a certain place in the ocean. The neophytes already regretted leaving sight of land and embarking on a seemingly endless voyage. They asked if the monster stories were true and, according to John Turnbull, "on being undeceived, gave a scope to their joy in the most extravagant manner, leaping and hallooing about the deck." They were still shaved at the equator, but the ritual seemed to make "a deep impression on the Otaheitans." Two young Hawaiians, Opukahaia and Hopu, experienced the rite aboard an American sealer entirely at night. Kept aft on the quarterdeck, they were told that Neptune was a god who could make his iron canoe and paddle float. One sailor went forward, dressed in an old great coat and sheepskin hair, and called out loudly through a speaking-trumpet, "Have you got my boys?" When the captain answered yes, both *kanaka*s had to go shake hands with the king or become his servants in the sea. Their reward for such courtesy was having seawater poured through his trumpet into their mouths. Alert Opukahaia held the trumpet against his cheek in the dark to escape swallowing, but Hopu vomited for a whole day.[39]

Status and Skills

Incorporating Pacific Islanders into the Euroamerican shipping circuit was a test of both its hierarchy and its meritocracy. Just as island chiefs might separate their white beachcombers into perceived categories, so a captain (like Surville) would divide Oceanian voyagers into either cabin mates or crewmen, according to their apparent status or utility. Islanders already knew about hierarchy, especially on long voyages, when the navigator's word was law.[40] The question was, would they enjoy the same rank aboard ship as they had on shore, or be allowed to earn it? Ennobled tourists sometimes assumed the same rank as ship's officers and this created class ambiguities. Ahutoru lacked high rank in Tahiti, but on Bougainville's vessel he acted as haughtily toward his French shipmates as a chief toward his subjects. Tupaia traveled with a native servant, but he apparently tested the limits of his shipmates' tolerance. A navigator of rank, he was said to have alienated white crewmates by expecting special treatment. In contrast, his young servant Tayota seemed to fit their Crusoean expectations, "being of a mild and docile disposition, ready to do any kind office for the meanest in the ship, and never complaining, but always pleased." Humble Tayota became "the darling of the ship's company from the highest to the lowest."[41]

Omai, too, tested the limits of privilege. His status, like Ahutoru's, derived only from favoritism, and when he drank too much and threw up, the common sailors taunted him. Kadu flaunted his new rank by asking the Russian sailors to wait upon him, but according to Kotzebue, "He once ordered the waiter to bring him a glass of water; the latter took him by the arm, led him to the water-butt, and gave him the cup out of which the others drank."[42] Some Maori chiefs sailed as common sailors on British ships and suffered from mistreatment. George of Whangaroa, after two years of wasted efforts and humiliation on a sealer, received no pay at Sydney. On his return voyage on the *Boyd,* he fell ill and was accused by the cook of stealing pewter spoons—which the cook himself had evidently dropped overboard by accident along with dirty dishwater. The captain had the Maori flogged and, when George protested that he was a chief, added insult to injury by calling him a "cokey" (slave). The Maori was also deprived of food and, before going ashore in Aotearoa, stripped of all his English clothes. When his outraged kin saw George's lacerated back, they massacred and ate the whole crew and burned the ship. The Maori chief Ruatara experienced similar abuse during seven years of voyaging on British whaleships until Marsden, the English missionary, came to his rescue. Morrell's "Sunday" got along well with everyone in his crew by wisely displaying "a most inveterate and praiseworthy habit of minding his own business."[43]

Living accommodations are one index of status, and on a ship, space was at a premium. Like officers, dignitaries had more comforts and slept in aft cabins, either in a normal berth or on a floor mat or hospital mattress. Their ability to eat at table with proper utensils was evidently considered a measure of their humanity. The English captain who took Te Pehi Kupe to London said of the Maori chief, "all the time he was on board he lived at my table. . . . The man is now cevelized." Hawaiian Chief Manui'a showed such skilled table manners that his Russian host concluded, "he had often been on board European ships." The same captain said of Kadu of Woleai that he "accustomed himself with incredible readiness to the use of knives and forks . . . as if he had been long associated with civilized people."[44] Yet even VIPs might be hesitant at first to enter the dark aft cabins. Those who did would not necessarily sleep well; they sometimes got restless or giggled all night because of their strange surroundings. Moreover, a belief that exotic objects had spiritual power could present protocol problems for newcomers. Two New Guineans on Morrell's ship revealed this issue, if we read behind Thomas Jacobs's mockery:

> When we placed them at the supper-table, they sat very uneasily, and, jumping up, examined closely the camp-stools upon which we had seated them.

Having satisfied themselves how they were made, and that there was no charm about them, they again were seated. The knives, forks, plates, cups, etc. underwent a severe scrutiny. They thought that tin cups, bottles, and tumblers were shells that grew upon the coral reefs and sand-spits in the moon. . . . [45]

Fitting Oceanians into a ship's class system could be a delicate process. Young Maori chiefs were usually willing to do cabin chores, such as washing plates or mopping the deck, as long as no one suggested that such work was beneath their station. Yet when Tupehi's own servant forgot to put sugar in his tea, as he had seen the English do, the chief sulked in his bed over the affront. Finally Marsden, his missionary mentor, delivered the sugar himself. Omai's Maori servants were sent to steerage, where only their own cloaks separated them from the bare deck. Cook also bedded his three Maori captives "upon the lockers" after a full meal, with Tupaia standing watch to comfort the boys. This accommodation was not terribly different from the hammocks the white crew slept in on the gun deck. At first, Kadu slept above deck on a mat close to the captain, Otto von Kotzebue, who was avoiding the heat of his cabin and also keeping an eye on his guest. Later, Kadu ate and slept with the officers in the aft cabin. Hawaiian and Tongan royals traveled as comfortably as white passengers, but lesser voyagers might be assigned to a sail on the half deck. The Tikopian commoners on Dumont's exploring ship slept in the cutter, but because they were simply traveling to Vanikoro, they could spend their days under an awning set up on the stern. Ennobled tourists might have little to do but chat, sing, or sleep, though a few helped with the pumps or even pulled ropes. Marsden's Maori protégés spent most of their time carving spear handles, cleaning their firearms from Sydney, or playing chess. [46]

For working *kanaka*s, however, training in shipboard duties usually consisted of being arbitrarily divided into watches and like other greenhands, "driven about mercilessly amid a perfect hurricane of profanity and blows." In the mid-1800s, half the seamen in the American whaling fleet were usually new recruits, whose seasoning could be trying for an officer. In 1840, Charles Wilkes regretted hiring so many Hawaiians to replace his discharged sailors: "Though well-disposed men, they are unfitted for service in men-of-war. They do very well when they are working in small parties, but are inclined to be idle, and disposed to let others do all the work . . . they are not apt at learning either the language or the ideas necessary for sailors." Most disliked going aloft but proved useful on the ship's boats. Still, he praised the Tahitians already employed in his naval squadron, who worked speedily and well. [47] Foreign mariners commended the rapidity with which "tractable" Oceanians learned terminology and work duties. Eating habits were yet another liminal test. *Kanaka*s often missed raw fish and fresh fruit, though they learned to soak hard biscuit in coffee and acquired a taste for salted meat. Some surprised their shipmates by eating leftovers and parts of animals that others disdained, and a few were accused of bringing vermin aboard.[48]

Timing could affect the quality of recruits. In 1848, Mullett said of two young Hawaiian recruits, "I took them both in my watch, and my first business was to learn them the English names of the ship's rigging, masts, spars, etc., etc., which they learned very readily, and long before the close of the voyage had become very handy." On another ship, two Hawaiian sailors quickly became able to "climb aloft with extraordinary velocity," and one learned to steer.[49] Yet during the peak of the 1849 California gold rush, the quality of Hawaiian recruits dropped after the experienced *kanaka*s shipped out. One shipmate complained that even raising the anchor was slow work: "All the long day we labored, expostulated and gesticulated." Old "John Gilpin" rarely understood orders: "If he was told to find even the main topsail halliards, he would turn in every direction, with a ghastly grin on his anatomy of a face, thrusting his hands in this way, and that." In 1851, the *Wanderer* left San Francisco with a mostly Oceanian crew that was amateurish—particularly a one-eyed Rotuman, Friday, who was said to watch the compass with his blind side and the rigging with the other.[50]

Yet many Oceanian sailors were able to transfer to ships traditional skills, such as boat-handling, swimming, and diving, all talents that their employers frequently praised. To bring his Russian hosts drinking water, Kadu "frequently went down to the bottom of the sea, where it is well known that the water is not so salty, with a cocoa-nut, with only a small opening." Tapeooe of Tahiti used his diving skill to repair a leak on the bottom of the *Plumier* and to gather bêche-de-mer from the waters around Palau. *Kanaka*s went with shore parties to gather coconuts from trees, "a task which they performed with much more ease than we could," to cut wood, or to load water into casks that had to be rolled to the beach, floated to the ship, and hauled aboard. But their specialty was boat handling, especially in difficult surf; such "landsmen" provided an essential link between ship and shore. In 1826, Anglo-Australian shippers recommended that Britain annex New Zealand, in part because Maoris "readily volunteer their services, and prove orderly and powerful seamen."[51]

Accurate spear-throwing ability translated readily into whale harpooning, true to the Queequeg archetype. *Kanaka*s were said to pursue whales with fearless enthusiasm, and on lookout duty their keen eyesight made them excellent whale spotters. One whaler claimed that Maoris "will go alongside a Whale more boldly than a British Man."[52] In Melville's story *Omoo*, an Islander called Bembo, who was based on real-life Maori shipmate Benbo Byrne, supposedly defied death by actually jumping onto a whale to make sure his harpoon hit home and lived to rise out of the foam. This classic sea story earned repetition in Arthur Thomson's 1859 history of New Zealand, as if it were fact. Tall, strong Harry the Marquesan, according to a fellow boatsteerer, "was an ideal man for this position and might well have posed for French's statue of the 'Whaleman.' " Harry's brother was another harpooner, but it was Harry who, on his two-hour watch atop the fore-topgallant yard, won the prize of twenty pounds of tobacco for being the first to sight a whale. [53]

Oceanians also served as cabin boys, personal servants, even cooks. Mesiol of Pohnpei scrubbed the decks, a daily ship routine, and because of his experience in slaughtering pigs, he helped the cook. Native divers were essential on bêche-de-mer and pearling ships, but their employment was irregular, and in the atolls they could easily be replaced. Most *kanaka* voyagers worked seasonally on merchant ships or whalers. By 1830, Northwest American fur trading vessels were manned largely by Hawaiians, and it became standard practice to send out only skeletal crews from Boston because Hawaiian hands were available. In the 1840s, as many as a thousand recruits left Hawai'i yearly, mostly on whalers. Similarly, Maoris and Tahitians made up significant numbers of Australian whaling personnel. By mid-century, ship crews might be two-thirds or more *kanaka* from various beaches, including Rotuma and the Loyalty Islands of New Caledonia.[54] Clearly, the liminality of seafaring was being indigenized.

Rewards

Oceanians came to occupy an important niche in Pacific shipping, but what can be said of their pay and chances for promotion in the purported meritocracy? In theory, showing a willingness to work and proper respect for officers and senior crewmates would permit any sailor to rise in rank. As historian Samuel Eliot Morison wrote, "a whaling skipper generally knew the record if not the pedigree of every man who sailed under his command." Yet the relatively poor English-speaking ability of nonwhites and other foreign nationals was sometimes used as an excuse to pay them less than native-born New Englanders.[55] African Kru-men and Indian lascars were usually hired as cheap, supplementary work gangs and discharged before the ship left their coasts. British laws to prevent their being stranded destitute in London actually discouraged their employment, which was already at lower pay than whites received. This pattern of discrimination seems to have extended to *kanaka*s as well, who were long considered relatively cheap replacements and regionally disposable.[56] But with experience, market demand, and, in the case of Hawai'i, some government regulation, the overall trend was for wages to gradually improve.

In 1789, the American fur trading ship *Columbia* hired Jack Atu of Ni'ihau as a seaman for one pound, ten shillings per month, its lowest greenhand wage; he served for only nine months. The job classification "landsmen" on whalers could prevent *kanaka*s from receiving a lay, unless they actually participated in the chase. In 1797–98, the sealer *Nautilus* recruited nine Hawaiians as "landsmen" for about half-pay, mostly in slops from its own store. Ten years later, such boatmen earned twice as much, but fur companies still admitted to hiring them because "they are less expensive than American seamen." In 1813, the fur trader *New Hazard* paid off its Hawaiian crew with slops, though the *kanaka* boatswain made 50 percent more than the men he supervised.[57] Maoris at first shipped out as common sailors on whalers or sealers (often the same ship did both kinds of hunting) with little or no payment, except in manufactured goods. Even after the British annexation of New Zealand in 1840, some whalers paid Maoris less than their white counterparts because, one captain argued, "they are satisfied with a smaller share." Some skippers cheated *kanaka*s out of the two or three pounds per month they were due. One commented, "They are only niggers, let them wait for their pay."[58]

Discrimination lingered long in Oceanian-Euroamerican maritime relations. In 1814, Marsden told the Maoris who made up half the crew of his missionary vessel, the *Active,* that he would pay them two months in advance at wages commensurate with their services, "the same as I paid the Europeans according to the work they did—at this they were astonished and much gratified." Yet he assured the London secretary of his mission that once he employed more Maori crew on the *Active,* "her expenses will not be on that account so great."[59] Dillon, known for his paternalism toward Oceanians, paid his Polynesian seamen about the same as his Indian lascars, which was less than what his European crewmen received. Relative frequency of contact with ships, an index of market demand, could create regional disparities in wages. In 1834 a Tahitian harbor pilot asked fifteen Spanish dollars for his services, eight going to his queen; fifteen years later, a New Caledonian piloted a British warship from Isle of Pines to Noumea and was satisfied with old clothes, pipes, tobacco, a blanket, and a sovereign.[60]

It is worth considering what Oceanians, perhaps picked up for a few months of regional employment and dropped off anywhere in "kanakadom," might have regarded as good pay. One man's pittance could be another's treasure, and what was the boundary between tangible and intangible rewards? For example, Hawaiian seamen working in the American Northwest might be paid off in slops (clothing and other supplies), but for a long time cash was useless to them. Instead, they would present such imports to their chiefs and receive in return land and horses enough to become "great men."[61] Many *kanaka*s wanted firearms, and in Micronesia sticks of tobacco became a popular currency into which they converted their pay. In 1849, Tom Kanaka of Rotuma shipped out of Pohnpei for ten pounds of tobacco a month. Timarare of Banaba went ashore after a three-year absence with a trade box full of tobacco and hardware and, according to John Webster, "had but to make his choice, and there was but little fear of any damsel refusing him." Kadu freely gave away his possessions and thereby earned chief-like status in the Marshalls. He was paddled to shore in the place of honor in a canoe and carried over the surf on the shoulders of his friends.[62]

Hawaiian commoners were often said to desire nothing more than their daily fish and poi, but modest pay advances, quickly spent, lured them onto the ocean. One Euroamerican resident lamented, "The natives either sailed the seas with the whaling fleet, or else they did nothing at all. Apart from their strong emotional attachment to the whaling industry, and to the opportunities for profits it offered, the Hawaiians confined their activities to cultivating their taro patches."[63] After 1841, Hawaiian laws regulating recruitment helped to raise the pay of native sailors to parity with that of Euroamericans. The government required not only a two-hundred-dollar bond guaranteeing the safe return of all Hawaiian sailors, but also a twenty-dollar pay advance and anywhere from five to sixteen dollars per month in wages. As whaling boomed, captains began paying Hawaiians a share of the oil profits, usually at the standard "long lay" of a greenhand, about 1/200. Ordinary or able-bodied seamen might receive as high as 1/125, and becoming a boatsteerer (harpooner) could raise their pay to 1/95. By the 1830s, Rotumans were also sought by whalers and, as time passed, they reportedly made the same wages as their white shipmates. In 1838, the whaler *Australian* paid its eight Maoris 1/160–1/170 lay, which was about average for ordinary seamen. A Maori named John William earned promotion from ordinary seaman to boatsteerer in six months, which nearly doubled his lay to 1/100, equal to that of his fellow harpooners. After reaching Sydney, he shipped out again at that same rating and pay.[64]

For an Oceanian to become a boatsteerer was a major promotion, but other advances were also possible. As early as 1811, Boatswain Tom, a veteran Hawaiian Northwester, was said to be ready to rope-whip or curse any compatriot for an extra five dollars a month. In 1853–54, the American whaler *Edgar* recruited Hawaiians every spring for north Pacific hunting and was so successful it promoted almost half its crew. Some *kanaka*s became adept at navigating the maritime frontier, up to a point. A Tahitian boatswain had to manage Hawaiian hands he could barely communicate with, and failed, but in the 1830s, a literate Maori named James Earl Bailey served as second mate and later as chief mate on the Australian whaleship *Earl Stanhope*. He was reputedly of "excellent character," both as a whaler and as an officer. Yet he was mentioned so often in texts that he suggests the token exception rather than the rule. Other Polynesians, such as a Tahitian called John Bull, became mates, and employers provided *kanaka*s with written recommendations, a valuable career marker. A few Maoris and Hawaiians even commanded their own trading schooners, and some Marshallese and Cook Islands chiefs owned vessels.[65]

By 1900, nearly every island in Oceania was colonized by an outside power, thereby institutionalizing racial inequality. In the South Pacific, discrimination revived as early as 1878, when Australian seamen's unions lobbied companies like Burns Philp not to hire or to promote nonwhites. Yet from the late eighteenth century onward, thousands of Islanders chose to sail on foreign ships, despite meager rewards. They had survived on marine resources for generations, so it should not be surprising that Tuamotuan divers began to use their skills to earn wages in clothing or whisky, sometimes paid in advance. In *Omoo*, Melville described a Marquesan recruit who wanted only a red shirt, a pair of trousers, a hat, a plug of tobacco, and a pipe. E Ware had whaling experience and skillfully took the helm as soon as he came aboard a New Zealand Company ship, but all he asked for in return were his meals and a little tobacco. Edward Wakefield wrote of this Maori *Kanaka*, "I have often seen him, in the violent gales which we weathered on various parts of the coast, out on the end of the yard-arm doing the work of the best man in reefing, and cheering the sailors to exertion by some broad joke or irresistable grimace. He was fully competent to do the work of an able seaman; and his good humour under all circumstances was invincible."[66]

～ 4 ～

Contested Decks

*He was marvelous to look upon, the whale rider. . . . Upon
that beast he looked like a small tattooed figurine, dark
brown, glistening and erect. He seemed, with all his strength,
to be pulling the whale into the sky.*

—Witi Ihimaera of Aotearoa[1]

Evidence suggests that Pacific Islanders acculturated to new ways on Euroamerican ships. Yet that process was not always easy, and working *kanaka*s, in particular, experienced alienation. Resistance to domination can take many forms, from overt violence to superficial cooperation. Even the way that orders are carried out can limit authority, as when a Hawaiian supercargo traded his ship's supplies for the favors of local women in the Tuamotus. The "lazy native" some Euroamericans complained about really had a subversive agenda: he had worked to survive for years and discovered subtle ways to "negotiate" foreign power.[2] The structure of the contest was often one-sided, but at times roles could change. Louis Becke described the potentially ambivalent relationship between *kanaka*s and bosses:

> "Tarawa Bob" and "Rotuma Tom," two huge, soft-hearted, hard-fisted able seamen, whose light brown skins were largely illustrated by fantastic devices in blue and vermillion, were the respective brothers-in-law of the gentlemen who officiated as first and second mates of the schooner—Messrs Joe Freeman and Pedro do Ray. And if, occasionally, their superior position made these officers in times of emergency address their tattooed brethren-in-law in vigorous and uncomplimentary language, emphasized by a knockdown blow, no ill will was either felt on one side nor engendered on the other. Therefore, in moments of relaxation, when the ship lay at anchor and there was nothing to do, the two white men seated on one side of the skylight and the two

60

brown on the other, with a large bottle of Hollands gin, between them, would endeavor to rook each other at cards.[3]

Strategies of Adaptation

It is impossible to know exactly what Oceanian voyagers felt, since foreigners kept most of the written records, but shipping out clearly tested *kanakas*' identity and loyalty. The liminal experiences they shared in the new seafaring circuit led some to describe themselves, at least in certain contexts, as "all the same white man." John Nicholas claimed that George of Whangaroa "had acquired, too, from his intercourse with European sailors, a coarse familiarity of manner, mingled with a degree of sneering impudence, which gave him a character completely distinct from his countrymen." Nicholas also noted that another Maori, who had left home at a very early age, became quite inept at traditional dancing: "civilization had cramped his limbs." John Steward, a Hawaiian who loved to dress in fine clothes, chose to return from London to Honolulu, but a shipmate wrote, "I can never believe he took kindly to old Arcadian habits again. There might have been a time when John could expend all his taste on the arrangement of his breech-clout, and took pride in wearing it, but that time was past."[4]

The records show that many Oceanians possessed, or perhaps developed, a peculiar talent that helped them to adjust: mimicry. Education in Oceania was already built on imitation, and in the *limen* that could be playful. Richard Henry Dana said that Hawaiians picked out their coworkers' quirks "before we had observed them ourselves." Kotzebue wrote of Hawaiians, "Their great talent is mimicry, and habit made it very easy for us to understand each other." Kadu of Woleai also demonstrated this quality. He tried to imitate Kotzebue's walk and mannerisms and amused the crew by following the captain around like a duplicate, until an annoyed Kotzebue finally prohibited the game. When he heard a shipmate counting in Spanish, Kadu quickly copied his voice (perhaps knowing some Spanish already from his contact with Guam).[5] Omai's Maori servant, Kokoa, made himself popular among the crew by copying their ways and showing "a very humorous and lively disposition . . . he afforded us much mirth with his drolleries." Seventy years later, another Maori, E Ware, won himself a job on a New Zealand Company ship as "Jim Crow" by "mimicking almost every one on board," and other Maori voyagers amused themselves "in imitating the particular manner of walking, or any singularity of attitude which they had observed among the different persons in the ship." Three Marquesans on an American whaler mimicked "the sailors' dances, the singing tone of the Sandwich Islanders, peculiarities of manner amongst the crew, or the English language; which last they considered was nearest approached, by combining with some 'unknown tongue' a constant succession of hissing sounds."[6]

Such parody risked offense, but Oceanians also endeared themselves to their shipmates in other disarming ways. For example, Euroamericans often commented that *kanaka*s were warmhearted, emotional, and generous. Native sailors were known for sharing whatever they had with compatriots who lacked, "no matter how small the portion received by any one." Wilkes considered this inclusiveness "one of the most pleasing of their social customs, and shows an absence of all selfishness." When *kanaka*s smoked tobacco, they took a couple of puffs and passed the pipe around to be sociable. Hawaiians introduced Dana to "Oahu puffs" that he said could serve for an hour or two: "Using pipes with large bowls, and very short stems, or no stems at all [they] take a long draught, getting their mouths as full as they can of smoke, and their cheeks distended, and then let it slowly out through their mouths and nostrils." Oceanians had thus refashioned a typical sailor pastime, and they did likewise in making music, dancing, singing, scrimshaw carving, and playing checkers or cards. *Kanaka*s enjoyed fishing as much as other seamen did, and they brought their love of gambling aboard, risking pounds of tobacco at poker.[7]

Storytelling was another Oceanian talent that fit in well with life among sailors. Tall tales helped seamen make their lives more exciting and passed the time on watch. It was the entertainment value of a story that counted, not its literal truth, although veracity was ritually insisted upon. As one mariner wrote, "The important thing is not that one lies, but how one lies." Said another, "The more heartily the auditor laughed, the more severe had been the sufferings of the narrator. . . . Seamen have a language of their own; a dictionary peculiar to themselves: the nautical terms with which they interlard their narratives produce a truly burlesque effect. They colour what we merely sketch; and their style is a series of images always correct and always striking."[8] A New England trader described storytelling as the sailor's chief glory:

> The sailor, after all, is not such an "unhappy-dog" as many imagine. And those who dwell on shore, whom he has given the "sobriquet" of "land-lubbers," "Jack" would not exchange situations with. Seated around his kid of beef and bread with his messmates, and in the interval of eating and drinking, holding a junk of beef in one hand, and his jack-knife in the other, assuming a serio-comic face as he commences spinning one of his "long yarns" to his brother tars, who break out into a broad and hearty laugh when he arrives at the climax of his tale; at such moments, he appears to be the happiest being in the world.[9]

Visitors had long praised Pacific Islander oratorical skills. These were crucial for transmitting oral records, and for renegotiating them in new circumstances. A modern Tongan humorist has even satirized indigenous genealogists as "expert liars." In the mid-nineteenth century, an Irish beachcomber once paid tribute to what he described as native blarney: "Adroit lying is regarded as an accomplishment, and one who is expert at it is sure of a comfortable subsistence and a friendly reception wherever he goes . . . and nothing but what is greatly exaggerated is likely to be believed."[10] In the context of normal sailor talk, however, such virtuosity was hardly a debit, or even exceptional. Wakefield enjoyed E Ware's entertaining his shipmates as the comical Jim Crow (a blackface racial stereotype), yet he also wrote rather hypocritically about E Ware's regaling his Maori kin about his travels: "Nothing can remind one more forcibly of the monkey who has seen the world, than a maori thus relating news. He is an incorrigible exaggerator, and swells each minute circumstance into an affair of state, taking delight in drawing repeated exclamations of amazement from the surrounding badauds, who . . . drink in his metaphors and amplifications."[11] Such sarcasm contained a hint of envy.

Euroamerican accounts themselves emphasized the exotic, so the actions of our double ghosts are at least twice-translated. Yet through all the layers of imposed otherness resonates a dynamism, distorted by and subtly disturbing to the white chronicler. Kadu was said to have thought Russian tales of hot-air balloons and horse-drawn coaches were absurd, but he enjoyed telling Marshallese about his own adventures. He guided three visiting chiefs around the ship and confidently pretended to explain the function of everything they saw, including snuff. "When, to make the matter quite plain to them, he took up the snuff to his nose," Kotzebue wrote, "he threw the box from him, and began to sneeze, and to cry immoderately, that his astonished auditors ran from him in different directions; but he soon collected himself, and knew how to turn the affair into a joke."[12] Hitihiti's tales of ice were received with such disbelief that Cook's astronomer wrote: "I have always thought the situation of a Traveller singularly hard: If he tells nothing which is uncommon, he must be a stupid fellow to have gone so far, and brought home so little; and if he does, why—it is hum,—aye—a toss up of the Chin; and,—'He's a Traveller'!" A century later, a captain declared, "your travelled South Sea Islander is always a liar—even if he were not, he would always get the credit of being one."[13]

Pacific Islanders sometimes recorded their experiences in chants or songs, which provided both private comfort and social currency aboard ship. Kadu learned songs in various languages wherever he went, which Kotzebue said, "served him, as it were, as a book, in which he sought explanation or confirmation of his assertions." He often sang a chant in honor of Don Luís de Torres, the governor of Guam who had reopened trade links with his native Woleai. Adelbert von Chamisso learned it and later passed it on to the governor himself. Chants could also inspire home-sick nostalgia, as a Maori sailor felt after hearing Marsden's dignitaries: "Poor Tommy was so much taken up with the songs and tales of his country-men, which most probably awakened in his mind some early recollections of a pleasing nature, that, during the whole voyage, he was of no service to us."[14] A shipmate praised his Marquesan harpooner's singing: "He had a rich, mellow voice and it was a joy to hear the sailor's yodel when he would assist in hoisting the topsails." Yet Alfred Tetens complained when his Yap-ese divers kept themselves happy "by incessant, ear-splitting singing." George of Whangaroa reportedly learned very little spoken English from his shipmates, but he "remembered some verses of the popular British songs, which he had learned during his service in one of our ships."[15]

Dillon used Oceanians like circus acts to promote his ventures. His Maori crewmen did their grimacing, tongue-wagging, spear-wielding *haka* chant on command, foreshadowing the commodification of native arts in the tourist industry. Three Marquesans entertained shipmates by "perform-ing, in unison, a slow, mournful chant, accompanied by an occasional clap-ping of the hands, their palms being kept concave to produce a hollow sound, which is varied to required keys."[16] When a U.S. warship's band played martial tunes on deck for visiting Marquesans or Tahitians in 1829, Charles Stewart said they crouched down "in perfect silence, as if under the influence of a charm." Yet Western-style instruments would gradually alter Oceanian music. Omai had learned to play a hand organ, and George Kaumualiʻi a bass viol. Hawaiian sailors soon began singing melodies and playing ukuleles to entertain passengers, and Maori boatmen chanted to pass the time. When an English companion began to put his own words to a Maori tune, "they all left off pulling to listen, so I was obliged to desist notwithstanding their reiterated cries of 'Tena! Tena!' (Go on! Go on!)"[17]

Oceanians brought their own spiritual beliefs on board and clung tena-ciously to them, despite skepticism. They held religious services and prayed for everything from good health to fair weather. Tupaia prayed to Tane for wind and claimed success, regardless of Joseph Banks's disbelief, and he told stories about Maui, the pan-Polynesian demigod, which Cook branded "absurd." Kadu was just as experienced a traveler, but he chose a different strategy. When he prayed for favorable winds, his hosts laughed, "and he soon laughed himself at these adjurations, which he afterwards only re-peated in joke, to amuse us."[18] One Sunday, Marsden prayed to God to end a storm, but it did not abate, so his Maori voyagers argued that their *atua* (gods) were more powerful. Oceanians explained their beliefs about star constellations, meteors, and comets; some likened the carved figures on ship bows or sterns to sacred icons. Yet as time passed, missionaries ashore produced seagoing Christians. In 1827, Dillon buried a *kanaka* at sea, "one of the Otaheitans on board, a christian of the Protestant persuasion, performing the funeral service extempore over the body."[19]

Birds at sea, for Oceanians, could be messengers or incarnations of spirit guardians. Hitihiti chanted solemnly to a heron, a bird sacred on Borabora, but Omai (no lover of Boraborans) ridiculed him and said the British ate his *atua.* Maori seamen saved white albatross feathers, which they regarded as valuable gifts for their kin back home. When Thomas Hopu of Hawai'i tried to draw up a bucket of water for washing dishes, he fell overboard. The ship turned about but took two and a half hours to rescue him. Though an excellent swimmer, Hopu was tiring, so he prayed to his guardian for help and offered it "a fine jacket, which I had received from my Captain, as a present." A bird came down out of a cloud, Hopu repeated his prayer, and the ship arrived. Another Hawaiian drowned trying to save a shipmate lost overboard, and an albatross landed on the spot where they both went under.[20] Timarare of Banaba was dumping out a tub of dirty water and fell overboard, so one bird perched on his head while others led the ship to him. "On reaching the deck," John Webster wrote, "he leaped about like one deranged, clapping his hands together and uttering loud cries. He then rushed to the side of the vessel, and gazing on the wild waters he broke out into a chant in his own language, the tones exceedingly wild at first, but ending in a voice very soft and plaintive." After a glass of brandy, Timarare said, "Te manu (bird) he speakee me, he say no mate (drown). In my country manu plenty speak to man."[21]

Risks and Resistance

Seafaring, for both Euroamericans and Oceanians, was always risky, because as a Massachusetts historian has said, "The ocean knows no favorites. Her bounty is reserved for those who have the wit to learn her secrets, the courage to bear her buffets, and the will to persist."[22] In the British navy, nine times as many seamen died from accidents or disease as from warfare against enemies. Sadly, Oceanian deaths litter the scanty records of their travels on foreign ships, particularly from disease, since they lacked exposure to Eurasian epidemics. One-fourth of the best-documented Islander voyagers in the records died prematurely overseas. The death rate could rise even higher: 70 percent of the Pacific Islanders taken to Mexico or Peru by Spanish explorers died; of eleven taken to Calcutta by Dillon in 1826, seven died there or soon after of illnesses ranging from tuberculosis to measles.[23]

*Kanaka*s also died in shipwrecks or suffered injuries on the job. In 1806,

Tom Hupea of Tahiti was washed overboard off New Zealand because, perhaps seasick, he had refused to go below during a storm. He fell asleep in the square sail and, when it was hoisted the next day, he disappeared into the deep. An i-Kiribati met the same fate in 1852. The captain noted, "We suppose he got to sleep on the rail and fell overboard and drowned." A young Hawaiian fell to his death in the Okhotsk Sea when the cold numbed his hands so badly he could not hold himself aloft while reefing the foresail. He was knocked from the yardarm by a sudden change of wind in a sail and hit the rail with his head before disappearing into the deep forever. Cold climates were known to weaken or kill so many Pacific Islanders that Cape Horn became a real barrier to their travels.[24] Arctic whaling was particularly hard on Hawaiian recruits. They sometimes drowned in the frigid waters off Japan. If they caught chest ailments, they were put in the sunshine on deck, if there was any. In 1858, William Kalama died just as the ship's *kanaka*s were enjoying warm weather again. The captain's wife noted,

> He has been off duty some time; did not complain but appeared to be running down. Samuel gave him medication and tonics. We had no idea that he was so low until they told us he was dead. He was on deck the day before. I went on deck at sunset to hear the funeral service read before he was consigned to the deep. It seemed rather aggravating after being so long from home to die as it were within sight of it.[25]

In the American Northwest, some Hawaiians found it difficult to adjust to the constant rain, sleet, and damp fog: "used to a dry, pure atmosphere, [they] sank under its influence." In 1811, when the fur trader *Tonquin* tried to sound the mouth of Columbia River, a riptide swamped its boat. Two whites drowned, but Stephen Weeks survived thanks to two Hawaiian boatmen who, "being expert swimmers," stripped off their clothes, dived to free him from the line that entangled his legs, pulled his clothes by their teeth to the boat, righted it, bailed it out, and recovered an oar. But both *kanaka* heroes soon became numb with cold, and one died that night.[26]

Even if the cold north spared Hawaiians, they risked Asian diseases in Canton, where those on fur traders tended to become ill. In 1788, a Hawaiian woman called Winee died just after leaving China and was buried at sea. Delano had his *kanaka*s vaccinated at Canton against smallpox, because in other voyages he had "seen many of these poor creatures die with that loathsome and fatal disorder in that place." In 1806, he experimented with a new serum using Hawaiian crewmen as guinea pigs, but as they recuperated from their temporary illness, he found it "very inconvenient as well as expensive to have them with me."[27] Of the three well-known diplomats, Ahutoru, Omai, and Lee Boo, who visited Europe with early explorers, smallpox killed the first and last; Omai was lucky to be vaccinated. Tupaia never made it past Java, where both he and his servant died. In Australia, Islanders picked up tuberculosis and dysentery; a Maori who died of the latter was wrapped in his mat and buried ashore in New Zealand. Melanesia had malaria, and kanakas caught venereal disease and suffered from scurvy. As Epeli of Rotuma said, "I went looking for money but got a fever."[28]

The death of compatriot shipmates could depress kanakas almost inconsolably, and when sick, their religious beliefs may have contributed to what many writers described as passive fatalism in the face of "disease"—supernatural attack in their view. Ill Maoris were said to give in quickly to death: "They say the Atua or 'Spirit' has seized them, and they will take no encouragement."[29] This may especially have been true when local remedies failed. A Maori caught tuberculosis on the *Dromedary,* so a compatriot shaved his head with a shell and quarantined him under strict *tapu,* but he died anyway. Marsden found Ruatara ill with a bloody cough, "wrapped in an old great coat, very sick and weak. . . . His mind was also very much cast down, and he appeared as if a few days would terminate his existence." Involuntary voyagers, of course, had even more reason to be depressed. A blackbirder complained, "Nurse our passengers as we would, they lay down, resigned to what they regarded as the inevitable, and gently passed away. None of the dark folk have the fighting spirit of white men."[30] A Hawaiian chant expressed the loneliness of dying far from home:

> Left in the misty air
> Are the bones of the traveler.
> My body lies sleepless,
> My eyes strain into the distance . . .
> Like a chilling fog is my bitter grief.[31]

Yet Oceanians were also known for their risk-taking on behalf of their shipmates. In emergencies, their swimming skills often came to the rescue, as in the case of the two *Tonquin* heroes. After a gale nearly capsized the Northwest fur trader *Lark,* a Hawaiian named Power kept the crew alive by diving to retrieve a new sail and food from the submerged portion of the ship. After nineteen days, the *Lark* reached Maui. In 1847, when the whaler *Mozart* wrecked at Christmas Island, three Hawaiians swam water casks from the ship to the crew ashore, and in 1854 a *kanaka* swam supplies from the whaler *Canton* to an atoll where its crew had assembled after running aground. Wilkes complained that his *kanaka* boatmen avoided danger by jumping overboard, but they rescued one of his lieutenants from drowning. Another Hawaiian saved his mate from drowning after their boat was smashed by a whale, but he reportedly did not receive any better treatment from that "rough and tough sailor."[32] Hunting whales in a small, open rowboat was a true test of courage and stamina. After helping to secure a whale after dark, one *kanaka* panicked and almost capsized his boat before the mate held a pistol to his head to calm him down. In another case, a whale "stove" (destroyed) the boat and killed three crewmen, but a *kanaka* kept alive by staying afloat until the ship turned about. Another, after four compatriots died of thirst and exhaustion in a lifeboat, became despondent. Near death, he turned to James O'Connell and "hesitatingly proposed to me to eat of him. I shuddered at the proposal and discouraged it with disgust, and my companion gave it over."[33] That tragic offer was an act of despair, but it also symbolized how expendable *kanaka*s may have felt in the foreign shipping circuit.

Records show that racism exacerbated the natural tensions of being crowded into a forecastle that was "black and slimy with filth, very small, and as hot as an oven." Harassment by "old hands" inducted greenhands into competitions among watches and class or ethnic solidarities whose boundaries were defended by force.[34] Minor disputes, even over food, reveal hidden antagonisms. One cook fed ten Hawaiians (a rather large number for a watch, hence probably "waisters") stewed beans from a communal pan. Rolling waves spilled the dish, so the cook scolded them for being "dirtier than dogs" and said he would find them a trough to eat from. But the *kanaka*s only laughed: "First, sundry diabolical grins were interchanged, then followed pantomimic action, and then barbarous words, and, at length, by way of pleasantry, they made feints to, and actually did lick the bean soup off from each other."[35]

Oceanians often subverted Euroamerican pretensions with such satirical clowning. After visiting Sydney, a Maori insisted on being called Governor Macquarie and wanted people to bow down to him, so that he could extend a hand to them with a slight nod, "as a mark of his condescension." Another asked an English shipmate wearing glasses at sea if he could see Australia with them: "This was considered an excellent joke by his countrymen, who laughed heartily at it."[36] George of Whangaroa found a ship's wine so liberating that he stripped off his clothes and "ran up and down the deck, nearly naked, exclaiming 'Me gentleman!' " Another Maori asked for some of the pikes and swords he saw on his ship; when told that they belonged to King George, he cleverly replied that the king, if present, would give them to him, or if not present, would never know they were gone. Even the chants that foreigners regarded as signs of "nativeness" could mock unsuspecting shipmates. Maori sailors who did their *haka* "observed, and with a degree of ridicule, that no two white men ever moved their arms or legs in the same manner." Dana noted that a Hawaiian showed his skill at improvisation among Americans: "By the occasional shouts and laughter of the *Kanaka*s, who were at a distance, it was evident that he was singing about the different men that he was at work with. They have great powers of ridicule."[37]

Like other sailors, Oceanians were flogged for stealing or deserting, but *kanaka*s sometimes seemed to suffer special mistreatment. Bembo, Melville's Maori harpooner in *Omoo,* was disliked by his shipmates for being aloof and moody. After fighting with a drunken ex-convict on watch, he tried vengefully to steer the ship into breakers, only to suffer a beating by the crew before being locked up at Tahiti. Such fiction was not far from fact. In 1849, a frustrated mate on the *Hampton* kicked a Hawaiian for hauling in a sail poorly and started a brawl. Later, the mate hit a Hawaiian over the head with an iron-belaying pin for steering badly, so the Hawaiian began to crush him in a bear hug and "chant a dismal song" until subdued by the captain. "John Gilpin" failed not only as a sailor but as a cook's assistant, so the captain smashed a gourd over his head and called him a "brown scoundrel." When the black cook also abused Gilpin, they wrestled until the crew pinned old John down. The mate then kicked him several times and the captain had him put in irons: "He lay still on his back, glaring at us with eyes as red as fire coals . . . all alone." After three-hundred-pound Big Man fell headfirst twenty feet into a hatchway and survived, Raymond Davis wondered whether a "thirty-two pound cannon ball, dashed by a human hand, [could] harm the head of a Kanaka?" For the record, one mate knocked out a Hawaiian crewman by hitting him on the head with a knotted rope.[38]

Cultural isolation could generate intense stress in close quarters. Language barriers frustrated the mates and resulted in abuse, lower pay, or even dismissal. Mesiol of Pohnpei had to learn by doing, but he knew so little pidgin English that he was "the brunt of many jokes." The shock of being separated from familiar things and thrust into the dark innards of a sailing ship could be traumatic. Dillon discharged a Tahitian he considered dangerous, and also a melancholy Marquesan called Peter, who attended muster armed with a club and shot his musket at a moving sail on sentry duty: "His madness, which was a kind of hypochondria, led him to suppose that a part of the sail which was quivering in the wind was an evil spirit."[39] An i-Kiribati sailor, "thought to have been deranged," lowered a whaleboat into the open sea, rowed two miles astern and vanished. Sam Kanaka of Nauru felt so lost, his captain wrote, "His eyes had a rather wild and worried expression. . . . He soon began to get excited and talked quite fast in his own tongue. I tried to calm him but he suddenly grabbed me by the wrist and gave me such a wild look that I wrenched myself free." Sam then stabbed two white shipmates, one fatally, and had to be shot in the forecastle as he leaped from bunk to bunk, shouting words in his own language that no one understood.[40]

Oceanians brought their own expressions of manhood to foreign ships.

Tattooing attracted the attention of white seamen, who had their own heritage of body marking. In 1835, evolutionist Charles Darwin observed of Tahitians,

> To see a white man bathing by the side of a Tahitian, was like comparing a plant bleached by the gardener's art, with one growing in the open fields. Most of the men are tattooed; and the ornaments follow the curvature of the body so gracefully, that they have a very pleasing and elegant effect. . . . I thought the body of a man thus ornamented, was like the trunk of a noble tree embraced by a delicate creeper.

Some white beachcombers underwent indigenous tattooing to assimilate into their host societies. Their later careers as carnival stars, combined with visits by native Oceanians, stimulated new Euroamerican interest in the *tatau*—a Polynesian term.[41]

Wrestling was a popular sport in Oceania. After public challenges, the object was to throw an opponent using sheer strength. Sunday, or Darco, was very successful against his shipmates: "He would smile pleasantly and open his arms, clasp them like a bear, and, with one tender hug, lay them sprawling and discomfited on the deck." On the *Hampton,* Big Man claimed he could throw a white shipmate named Joe with one hand. "Not with both, big as you are," Joe bragged back. "Spose try," Big Man said. But Joe knew how to trip and threw the Hawaiian hard onto the deck, twice. Then another white sailor threw Joe down, whereupon Big Man egged Joe on to further duels: "Where your smart? You no put him down. Where your brag?" One *kanaka* was remembered in whaling lore for being the largest of a boat crew of six unusually big men, each of whom weighed over 225 pounds.[42] Size and strength had *mana* on the liminal deck.

Some voyagers jumped ship soon after being recruited, or wished that they had. Tamana Jack made the mistake of repairing his new pants with part of a shipmate's blanket. After being chastised, Jack leaped overboard at the next island. So did Tetens's "Herman Vesta." During his seven-year odyssey, Ruatara was paid nothing at Sydney after working on the whaler *Argo;* he suffered from the cold and lack of provisions when stranded to kill seals on Bounty Island with thirteen shipmates. Moreover, he rarely got ashore while his ship was at London and was twice more cheated out of his pay. By the time Marsden rescued him, "the English sailors had beat him very much, which caused him to spit blood."[43] Oceanians sometimes refused to work on whaleships for fear of mistreatment, griping "Too much work . . . too little eat." A Maori jumped ship in Tonga but was recaptured. He went unpunished, because "he said and proved that one of the white men beating him was the cause of him running away." In fact, violence was commonplace on ships. An employer considered *kanaka*s "extremely tractable, free and ingenuous—and if they became vicious the fault is not their own."[44]

The ultimate form of resistance was mutiny, and tales of *kanaka*s in revolt filled newspaper stories and journal entries of the nineteenth century. In 1813, a Ra'iatean named Fa'anuhe returned from Sydney as a pearl diver for a ship in the Tuamotus. Once there, he led the divers in a mutiny, axed two mates personally, and turned the ship over to his chief on Ra'iatea. After a voyage to New Guinea in 1866, Yapese pearl divers tried to seize Tetens's ship, only to be driven off with cannon. "They were disgruntled," he wrote, "because I refused to let them take the pearl shells to use as small change."[45] Unlike the *Bounty* mutineers, some of whom later hanged, *kanaka* rebels did not release their captains in a lifeboat. In 1834, the Hawaiian crew of the schooner *John Little* killed their captain, threw him overboard, and burned the ship at Fanning Island. In 1853, harpooner Oahu Harry led the entire *kanaka* crew of fifteen in a mutiny on the whaler William *Penn,* armed only with lances and whaling spades. He killed the captain, cook, and steward and told the surviving whites, "I have killed all I want to, and if you will give me fifteen muskets and a keg of powder, and let me take what provisions I want, I will leave the brig when I see land; but if you do not consent, I will set fire to her and burn you all up." The victors left in two boats with muskets, powder, and one thousand dollars in cash, but Harry himself was killed later in a fight on Abemama.[46]

One tactic was to seize the ship while most of the crew was dispersed in longboats hunting whales. Two i-Kiribati on the *John* mutinied during a chase, their captain "having ill used them." The rebels managed to kill him, the cook, the cooper, and, incredibly, most of two returning boatcrews. They allowed three shipmates to leave on a longboat without compass or food and vowed to sail the ship to a beach "where no white man lived." Six other Micronesian mutineers (an alliance of Pohnpeians and i-Kiribati) were less successful on the *Sharon* in 1842. While most of the crew was chasing a whale—and getting paid a lay, unlike the *kanaka* waisters—they killed the captain. When the boats returned, a fierce battle developed. At one point, a white third mate put out a Pohnpeian's eye with his knife and tried to saw off his head: "One of his eyes hung upon his cheek and his body was covered with gore; he was still alive but did not move. One of the men stabbed him twice with a boat spade and Mr. Smith discharged a musket at him; he was then caught by the hair, dragged upon deck and thrown into the sea."[47] Such vicious behavior had obvious racial overtones and probably reveals the cause of the mutiny.

Yet along with these cases of revolt, there were many examples of *kanaka* loyalty to their ships. An i-Kiribati oarsman in a returning whale-boat refused to join in the *Sharon* mutiny and was axed in the back, a tragic price to pay for the lay he had hoped to receive. During the *Globe* mutiny, a

Hawaiian sided with the captain, was marooned on Mili with several other loyal shipmates, and died at the hands of indigenous Marshallese. His fate demonstrates that Oceanian seamen often found themselves caught in a deadly crossfire between ship and shore and had to choose sides. Even kidnapped Lova Saregua asked for a bow and arrows from Surville's cabin in order to help fight off other Solomon Islanders, "letting me understand that he would not miss his mark." A Tahitian steward on the mission-built *Haweis* brought up cutlasses for his crew when they were attacked by Maoris. In the ensuing fight, he died of five gunshot wounds, and a Maori preserved his head and tattooed it for sale. When their ships were attacked from shore by other Pacific Islanders, *kanaka* seamen sometimes took control of the vessels and steered them until rescued by passing whalers. One helped a lone white survivor to sail a burning ship, and another took the vessel out to sea and safety.[48]

For seamen, whether foreign or native, their ships were safe havens in strange waters, like lonely spacecraft. The physical limitations of the vessel itself forced a degree of cooperation even in difficult circumstances; if survival was not motive enough, profit might be. Tahitians had a reputation for fidelity, if the pay were "liberal." A Russian explorer wrote that Hawaiians were "eager, obedient, reliable, and intelligent workers, and always loyal to their superiors. The captains of American ships, when suspecting the crew of some dangerous plot on their trips to the northwest coast of America, take along several."[49] First mate J.C. Mullett helped smuggle two Hawaiian *kanaka*s onto his whaler in Honolulu, and one night they warned him about a mutiny plot. The captain threw the ringleader overboard and sent his accomplices to rescue him in a boat, whereupon the ship set sail. Mullett wrote, "the captain and myself had many a hearty laugh over this night's transaction, not forgetting to befriend the natives who betrayed the rogues." Both men stayed by his side even when he switched to another ship, declaring, "where I went they would go also."[50]

Personal bonds could thus help to determine allies when far from home. Te Pehi Kupe told the English captain he had persuaded to take him to London, "if he was seperated from me before he got a passage out again he would put an end to his existence, which I verily believe he would. His affection for me is very great." Brian and Morgan, Dillon's traveling Maoris, refused to undergo a medical examination by Doctor Tytler, who was feuding with their mentor. Ever the self-promoter, Dillon put these words into their mouths:

> You are our friend, and protector; you have brought us from our native country over a sea three months long (referring to the length of the voyage from New Zealand), and you have victualled and clothed us: you have also

loaded us with presents to take to our country; you are the relation of our fathers and friends in New Zealand: we are therefore directed by our god to fight for you. Those men that are not your friends cannot be ours. We will not speak to the Doctor. We will kill and eat him if he lands in our country.[51]

Between Ship and Shore

Like other cross-cultural travelers, *kanakas* developed multiple layers of identity, and their communication skills helped the maritime frontier to function. Even if hired as common seamen, Oceanians were still expected to be guides and interpreters within the region. But translating was not always easy, because local cultures differed. Omai, for example, could not speak with Maoris as well as Cook's own veteran English sailors did, and none of Cook's Society Islanders could understand Tongan very well. Stewart wrote that Hawaiian and Tahitian sailors in the Marquesas found it difficult to bridge "an imperfect knowledge of English, and a variance between this dialect of the Polynesian tongue and their own." A white beachcomber did the job better. Nor was mediating necessarily simple even for a fluent speaker, as Hitihiti of Borabora found on Tahiti. When he tried to help Cook retrieve a stolen musket, he became so embroiled in local politics that he considered deserting the ship.[52]

Evidence suggests some overlap between older forms of voyaging and that by *kanaka* seamen. Guides for exploring ships might already have been victims of circumstance or footloose volunteers, making the journey an extension of their exile. The cases of Moac and Digal demonstrate this ambiguity. Storms often blew canoes from Micronesian atolls to Guam or the Philippines, where Spanish Jesuits proselytized among the castaways to train intermediaries. In 1708, Chief Moac of Palau landed in the Philippines with ten companions, including his wife and son. In Manila, he converted to Christianity and was baptized José Miguel. By 1710, the Jesuits decided to take him to the atolls as an interpreter, but a Spanish vessel took Moac and two Jesuits to Sonsorol, not Palau. Moac revealed his tattooing to the natives and said something that made them dance and carry the Spaniards on their shoulders, but the ship was driven off by strong winds and had to return to Manila, abandoning the priests and Moac to their fate. Two years later, Bernardo de Egui sailed from Guam to find them, but despite kidnapping guides from Ulithi and Palau he failed to reach Sonsorol and went on to Manila. Later castaways said that Moac had turned against his Jesuit mentors. Though never confirmed, this rumor made Moac an apostate in Jesuit eyes.[53]

Digal of Woleai, a castaway rescued at sea by a Spanish ship in 1725, spent four years serving the governor of Guam. He devoted himself to the

Jesuits and was baptized Gaspar de los Reyes. In 1731, he went with two priests to Ulithi, not Woleai. After a short stay, one Jesuit returned to Guam for supplies, but Father Antonio Cantova stayed on Ulithi with Digal. Cantova sent along a letter with the ship, saying that native priests opposed the mission. Even the chief had become less friendly after a canoer from Woleai brought negative reports about the way the Spanish garrison on Guam had treated Chamorros and Carolinians. No doubt the murders and kidnappings perpetrated by Egui also rankled in Ulithian memory. When the priest who went to Guam finally returned two years later, a captured canoer revealed that Cantova had been murdered by armed natives who complained, "You have come to change our customs." The Jesuits, without direct proof, blamed Digal for treachery.[54] Moac and Digal may have been caught in the *limen* or indeed been wily survivors who used the Spanish to their own advantage, just as the Spaniards tried to use Oceanians.

Perhaps the most astute guide was Tupaia of Ra'iatea, who not only helped as a pilot in the Society Islands but also interpreted between Cook and the Maoris of Aotearoa. Tupaia was already a refugee who had found a niche serving a Tahitian chiefess. When the political tide turned against him, he joined Cook's first expedition in 1769. A trained navigator, Tupaia drew charts of islands, named directional stars, and predicted landfalls and weather, but as he went farther from home, he had to improvise. In New Zealand, Cook praised his utility as a translator so wholeheartedly that it is tempting to ask which of them really explored the place for Britain? Tupaia reportedly impressed Maoris by displaying his hip tattooing and by offering them Tahitian *tapa* made from paper mulberry bark, which they seemed to prefer to English cloth. According to Banks, while ashore with a watering party, Tupaia discussed theology with a priest: "They seemd to agree very well in their notions of religion only Tupia was much more learned than the other and all his discourse was heard with much attention . . . whenever he began to preach as we calld it he was sure of a numerous audience who attended with most profound silence to his doctrines." Tupaia became so popular that children were named after him, and Maoris over a wide area knew his name and asked for him "incessantly." When Cook revisited New Zealand in 1773, Maoris who had never met Tupaia asked for him and lamented the news of his death on Java.

Yet Tupaia actually played an ambiguous role because he was far from home on a British ship. To prevent a fight, he justified the flogging of a Maori thief, and in a pinch, he himself shot Maoris or helped to kidnap them for Cook. When Maori canoers threatened him, Tupaia said, "while we are at sea you have no manner of Business with us, the Sea is our property as much as yours." He also explained that Cook had come to raise the British flag and claim Aotearoa by right of discovery. Tupaia asked Maoris about their geographic knowledge, but when they answered that their ancestors had sailed northwest to a large country where people ate hogs, he claimed they were liars because their ancestors had obviously brought no hogs back. When an old man named Topa'a claimed that his ancestors had come from Hawaiki (the mythic homeland of many Polynesians) and that two other western-style ships had once visited New Zealand and been destroyed, Tupaia told Banks, "they are given to lying."

Tupaia demonstrated that indigenous voyagers were not necessarily any more sympathetic or adept at interpreting local cultures than Euroamericans were. He condemned Maori cannibalism and head-preserving, though he admitted that Ra'iateans committed human sacrifice and saved the jawbones of their defeated enemies. He criticized the treatment of Maori women, and he mistakenly thought that Maori *pa* (forts) served the same function as Tahitian *marae* (temples). In Australia, he regarded Aborigines as so poor that they were fit only for sacrifice, but despite the language barrier he still managed to befriend a few. Nevertheless, he revealed his own autonomy in the *limen* when the British rescued his Tahitian servant from would-be Maori captors: Tupaia blessed a fish and had the boy toss it into the sea as an offering of gratitude to the *atua* (gods)—not the British.[55]

Peter Dillon carried a wide variety of Oceanians as crew and interpreters. In 1813, while sandalwood trading in Fiji, he rescued three native wives of white beachcombers who had died in battle. At Tikopia, one fought with a native man trying to steal the ship's compass; she seized him by the throat and crotch and choked him until Dillon separated them. In 1827, he needed interpreters for his interpreters when trying to solve the mystery of French explorer La Pérouse's disappearance in Vanuatu thirty years earlier. After discharging a Tahitian and a Marquesan in Tonga, he added two Cook Islander castaways to his mixed crew. He also took along four Tongans to Rotuma to inquire what had happened to canoes a Tongan chief had sent there to collect tribute. At Rotuma, one of Dillon's Rotuman crewmen learned that the Tongan canoes had already gone to Fiji, so Dillon went on to Tikopia and picked up Rathea, who said he knew of La Pérouse's fate. The omnibus then continued on to Vanikoro, where his Tongan and Maori women passengers helped to befriend native canoers. Dillon finally found the shipwreck site of La Pérouse, and sailed to Bay of Islands, New Zealand, where the Tongans and Tikopians found other ships home again.[56]

In the resource-poor Tuamotu atolls, a long tradition of killing new arrivals made it difficult for some guides to approach threatening natives. Yet the profit motive on both sides finally regularized trade, so that divers from Ana'a translated for pearlers at other Tuamotu atolls, and gift-bearing

Tahitians befriended suspicious Austral Islanders. In Micronesia, bêche-de-mer traders used their *kanaka* divers to gain permission from other atoll-dwellers to harvest the lagoons. Palauans mediated with Yapese, who later mediated with other Carolinians, though conflicts continued.[57] In 1851, Timarare of Banaba could translate at other islands in Kiribati, but in culturally diverse Melanesia, mediators were a hit-and-miss gamble, depending on the cove in which the ship was anchored. Jacobs described how ineffective Morrell's Melanesian captive was in communicating with New Guineans: "Prince Darco mounted the taffrail and harangued them in return, while we held up, and made a great flourish with condemned beads, looking-glasses, calico, and old rusty iron hoops." Like the Malagasy "kaffirs" Surville had once dressed up as Solomon Islanders, Darco was in effect just another outsider hustling trinkets until he reached home.[58]

Reports of fights between ships and Pacific Islanders reveal a maritime frontier constantly in flux, a moving zone of collision and entanglement between foreign and indigenous desires. "John Brown" of Beru shipped out on the whaler *Triton,* only to jump overboard four days later at Abemama. He feared that the Abemamans would kill him, however, so he allowed himself to be brought back to the ship. That same night, when the watch changed at 3 A.M., he went "insane" and stabbed three of his watch-mates. He tried to hide but was found and when pursued, fell overboard and disappeared in the deep. Two Tahitian sailors were captured and badly disfigured by Fijians after their vessel fired on a local canoe, and three Hawaiians died at Butaritari when their captain refused to sell his double-barreled gun for a cask of coconut oil. When the sandalwood tradeship *Sovereign* shipwrecked at Efate in 1847, a Tannese crewman was able to escape the ensuing massacre. He hid ashore for a month until he could swim off to the passing *Isabella.* Yet that same year at Efate, white sailors of the *Cape Packet* fought with Maori, Tahitian, and Hawaiian shipmates over access to local women. The *kanaka*s then deserted and allied with natives to massacre the crew—including some Tannese. Chief Matuku of the Isle of Pines was insulted by white sailors from the *Star,* so he had the entire crew massacred, including two Marquesans, two Mangaians, an Aitutakian, and a Maori, as well as three Polynesian missionaries.[59]

Hoping to avoid such conflicts, Wilkes took aboard Oahu Sam, a Hawaiian ex-seaman who had been serving for several years as a chief's barber in Fiji. Sam spoke Fijian and helped the expedition to resupply in those islands, but he still could not prevent a bloody misunderstanding between a shore party and the natives of Malolo. In the condescending tone of his era, Wilkes summed up the challenge for *kanaka* intermediaries when he described a verbal exchange in the Tuamotus between his Maori crewman and the chief of Reao:

> John Sac was truly a savage, although he had imbibed some feelings of discipline, and was generally a well-disposed fellow. . . . At times it was difficult to control John's movements. On this occasion he soon became provoked by the chief's obstinancy; and the idea of their receiving all our presents so greedily without even thanks in return, excited his native fire; his eyes shone fiercely, and his whole frame seemed agitated. Half naked as he was, his tattooing conspicuous, he stood in the bow of the boat brandishing his boat-hook like a spear with the dexterity of a savage. It was difficult to recognise the sailor in the fierce majestic-looking warrior before us. The chief and John kept passing words until both were becoming vociferous, one appearing as savage as the other.[60]

～ 5 ～

Crosscurrents in Oceania

I have been brought up with white men. I have sailed the
sea in their ships, and lived in their houses on shore. I
know the white man loves to trade. . . .

—Chief Henele Ma'afu, 1858[1]

The new maritime circuit was to some extent a shared adventure, and *kanaka* voyagers were frontline "negotiators" in an increasingly interdependent world. When voluntary recruiting began to outweigh kidnapping, it became clear that Pacific Islanders were using foreign ships for their own purposes. As we have seen, they underwent initiations that gave them multiple layers of identity and insight, like a fifth column within Euroamerican ranks. But what about those who left their ships and took their cross-cultural baggage with them to another island? Pacific historians regard white beachcombers as "cultural brokers" who played a crucial role before seaport communities developed. They crossed the beach alone, without the support of a warship, and had to adapt to the ways of their hosts. To survive they learned the language, got tattooed, and married locally, but to attain status they had to offer services as advisers, interpreters, shipbuilders, and gunsmiths.[2]

Yet thirty years ago, Harry Maude pointed out that indigenous sailors, as seasonal, regional hires, were even more likely to wind up on strange islands than their better-documented white counterparts. The explorations of *kanaka* seamen were more than geographical, and they could use the same strategy as other beachcombers: sharing the skills they had acquired on foreign ships and shores. A Joseph Conrad character once referred to a shipmate he described as "the secret sharer of my cabin and thoughts, as though he were my second self." That alter ego slipped away one night, "a free man, a proud swimmer striking out for a new destiny."[3] Indigenous beachcombers were native to Oceania but not to the particular island where

78

they disembarked. They were oddly commensurate and novel at the same time, and like true chameleons they could look in more than one direction and use a wider range of adaptive strategies. Crossing the cultural beach "did violence to a man in all his parts," and they did it, by definition, more than once.[4]

The Polynesian Triangle

Beachcombers from foreign vessels helped to reopen contacts between Tahiti, Hawai'i, and Aotearoa. Pomare I employed Hawaiians as attendants, "from their superior skill and warlike disposition." As early as 1792, he enticed Kualelo, who was returning to Hawai'i from England with George Vancouver, to desert and become a warrior and gunsmith in his entourage. Vancouver, however, forcibly recovered Kualelo so that he could represent Britain in Hawai'i instead.[5] Four years later, three Boraborans from an American fur trading ship disembarked in Hawai'i, where they urged Kamehameha I to sail his fleet to the Society Islands—probably so that they could go home again. He apparently considered the idea before his invasion of nearby Kaua'i failed, and he proposed to Pomare I that they marry their daughters to each other's heirs. In 1803, Tahitians deserted from a British ship in Hawai'i. They swam ashore at night and seemed to feel at home among Hawaiians, "whose language, complexion, and manners, so nearly resembled their own." The Tahitians boasted about the power and wealth of their king and showed off their *tapa* cloth, which the Hawaiians admired. The hospitality they had received seemed to give the deserters visions of living in chiefly leisure, but a short stay disappointed them, for they soon shipped out for home.[6]

Disillusionment was a common feature of beachcombing. When the British privateer *Betsey* called at Papeete in 1799, Pomare I asked for volunteers to join the crew: "Tapeooe, who had been much in company with the Missionaries, and having a thirst for knowledge, immediately replied that he would, and accordingly was taken on board." The vessel visited Tonga and then Australia, where English officials and missionaries received Tapeooe warmly. Rather than continue on to England, however, as he expected, the *Betsey* sailed east to hunt for Spanish prizes off South America. Tapeooe jumped ship in Tonga to join a fellow Tahitian, but they spent two years caught in bloody civil wars. Finally, he shipped out again on the *Plumier,* one of the *Betsey*'s prizes, only to have the crew mutiny, stop at Guam, and get arrested by the Spanish. Tapeooe was released from jail and eventually made it to England, but he died of dysentery in Sydney.[7] Hundreds of other *kanaka*s would circulate between Pacific beaches, often ending their lives abroad as Tapeooe had, but a few achieved fleeting notoriety.

The career of Tama of Hawai'i was typical. In 1798, "Owheve" or "Ouhwe," called Sam by the Americans and Tama by Oceanians, disembarked in the Marquesas from a Boston ship. He spoke broken English, so the captain left him at Tahuata to learn to read and write and assist an English missionary. Tama came ashore, however, with exotic capital that made him a factor in local politics: a chest of clothes, including a suit of military regimentals, a musket with ammunition, and enough English words to trade with foreign ships. He could also throw a spear farther than any Marquesan, and he entertained his hosts with tall tales about the wider world. Though of low rank in Hawai'i, he was adopted by a chief and became *toa,* or war leader. Tama then forged an alliance between two groups and led bloody expeditions of nearly one thousand warriors and thirty double-hulled canoes against Hiva Oa. At first mildly supportive of the English missionary, Tama soon told the Marquesans he had seen firsthand that whites had no gods—Hawaiians did, however, so he demanded pigs for his deities. After Tama was wounded by a stone in battle, his career declined, and he died in despair on Hiva Oa after trying to strangle himself.[8] Melville, in *Typee,* suggests that by the 1840s resident Hawaiians were trading for ships at Nukuhiva, because their local exchange partnerships made them "tabooed kannakas" who had freedom of movement.[9]

The Tahiti-Hawai'i connection would persist because of their strategic locations on commercial shipping routes. Between 1818 and 1826, several Tahitian missionaries came to Honolulu. Toketa and Kahikona arrived as sailors, but they used their previous religious instruction to gain entrance to Hawaiian chiefly circles. Chief Ke'eaumoku had a Tahitian steward who was related to a native teacher, and Kaomi, the son of a Tahitian beachcomber and a Hawaiian woman, became a prominent member of King Kamehameha III's *hulumanu* drinking entourage. Other Society Islanders came with LMS missionary William Ellis on the *Prince Regent,* a six-gun schooner that Vancouver had promised to have built for Kamehameha I thirty years earlier. Ellis's Tahitians brought along their wives and helped to translate sermons into the Hawaiian language. Most notable among them was charismatic Auna, a descendant of Ra'iatean priests. Auna left after two years because his wife was ailing, but Kahikona and Kuke lived in Hawai'i for over thirty years.[10]

Beachcombers could be colorful transculturists. In 1825, a visitor to O'ahu met a well-dressed, English-speaking Tahitian at the Nu'uanu Pali lookout. He claimed to have left Tahiti as a boy to serve on a whaleship: "Afterwards he was in the British navy, till he was wounded at the battle of Algiers, when he was discharged as unfit for service with a pension of twenty-five pounds a year." The same visitor also met a Tahitian attendant

of Queen Ka'ahumanu, "an old cunning fellow, 'Jack Bligh,' native of Otahite, who spoke a little English, and had, he said, been with Captain Bligh in
the *Bounty* at the time of the mutiny."[11] Four years later, Hawaiian Chief
Kamanohu and his wife opened a trade shop in Tahiti, which sold "Chinese
goods, blank books, stationery slates, pencils, etc., and various articles of
hardware, all in demand here, and purchased for cocoanut oil and arrow
root." But while his wife handled the business, Kamanohu squandered much
of the profit on social gatherings with his Tahitian hosts. By the 1840s, an
estimated four hundred Hawaiians resided in Papeete and two hundred
Tahitians in Honolulu, and like other sailors, their rowdy behavior in port
sometimes got them into trouble with missionary-influenced regimes.[12]

Some *kanaka*s were able to retire to a favorite beach after a long career.
In 1814, for example, an old Hawaiian called "Babahey" disembarked on
Rotuma. He died five years later, leaving behind a wife and twelve-year-old
daughter—indicating that like many sailors he had already started a family
ashore. He had worked as an interpreter for Sydney-based vessels trading in
Northwest America, Tahiti, Fiji, and Hawai'i, and on Marsden's mission
ship, the *Active,* in New Zealand, before he finally decided to settle down at
Rotuma with his trade goods. His Hawaiian name may have been *Papa he'e
(nalu),* or surfboard, an appropriate metaphor for such a voyager.[13] Not all
*kanaka*s ended their voyaging as they pleased, however. A Hawaiian
stranded by a whaler in the Australs was able to parlay his knowledge of
English and the atolls into a job as supercargo on a pearling ship in
1841. "Since childhood," his captain said, "he has been sailing about. . . .
At the close of voyages he has been set ashore at different islands, and in
this way I came to pick him up at Rapa." He apparently traded ship's
supplies on the side, portraying himself as a "partner" in the business. For a
time, he enjoyed hospitality in the Tuamotus, including the favors of young
women in every lagoon—until his captain caught on and fired him.[14]

The Marquesas were linked to Hawai'i by sandalwood and whaling
ships. One Marquesan sailor who arrived in Honolulu claimed he could
understand the Hawaiian language as soon as he arrived, "and in a short
time, it was as familiar to him as his own." In 1819, an American whaler
tempted Thomas Patu away from his father, a Marquesan chief. Patu
feigned going fishing with his brother and then switched canoes on the
beach to escape. In Hawai'i, Patu joined the royal guard of Kamehameha II,
who doted on his tattooed warrior. But the heavy-drinking young monarch
abused Patu and, when Patu asked to leave Hawai'i, gave him a pay raise
instead. After several unhappy months, Patu escaped with the help of night
sentinels and caught a ship to Canton and Boston.[15] In 1852, a Hawaiian
named Pu'u left an American whaler at Fatuhiva and married a local chief's

daughter. Pu'u bragged so much about Hawai'i that the chief went there with him to fetch missionaries, hoping to acquire firearms. As a result, Hawaiian families like the James Kekelas, Samuel Kauwealohas, and Zachariah Hapukus spent the rest of the century in the Marquesas, preaching despite opposition or indifference from the indigenous people, most of whom had become Catholic. In 1858, "Johnny Boy" of O'ahu jumped ship at Ua Pou. The New England captain's wife wrote how sad it was "for a Kanaka that has been brought up among partially civilized people to run away in such a place as this."[16]

Tupaia reopened contact between the Society Islands and Aotearoa in 1769, and eight years later, Omai recruited two Maori boys to be servants on his homeward voyage. Cook's surgeon wrote that teenaged Tiburoa, or Te Wherua, "being a good natured honest young fellow was taken more notice of by us now than any of the rest, which probably first induced him to place such confidence in us to embark." His father had died in battle, so he and a younger friend attached themselves to Omai when he flaunted his wealth and travel stories. Despite warnings that he would never return home, Tiburoa was determined to go. His companion soon changed his mind, but Tiburoa's kin found a replacement named Kokoa. Cook took both boys ashore to give them one last chance to stay, and Omai warned them that they would only be servants in Tahiti. Still, Tiburoa wanted to go, even though his mother wept and cut herself with shark teeth. Kokoa was rumored to be a slave and wept for a week after sailing. Both boys wept at Huahine when the ship left them with Omai. Cook actually had to evict them by force, "which was no easy matter, the eldest now near sixteen, being of an athletic make, and of prodigious strength, and the youngest about eleven, being likewise giant for his age, were not easily managed." Tiburoa generally got on well with the Society Islanders, whereas young Kokoa lost several fights against local boys. Once a girl mocked his reputed cannibalism by pretending to bite her arm, so he imitated eating a louse from his hair as he had seen Tahitians do. Omai and his two Maoris "died a natural death" not long afterwards.[17]

Other Maoris also wound up in Tahiti, as a result of whaling and the pork trade with Australia. In 1829, New Zealand missionary Thomas Kendall visited Papeete, where two Maoris who had once been his pupils walked thirty miles over the hills to see him, and twenty years later, two English-speaking Maoris called Bob and Friday were acting as local guides for ship captains at Tahiti.[18] The Tahiti-Aotearoa connection also worked in reverse. In 1800, Tapeooe helped the *Betsey* to obtain spars in New Zealand, and after hearing about the Tahitian monarchy, the enterprising Maori chief Whetoi took the name Pomare. Another Tahitian called Jem went to

Sydney at the age of eleven and led a comfortable life there as a literate house servant. As he grew older, however, he sought higher status and worked his passage to New Zealand, where he fought in three local wars in five years and married a chief's daughter. When Marsden visited New Zealand on the *Active* in 1814, he found Jem carrying a musket and wearing a Maori mat and feathers. In return for gifts for himself and his father-in-law, Jem traveled with the *Active* along the coast as an informant and provision buyer. He was still available as a ship mediator at Bay of Islands in 1827.[19]

In the central Pacific, Chief Finau 'Ulukalala II of Tonga employed Hawaiian beachcombers in his wars. Tuitui, for example, had sailed on an American ship from Hawai'i to Manila to Tonga and knew a little English. In 1806, he enticed the captain and half the sailors of the *Port au Prince* ashore. Finau's army massacred the crew, stripped the ship, and burned it, reportedly in revenge for an affront they had suffered from a Manila vessel (Tuitui's?). Eight other Hawaiians the *Port au Prince* had hired in Honolulu joined Finau's forces. The only white survivor, William Mariner, saved his life by saying "aloha" to Tuitui. Finau placed several of the ship's cannons under Tuitui's command, and he showed confidence in his new Hawaiian musketeers by telling one to shoot a Tongan commoner who was cutting iron from the topmast. "Without the least hesitation," Mariner wrote, "the Sandwicher levelled his piece, and instantly brought him down dead; upon which Finow laughed heartily, and seemed mightily pleased at the facility with which his order had been obeyed." Tuitui warned Finau to burn all of Mariner's written materials, lest their "magic" harm Tonga, and to intercept letters Mariner wrote to passing ships.[20] Mariner had reason to dislike the Hawaiian beachcombers in Tonga, but like Tama they were using their wits to survive.

The new maritime frontier could produce some ironic twists of fate. A Samoan chief named Tuvai arrived at Wallis Island (Uvea) in 1840, but not by choice. He had been arrested in Samoa and "deported" by U.S. naval explorer Charles Wilkes for killing an American. In captivity, Tuvai had expressed fear about being exiled to a place that had no coconut trees, so Wilkes decided to put him ashore at Uvea. Yet Wallis and nearby Futuna were first settled by Tongans and Samoans, and Wallisians regularly shipped out as sailors on whaleships, so Tuvai must have regarded it as a very convenient place indeed to be marooned. Placed in a canoe with a Wallisian who spoke English, and laden with rolls of *tapa* cloth for the local king, Wilkes noted that "Tuvai seemed delighted at being released from his confinement on shipboard, and took his leave by shaking hands with the sentry." Wilkes also arrested a Fijian chief, Vedovi, for attacking an American ship and took him all the way to New York, where he died. The chief's personal barber, Oahu Sam, had once sailed on whalers and was able to serve Wilkes as a translator in Fiji and Samoa, finally disembarking in his native Hawai'i. Another Hawaiian called John Adams would stay in Samoa, working as harbor pilot at Pago Pago from 1846 to at least 1873. He married a Samoan woman and had eight children by her.[21]

Hawai'i's relationship with the central Pacific varied. In the 1820s, George Manini, a part-Hawaiian, sailed in the *Kamahaolani* to Alaska to trade salt for timber, and to South Pacific islands for bêche-de-mer, tortoise shell, coconut oil, and sandalwood. In 1830, he returned from the "Feegees" with five Wallisians, including his wife and chiefly father-in-law. Hawaiian historian Samuel Kamakau wrote, "This was the first time that any Wallis islanders had been seen in Hawaii. They appeared to be somewhat civilized as they wore dresses woven like cloth. . . . The little fingers of the hands were amputated." With a new ship whose "Dutch" (mixed) crew included Hawaiians and Tahitians, Manini returned to Wallis to establish a bêche-de-mer station. The Wallisians at first welcomed "Siaosi" Manini warmly, and three locally married Hawaiians negotiated the "purchase" of an islet. But Old Slade, his white business manager, complained that Manini had "Napoleonic" ambitions, having sold guns to rival factions in Samoan and Fijian wars: "His mind was wandering over the ocean continually, dwelling on scenes of danger and blood." On Wallis, Manini built a two-story fort with nine cannons, as well as bêche-de-mer smoking sheds, storehouses, and thirty residential dwellings.

Wallisians soon disputed the property sale, however, and they resisted forced labor at low wages. Manini also drank too much and beat his pregnant Wallisian wife until she apparently gave birth prematurely. Wallisian tradition records that a dozen armed Hawaiians enforced Manini's authority, but Tongan beachcombers from Samoa, led by a man named Vuna, sided with the Wallisians. Manini killed their negotiator and defeated their army, burning a village and shooting many people. Then he made his father-in-law king, imposed taxes, and chose the prettiest young women as wives for his loyal henchmen. Finally, a local warrior named Hua chopped off the tyrant's head as he came out of his house. That killing started a massacre of all the Hawaiians on the island. By the time Manini's ship reached Hawai'i with seven hundred pounds of tortoise shell and one hundred piculs of cured bêche-de-mer and proclaimed him "king of the Island of Uvea" by right of conquest, his body already lay buried in a coconut grove by the beach.[22]

Yet the Hawaiian kingdom also expressed solidarity with fellow Polynesians as Euroamerican imperialism intensified. In 1866, Anglican priest

William Hoapili stopped in New Zealand on his way home from Europe and met with Maori chief Tamehana, who had just lost a war of resistance against the British. Despite objections by some Maoris, Hoapili was reportedly able to persuade "several thousand" to migrate to Hawai'i, which still had a Polynesian king, because "their country was virtually lost to them." But Kamehameha V was opposed to the idea. Part-Samoan Emma Coe Forsayth, later called "Queen Emma" when she built a copra empire in New Guinea, stopped in Honolulu in 1875, on her way home from California. She befriended Hawai'i's own Queen Emma, the widow of Kamehameha IV, and King David Kalakaua voiced pride that both ladies carried royal Polynesian blood—but the visiting Emma had just signed over Pago Pago harbor to the United States in a San Francisco hotel.[23]

By 1880, the U.S. consul complained that Kalakaua had become "inflamed by the idea of gathering all the cognate races of the Islands of the Pacific into a great Polynesian Confederacy." In 1887, Kalakaua's part-Hawaiian envoy John Bush negotiated Articles of Confederation with Samoan high chief Malietoa Laupepa. The Hawaiian cabinet, led by Walter Murray Gibson, ratified the treaty, and Kalakaua sent the gunboat *Kaimiloa* with King's Guards to salute Malietoa in Samoa. But a German warship opposed the union, warning that if Kalakaua persisted in meddling in Samoan affairs, "we should shoot his legs in two." The *Kaimiloa* steamed sadly home, yet Samoan oral tradition records that three Hawaiian seamen deserted at Tutuila with ship's arms. Two, Aniani and Mahelona, joined Manoa, a resident Hawaiian shopkeeper on the islet of Aunu'u, to defend the village from enemies. Using *Kaimiloa* rifles and cannons, they became heroes and married local women. Kalakaua's pan-Polynesian dream was thus fulfilled in microcosm, as the beachcombers' names live on in the present generation of their descendants.[24]

The Western Pacific

The new maritime circuit took longer to have an impact on Micronesia and Melanesia, but in the late eighteenth century British East India Company vessels began passing through the western Carolines on their way to China. After the British befriended the *ibedul* of Koror, John McCluer settled in Palau, which he regarded as "a perfect paradise." In 1794, he took three Palauans, including a chief's son, to New Guinea as trade mediators, but they died in Indonesia. A year later, McCluer abandoned Palau, taking away seven women as maidservants for his wife. In 1818, Chamorros asked Russian explorers at Guam "repeatedly to take them into service, and one very nice young man was even willing to leave his wife and two children in order to get away. They knew that we were proceeding to Manila and wanted to come along in order to jump ship there."[25] Some left less than voluntarily, as when an American whaler seized sixteen-year-old José Taitano, but by the 1840s, tortoise shell and bêche-de-mer traders were hiring Micronesian crew and divers and whalers cruised through the eastern Carolines toward the Japan grounds. Voyagers from other parts of Oceania mingled with local Islanders, and a Marshallese chief took the name Kaibuke, since a *kanaka* told him it meant "ship" in Maori.[26]

Kadu of Woleai, a navigator like Tupaia, was a transfer from canoe-borne voyaging to foreign vessels. He sailed as an emissary for his chief from Woleai to other atolls, but in about 1814, he and three other companions were blown off course and marooned at Aur in the Marshall Islands. In the next three years, Kadu traded his Guamanian iron for food, came under the protection of a local elder, married twice, and fought in wars for his hosts. Then a Russian exploring vessel, the *Rurick,* appeared off Aur. The Marshallese sent for Kadu to mediate, because he had told them stories about such ships. In reality, he had only heard of them secondhand, but he reassured the Marshallese that whites did not eat "blacks" as their oral traditions recorded—perhaps a distant memory from Magellan's visit to Guam? Kadu was fortunate that the *Rurick*'s German officers, influenced by the Enlightenment, still had notions of "noble savages" in their minds. Adelbert von Chamisso found in the Marshallese "pure, uncorrupted customs, charm, grace, and the gracious bloom of modesty," and he would later call Kadu "one of the finest characters I have met in my life, one of the people I have loved most." They treated Kadu kindly, which further enhanced his status among the Marshallese.

When he first came on board, the Russians asked him about his tattooing, so he blurted out an incomprehensible tale of hardship in his own language. His "agreeable countenance" earned him pieces of iron hoop from Captain von Kotzebue—whom he then clung to constantly, fervently asking to stay with the ship. Kadu's Marshallese and Woleaian friends tried to change his mind, twice by physical force, but he knew what he wanted. Skilled in celestial navigation, Kadu at first thought that Kotzebue's apparent wandering across the Pacific meant the *Rurick* was lost. Then he saw that a compass enabled his Russian hosts to predict landfall accurately and realized, in Chamisso's haughty words, "our superiority depended upon our greater knowledge." Thereafter Kadu helped in their research, especially observing sea lions, whose warfare he mimicked comically. He visited Unalaska Island, one of many Russian fur trading stations in the northern Pacific, but he disliked the treeless terrain and harsh air. He made it clear he preferred life in the Marshalls and Carolines and missed his coconuts and breadfruit.

Nor did he find Aleut Indian underground dwellings appealing—he asked if the Russians lived that way in St. Petersburg. On St. Lawrence Island, near the Bering Strait, he doubted the native people were really human, "on account of their fur-clothing," and he warned Kotzebue that they had knives up their sleeves. Nevertheless, Kadu was fascinated by whales, and he followed cattle around and sang to them.

When the *Rurick* arrived on the Kona coast of Hawai'i, Kadu fell in love with an attractive *wahine* who paddled out alone in her canoe. As Kotzebue wrote, "expressive gestures explained her object, and she was very angry when she saw herself laughed at." The captain refused to allow her on board "for good reasons," but Kadu tried to communicate with her in every language he knew, without success. He had to content himself with tossing her all his glass beads and nodding amiably until she was out of sight. Kadu was introduced to the Hawaiian leadership as the inhabitant of "a newly-discovered island" and received many gifts. King Kamehameha I found the tattooed Carolinian intriguing, and Queen Ka'ahumanu was particularly fascinated by his long earlobes. Kadu, "on his part, treated the king with the greatest respect, whose splendid possessions, in his opinion, rendered him the first tamon [chief] in the world." Kadu was glad to see coconut trees again, but the sight of a man on horseback startled him. He asked questions about Hawaiian farming techniques and cloth making and enjoyed the attention paid to him by the Hawaiians, especially two young female guides.

Chamisso wrote that "our friend was shy, but quite poised and well-mannered . . . and he mixed happily with the people." At Honolulu, he "disappeared among the natives, who liked him, and with whom he soon learned to make himself understood." Kadu traded what the Russians had given him for new souvenirs to give to his Marshallese friends, and he helped the Russians gather animals and plant seedlings for the Marshalls. Yet he voiced disapproval when a married woman offered herself to him, comparing it to the immorality he had seen in Palau since foreign contact. Chamisso praised Kadu as an experienced traveler who "always remained within the bounds indicated to him." But Kadu also knew how to expand those bounds to appropriate, in his own way, the Euroamerican adventure in the Pacific. Once back in the Marshalls, after nine months of travel, he showed off his clothes again, saying, "Look here! I am Kadu, do you know me still?" When chiefs and commoners sat around in a circle to listen to Kadu's stories, "his eyes sparkled." Kotzebue noted that "Kadu, who supped with us, explained to them the use of the several utensils, and must have expressed himself very wittily, as they laughed heartily." When Marshall-ese expressed disgust at the taste of wine, "Kadu called them fools, who did not know what was good; they should follow his example as he was a man of experience; at the same time he emptied the glass in one draught."

He soon shed his foreign clothes, such as the boots he disliked so much, but during the after-dinner dance, Kadu stepped into the circle and demonstrated Russian steps to the delight of the crowd. He reportedly introduced yams, taro, plantain, goats, and pigs to Aur, and young women sang his praise around evening campfires. As the Russians prepared to leave, Kadu expressed concern the Marshallese might steal his treasures, so Kotzebue put on a cannon and rocket display, complete with oratory about the power of the czar to punish anyone who stole from Kadu. As the *Rurick* sailed away, Kadu wore a white shirt and saber and waved to the Russians with a white handkerchief. Chamisso reflected that the *Rurick* had left Kadu at Aur, by his own choice, instead of taking him home to Woleai or even on to Russia:

> You, my friend Kadu, made the better choice: you parted from us in love . . . upon your second father-land . . . But what would you have done in our old Europe? We would have played a vanity-satisfying game with you, we would have exhibited you to princes and potentates; they would have hung medals and tinsel around your neck and then forgotten you . . . you would have found yourself forsaken in a cold world.

Yet he admitted, "We must confess that our friend stands alone, exposed to the envy of his equals, the greed and power of his chiefs, and the treasures that our love has heaped upon him will draw a storm upon his head." As it turned out, Kadu married a chief's daughter and became a war leader. He fought in a red cap and white shirt with his saber, and his iron weapons tipped the balance in favor of his side. Kotzebue learned this news on his 1824 expedition from the Marshallese chief Lagediack, who asked Kotzebue to take his son to Russia but was politely refused.[27]

On Pohnpei, oral tradition records quite a different story, the misadventures of Mesiol. A diminutive young man, he was transporting cargo between ships and shore, and one day a captain invited him on a tour of the deck and the cabin. Once below, Mesiol saw that the ship was sailing, but he was too short to escape through the porthole. He had to scrub decks and help the cook until he reached Hawai'i, where the captain locked him up in the hold with plans to sell him in California. That scheme failed, however, again because Mesiol was so short, so the captain abandoned him in San Francisco. Mesiol wound up in jail as a vagrant until a sailor with experience in the Carolines helped him to escape one night and stow away on a ship. The captain was angry to discover Mesiol three days later, but he allowed him to assist the cook in killing pigs. Mesiol reached Honolulu for the second time and disembarked, but no one understood him. Finally, a missionary who had taught on Pohnpei recognized Mesiol and, after nursing him to full strength, arranged his passage home. Mesiol returned to Pohnpei to find that his death had already been formally mourned. Yet many young Pohnpeians shipped out voluntarily, knowing they might never return. One called Joe lived for a year in Oakland as a whaler's houseboy.[28]

Missionary vessels brought waves of Polynesians to the western Pacific. Early converts helped to spread the faith from island to island, until Hawaiians were preaching in Micronesia and Samoans and Tongans in Melanesia. In 1830, John Williams launched the *Messenger of Peace* from Rarotonga under the LMS flag with a crew of native sailors. Chief Makea went with him to Samoa, where Williams presented him, "dressed in European costume, with a red surtout," as a king. High Chief Malietoa Vai'inupo of Samoa "viewed him with an eagle's eye, made many inquiries about him and then called him a handsome man and said he was not able to be equalled by any chief of the Samoas." After sailing with Williams as far as Tonga, Makea decided to outfit his own trading vessel. Williams found a visiting Samoan chief in Tonga, converted him and his wife, and used them as envoys in Samoa. He even kidnapped two Niueans to "keep them for a short time, load them with presents of useful articles, and then restore them to their home." A newspaper criticized Williams, questioning "whether one man has a right to do another a kindness against his own will." In 1839, Williams was murdered on the beach at Erromanga, in Vanuatu.[29]

In the 1850s, a succession of vessels named *The Morning Star* began to take Hawaiian missionaries to Micronesia. In 1868, Hiram Bingham Jr. brought two Hawaiian teachers to Tabiteuea atoll in Kiribati. But Bingham's own preaching inspired a local prophet to start a Tioba (Jehovah) cult, and the Tiobans opposed the work of the Hawaiians, Kapu and Nalimu. In 1880, some Tiobans threatened Kapu while he was preaching, so he organized a military expedition against the southern part of the atoll. Kapu taught his Christian soldiers a fighting song: "Oh, do not be discouraged, for Jesus is your friend. He will give you grace to conquer. . . . Yes, I'm glad I'm in this Army and I'll battle for the School." In a pitched battle the Christian force surrounded and pushed together the Tiobans and other non-Christians, then slaughtered and burned them. The victors enslaved the survivors and confiscated their lands. A mission board investigation could not establish culpability, but local oral tradition blamed Kapu for the tragedy. Dismissed from mission service in 1886 for trying to communicate with the spirit of his dead wife, he remained a lawgiver on Tabiteuea until 1892, when a British warship deported him.[30]

Mission ships with *kanaka* crews also took hundreds of Polynesian teachers to Melanesia, where half died of malaria or violence and others "backslid" into indigenous custom. Tongan historian Sione Latukefu has argued that Polynesian missionaries in Melanesia adapted more readily to island life than white missionaries did and even introduced their own customs to their host communities. Yet linguistic diversity was always a challenge in Melanesia, so Anglican Bishop George Selwyn rounded up as many native boys as he could to take them to New Zealand for conversion: "Steering his own little vessel, he stood surrounded by the black heads of his disciples."[31] After sandalwood trading opened up Melanesia in the 1840s, canoe voyaging, missionary work, and seafaring on commercial ships overlapped. For example, Sualo of Samoa drifted by canoe with compatriots fleeing a civil war to Vanuatu, where he joined a Maori beachcomber and fought in wars for chiefs. Sualo became a middleman between Efate and sandalwood ships, and he helped to welcome the first Samoan missionaries. Perhaps the most dramatic case of Polynesians converting Melanesians occurred in Fiji. In 1853, King George Tupou I of Tonga journeyed to Sydney on the Methodist vessel *John Wesley* and stopped en route to urge Chief Cakobau of Fiji to accept Christianity, adding a promise of military support. Surrounded by old enemies, the Fijian finally converted the following year, so Tupou sent thirty Tongan war canoes and three thousand warriors to help Cakobau to victory in a bloody battle at Kaba.[32]

European explorers had regarded Melanesians as "ignoble savages," and malaria long kept most traders away. Fiji lacked malaria, but it had a bad reputation for warfare and cannibalism. Beachcombing there could be risky, as when Pemi of Tahiti was killed in battle and eaten. Yet ships buying pork from Tahiti passed through Fiji, and in 1804 they discovered sandalwood there. By the 1830s, Fiji was exporting cured sea slugs to China, and Polynesian *kanaka*s arrived in larger numbers. Fijians and Tongans of the Lau Islands soon became pilots and mediators for foreign ships. Takai and Langi, for example, voyaged to Australia and Tahiti, where they became Christians, and in 1840, Takai earned a piloting job by presenting written recommendations. Shipping out also overlapped with the ancient Fiji-Tonga exchange circuit. Tongan chief Palu Mata Moina and his wife went by canoe to Fiji and then took an English sandalwood ship to Sydney. Tupou Tutai, a Tongan canoe builder and pilot at Lakeba in eastern Fiji, went to Sydney as a guest of the English governor and returned to serve as interpreter for Chief Tanoa of Bau.[33]

Tongans, Hawaiians, and Rotumans would help to expand the trade frontier westward to Vanuatu. In 1829, when Hawaiian sandalwood was running low and foreign warships were demanding that the monarchy pay its debts, High Chief Boki took four hundred Hawaiians and one hundred Rotumans to cut sandalwood on Erromanga. He also intended to annex "Certain Islands in the South Seas which are now in an Uncultivated State."

But Boki's ship disappeared at sea, and Manui'a, commander of a second vessel, died of disease at Erromanga along with most of his crew. The Hawaiians clashed with the natives, since they were cutting trees without approval, and malaria soon invaded their fortified tent camp. Dying young men crawled down to the beach to watch in vain for Boki's ship, and of those who got away, twenty were left at Rotuma on an islet that became known as "Oahu." That same year, Tahiti-based trader Samuel Henry took nearly 250 Tongans and Rotumans to Erromanga to cut sandalwood, but again indigenous hostility and malaria took their toll on the Polynesians, and few lived to see their homes again.[34]

Despite the murder of John Williams on the beach at Erromanga in 1839, in revenge for the earlier depredations by sandalwooders, Henry returned in 1842 with sixty-seven Tongans led by young Chief Ma'afu. After three days of cutting, a fight over thefts led to the deaths of an Erromangan and a Tongan, so the ships left with four Erromangan captives. At nearby Efate, the Tongans cut wood for another three days. Then the inhabitants began to harass them for harvesting coconuts and singing irreverent songs. Under Ma'afu's leadership, the Tongans used their firearms to take a fort, killed sixty Efateans, and smothered another eight in a cave by lighting a fire outside. Seven years later, an Erromangan captive was still alive in Tonga and missed his homeland. Meanwhile, a Tongan named Toriki Rangi remained at Erromanga and helped Henry to procure sandalwood into the 1860s. Rangi became prosperous enough to buy a thirty-foot boat from Sydney, marry nine local wives, build himself a fine house, and raise livestock. Ma'afu went on to become a major power broker in eastern Fiji, and in 1858 he boasted to the British that he could hand over all of Fiji to them. Later, on the eve of British annexation in 1874, Ma'afu came aboard a British warship for lunch and impressed James Goodenough, who wrote, "He is a man of the world, and we were soon on winking terms."[35]

After the discovery of sandalwood on the Isle of Pines in New Caledonia in 1841, ambitious Loyalty Island leaders like the Naisselines of Mare organized cutting parties and sold to Anglo-Australian vessels. James Paddon gathered Melanesians from their home islands to work at sandalwood stations and also hired Melanesian sailors for his ships. Loyalty Islanders, in particular, were said to have a "love of wandering." In 1849, a teenager called George Havannah persuaded a ship to take him to Sydney. John Erskine wrote, "the Loyalty islanders ... are ready to embark in English vessels, where they not only quickly acquire the language but are said to make excellent seamen." One met an English missionary while serving on a sandalwooder and asked for Christian teachers on his island, and two chiefs went to Sydney and learned "enough English to make conversation." Yet in 1853, it was France that colonized New Caledonia, and Tahitian troops defeated and deported Bwarat, a chief who had been hailed in Sydney as the "King of New Caledonia."[36]

Rotumans too became very active in foreign ship crews. By 1829, two hundred were enlisting in Henry's sandalwood-cutting voyage to Erromanga, explaining: "Rotuman man want to see new land." Rotumans developed a sense of pride in rounding Cape Horn and bringing back information about the outer world. One father wanted his son to see the world "for the boy's own good," since Rotuma was so small and isolated.[37] Rotumans began to abandon their sailing canoes and bought Australian whaleboats as status symbols. In 1851, Rotumans "Tom" and "Friday" sailed aboard the *Wanderer* from California to the Solomons, where the captain noted, "Our islanders look with great contempt on these people, and consider them an inferior order of beings." The repetition of *kanaka* nicknames in the records makes it impossible to be certain, but the *Wanderer*'s "Friday" may have had unpleasant memories of Melanesians. He had only one eye, and two years earlier, New Caledonians had massacred the entire crew of the *Mary,* except for a "near-blind" Rotuman. Meanwhile, by the mid-1850s, a Rotuman Tom was piloting ships at Kosrae and selling pigeons to their cooks.[38]

In the 1860s, a cotton shortage caused by the American Civil War stimulated speculators to start plantations in the Pacific. They often acquired land by collecting debts owed by chiefs and recruited Oceanian labor according to Paddon's strategy of removing *kanaka*s from their island to keep them from slipping away when they were fed up or had reached their target in wages. In 1863, sandalwood trader Robert Towns began to recruit ni-Vanuatu for work in Queensland, Australia, saying, "We have land, but land is of no use without labour; we must have labour, get it as we may." He claimed that his workers were "as fat as pigs and as merry as crickets."[39] When cotton planting waned after 1865, sugar or copra replaced it. By 1900, over 120,000 Pacific Islanders, mainly from Melanesia, had gone on indenture contracts to plantations in such places as Queensland, Fiji, or Samoa. Recurring abuses marred recruiting, most notably the Peruvian slave raids of 1862–64, which took thirty-five hundred people from islands across the South Pacific, and the massacre of rebellious captives on the *Carl* in 1871. The British began to regulate South Pacific recruiting in the 1870s, but many *kanaka*s died working on distant plantations, and kidnapping never entirely ended, especially the "cultural" variety.[40]

The increasing scale of trading and recruiting could compromise the status of *kanaka* sailors and their relations with local natives. In 1855, the sandalwooder *Two Brothers* sold ten Loyalty Islander crewmen as slaves on

Pohnpei, and a German copra trader later threatened to land one hundred Solomon Island laborers on Kosrae to force the local king to pay off his debts. The range of options between ship and shore drew Oceanians into a liminal no man's land. When three Palauans arrived at Tobi in a whaleboat with the shipwrecked crew of the *Mentor,* the natives kept them all prisoners for three years and treated the white men with more deference than the Palauans. Yet when Nauruans massacred the American crew of the whaler *Inga* in 1852, "A part of the men were Kanakas, from different islands. The natives spared their lives, and they are on the island still." In 1865, thirteen *kanaka*s, mostly Hawaiian, had to join the Confederate navy when the raider *Shenandoah* sank four New England whalers in Pohnpei harbor. Stranded while ashore, they had no other way to get home. In 1866–67, bêche-de-mer trader Tetens recruited one hundred Yapese divers, who not only dived for him but fought with local inhabitants in New Guinea, Chuuk, Ulithi, and Losap. Tetens persuaded the Yapese not to decapitate their wounded prisoners for trophies, but after winning a fight at Chuuk they helped themselves to the favors of local women.[41]

Perhaps the most tragic entanglement was when *kanaka* seamen helped to "blackbird" other natives in return for trade goods. Rotumans and Tannese seem to have been notorious in that role. For sixteen years, Nomu of Tanna helped Australians to recruit other ni-Vanuatu, often by less than honest means. In 1882, while interpreting for the *Ceara,* he offered tobacco or asked for water to entice Erromangans into approaching his boat, then kidnapped them. Nomu also seized a chief's daughter and killed her brother and father with a revolver. A blackbirder wrote of Tannese, "They were a decent and faithful lot of men . . . we knew that they would have fought at our sides until their shirts bled—had they worn any." On one occasion, loyal "blackboys" had to right a swamped boat and dive for its valuable trade box while natives on the beach were shooting at them. Even Oceanian passengers might be sold by unscrupulous captains. Such kidnappings caused vengeful massacres of visiting ship crews, which in turn invited reprisals by warships.[42]

Cross-Fertilizations

Most Oceanians who worked or traveled on Euroamerican ships stayed within the Pacific basin, so the new maritime circuit intensified interaction among indigenous peoples. The results could be quite benign, such as the relations established by French Catholic missionary vessels between Micronesia and the Gambiers (south of Tahiti) in 1838. Two Mangarevans settled on Pohnpei and married local Christian women, and two Pohnpeians did the reverse.[43] Yet cross-cultural contact could also produce shock. For example, Maoris' martial reputation spread around the region as they shipped out. Their elaborate facial tattooing fascinated other Islanders, but Tahitians, Samoans, Tongans, Rotumans, and Tikopians expressed disgust at Maori sailors' cannibal image. Tahitians fled from Maoris' grimacing, aggressive "war dance" (*haka*), but Dillon used his Maori *kanaka*s like a carnival showman and had them perform their *haka* in places like Tonga. Wilkes had John Sac, or Tuati, a Maori seaman in his expedition, perform a solo *haka* in Fiji, "which excited great astonishment among them. John's dance was one of great energy and violence, and as opposite from that we had just witnessed as could well be conceived."[44]

In 1836, a Tongan chief enticed a Maori seaman to desert from his whaleship to be a warrior in his entourage. He returned him only when the captain offered axes, knives, fishhooks, and cloth in exchange—a rather graphic measure of *kanaka* beachcomber (and seaman) worth.[45] Tuitui, Tama, and Jem all achieved prominence in their host societies because of their martial skills, but Tapeooe finally fled from his wartorn Tongan interlude, and Patu had to escape at night from being a Hawaiian king's favorite guard. Kadu and Tupaia seemed to transfer older forms of beachcombing to the foreign ship circuit with finesse, and Babahey and Jack Bligh settled down on strange beaches, having become liminal chameleons in their travels. Yet Temoana languished for three years in rags in Samoa, where people viewed him as an outsider. He failed as an assistant to missionary Thomas Heath and went home to Nukuhiva with another LMS preacher, where the French made him "King of the Marquesas." White beachcombers were most valued before 1840, by which time they had evolved from chiefs' "pets" to commercial agents. They usually lost their historical role when Euroamerican beach communities developed, and when local inhabitants learned most of their skills.[46] Yet as late as 1887, as we have seen, Aniani and Mahelona became heroes in Samoa, so the relative "invisibility" of indigenous beachcombing in the records may conceal continuity with precontact voyaging.

Euroamerican shipping relocated many Oceanians to new islands in dependent roles. American fur traders repeatedly tried to establish Hawaiian men and women in the Marianas to grow ship provisions, but the Spanish kept removing them to Guam. Another "colony" of Hawaiian provisioners took root in the North Bonin Islands, while still others hunted seals in the Juan Fernandez Islands off Chile. In 1820, Fanning Island in the Line atolls became a place of exile for "riff-raff" not clearly under any Hawaiian chief's control, and by 1832, a dozen Hawaiians lived there, working as divers for ships. The Guano Act of 1856 sent American and Hawaiian vessels to the Line atolls to scrap up bird manure for farm fertilizer. A captain wrote, "The Kanakas make the best kind of laborers, being quiet, and good strong fellows to work. We were at [Howland] island 21 days altogether, during which time we discharged 600 tons of ballast and took in and stowed 1,500 tons of guano. They gave us one hundred tons per day whenever we could take it."[47] Conversely, from 1868 to 1887, the Hawaiian kingdom made attempts to import plantation laborers from the western Pacific, partly to replenish its declining population, but most died or went home. Judith Bennett has noted, "One pathetic commentary on the state of the native Hawaiian population was the attempt by Hawaiians to persuade the Gilbert Islanders to give them their children."[48]

Maori *kanakas* hunted seals on cold, barren outcrops like Bounty Island, and Maori women accompanied their white husbands to Three Kings Island, Lord Howe's Island, and Sunday (Raoul) Island to grow potatoes, cabbages, and pigs for passing ships. Tahitians caught turtles on the Phoenix atolls, planted coconuts in the Tuamotus, or killed seals on Bounty Island, and by the 1850s, part-Tahitian Henry English managed a copra plantation on Fanning Island with a hundred Tahitian workers.[49] In the 1870s, missionaries moved 250 Easter Islanders to Tahiti to work on church farms, but disease reduced their numbers until the most marriageable survivors went home before Chile annexed Easter Island in 1888. In 1837, about twenty Pohnpeian men "colonized" Ngatik Island, along with some white sailors, when Charles "Bloody" Hart massacred the local men to acquire their tortoise shell. The local women, part of the spoils, recorded the invasion in oral tradition. Just as tragic was the Maori conquest of the Chatham Islands in 1835, using a hijacked English ship and firearms. The native inhabitants were killed or enslaved.[50]

Oceanian beachcombers often had to compete against white rivals. Tuitui seemed to keep the upper hand in Tonga, but on Pohnpei in 1843, several Maoris took local wives, only to have Euroamericans try to steal the women away. The Maoris killed two white men, but other white residents—who dominated the local ship trade—killed two Maoris. The rest had to flee to a nearby islet.[51] In addition, *kanaka* movement to new regions carried serious health risks. Several were put ashore at the nearest island when they were gravely ill. Dillon's guide to Vanikoro, Rathea, died in New Zealand, and Dillon put these words into his mouth: "Had I cocoa-nuts, bread-fruit, bananas, etc., which I have been accustomed to, I might once more see Tucopia; but as it is, I cannot live." Dumont d'Urville, who traced Dillon's path, kidnapped five Tikopians. One was a Wallisian castaway called Brini-Warrou, who translated for Dumont at Vanikoro but refused to stay ashore because of a deadly fever there. When a Tikopian contracted the illness,

Brini-Warrou acquired a canoe from a Vanikoro chief, and the five sailed off, apparently never to reach home. The weather was stormy, and as Dumont noted, "The sick man was lying near a small fire under a shelter they had rigged up for him on the platform of the outrigger."[52]

Oceanian women also became beachcombers. In 1846, Queen Pomare IV of Tahiti had a Fijian female attendant who had, said a visitor, a "most savage & ferocious aspect." "On one occasion," he wrote, "having a quarrel with Mr. Lucett, the father of her child, she coolly told him if ever she caught him in a Feejee land she would eat him." A female Cook Islander bore the word "Murderer" tattooed across her face. She said she had killed her first husband on Rarotonga, but missionary John Williams had saved her from being executed for her crime. Instead, she accepted the branding and fled to Tahiti. "Time has made her callous to the gaze of strangers," the visitor wrote. "She has married a second husband, & looks very much as tho' she would treat him as she did her first." In Fiji in 1840, Wilkes met a Rotuman woman named Henrietta. She had married a Tahitian sailor, left Rotuma with him to visit Tahiti, and then sailed for home again on an American bêche-de-mer ship. At the small island that Wilkes was visiting, fellow Rotuman beachcombers enticed Henrietta and her husband to disembark. A Fijian chief took a liking to her, killed and ate her poor husband, and forced Henrietta to marry him. Unsurprisingly, Wilkes found her "occasionally . . . in ill-humour."[53]

Tahitian women who went to Pitcairn with the *Bounty* mutineers also had a strange adventure. The Tahitian male servants twice plotted revolt in order to have a larger share of women, and they finally killed five white men in one day. The surviving mutineers retaliated by killing all the male servants. That left four white men with all the women, who soon became dissatisfied with their lot, moved from man to man, and attempted to escape in a boat but were caught. Premature death eliminated all but one of the mutineers, John Adams. Suddenly, the harsh history of the *Bounty* women on Pitcairn changed: Adams converted the women and children to Christianity and instituted a puritanical lifestyle with daily prayers. Discovered by an American ship in 1808, the mixed descendants befriended sailors who had the same first names and guided them up the steep cliffs from Bounty Bay. In 1817, Jenny Teehuteatuaonoa managed to return from Pitcairn to Tahiti in a whaleship, and the other Pitcairners followed in 1830 on British ships, at their own request. Queen Pomare IV granted them land, but twelve out of eighty-seven migrants soon died of disease, and the rest pined for "home." An American ship took them back to Pitcairn, but in 1856 they sailed to Norfolk Island, where two-thirds chose to remain. Today, there are only fifty-five Pitcairners on the last remaining British colony in the Pacific.

They live from stamp sales, sporadic cruise ship visits, and donations from worldwide fans of the *Bounty* story.[54]

As indigenous beachcombers circulated around Oceania, so did their knowledge. Hawaiian and Tahitian beachcombers introduced the idea of centralized monarchy to Marquesan chiefs, and Tahitians and Maoris helped Fijians to cope with Euroamerican ways of business. During the whaling era, Rotuman *kanaka*s learned how valuable *tabua* (whales' teeth) were in Fijian alliance-building rituals, so they exchanged them for tobacco, thereby causing a kind of inflation that may have contributed to the rise of chiefly confederations. Hawaiians learned from Australian convict deserters how to distill ti-root liquor, and their beachcombers taught it to Tahitians, who taught it to Fijians, in return for wives and other gifts.[55] Foreign captains did not always approve of such transfers. In 1873, one observed that twenty Nauruans at Kosrae "had lighted on the place like a pestilence. . . . To carry them to any island would have been to convey a plague to the unfortunate inhabitants; and it would be far better that they should drink themselves to death where they are." But the new maritime circuit created a pan-Pacific network of "kanakadom" that spread the Hawaiian word itself to places like New Caledonia, where it became the collective term for a modern nationalist identity.[56] What of *kanaka*s who voyaged to Asia and beyond the Pacific? Could they become as commensurate as they needed to be to survive, or was their very difference essential for success?

∼ 6 ∼

From Rim to Shining Rim

When he [Ka'iana] first beheld the ships at Wampoa, his
astonishment possessed an activity which baffles description,
and he emphatically called them the [ships] of Britanee. . . .
—John Meares, 1787[1]

Fantasies about the wealth of Asia had first brought European explorers and traders to the Pacific. Portugal took the eastward route around Africa, but Spain went west and found the Americas. In 1513, Portuguese ships arrived in China, and that same year Vasco Núñez de Balboa hacked through the jungle of Panama to what he called the "South Sea." Magellan completed this appropriation of the ocean basin by naming and crossing the Pacific in 1520–21. For two hundred years, Spanish treasure galleons traded Mexican silver for Chinese silks and other luxury goods in Manila. In fact, China bought silver at twice the world price, thus creating a ripple effect that stimulated global trade and changed world history. Spain soon faced competition, first when British and French buccaneers raided American coasts and ambushed the galleons. The Dutch seized the Portuguese spice islands of Indonesia in the 1600s, and by the 1780s, British and American ships were selling furs, sandalwood, bêche-de-mer, and tortoise shell to China.[2] Growing regional commerce brought *kanaka*s into contact with native peoples of the Pacific rim and also brought Bengali lascars, "Manila-men," and Asian plantation laborers into Oceania.

Silks and Silver

Spanish and Russian commerce bridged Asia and America by exploiting the labor of native fur hunters, miners, and farmers. Conquistadores seized

98

Mexico and Peru and looted their mineral resources, while in Alta (upper) California, Spanish troops and missions used Indian labor to export ship provisions, grain, horses, beef, tallow, and hides. In 1790, however, Spanish warships failed at Nootka Sound to reassert their claims over Northwest America. The coastal trade was increasingly passing into the hands of non-Spanish vessels. Meanwhile, colonial exploitation and Eurasian diseases cut native populations drastically, and Mexican independence only transferred power from monks to even harsher officials. In the 1740s, Russian fur traders expanded eastward from Kamchatka to Alaska, where they forced Aleut kayakers to hunt sea otters for pelts. By 1812, they established a post in northern California, but Anglo-American traders dominated the isolated Russian colonies. Kadu visited Unalaska and St. Lawrence Island on a Russian vessel, as we have seen, but he did not linger in near-Arctic waters. Farther south, Manila galleons had long been circulating Filipino, Chinese, African, and Native American seamen from rim to rim.[3]

Spanish America could be deadly for Oceanians, who had little protection against alien diseases. As early as 1606, Quiros brought kidnapped Pedro and Pablo from the "Solomons" to Acapulco, the eastern terminus of the galleon route. After learning a bit of Spanish, the Melanesians dutifully reported on the resources and customs of their islands, joined in Catholic services and died within a year. In the "enlightened" 1770s, the viceroy of Peru had eight Tahitians brought to Lima to impress them with Spain's wealth and power, but most died even though he clothed and entertained them at his palace "in more than commonplace decency." Only one survivor wanted to stay in Peru.[4] Jack Naihekukui of Hawai'i died of smallpox at Valparaiso, Chile, in 1825, on his way home from London, where measles had killed his king and queen. In the 1860s, Peruvian labor vessels blackbirded over three thousand Oceanians from as far west as Kiribati. Most victims died of hard labor or disease—or were sent home with smallpox. Easter Island was nearly depopulated, and Tokelau's chiefly system never fully recovered.[5]

Nevertheless, some Pacific Islanders survived their exposure to Latin America. In 1770, the French explorer and kidnapper Surville drowned in the surf at Peru, but his teenaged Solomon Islander captive, Lova Saregua, went with shipmates to Lima, a coach ride away from the crowded port of Callao. Amazed by the size of the Spanish houses, Lova melodramatically tried to shake their walls. His French at first mingled with Spanish, but soon "he managed quite well to make himself understood in both languages." He lived long enough to visit France. In 1823, Dillon brought two of his traveling Maori chiefs to Callao, where he provided them with guns and ammunition, and a year later, Maori chief Te Pehi Kupe visited Lima on his way to

England. He stayed very close to his British captain while ashore in his first urban centers. Valparaiso, Chile, was an important port for nineteenth-century Pacific shipping, especially vessels that rounded Cape Horn. In 1825, Dillon took a crew of Tahitians there, but miscommunication between them and his drunken first mate caused the *Calder* to wreck in a storm. Mary Lucatt of Ra'iatea had a more enjoyable visit twenty years later with her merchant husband: "She was delighted with the scenery, gardens, birds, cattle, flocks, etc., and all the novelties that met her eye."[6]

Manila, at the other end of the galleon route, was Spain's link to Asia, though Chinese shippers, craftsmen, and shopkeepers dominated Manila's commerce. Between 1526 and 1606, Spanish blackbirders brought at least thirty Pacific Islanders to the Philippines, and castaways also arrived by canoe. As more ships began to pass through Manila, they often hired quasi-Malay "Manila-men" for crew, some of whom turned out to be stranded Micronesians. In 1844, bêche-de-mer trader Andrew Cheyne found a Pohnpeian boy in Manila who had survived a shipwreck and returned him home. Another sea "escargot" trader, John Eagleston, brought two Fijians to Manila, apparently at their own request. Oceanian tourists had mixed experiences in the Philippines. Chief Ka'iana of Hawai'i obtained a medicinal bark while ashore at Mindanao and was able to recover from a fever there, yet "Kakawaki" of Palau failed to befriend turtle hunters in the Babuyan Islands—the more he chased after them, the farther they ran away. Phebe, a Fijian servant girl traveling with a ship captain's wife, visited Manila in 1848 and 1850. She was vaccinated against smallpox during an epidemic and then rode in a carriage to see Chinese shops and Malay cockfights. But her Protestant mistress would not allow her to participate in Manila's Catholic Christmas festival.[7]

The Hawaiian Connection

Because of the strategic location of their islands, Hawaiian voyagers became prominent in trans-Pacific trade. In 1787, Chief Ka'iana of Kaua'i arrived at Canton, China, with British fur trader John Meares, who in the language of the age called him a "child of nature." Ka'iana was disappointed when the harbor turned out not to be London, as he had first guessed. According to Meares, he expressed disdain toward the Chinese: "Their bald heads, distended nostrils, and unmeaning features, had raised in his mind the strongest sensations of contempt." He was surprised at the plight of Chinese beggars in sampans and gave them his food leftovers. Ka'iana valued iron more than money, so he tried to buy oranges from a woman with a nail, which she did not appreciate. He resented the fact that the Chinese hid their young women from him, and he once tried to throw a Chinese harbor pilot over the side for a perceived insult. Local crowds regarded him with fear and made way for the six-foot four-inch giant when he donned his chiefly feathered cap and cloak and carried a spear through the streets.

At Nootka Sound in the American Northwest, Ka'iana had to wear a fur cap and warm clothing and became homesick. As in Canton, he was said to feel superior to the natives, including an American Indian chief who had traveled with him from China. Meares wrote, "when he, with his fine colossal figure, stood by Maquilla, who was rather of a low stature, the difference was such, as not only to strike every beholder, but even to affect themselves with the different sensations of an exulting or a wounded pride." When Meares's Chinese carpenters built a new vessel, the *Felice,* to sail to Hawai'i, Ka'iana clapped his big hands in joy, saying "Myty, Myty" [*maika'i,* good].[8] The Anglo-American fur trade between Northwest America and China carried many other Hawaiians as boatmen, servants, and bodyguards. Some, like Atu and Opai, shipped out more than once.

In 1789, Jack Atu of Ni'ihau was hired as a greenhand by the *Columbia.* The fur ship's captain, Robert Gray, gave its name to a river he found in Oregon. Along with another Hawaiian named Opai, Atu would travel to Boston and play the role of ennobled diplomat, as we shall see in chapter 7. In 1791, the *Columbia* took Atu to Vancouver Island, where he tried to desert "and go among the natives." But Gray lured a local chief onto the ship and took him hostage to get Atu returned; then he publicly flogged the *kanaka* to punish him for desertion. During another visit less than a year later, the same Indian chief, vengeful about having been taken prisoner, tried to entice Atu to help him capture the ship. He no doubt assumed that the young Hawaiian had resented being flogged, so he promised him power and wealth if he would wet the ship's guns. But a ship's officer saw the two talking together, separated them and scolded Atu. The Hawaiian reportedly blurted out, "What is Mr. Smith mad with me for, does he think I talk with Tootoocheetticus to come and take the ship?" Thus the plot was discovered, and Atu never got the sea otter skins he had been promised by the chief. Opai, or Kalehua, had gone to Boston with Atu and took the name of the American captain who brought him back to the Pacific, Jack Ingraham. In 1792, he arrived at Nootka on Vancouver's *Discovery,* having helped the British provision in Hawai'i. Ingraham's *Hope* was anchored there, and Kalehua tried to desert to it, but Ingraham had no need of him and sent him back to the British vessel. He credited Kalehua's motives to "a restless disposition."[9]

Hawaiian *kanaka*s were sometimes caught up in regional politics. In the

Nootka Incident of 1789, Spanish warships seized several foreign fur trading ships in the Sound, including the British *Argonaut,* which had a Hawaiian cabin boy. The viceroy of New Spain decided that Hawai'i, like Tahiti,
was in danger of being taken over by the British, so he had "Matutaray"
brought to Mexico City and placed in the care of Franciscan friars.
Matutaray was the son of a Ni'ihau chief and had sailed on a fur trader to
China, where Captain James Colnett hired him. Amid talk of international
war over the Nootka affair, Colnett kept writing letters until he won his own
and Matutaray's release. Matutaray had meanwhile grown "accustomed to
dress very neatly in the Spanish fashion," but he rejected Catholicism. In
Colnett's unsympathetic words, the padres told Matutaray that his countrymen would burn in hell for wickedness, and that "he must not have a wife in
this world or the next and starve two or three days in a week." Before
leaving Mexico City, Matutaray had a chance to express himself at a theater. He reportedly amused the audience by shouting out encouragement to
an actor who was romancing a young lady. Unfortunately, the young
kanaka died in late 1790, aboard Colnett's ship off the wintry Northwest
American coast.[10]

Even kidnapped Hawaiians, if treated well, seemed able to acquire a taste
for voyaging on foreign ships. In 1795, the *Mercury* seized several Hawaiians to replace deserters. After being confined below until the ship left
Hawai'i, the captives served as armed guards while the ship traded with
Indians in the American Northwest. When they finally returned home, the
Hawaiians received pay in clothing and also letters of recommendation
from the supercargo of the *Mercury.* They later held up those letters when
the *Ruby* arrived at Ni'ihau and clamored to go to "Pretannee," but only one
was selected for the China cruise. *Kanaka*s also worked as boatmen on
seal-hunting ships. As a captain explained, "The Sandwich Islanders will
serve to man the Cannoes to bring the skins in small parcels through the
Surf to the boat outside, which, man'd by 4 others, ply to the Ship with
them." In 1807, Opukahaia and Hopu, serving as sailor and cabin boy,
visited the Northwest on an American sealer before traveling to China and
on to New England.[11]

By the 1810s, Hawaiians in the Northwest were serving on ships, at
shore stations, and alongside French Canadian and Iroquois *voyageur*s in
fur-trapping expeditions. Their swimming ability made them useful on inland canoe journeys. An employer wrote, "little of our effects are lost
beyond recovery that accident now and then consigns to the bottom of the
water in our perilous navigations; and it is next to impossible for a person to
get drowned if one or more of them are near at hand." In the mid-1840s,
five hundred Hawaiians were working on the Columbia River and another

three thousand were sailing the Pacific in whaleships.[12] The Russian American Company, based at Sitka, also employed Hawaiians and actually considered recruiting more to replace the Aleuts working on the islands of St. Paul and St. George, north of Unalaska.[13] We can imagine Kadu's probable advice, if he encountered such recruits.

Soon after his visit to Hawai'i, seven Hawaiians came to Sitka on a ship, but only after a long sea adventure. In 1818, two anti-Spanish privateers, the *Santa Rosa* and the *Argentina,* had recruited eighty Hawaiians in Honolulu for a raid on the California coast. The rebels then bombarded San Francisco and captured, looted, and burned Monterey. The Hawaiians, dressed in Spanish clothing, were said to have led the assault on the presidio of Monterey with a phalanx of pikes and been the first to haul down the Spanish flag. Before leaving, the insurgents seized a Spanish vessel in Monterey harbor, the *Fortuna.* But there was soon a mutiny on the rebel frigates at sea, and the ringleaders told seven Hawaiian sailors to follow them on the *Fortuna.* The *kanaka*s fell behind, so they decided to sail for home and present the ship to King Kamehameha I. Unfortunately, they could not tell directions at sea well and wound up at Sitka eighty-two days later, short of food and water. The Russians confiscated the schooner, detained the Hawaiian "captain" and his assistant, and sent the five crew home on a company ship.[14] Kamehameha II soon sent his own brigs, manned by Hawaiians, to Kamchatka and Russian America to sell salt for the fur trade. Russian officials received them cordially, but they brought back only exotic gifts of deer and bears.[15]

The northern climate could be hard on *kanaka*s. In the winter of 1845, four Hawaiians on a whaleship died at Kamchatka. Hawaiians seemed to like the *voyageur* diet of venison and fish, ate dogs and horsemeat without complaint, and introduced a new dish to Hawai'i by bringing home salted salmon as part of their pay. They also communicated with a pidgin of Chinook, English, and Hawaiian, and married Native American women, who sometimes assimilated them into Indian society. The damp, rainy climate; frigid winters; and alien diseases took their toll on Hawaiians, but many adapted to forest life and became good lumberjacks, sawmill workers, and livestock keepers. They worked as field hands and house servants more willingly than Indians, both for the Hudson's Bay Company and for missionaries. Sadly, they encountered growing racial discrimination as American and Canadian settlers expanded to the Pacific, even though some Oregon politicians proposed that the United States annex Hawai'i and bind it to the economy of their state.[16]

The story of "John Coxe" exemplifies the adventures Hawaiians could have in the American Northwest. In 1811, John Jacob Astor's *Tonquin* hired twenty-four Hawaiians in Honolulu, twelve for ship work and twelve for fur-trading posts. They helped the Pacific Fur Company to found Astoria at the mouth of the Columbia River and Fort Okanogan farther upstream. One *kanaka* was nicknamed John Coxe because he resembled a white shipmate on the *Tonquin.* Indians blew up the ship, killing half the Hawaiians, but "Coxe" traveled inland with an expedition to acquire furs. There his "wit and humour" charmed the commander of a British Northwest Company party, who swapped a French Canadian for him. Coxe then voyaged overland with the British to Fort William (Thunder Bay) on Lake Superior and by water to England. In 1813, he returned to the Columbia as a pilot for the British warship *Racoon,* whose mission was to seize Astoria! Astor soon sold his holdings to the British, so Coxe returned to Honolulu in 1815. There he told stories about getting drunk in London and being arrested, and about burning his nose when gun powder blew up on the *Racoon.* He later returned to the northwest coast with the Hudson's Bay Company, after it absorbed the old Northwest Company. Coxe worked for several years at Fort Vancouver before retiring. He finished out his days as a swineherd on the Columbia River and died of tuberculosis sometime around 1840.[17]

Despite adapting to their assigned roles, Hawaiians also seem to have kept their own identity in the American Northwest. In 1811, a riptide swamped the *Tonquin*'s boat as it attempted to sound the mouth of the Columbia River. Two Hawaiians rescued a white shipmate, but one of the heroes died of exposure from the cold water. His fellow Hawaiians buried him on shore under the direction of a *kanaka* who acted as priest. Beside a dense forest, they dug a deep pit in the sand, put sea biscuit under the dead man's arm, pork lard under his chin, and tobacco under the genitals. After burying the body, they knelt in two rows facing eastward. They received a libation of sea water from the priest's hat and prayed together, then they rose and walked away without looking back. Some aspects of this ceremony, most notably the sprinkling of sea water on a row of seated mourners, conformed to traditional Hawaiian burial customs, indicating some cultural persistence within the shipping circuit.[18]

Far from home, Hawaiian soldiers and trappers sometimes helped their employers against Native Americans. In 1812, twenty *kanaka*s went with a brigade from Astoria to Nez Percé country. Ross Cox wrote, "Owing to the extreme heat, the Sandwich Islanders had thrown off their jackets and shirts during the day, and their swarthy bodies, decorated with buff belts, seemed to excite the particular attention of the Indians, who repeatedly pointed towards them, and then spoke to each other with considerable animation." Six years later, thirty-two *kanaka*s helped to establish a British Northwest

Company fort on Nez Percé land. "The natives," Alexander Ross said, "were offered such terms as were given in other parts of the country. That they should have the choice of cultivating a peaceable understanding with us and might profit by a friendly intercourse, or lay their account to undergo the vengeance of all the whites and ever after be deprived of the benefit resulting from a trade established among them."[19] Fort Okanogan was once defended only by three Hawaiians nicknamed Bonaparte, Washington, and Caesar. Six other Hawaiians later told Cox they would gladly fight against threatening Walla Walla warriors: "Missi Keit, we kill every man you bid us." An Indian chief offered peace to avert battle, because the Nez Percé did not "half relish the worthy aspect of these invincibles." On the Snake River, a half dozen Hawaiians won a tense standoff against Indians by leveling their guns and vowing to George Simpson, "Me broke him."[20]

Although they were considered more trustworthy than the Iroquois or French Canadian *voyageurs*, Hawaiians might still desert, like Atu, if someone paid them better. In 1816, a Russian renegade persuaded a dozen Hawaiians to leave Fort George (Astoria), but they soon returned after three days of arguing. In 1834, twelve Hawaiians grew tired of walking through the snow while their white bosses rode on horseback, so they deserted one night with the horses. Five died from drowning, frostbite, or conflicts with Indians before the survivors decided to turn themselves in. Like Kaʻiana, many Hawaiians were said to express contempt for Indians, even when outnumbered. Ross claimed, "if they were let loose against them, they rush upon them like tigers." In 1819, however, three *kanakas* were ambushed and killed while trapping beaver along a river in Washington that was then named the Owhyhee.[21]

By the 1830s, ships with mostly Hawaiian crews were sailing along the coast of Alta California. *Kanakas* usually manned surfboats, which they loaded with dried bullock hides and bags of tallow from oxcarts manned by mission Indians. At San Diego, Hawaiians mixed with other sailors, including Tahitians and Marquesans, in adobe grogshops and rented horses to ride around the countryside. A small Hawaiian community lived there on the beach, curing hides gathered by ships from other parts of the coast. In 1835, a Mr. Manini was their quick-witted spokesman and finest singer, though another Hawaiian, elderly "Mr. Bingham," held the position of patriarch. Several inhabited a large, abandoned bread oven. They fished for food and spent free time drinking, smoking, and gambling at cards. Richard Henry Dana wrote, "So long as they had money they would not work for fifty dollars a month, and when their money was gone they would work for ten." Dana spent four months living and working with them and learned to admire the way that they shared everything according to the principle,

"Kanaka all 'e same a' one!" In keeping with their custom, he developed a special friendship with one *'aikane* (friend), a Hawaiian nicknamed Hope after a ship he had served on. Dana taught Hope letters and numbers and saved him from an illness with ship's medicines. When Dana parted with his friends for the last time, "Old 'Mr. Bingham' and 'King Mannini' went down to the beach with me, shook me heartily by the hand, wished us a good voyage, and went back to the oven, chanting one of their deep, monotonous, improvised songs, the burden of which I gathered to be about us and our voyage."[22]

In the 1840s, every port in California had its *kanaka*s. Hawaiians made up 10 percent of the small population of San Francisco and took over much of the boat handling in the bay from local Indians. John Sutter arrived in California with ten Hawaiians to work on his land, and the ensuing 1849 gold rush brought so many Hawaiians to California that ships found it harder to hire seamen in Honolulu. Hawaiian gold seekers could dive in rivers and thus aroused jealousy in white miners. Despite such opposition, Hawaiian "Diggers" formed their own communities, called Kanaka Flat or Kanaka Glade. They intermarried with Indian women, some of whom learned to speak and read Hawaiian, and they started their own churches.[23] William Kanui and Thomas Hopu, who had come home from Boston with the first missionaries to Hawai'i in 1820, both went to the California gold fields. Kanui opened a restaurant near Sutter's fort and was soon able to deposit six thousand dollars in gold in a San Francisco bank, which unfortunately failed a few days later. Many Hawaiians became so indebted to shopkeepers that they could not pay for food or medicines and died in the winters. Others prospered by selling fish in Sacramento and built houses. A clergyman complained, "Gold is their god, as it is the god of many a white man."[24]

Foreign ships also took Hawaiians farther south. In 1817, six Hawaiians deserted from the Boston merchantman *Bordeaux Packet* in Mexico. Two years later, five Hawaiians in a fishing canoe were kidnapped by a short-handed American vessel, which in turn was captured by a Spanish privateer in the Gulf of California. At San Josef, Spanish authorities killed two of the Hawaiians, and another paddled desperately out to sea in a canoe. The two survivors, Busohu and Tuana, were forced to do slave labor, first in a silver mine, then as pearl divers. They finally escaped on a whaleship that took them to London.[25] In 1842, Hawaiian envoy Timothy Ha'alilio traveled overland through the mountainous Mexican interior with William Richards, in order to avoid being intercepted by powers who might oppose their mission to seek guarantees of Hawaiian sovereignty. Four years later, when Mexico was at war with the United States, a Hawaiian naval ship, the *Don Quixote,* arrived in Acapulco. The harbor defenders did not know the Hawaiian flag and prepared to do battle, but just in time, Hawaiians ashore explained the ship's nationality. Fifteen had just spent a year serving in the Mexican navy! That same year, an estimated fifty Hawaiians were reported at Paita, Peru.[26]

Hawaiian *kanaka*s also wound up on the other side of the Pacific, in the Bonin Islands, or Ogasawaras, near Japan. In 1830, Nathaniel Savory, an American under British auspices, founded a colony on North Bonin Island with four other white settlers and twenty-five Hawaiian men and women. Their purpose, like those earlier failed settlements in the Marianas, was to grow provisions for passing whaleships. Ten years later, however, the Hawaiian population had declined to fifteen, mostly female. Meanwhile, Japan's closed-country policy caused hardship for eight Hawaiian *kanaka*s in 1848, when they deserted from the whaler *Ladoga* because of harsh treatment by their captain. With ten white shipmates, they were kept in cages and transported to the Dutch station at Nagasaki for deportation, the standard response to interlopers. One Hawaiian hanged himself, but his body was not removed from the cage for two days and was denied burial. In 1853, U.S. Commodore Matthew Perry bought land on North Bonin for a coaling station on his way to force Japan to open up to foreign trade. Ironically, his naval threat caused a change of government in Japan, the Meiji Restoration, and a new era of modernization and expansion. In 1875, Japan annexed the Bonin Islands, along with the remaining Hawaiians. Today, Hawaiians are credited with introducing the outrigger canoe to the Ogasawaras.[27]

Maritime East Asia

Vast and practically impenetrable by outside powers until the Opium Wars of the mid-nineteenth century, China was a different kind of encounter for Oceanians. Foreign ships often stopped at Portuguese Macao before going upriver to trade at Canton under closely regulated conditions. As many as two hundred Chinese war junks might be in port to ward off coastal pirates and to protect shipping routes to Manila, Japan, and Singapore. Like Ka'iana in Canton, Lee Boo of Palau was impressed by the number of trade ships in Macao, and he too gave some of his food to Chinese mothers begging from sampans. His compatriot Kakawaki, in 1791, was more adventurous: he bargained alone with Chinese vendors in the market and bragged about his great deals—though John McCluer claimed that Kakawaki actually paid four times the fair price. One day a pickpocket tried to rob the Palauan. Kakawaki quickly grabbed a hatchet and chased the thief through narrow lanes until confronted by a Chinese gang, which clubbed him unconscious with bamboo sticks. Later, he wanted to kill the

Chinese in revenge, but McCluer showed him a Portuguese prison dungeon, which the Palauan pronounced "a place of evil spirits."[28]

Islander views of China come to us only through the written records of their white mentors, which are filled with biases and self-serving accounts of Oceanian naiveté. Yet in Asia, *kanakas* were crossing yet another cultural *limen*. Lee Boo had a harbor-view room in Canton and was said to express wonder at the square, flat ceilings of the building and at the decorations, especially glassware. When handed a mirror, he reportedly looked behind it to find the young man who stared back at him—perhaps jokingly? At meals, he was amazed at how many servants waited on table and changed plates between each course. Both Lee Boo and Kakawaki, like true "tygers," were asked to demonstrate their spear-throwing abilities and obliged their hosts with great skill. The Palauans were at first afraid of horses, but Lee Boo finally agreed to ride one. McCluer's travelers barked to mimic Chinese dogs, and George Mortimer said that Ka'iana spent hours on the floor of a room playing with two white rabbits, "running after them, and imitating their motions by crouching and squatting upon his hams." Lee Boo reportedly liked tea but not the smell of coffee, and the sight of a drunken sailor, according to George Keate, turned him against liquor. Kakawaki's attempt to smoke a Dutch pipe sent him running away into the Chinese market.

Oceanians underwent a number of initiations in China. One was vaccination against smallpox, a precaution taken by more than one captain to keep alive his ennobled tourists or *kanakas*. Because smallpox killed Lee Boo in London, McCluer had Kakawaki inoculated in Macao. When a trickle of blood flowed from the wound, Kakawaki asked, "Is that all?" He was accustomed to tattooing and offered the doctor a carving knife, saying "Cut away." When the doctor insisted that it was not necessary, the Palauan only laughed. In Canton fifteen years later, Amasa Delano used his Hawaiian crewmen as guinea pigs for a new cowpox vaccine: "I had in my previous voyages seen many of these poor creatures die with that loathsome and fatal disorder in that place." It was in China that Ka'iana learned how to wear European clothes, after some initial reluctance, as did Lee Boo, and the three Palauans with McCluer. Ka'iana attended Catholic masses in Macao and imitated the worshipers, like an anthropologist. Lee Boo seemed to find the European women he met enchanting and allowed them to examine his tattooed hands. Kakawaki reversed that gesture by probing at a white woman; when she pushed his hand away, he struck her twice with a cane. McCluer rented a house for his three Palauans and provided them with servants and sumptuous meals, but Western-style musical concerts did not appeal to the visitors, who preferred to gaze up at the hall's sparkling chandeliers.[29]

Jeoly, a castaway from Miangas who was taken as a slave to England by William Dampier in 1691 and died of smallpox. This carnival advertisement claimed that the tattoos of the "Painted Prince" chased away snakes and scorpions. *Photograph courtesy Tricia Allen, Honolulu.*

Omai of Huahine, who traveled as a "Tahitian" ennobled tourist with James Cook to England and back, 1774–77. *Mezzotint by John Jacobi from oil painting by Sir Joshua Reynolds, Dixson Library, State Library of New South Wales, Sydney, Australia.*

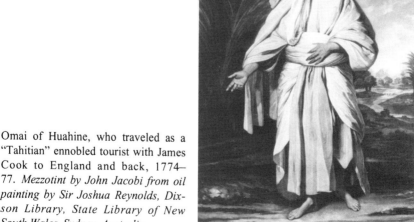

Hitihiti of Borabora, who traveled with James Cook, 1773, and with *Bounty* mutineers, 1789. *Chalk drawing by William Hodges, National Library of Australia, Canberra.*

Lee Boo of Palau, who went to England with Henry Wilson and died, 1783. *Lithograph by G. Keate, Bishop Museum, Honolulu.*

Chief Ka'iana of Kaua'i, who traveled with John Meares to China and Northwest America, 1787–88. *Bishop Museum, Honolulu, HI.*

Winee, a Hawaiian servant woman, who traveled with John Meares to China and died, 1787. *Engraving after John Webber, Bishop Museum, Honolulu, HI.*

King Kamehameha II (Liholiho) of Hawai'i, who traveled to England and died of measles, 1824. *Lithograph by John Hayter, Honolulu Academy of Arts, Gift of George R. Carter.*

King David Kalakaua of Hawai'i, who traveled to the U.S. in 1874 and around the world in 1881; stripped of authority in 1887. *Lithograph by J.H. Bufford and Sons, Bishop Museum.*

King Kamehameha II, Queen Kamamalu, and their entourage, including Boki and Liliha on right, at the Theatre Royal in London, 1824. *Lithograph after J.W. Gear, State Library of New South Wales, Sydney, Australia.*

Henry Opukahaia (Obookiah) of Hawai'i, who worked passage to New England and died there, but became a martyr for missionaries. *Bishop Museum, Gift of Donald Angus.*

"Old Coxe" of Hawai'i, who worked for fur companies in the American Northwest and visited England. *Sketch by Paul Kane, Royal Ontario Museum, Toronto, Canada.*

Kadu of Woleai, who traveled with Russian explorer Otto von Kotzebue, 1817–18. *Bishop Museum, Gift of Donald Angus.*

Vedovi (Vidovi), a Fijian chief arrested by Charles Wilkes, who died in New York, 1845. *Engraving by A.T. Agate, Bishop Museum, Honolulu.*

Maori Actors in the Limen, from High Chief (with elaborate facial tattooing) to Commoner (with none)

Te Pahi, a Maori chief who visited Australia in 1805. *Etching from a drawing by G.P. Harris, Rex Nan Kivell Collection, National Library of Australia, Canberra.*

Te Pehi Kupe, a Maori chief who visited England in 1826. *Rex Nan Kivell Collection, National Library Australia, Canberra.*

Maui, or Tommy Drummond, a Maori who lived for years in Australia and died in London. *Rex Nan Kivell Collection, National Library of Australia, Canberra.*

Nayti, a Maori commoner who worked passage to France and England in 1836. *Ferguson Collection, National Library of Australia.*

New Hebridean (ni-Vanuatu) seamen and plantation labor recruits, 1880s. *From W.E. Giles,* A Cruize, *State Library of New South Wales, Sydney, Australia.*

As time passed, many more Pacific Islanders visited Asia, most as common sailors bringing furs, sandalwood, and culinary delicacies like bêche-de-mer to Canton. In 1808, Hopu and Opukahaia of Hawai'i, typically, found the number of ships at Macao astonishing. Arriving on an American sealer, they were arrested by a British warship but soon released. Both men spent six months in Canton, waiting for their ship to trade sealskins for tea, cinnamon, nankeens, and silk before sailing on to New York. King Kamehameha I sent his own sandalwood shipments to China in ships manned mainly by Hawaiians, and Canton charged him such ruinous harbor fees that he instituted port dues at Honolulu. In the 1820s, Boki of Hawai'i sent his aide Manui'a to Manila and Canton with the royal brigs *Koli* and *Ainoa*. Manui'a sold not only sealskins and sandalwood but also the *Ainoa* to help pay off the royal debt to merchants. Unfortunately, he also bought goods worth twelve hundred dollars more than his cargo and paid the balance with drafts on the royal treasury—adding to the debt.[30] Half a century later, bêche-de-mer trader Tetens brought ten Yapese to Hong Kong. Their chief admired the silk top hats worn by English merchants and wanted one. Tetens wrote, "it now became almost impossible for me to lead my Yap company through the streets. The sight of the naked prince with his inevitable silk hat squashed on his head produced a sensational effect." Moreover, during a vigorous dance they performed at a German merchant's house, all ten Yapese suddenly tore off their loincloths: "Before the dance came to an end, the entire company of ladies, shrieking and laughing, had surged from the hall."[31]

Few Oceanians visited Japan before 1854 because of its closed-country policy, but in 1881 King David Kalakaua of Hawai'i was able to travel to Japan, China, and Southeast Asia as a dignitary, exchanging decorative medallions with every monarch he met. Ironically, it was his white valet who wore a traditional chiefly feather cloak at receptions. Kalakaua promoted the recruitment of Chinese and Japanese plantation laborers for Hawai'i, a migration that would transform its demography. He also proposed that his niece, Princess Kaiulani, wed a Japanese prince to unite their royal families, but the Japanese emperor was less than enthusiastic. In contrast, both the king of Siam and the maharajah of Johore, under pressure themselves from foreign powers, approved when Kalakaua asserted that they were "long-lost brothers" because of linguistic and physical similarities. Kalakaua sent three young Hawaiians to study in Canton and Tokyo in 1882. His diplomatic efforts in Asia showed a desire to earn respect for Hawai'i and the rest of Oceania in an increasingly interconnected region.[32]

The Dutch East Indies remained a key source of spices and the gateway to the Pacific for ships coming from Europe, but disease made it deadly for

Oceanians. Batavia, on Java, was praised by visiting captains as a fine colony, but the climate was so humid and unhealthy that after work European residents retreated to hilltop villas outside town. Its slave population included Papuans, who likely had resistance to malaria, but Joseph Freewill died in Indonesia in 1767. The next year, Ahutoru fell ill in Batavia, along with many of Bougainville's crew. He took his medicine willingly and survived, but he called the fever-ridden port "the land which kills, *enoua mate.*" Cook's crew also suffered from sickness there, but Tupaia refused to take any medicine. He died in a tent on the beach after his beloved servant Tayeto did, calling out the boy's name in despair and expressing regret that they had ever left Tahiti. Illness killed all three Palauans that McCluer took to Indonesia in 1791.

Nevertheless, the Dutch East Indies did impress some early Pacific Islander visitors. At Buru, Ahutoru became curiously self-conscious when Bougainville unexpectedly did not take his Tahitian "guide" ashore. The French captain wrote that Ahutoru "imagined it was because his knees are distorted, and absolutely wanted some sailors to get upon them, to set them to rights." Once ashore, Ahutoru was said to admire the trade station's houses and gardens and the dress and manners of its European residents, whom he tried earnestly to imitate. He presented himself as a great chief on a pleasure cruise and asked if Paris was as fine as Buru? McCluer's Palauans enjoyed touring the European-style houses at Timor and at Amboina, where a host entertained them with sleight-of-hand tricks. Unlike the two young women, Pimu managed to sneak out for "night games." He bathed twice a day and ironed his own shirts, but he died of smallpox about a month after fever had killed both the women. Batavia amazed Tupaia and Tayeto, particularly the boy: "Houses, carriages, streets, in short every thing were to him sights which he had often heard describd but never well understood, so he lookd upon them all with more than wonder, almost mad with the numberless novelties which diverted his attention from one to the other he danc'd about the streets." Tupaia saw that people dressed in their own national style, so "He desird to have his, on which South Sea cloth was sent for on board and he cloathd himself according to his taste."[33]

Australia

In 1770, Aborigines at Botany Bay shouted and threw spears at Cook's longboats, but the British left gifts in some abandoned huts. By 1788, when the first convict ships arrived, Aborigines accepted whatever foreign goods they could get. Yet they also killed encroaching settlers and livestock and speared a governor who had tried to "civilize" an Aborigine by renaming him, tying him to a leash, and forcing him to dine at table. In the 1800s, Aborigines came into Sydney each day to beg or to work for low wages, but they also stuck stubbornly to their own ways. Perhaps twenty thousand died resisting conquest, and disease reduced their numbers by 80 percent in a century.[34] Sydney became a magnet not only for English convicts and settlers but also for seamen, and trade so increased the number of Tahitians, Hawaiians, and Maoris in port that the government began to regulate their employment. A benevolent society attended to South Sea Islanders in New South Wales after 1814.[35]

To many Oceanians, Australia represented England, or "the white man's country." As in China, written sources repeatedly record that the "forest of shipping" in Port Jackson impressed Islanders, as did the windmills and horse-drawn carriages. Many apparently wanted to see Sydney after hearing about it from friends. Tuki and Huru, as we have seen, traveled involuntarily from New Zealand to Norfolk Island in 1793, when Lieutenant Governor King wanted his convicts to learn flax weaving. Although they lived in comfort in King's residence, they repeatedly asked to go home and even threatened suicide. He wrote that, unlike Tuki, Huru was not curious about what he saw: "Like a true patriot [he] thinks there is no Country, People, or Customs, equal to his own." Yet a decade later, Te Pahi sailed from Bay of Islands to Sydney with his five sons to meet King, having heard about him from Tuki.

The tall, proud Maori chief wore his traditional mats, presented now-Governor King with handicrafts and a war club and rubbed noses with him. "He spared no pains," King wrote, "to convince us that the customs of his country were in several instances better than ours, many of which he looked on with the greatest contempt." When an English gentleman made fun of his facial tattoos, Te Pahi pointed to the powder and grease on the man's own hair. He urged King not to execute three white convicts caught stealing pork—arguing that only the theft of something nonperishable and rare like iron should merit such harsh treatment. His own people, Te Pahi argued, always fed the hungry. Perhaps, he said, captains who flogged Maori sailors or stole potatoes from New Zealand should be punished! Te Pahi admitted he killed one of his wives "for having a troublesome tongue; nor could he help testifying his surprise that many of the women here did not suffer the same fate." When a lady complained that he had passed along some earrings she had given him to a younger woman, he angrily returned everything to her and insisted that it was his own business what he did with his presents. Te Pahi took home an English beachcomber to marry his daughter and command his army, and King gave him presents to assure "advantage to our whalers."

Te Pahi and the British shared some notions of class distinctions. King proposed employing lower-class Maoris stranded in Australia as shepherds, but Te Pahi opposed the idea and "insisted on sending the middling order of people, who would be more expert at labour and tractable than the emokis or lower class, who were too idle and vicious to send here and from whom no good could be got." Te Pahi and his son also attended an Aboriginal funeral outside Sydney that resulted in a battle among the mourners. A man targeted for vengeance warded off spear after spear with his shield, but Te Pahi exhorted the attacking Aborigines to finish the job and even asked to participate. He admired the Aboriginal throwing stick for giving greater velocity to their weapons, but he said that a warrior should be able to deflect spears bare-handed. Te Pahi and his son regarded themselves as superior to Aborigines, because the latter went naked and lacked permanent shelter or Maori-style military prowess. For their part, Aborigines seemed to dread the approach of the two Maoris, especially when Te Pahi's son demonstrated his own spear-throwing technique.[36] The Maori connection with Australia was clearly through its British colonizers, not the marginalized native peoples.

Oceanians had mixed success in relating to Aborigines. Like Te Pahi, other Maori visitors commented on Aboriginal poverty and nakedness and asked if they planted any crops or raised pigs. Some Maoris tried to befriend Aborigines by rubbing noses, Polynesian-style; shaking hands; dancing and singing for them; and presenting tobacco. When one Aborigine tried to sing back but choked on the tobacco in his cheek, "The New Zealanders stared at him in astonishment, and thought he was mad ... to the mirthful surprise of every body present." Yet after seeing what had happened in Australia, some Maori travelers recognized the danger to their own sovereignty.[37] Tupaia described Aborigines as fit only for sacrifice, yet Cook expected him to act as intermediary. Unable to communicate verbally, the Ra'iatean offered them gifts and gestured that they should put aside their weapons and sit down with him. They slowly began to like Tupaia, visited his tent, and brought roots that helped to cure his scurvy. Omai proved useless in Tasmania and scared the natives off by shooting a musket. Yet Tahitians at Port Jackson later asked for and received fish from Aborigines. In 1853, King Taufa'ahau Tupou I of Tonga visited Sydney and was at first impressed, but the sight of so many native beggars convinced him to keep Tongan land in Tongan hands.[38]

British whalers and missionaries developed almost a shuttle service between Bay of Islands and Sydney for Maori chiefs. Chief Ruatara visited New South Wales five times, as a mistreated *kanaka* on whalers and an honored dignitary on church vessels. Missionary Samuel Marsden regarded

English convicts as worthy of nothing but a good flogging and as "the most degraded of the human race," but after meeting several Maori chiefs at his Parramatta farm outside Sydney, he decided that they were a "noble and intelligent" people: "Their minds appeared like a rich soil that had never been cultivated, and only wanted the proper means of improvement to render them fit to rank with civilized nations." When Ruatara nearly died from mistreatment on a British whaler, Marsden nursed him back to health. Ruatara studied wheat farming at Parramatta and in 1810 left for New Zealand on the whaler *Frederick* along with three other young Maoris, including one of Te Pahi's sons. After still more misadventures, he finally planted wheat in New Zealand with Marsden's technological help. According to Marsden, Ruatara had a dream: "I have now introduced the cultivation of wheat in New Zealand. It will become a great country; for, in two years more, I shall be able to export wheat to Port Jackson, in exchange for hoes, axes, spades, and tea and sugar."

The *Boyd* incident of 1809 caused a temporary break in contact between Australia and New Zealand. George (Te A'ara) of Whangaroa had been flogged on the whaleship *Boyd,* so his kin massacred and burned the ship. Te Pahi, who had returned to Bay of Islands two years earlier, was trading fish at Whangaroa that day, and his complicity was suspected. Three white survivors and Chief Tara of Bay of Islands (who earned a boat for his testimony) blamed Te Pahi for leading the attack, while chiefs Hongi Hika and Ruatara later blamed Te Puhi of Whangaroa—suggesting a case of mistaken identity. Vengeful British whalers burned Te Pahi's village, killing sixty people and wounding the old chief. Marsden wanted to reopen contact with Bay of Islands and establish a mission there, so he did what he could to redeem Te Pahi's name, claiming that the friendly chief had actually tried to save the lives of some of the *Boyd* crew but failed. Te Pahi, however, may well have cooperated with the Whangaroa Maoris to avenge the kidnapping and abuse of his sons by English ships, as well as the clandestine departure of his favorite daughter with her beachcomber husband the previous year.

At the age of eight or ten, Maui shipped out from Bay of Islands to see Norfolk Island, having heard about it from Tuki and Huru. He was adopted by the harbormaster, a Mr. Drummond, who dubbed the boy Tommy and sent him to school to learn to read and write. When the Drummonds moved to New South Wales, Tommy joined Marsden's flock at Parramatta. In 1814, Marsden's *Active,* with Tommy Drummond on board, took presents to Bay of Islands chiefs. Several then visited Parramatta and returned home with Marsden as goodwill ambassadors. Marsden was able to negotiate peace with the Whangaroa people with Ruatara's help, though the chief died soon afterwards of a stomach ailment. After establishing a mission station on Te Pahi's land, Marsden began to rotate young Maori chiefs between Bay of Islands and Parramatta:

> Many solicited to go with me to Port Jackson, whom I was obliged to refuse, partly because we had no room and partly on account of the heavy expense of maintaining them on their passage to and from New Zealand and while the vessel lay at Port Jackson. I told them I would at all times permit a few to have a passage, but that should be in turns, which satisfied them.[39]

By 1819, he wrote: "Two are learning to make bricks, 1 nail-making, another in the blacksmith shop, and the others will be employed . . . in some useful work." Marsden said he hoped to build unity among the Maori: "By the sons of chiefs living together in civil life, and all paid equal attention to, they will form attachments that will destroy the jealousy which has kept their tribes in continual war." Maoris remained disunited, but Marsden saw his guests as guarantors of the security of English missionaries in New Zealand. Marsden also employed Maoris on the *Active,* not always by their own choice, as when a well-traveled sailor named Wari, "an expert proficient in turpitude," was flogged for seducing one of Ruatara's wives and condemned to three years of service on the *Active.* But most traveled with Marsden as ennobled diplomats. A young chief named Tuhi went on the *Active* to Parramatta twice. In 1818, Marsden sent him and Titore on to England as literate showpieces, because "Tooi is a fine man, well informed and well disposed, and has a love of our religion." Te Morenga was another informant and confidant for Marsden and, like Te Pahi a decade earlier, advised training only chiefs' sons, not commoners who "would never rise higher in rank than their parents." In 1820, Hongi Hika sailed with missionary Thomas Kendall to England, insisting, "he should die if he did not go—that if he once got to England, he was certain of getting twelve muskets, and a double-barrelled gun."[40]

Other Oceanians also underwent cultural initiations in Australia. A Tahitian arrived on Norfolk Island on a trade vessel in 1801, quite proud of his own country and dressed in fine Tahitian *tapa* cloth. Yet he was still impressed by the colony, notably its well-provisioned homes where white families welcomed him warmly. He met a compatriot, Oreo, who had worked his way to England and back on the *Albion* and was "smartly dressed in the style of an English sailor." Oreo also had guns, metal tools, and travel stories to tell, all of which gave him status in his compatriot's eyes. In 1798, Governor King treated Tapeooe of Tahiti as Pomare I's ambassador, and on his way home from England a decade later, Tapeooe had a passenger's berth in steerage while Tomma, a compatriot, had to work his passage. At Parramatta, Tapeooe was a guest of Marsden, but most of his property was stolen and he soon died of dysentery.[41] According to Tongan oral tradition, Chief Palu Mata Moina and his wife Fatafehi did not have a warm welcome in Sydney. They were put to work sweeping floors at the governor's house. No one understood their protests about being chiefs or would even invite them inside to eat, unlike in Tonga. When Palu saw people coming out of a shop with food, he went in and waited for a share, but the white owner assumed Palu was a thief and chased him outside. The Tongan later said he learned that "money made a man a chief" in Sydney. Forty years later, a twelve-year-old Loyalty Islander was making his living selling oranges in Sydney, "every body preferring to buy from this witty little urchin." Sometimes young *kanakas* were taken in by English gentlemen to be educated and "civilized," in return for servant duties. Yet in typical sailor fashion, Epeli of Rotuma left his ship to "play around" and spent all his money on rum and prostitutes in Port Jackson bars.[42]

Military parades entertained visiting Oceanian chiefs, and some donned red British officers' uniforms, complete with swords. One Maori delegation mistakenly put on convict clothes for their meeting with the governor until advised to wear traditional costumes. A Fijian chief said he first thought all of the inhabitants of Sydney were preachers, because they wore white shirts like those of native teachers at home.[43] Dillon introduced Takai as a Fijian admiral and Langi as a Tongan prince and had cards printed up for them to present to Australian well-wishers. They stayed at the shop of a large-sized man named Robert Cooper, whom they at first mistook, according to Dillon, for the king of Sydney. Impressed by a steam engine, cutlery, and firearms, they asked for presents from the people they met in high society. Dillon also brought Tongan chief Tupou Tutai to Sydney in 1838. He visited Government House and attended the usual balls and dinner parties, where he apparently received plenty of attention from the ladies. Wilkes later wrote, "He said that they had admired him very much, and called him a very handsome man." He hired Tupou Tutai as a pilot in Fiji in 1840 and found him to be polite and fairly fluent in English, with "all the grace and elegance of a finished gentleman, if one can imagine such a being in a Tongese Islander. . . . He was a professing Christian, and might be called more than half civilized."[44]

Yet the white man's country could be taxing. Maori chiefs at a dinner party became drowsy and uncomfortable in their chairs, so they retired to an adjoining room and curled up on their mats on the floor to sleep. Oceanians tended to dislike the barren, cold climate at Sydney; Te Pahi's daughter died there at the age of eighteen. Despite protective government decrees, some *kanakas* died of exposure instead of going to the local Benevolent

Asylum, where two hundred indigent inmates lived under strict rules. Sydney also had a maritime court. The American whaler *Sharon* brought a Pohnpeian there in irons, on charges of mutiny and murder, and a Maori once interpreted for a Hawaiian who was giving evidence in a Sydney law court.[45] In 1850, nine Fijians returned home from Sydney, where eleven compatriots had died in less than a year. One returnee entertained his chief at a *kava* party with stories of the "white people's country." He said his black skin had brought him hardship: his boss had made him eat and sleep with the pigs, not in the house, and work at the forge with a hammer much heavier than that used by white men—it sent sparks flying into his face and left holes (which looked to John Erskine like those made by smallpox). Other Fijians told Erskine, "Too much work at Sydney, too little eat!" Plantation and dock work brought one hundred thousand *kanaka*s to Australia in the late nineteenth century, but after 1901, a "White Australia" policy caused the deportation of most. Those few South Sea Islanders who remained behind became as marginalized as Aborigines.[46]

~ 7 ~

In the Belly of the Beast

Can it possibly be that these light hearted happy people are all going to Hell? All enjoying nature as nature's best gift? Surely not!

—King Kalakaua in Paris, 1881[1]

In this age of modern air travel, it may be difficult to imagine spending a year or more on a dangerous voyage to the other side of the world. But North Atlantic seaports are more than fifteen thousand miles from the Pacific, and one-third of the best-documented Oceanians who left their region died prematurely, mainly of Eurasian diseases. Nevertheless, many reached the cores of the emerging world economy as ennobled tourists or working *kanaka*s, like disguised spies. Just as Euroamericans came to Oceania in search of romantic adventure or exotic wares, so Pacific voyagers crossed three oceans to explore the sources of the technology that had impressed them. The question was, would their shipboard initiations and visits to colonies along the way prepare them for what they encountered? Would they convert to the "civilization" whose ships had carried them so far, as their white mentors expected, or would they become disillusioned? We know mainly what their hosts wrote, but even secondhand, refracted testimony can be revealing.

The Indian and Atlantic Oceans

Most *kanaka* seamen spent their careers circulating in the inner Pacific, or possibly in key rim ports like Canton or Sydney. But a few slipped outside their region into the sea-lanes of the Indian and Atlantic Oceans, which led to Europe and the United States. The Indian Ocean had been traversed since ancient times by Indonesians migrating to Madagascar; by Arab, Indian, and Chinese trading fleets; and in the 1500s by armed Portuguese caravels. Yet Vasco da Gama needed a Muslim pilot to guide him from East Africa to India, and European tradeships had to replenish crews far from home. The new maritime frontier thus became liminal for foreign seamen, as they came to depend on hiring African "Kru-men," Indian lascars, "black Portuguese" from the Cape Verde Islands, and "Manila-men."[2] Oceanians would join this international circuit and on the way to London or Boston they followed a trail of colonies.

The first Pacific Islander of record to see the Indian Ocean was Jeoly of Miangas, who arrived in Madras, India, in 1690 on a clove ship. Both he and his mother were slaves. William Dampier bought a half-share in them and sailed to western Sumatra, but there the mother died of disease, while Jeoly traveled on to England and death from smallpox.[3] Late eighteenth-century voyagers like Ahutoru and Lee Boo would succumb to the same illness, but Omai and Kualelo survived London and returned home. In 1809, two Oceanian women, Mary Bruce (Te Pahi's teenaged daughter) and Ena Robarts of the Marquesas, entered the Indian Ocean as wives of roving white beachcombers. At Malacca, on the west coast of Malaya, Mary was abducted by a sea captain to Penang. Her loyal husband managed to rescue her and take her on to Calcutta and then back to Sydney, where she died. Ena lived with her husband for a year in Penang, where she bore him a third child with help from a Tahitian midwife. In 1810, they moved to Calcutta, where, sad and sickly, Ena gave birth to two more children before dying in 1813. Her husband later wrote, "my daughters told me that for some time before she died, when I was absent every day on my duty, that she would go into her chamber and weep, and, when the time drew near for my return, she would wash her face and be cheerfull, strictly chargeing the children not to tell me. She had often expressed a desire to return to her native Island." Within a decade, his children too all died, except one.[4]

India was thus not much healthier for Oceanians than Indonesia. In 1795, John McClure took half a dozen Palauan women to Bengal and Bombay as servants for his wife. Three died of smallpox before the British East India Company could repatriate the survivors.[5] Of eleven Islanders who went to Calcutta with Dillon in 1826, four died of tuberculosis and three more of measles soon after leaving. Yet Dillon's two Maori chiefs, "Brian Boroo and Morgan McMurragh," helped him to win official support for his La Pérouse expedition. In Calcutta, they dressed in traditional regalia and did "war dances" on command. British Indian newspapers covered the visit with mixed curiosity and condescension. At a hotel restaurant, a reporter asked Brian about the purpose of his visit. The Maori did not understand but pointed to some cold cuts and said "good." When the reporter asked about the political situation in New Zealand, Brian asked for more mustard. Tongue-in-cheek, the newspaper said, "He is rather modest in his demeanor for a Prince, and very guarded in his conversation, as men of rank, birth and station ought to be." Morgan, it reported, thirsted for knowledge, while Brian wanted only guns and ammunition. Brian saw so many Indian servants waiting on the British, he said via Dillon, "Ah, you will come and take my country too, I have no doubt, as you have taken this."[6]

By the 1850s, Hawaiian *kanaka*s were passing through Calcutta. Old John Gilpin, sailing on an American merchant ship, wound up in prison there. He had fought with the ship's cook, so the Calcutta police took him in irons to prison, where he soon died of a fever. Eight other Hawaiian crewmen from the same vessel took their liberty money ashore and deserted. They had already mutinied once because of physical abuse by a mate.[7] In 1881, on his tour around the world, King David Kalakaua of Hawai'i arrived in Calcutta after visiting the British establishments at Malacca, Penang, and Rangoon. In Southeast Asia, he had ridden elephants and seen Buddhist pagodas. He wrote his sister Lili'uokalani, "All these places we have visited ... so familiar to us during our school days in our geography, strange that I should live to be able to see them, has been a complete wonder." He traveled by train across India, seeing the holy city of Benares, the Taj Mahal in Agra, and the "Towers of Silence" in Bombay where the Parsees exposed their dead. Before he left India, according to William Armstrong, Kalakaua bought "a striking image of Buddha, for the purpose ... of showing to his own people that nations with some high civilisation used a variety of idols as well as the Hawaiians. His people, he said, were not the beastly pagans that the travellers and missionaries had represented them to be." In Cairo, he visited the pyramids and noted, "the Egyptians, like the Japanese, the Chinese, and the Siamese, traced the origin of their sovereigns to a divine source." At Alexandria, the king drank an ironic toast to Cook's fatal ship, the *Resolution,* by then a rusty coal barge in the harbor.[8]

Before the opening of the Suez Canal in 1869, Mauritius and Capetown were often visited by Pacific Islanders on the way to and from Europe. Ahutoru saw the former in 1768, on his way to France, and he stayed there for ten months in 1770, on his way home to Tahiti. In contrast to the way local African slaves lived, he was treated like a celebrity by French residents, but he caught smallpox and died before the ship could finish provisioning at Madagascar. Moehanga of Aotearoa passed through Mauritius in 1806, before Britain captured it from France and introduced Indian indentured labor; Morrell's Darco, himself a captive, saw it on his way home in 1834.[9] Like other colonies en route, Capetown was an introduction to Europe itself. Feeling peculiarly vulnerable in a Dutch slave-owning society, dark, flat-nosed Omai called himself a chiefly attendant of the Tahitian king, not a commoner. He was apparently quite taken by a young Dutch lady and parted from her reluctantly. On his return voyage, Omai scratched his autograph on a window pane in Capetown, like a tourist seeking immortality. He also recovered from "the French pox" there, along with many of Cook's sailors. In 1791, Kualelo of Hawai'i passed through Capetown with Vancouver and received gifts of a sword, two pistols, and a rifle.[10]

Once around the southern capes of South America or Africa, ships often stopped at St. Helena in the south Atlantic. Tattooed Jeoly went ashore there in 1691, Dampier said, and "he was very diligent to pick up such things as the Islands afforded, carrying ashore with him a Bag, which the People of the Isle filled with Roots for him. They flocked about him, and seemed to admire him very much." A century later, Lee Boo admired the British warships in the harbor and the fort's cannons and soldiers. He visited a school, where he said he envied the boys' learning. He rode a horse into the country and enjoyed the shade of an English garden, saying, in George Keate's self-satisfied words, "on this island they had but little wood, yet applied it to a good purpose; that at PELEW they had great abundance, and knew not how to use it."[11] Moehanga was on St. Helena in 1805, glad to be away from wintry Cape Horn. He had just escaped being eaten by a shark while swimming in warmer waters. Moehanga too admired the ships and the vast amount of iron, and he sang for joy until a cannon salute from the fort sent him diving to the deck. Ashore, he inspected people's clothing so closely he almost started a fight. The governor's regal appearance impressed the Maori most, oxen and horses made him laugh, and the regimental band entranced him. But the barren island became boring, so Moehanga spent the remaining time in port on the ship, barely escaping another shark attack while bathing. Ironically, Temoana of Nukuhiva, whom the French would make king of the Marquesas, paid his respects to Napoleon's tomb at St. Helena.[12]

The Atlantic could offer *kanaka*s a last chance to be "Islanders" before reaching Western urban centers. Ahutoru and his French shipmates caught turtles at Ascension Island, and a young Maori named Pomare caught scavenging pigeons near Cape Horn with a hook and line. Tropical zones could also provide a refreshing change from the colder extremes of the Atlantic. The balmy Cape Verde Island of St. Jagos reminded Opai of his native Hawai'i. Having tired of Boston and shipped out for home, he appreciated seeing coconuts and plantains again. Opai bought a monkey and took seeds from orange, lemon, and lime trees to plant on Kaua'i. Morrell's poor captive Darco, peering from the masthead for familiar land on his way back to Melanesia, also thought the Cape Verde Islands looked like home.[13] The Caribbean, however, could be risky. In 1793, young "Jacket" of Tahiti traveled by way of St. Helena to Jamaica, to help Bligh deliver the Tahitian breadfruit. After assisting the British scientists with the new crop, Jacket died—and the African slaves on Jamaica did not like the plant brought with so much trouble from the Pacific to feed them. Thomas Hopu of Hawai'i worked on American ships in the West Indies and was twice taken prisoner during the War of 1812. In fact, he survived because African slaves offered him their food and water.[14]

The Atlantic could initiate Oceanian voyagers into a harsh seafaring world. In 1820, Marquesan Thomas Patu had the misfortune to work on a sealing ship in the South Shetland Islands. One day the shrouds gave way under his feet while he was working aloft, and he fell into the frigid sea. Patu had to cut off his boots with a knife to keep afloat until the ship turned about to rescue him. He wound up in Boston Marine Hospital. On a Russian vessel about the same time, Lauri of Hawai'i experienced what Hitihiti had discovered in cold southern waters with Cook: ice and hail. According to explorer Vasilii Golovnin, Lauri "thought that stones were falling from heaven and immediately began to collect the hailstones in his handkerchief, explaining that he wanted to show them to his compatriots later. When they started melting, he thought that they had gotten wet and started drying them with his handkerchief; it is impossible to describe his astonishment when he discovered that the supposed stones were nothing more than solidified water." When the Russian crew laughed at nature's joke and teased Lauri by bringing more hailstones for his vanishing collection, he became angry and complained to Golovnin.[15]

Europe

In 1769, when Parisian intellectuals were debating the notion that people once lived in a pure state of nature before "iron and wheat" enslaved and corrupted humanity, Bougainville brought a specimen from Tahiti. Ahutoru was not their first exotic visitor, but compared to the Chinese and Siamese who had preceded him, who were categorized as barbarian or civilized, he represented a different kind of "other," a Pacific exemplar of "noble savagery." Ahutoru spent nearly a year in Paris under constant scrutiny. "The desire of seeing him," Bougainville wrote, "has been very violent." Critics called Ahutoru stupid for not learning better French, but fans called him intelligent because he figured out what to do with objects placed before him. He developed a kind of sign language and helped to compile a Tahitian vocabulary, but his main interest was apparently French women. After all, it was Ahutoru who had discovered among Bougainville's crew a French woman disguised in male dress. In France, the duchess of Choiseul became his benefactor and close friend; she would help to finance the tools, seeds, and cattle that he took on his homeward voyage.

Ahutoru seemed to adapt well to life in Europe. He went for daily walks around Paris alone without getting lost and paid fair prices for the souvenirs he purchased. He always carried a watch, and he knew the days when the opera performed. After buying the cheapest ticket, he would peep through little windows in the back walls of the expensive boxes for a better look at the actors. Afterwards, with characteristic enthusiasm, he mimicked the songs.[16] Still, Diderot criticized France for opening up Tahiti to perverse "civilization" and disease and predicted that Ahutoru would be considered a liar anyway when he returned home. Though a celebrity in Europe, Ahutoru was of relatively low rank in Tahiti. He was expendable, and he would die on the Indian Ocean, leaving philosophers to debate his significance.[17] Half a century later, two Maoris had to work their way from New Zealand to Le Havre as common seamen on a French whaler in order to meet King Louis-Philippe. Another whaleship brought Hawaiian crewman Joseph Maheo to France to stand trial for criminal behavior. But in 1849, Hawaiian Prince Alexander Liholiho encountered echoes of the "noble savage" vogue when he visited France and had to answer "a great many queer questions" at social gatherings.[18]

London, as capital of the expanding British Empire, was the major European magnet for Pacific visitors. As early as 1691, Jeoly arrived in England, to be sold and displayed in carnival sideshows as an exotic "Painted Prince" until he died at Oxford. Printed handouts, with a fanciful drawing and description, immortalized his long captivity.[19] More celebrated than Jeoly but hardly less appropriated was Omai, who came to London in 1774 on Cook's companion ship, HMS *Adventure.* John Hawkesworth's literary rendition of Cook's first voyage had already excited English intellectuals about meeting a South Sea Islander. The young Ra'iatean first stayed with Joseph Banks, the same scientist who had been responsible for Tupaia's martyred "tygerhood." Omai was happy to find that Banks and Dr. Daniel Solander remembered their Tahitian, because he had learned very little English. They wisely inoculated Omai against smallpox, thus enabling him to survive his two years in England. The cold climate displeased him, however, and he suspected Hertford graveyard was filled with patients the good doctor had vaccinated.

Omai dressed carefully, attended the theater in the upper boxes, and learned polite table manners. The renowned scholar Samuel Johnson found it hard to tell Omai from Lord Mulgrave in bad light, saying, "there was so little of the savage in Omai, that I was afraid to speak to either lest I should mistake one for the other." Johnson credited Omai's poise to his having circulated "only in the best company; so that all he had acquired of our manners was genteel." Like Ahutoru in Paris, Omai enjoyed the company of upper-class ladies, and he seemed to play his romantic role well. He once accepted a handkerchief from the duchess of Gloucester, and when she glanced furtively at him afterwards, he kissed it warmly. When introduced to Fanny Burney, his favorite shipmate's sister, Omai bowed graciously. He offered her a chair and pulled his own up close to hers. Without many words, he apparently convinced her that he cared deeply about her welfare. After supper, however, he surprised her and left in a coach to visit, he said, "twelve woman!"

Omai loved to rhapsodize about the beauty of the aristocratic women he met, and he took great interest in their appearance. For example, he pointed out to one lady that she had let two of her hair curls become unpinned in public. To amuse his hosts, he displayed the usual Islander skills of mimicry and storytelling, though his traditional chants apparently did not please English ears. He met King George III and heard him speak to the House of Lords. Omai walked around London alone, as Ahutoru had in Paris, and he lived by himself on Warwick Street. Yet the more he shed his Oceanian ways and learned correct English, the less interesting he became to his hosts. Even if he communicated in his own language through a translator, Miss Burney wrote, "it rendered Omiah far less entertaining than . . . when he was obliged, despite of difficulties, to explain himself as well as he could [in broken English]."[20] "Noble savages" had to fit Melville's description of Queequeg as "a creature in the transition state—neither caterpillar nor butterfly." It was incomplete, vulnerable liminality that appealed.

In 1784, Lee Boo of Palau arrived in London and was quickly befriended by George Keate, a friend of Voltaire's. Keate portrayed the young man as a princely "savage" with stoic humility and proper temperance. For his part, Lee Boo seemed surprised that Englishmen lived in countless boxes, from ship cabins to wheeled carriages to stacks of what he regarded as separate houses, each of which seemed to contain four-posted beds. He lived as a member of Captain Henry Wilson's family in Rotherhithe, a typical London seaman's parish, and attended church and school. Lee Boo took care to imitate proper table manners and entertained his hosts by mimicking other people's peculiarities. His own singing was evidently as unappreciated as that of Omai before him. He sometimes had the help of a translator, but his lively eyes and expressive gestures helped him to communicate as he learned English. Lee Boo retained his long hair but dressed and acted the role of an English gentleman.

According to Keate, the Palauan expressed sympathy for beggars, as he had in Macao—except for the young healthy ones who he said should work. He visited public buildings but was kept away from crowds, because Wilson claimed to be hesitant to inoculate him until he could explain why to him in English. After only six months in England, twenty-year-old Lee Boo learned the hard way about smallpox and died of it. He was buried in Rotherhithe churchyard, just after Christmas. Once, when viewing a miniature portrait of Keate, Lee Boo had said, "that Misser KEATE die—this Misser KEATE live." Keate immortalized the Palauan with a romantic account that amended the young Oceanian's epitaph, "Stop, Reader, stop!— let NATURE claim a Tear—A Prince of Mine, LEE BOO, lies bury'd here." That possessive pronoun showed the plight of such double ghosts. In 1793, Maititi of Tahiti arrived with Bligh, but he died in a few weeks— even faster than Lee Boo, and essentially unremembered.[21]

In 1799, Temoteitei arrived from the Marquesas on the tradeship *Butterworth,* hence his monicker John Butterworth. He was followed by another Marquesan, Hekenaeke (or Heko), and the Tahitian Harraweia. The cold climate adversely affected the health of all three Oceanians, but Temoteitei had sailed with a missionary and was inoculated against smallpox. He underwent the ordeal with twenty-four Africans from Sierra Leone. "Over these," wrote the missionary, "he assumed a superiority, proportioned to the difference of his complexion; and made suitable reports of their behavior." Temoteitei had lost his father in a war, so he appreciated boarding with a paternal director of the British East India Company in London. Still, he fell ill in the city and was taken to the country to recover. Temoteitei adopted English manners but had no interest in the language. His hosts translated their words and prayers into Marquesan for him, so he concluded that they had no language of their own worth knowing. He also disliked monogamy and saw nothing wrong in cannibalism. Temoteitei resented attempts to convert him to Christianity and told a missionary that at home he had heard gods "whistle among the trees, and in the thatch of the houses; but we [the English] have no gods in our country." Nevertheless, the missionary admitted that Temoteitei was a shrewd judge of character and could remember faces well.[22]

The same was said of Moehanga, who came to England from Aotearoa in 1805. "He was a great physiognomist," wrote surgeon John Savage, "and approved or disliked at a first interview." Moehanga loved to watch people in London and pointed out their peculiarities, often belittling their appearance, saying "good for nothing" or laughing at the lame, particularly those with wooden legs. He worried at first how so many people could feed themselves without cattle or gardens, but he felt reassured when he saw noisy markets, wagons of provisions, and droves of oxen going by in the street. The sight of a fat passerby led him to comment, "That man has plenty to eat." Moehanga's facial tattooing attracted the attention of Londoners. He would offer them his hand and say, as his sailor shipmates had taught him, "How do you do, my boy?" Ironware and clothing shops, the height of church steeples, the numerous ships in the Thames, and horse-drawn carriages all impressed him to the point where he voiced concern over his own status as a lower-class Maori in such a vast metropolis.

Yet the ironically named Dr. Savage introduced Moehanga as a chief to Earl Fitzwilliam and Lord Milton. He pulled up a chair to study closely a marble bust of the earl, the lines of whose face pleased him very much. After all, Maori facial tattooing defined identity. Yet instead of admiring the earl's paintings and mirrors, Moehanga counted chairs. Using a stick that he broke into segments, he concluded, "A great number of men sit with the chief." He enjoyed the monuments that England had erected to its national heroes, but he was disappointed when King George III was an odd old man, not a vigorous young warrior. Moehanga frightened the queen with a war-like *haka,* but she still gave him some gold guineas. These he quickly traded one-for-one for silver shillings. As he later told Peter Dillon, "I thought the people in England very foolish to give so many white monies of the same size for the red one of Queen Charlotte." But before his guineas were gone, Moehanga said, he spent some on a "wife" named Nancy, perhaps a prostitute. "She was very fond of me," he told Dillon, "and proved pregnant. She used to ask me if the child when born would go to New Zealand, and if it would have such marks on its face as mine." Dr. Savage sent Moehanga home with an "ample stock of tools," many of which he had learned how to use, but the Maori long regretted that he had not asked for firearms instead.[23]

Other Maoris came to London in the early 1800s, but some felt as captive as Jeoly. They found themselves in a damp, cold city that treated even Englishmen badly. In 1807, Te Pahi's son Matara met King George, who graciously took off his hat for the young chief; however, Matara caught tuberculosis and died soon after his return home. Ruatara, after many misadventures as a common sailor, reached England in 1809 on the sealer *Santa Anna,* only to be disappointed in his desire to meet the king. He was allowed to go ashore only briefly, denied the wages due him, and beaten. He fell seriously ill and was transferred "naked and miserable" to the Australia-bound convict ship *Ann,* where Marsden nursed him back to health. Maui, or Tommy Drummond, had worked on whaleships and lived in Australia before he set out for England as a common sailor on the whaler *Jefferson* in 1815. Protected and schooled by Anglican missionaries in

London, he converted to Christianity, but within a year he too died of tuberculosis. In 1816, Marsden sent Tuhi and Titore to England. They wrote back letters filled with proper piety: "I go home tell my countrymen, that Jesus is the true God. Atua is false—no God, all nonsense. I tell my countrymen, Englishman no hang his self—not eat a man—no tattoing—no fall cutting his self." But Tuhi became very ill and died shortly after his return home.[24]

In 1806, wandering Tapeooe of Tahiti arrived in London on the *Warley,* captained by the son of Lee Boo's mentor. The mission society would not support Tapeooe, so he stayed with a sea captain until a sailor named Kelso, who had known the Tahitian on Tongatapu, lured him into the exhibition circuit. Commodified like Jeoly, poor Tapeooe spent a year helping to raise money "from many humane individuals." But Kelso kept him illiterate and once hit him with a chair when he tried to quit. Finally, a surgeon rescued Tapeooe and put him in school, after which a committee raised enough money to send him to Australia as a passenger on a convict ship in 1810. The seat of empire attracted exoticism. In 1816, Thomas Raffles brought from Java a ten-year-old Papuan slave nicknamed Dick. He was studied by two scientists of the Royal Society as "the first individual of the woolly haired race of Eastern Asia who had been brought to this country." The boy had apparently grown up in captivity, and linguist William Marsden noted, "he had scarcely any recollection of his native tongue." After a year, Dick went back to Indonesia with Raffles, who would found the English colony at Singapore. In 1830, a businessman brought two tattooed Maoris to England and exhibited them around the country like Jeoly. The Maoris did their famous "war dance" and made fire by rubbing sticks together, but their employer abandoned them when they caught the measles. Fortunately, they won support from church charities and returned home in good health. Temoana of Nukuhiva was exhibited like a tattooed animal in London, a humiliation he never forgot. Rescued and semi-educated by Protestant missionaries, he would later be made "King of the Marquesas" by France.[25]

Yet ennobled tourism was still available for those who knew how to exploit it. In 1820, Hongi Hika and Waikato went with missionary Thomas Kendall to London, supposedly to finish work on a Maori alphabet and vocabulary that Tuhi had begun. Neither chief spoke much English, but they were introduced to "many distinguished persons" at Cambridge University. The *Church Missionary Register* described them as "manly [but] interesting strangers." The *Sydney Gazette* reported that they met King George IV, "who treated them with the greatest condescension and affability, conducted them to his armoury, gave them several valuable presents and allowed them the honour of kissing his hand." Hongi was proud of his double-barreled gun, helmet, suit of armor, and sword and would use them all in battle back home. They also visited the British Museum, the Tower of London, and the House of Lords and asked for "at least one hundred" English miners, carpenters, blacksmiths, soldiers, settlers, and preachers, plus cattle and plenty of guns. They lived with Kendall's family to control their diet, but the climate still made them ill before they sailed for home.[26]

Te Pehi Kupe imitated Hongi's quest for weaponry by foisting himself on a captain and demanding to go to England to see King George. There he visited public buildings and factories in London, Liverpool, Birmingham, and Gloucester and was said to be fascinated by steam machinery and water mills. Te Pehi wanted not only firearms but also farming tools, and he laughed when he saw a flax plant, so common in New Zealand, growing in a flower pot. People crowded around wherever he went, but he apparently made little progress in English. His mentor inoculated him against smallpox, fed, clothed, and sheltered him, but Te Pehi caught measles and chicken pox. In the end, the government provided money for his expenses and safe return.[27] A decade later, the New Zealand Association brought two young Maori commoners to England from France. Nayti and "Jacky" had worked their way to Le Havre as seamen to meet King Louis-Philippe, and now they would get home by helping Edward Wakefield with his colonization plans. He took them by hackney coach to his house in Chelsea and pointed out the passing shops, crowds, and public buildings: "They gazed for some minutes in mute astonishment on the bewildering sight, and then, by apparently unanimous impulse, covered their faces with their hands, and leant back in the coach, as though they could not conceive, and refused to be forced to see, any more. . . ." Jacky died of tuberculosis, but Nayti presented himself as a chief and walked around London sightseeing. He skated on the Serpentine, rode horseback in Hyde Park, attended church dinners and the House of Lords, and befriended the duke of Sussex. Nayti sailed back to New Zealand with Wakefield's first settler vessel in 1839 and lost all his status.[28]

Oceanians continued to arrive in London like recurring themes in the English records. The August 1800 *Evangelical Magazine* reported the arrival of a ten-year-old Tahitian, in the company of a missionary couple. It said they were teaching him to read and write in English, though the boy had already picked up "the Moor's slang" and a bit of Dutch on his passage via Bengal and Capetown. A teenaged Easter Islander arrived on the whaler *Adventure* and lived for six years in Rotherhithe, Lee Boo's resting place, where he was baptized Henry Easter. A Tahitian whaling veteran served in the British naval bombardment of Algiers in 1824 and took his pension to

Hawai'i, while a Tongan kidnapped by a whaler became a bass drummer in the duke of York's band.[29] Two other Tahitians were discovered in Gibraltar harbor on the *Calypso*. They had been kidnapped by an English ship to Lima, caught a Spanish ship to Cadiz, and finally escaped to the *Calypso*. Fortunately, they came to the attention of Peter Heywood, who had gone to Tahiti with the *Bounty* and could greet them in their native language. He described them as ill-treated, untutored "children of nature" and asked the navy to put them on a vessel bound for Pitcairn Island. They reminded him of his own romantic adventure twenty-five years earlier in Tahiti, "where plenty and content are the portion of all, unalloyed by care, envy, or ambition—where labour is needless and want unknown."[30]

Hawaiians had a special fondness for England ever since Kamehameha I asked his friend George Vancouver for British protection against foreign powers. In 1789, Kualelo of Hawai'i came to London on the fur trader *Prince of Wales*. He received good treatment and some schooling before being sent home two years later. Banks arranged for Vancouver to return Kualelo to Hawai'i with clothing and whatever else he wanted "to an unlimited amount," hoping he would be a pro-British adviser to the king. In fact, a "sprightly" son of Kamehameha arrived in 1802. American sealer Amasa Delano had taken young "Alexander Stewart" to Canton, vaccinated the boy against smallpox, and allowed him to transfer to a British vessel where Alex had made friends with a sailor. Delano heard the boy was "taken notice of on his arrival in England by a gentleman of consequence, who took him to his own house with an intention of giving him an education."[31] In 1812, fur trapper "John Coxe" voyaged from Quebec to Portsmouth, England, on the *Isaac Todd*. Tempted by his shipmates into drinking and womanizing while in port, Coxe joined a rowdy group that rowed a small boat around the harbor until they were caught by a navy press gang and almost assigned to a new ship. Coxe then sailed around Cape Horn to help the British capture Astoria. In 1820, two Hawaiians arrived in England after another long adventure. Blackbirded by an American ship and enslaved by Spaniards in Mexico, they had escaped on a British whaler.[32]

Half a dozen Hawaiian monarchs and their entourages also visited England in the nineteenth century. The first were King Liholiho (Kamehameha II) and Queen Kamamalu, who arrived with other chiefs on the whaler *L'Aigle* in 1824 to repeat Kamehameha's request for protection. Unfortunately, the young king had already gambled away 60 percent of his expense money in Rio de Janeiro, so the British put the remaining ten thousand dollars in the Bank of England for safekeeping. The Hawaiian party stayed in a fashionable hotel and went sightseeing. At the theater, they occupied the royal boxes. But before Liholiho could meet King George IV, he and

Kamamalu both died of measles. Chief Boki negotiated with the British monarch, who agreed to see to Hawai'i's protection without interfering in its internal affairs. The foreign office appointed a consul for Hawai'i and sent home the royal caskets and surviving diplomats in a warship, HMS *Blonde*. The tragedy was a heavy sacrifice, and Kamamalu's mournful chant as she had departed from Honolulu echoed in her people's memories.[33]

More assurances were needed after foreign warships, including HMS *Carysfort,* threatened Honolulu. In 1843, royal secretary Timothy Ha'alilio traveled with American missionary William Richards to London, Paris, and Brussels to negotiate formal recognition of Hawaiian sovereignty. The diplomatic effort succeeded, though Ha'alilio seemed to be a token "silent partner." Sadly, he caught a winter cold that killed him before he reached home again. Seven years later, Princes Alexander Liholiho and Lot Kamehameha came with Dr. Gerrit Judd for more assurances.[34] In 1865, Dowager Queen Emma of Hawai'i, herself part-English and educated by an English governess, visited Queen Victoria, with whom she had corresponded since the death of her son and husband in 1862–63. Emma was accompanied by William Hoapili, the first Hawaiian Anglican priest, who with his wife Ha'auwai sang Hawaiian songs for Alfred Lord Tennyson at his home. The party spent a night with the royal family at Windsor Castle before visiting other parts of Europe. Twenty years later, Hawaiian envoy Curtis 'Iaukea visited London, Paris, Vienna, Belgrade, and Rome, often checking on Hawaiian students. He also attended the coronation of Czar Alexander III in Moscow and was fascinated by the czar's Asiatic subjects: "These primitive warriors . . . presented a dazzling kaleidoscope of human beings and horseflesh."[35]

In 1881, King Kalakaua arrived in Europe on his round-the-world tour. In Italy, he visited young Hawaiians he had sent to military schools, and he approved of their physical and social improvement. In Berlin, he received royal favor and conferred decorations of the Order of Kalakaua. But when he experienced the lighthearted social life of Paris, Kalakaua felt bitter that American missionaries had turned Hawai'i into a "miserable bigoted community." He wrote to his sister Lili'uokalani that Hawaiians should make Sunday a day of mockery instead of observing a Sabbath prescribed by puritans who were "all sober and down in the mouth" and taught nothing but rubbish. In England, Kalakaua assured Queen Victoria that Emma was well, toured Windsor Castle, and enjoyed the "magnificent" horses at the Royal Stables. He met the Princess of Wales at a soirée and wrote, "It was one of my proudest moments to have had the honor and pleasure of walking under my arm the future Queen of England, who is very much beloved and respected by all classes." A composer himself, Kalakaua attended the opera and handed a female singer a bouquet. He also told Baroness Burdett-Coutts about Hawaiian traditions. Kalakaua later claimed to have acquired an English accent during his visit, yet he was puzzled that the English kept a monarch on the throne without allowing her to rule. In 1887, his consort Queen Kapiolani went to England for Victoria's fifty-year jubilee, along with future queen Lili'uokalani, who had composed a special song for their hostess. While in London, however, they heard the sad news that armed American residents in Hawai'i had forced King Kalakaua to sign away his power.[36]

Hawaiian sailors reached other countries in Europe such as the Netherlands, and a few even reached the Baltic Sea. In 1819, "Lauri" went to St. Petersburg with Russian Golovnin, who had nicknamed him after a Russian Orthodox saint. Described as "jolly and quick," Lauri had stowed away on Golovnin's ship and begged the captain to take him to Russia. "I took him on," Golovnin wrote. "It occurred to me that if he learned the Russian language he might prove very useful to the Russian-American Company in its dealings with the Sandwich [Hawaiian] Islands." In St. Petersburg, Lauri lived "in one of the houses of the Russian-American Company, near the Semenovsky bridge." He walked around the city without getting lost—a common measure by Europeans of Oceanian intelligence! He also made purchases on his own, sometimes paying prices that were too high, like many tourists. Lauri would wait until all the more important people in a room sat down before taking a seat himself, and he always carried his wolf-skin fur coat on his arm to avoid dirtying it. He performed "native dances" on command, but unlike Kalakaua he found an opera singer quite boring. The huge buildings, plentiful ships, and splendid clothes duly impressed him; he liked sweets, but he did not like alcohol, beards, losing money at dominoes, or the Russian winter, which gave him a cough. After the novelty wore off, he missed O'ahu and went home on a company ship.[37]

The record for longevity in Europe was probably set by Kaparena, or Harry Maitey, who lived in Prussia from 1824 to 1872. An orphan, Maitey had come on board the *Mentor* at Honolulu in 1823 and fervently asked to join the crew. The ship needed no extra hands, but the German supercargo was aware of the political implications of Liholiho's recent departure for London and decided to take Maitey to Berlin. From a Baltic port, the Hawaiian was taken by carriage to the Prussian capital. There he spent six years preparing for baptism on the pretext of better serving King Frederick William III. But first he was treated as part of the "exotic bounty" brought back by the first Prussian ship to circumnavigate the globe. The *Seehandlung*, or Maritime Company, displayed him in an exhibition with other artifacts and curios from the voyage. He performed a hula for a crowd that joked about his probably being a cannibal. Maitey lived with the president of the *Seehandlung* as a house servant and became part of the family. He also attended a school for wayward children, where he had status because he was able to eat and dress better than the other students.

In 1829, a Hawaiian called Jony Kahopimeai joined Maitey at the school. He had come with the second Prussian circumnavigation; a third young Hawaiian died of dysentery on that voyage. Jony proved even more promising a learner than Maitey, but he died of pneumonia during his second winter because he had to wear a thin student uniform. After his baptism in 1830, Maitey worked as a salaried assistant to the steam water-pump engineer on Peacock Island, a royal retreat on a Berlin lake. For the next forty years, in company with a giant, two dwarfs, several peacocks, and a lion, Maitey entertained Prussian nobles by building miniature castles on that island. He married the animal-keeper's daughter and sired three children. After half a century of living as a Prussian, however, Maitey died of smallpox in 1872 at the age of sixty-four. The disease arrived with French prisoners-of-war who were planting trees along the Havel River. Unfortunately, no one had ever vaccinated Harry; his working on an island had probably saved him from the Berlin cholera epidemic of 1831.[38]

It is worth noting that during Maitey's long education in German, experts decided that a "clumsy and not fully developed vocal apparatus" caused him difficulty pronouncing consonants. Similarly, the French had accused Ahutoru of having a speech impediment, and in England, Tapeooe received special tutoring "in the articulation of the difficult sounds of our language, which are usually so insurmountable to foreigners, on account of the number of consonants."[39] Europeans clearly did not consider Oceanian fluency in their own languages to be a true test of their humanity. Nor were abundant gestures, skillful mimicry, or sailor pidgin valued as "civilized." "Enlightened" Europeans like Fanny Burney wanted evidence that "nature can do without art," or as George Keate put it, "*natural* good manners is the *natural* result of *natural* good sense."[40] Yet the proof of "natural" virtue was to learn proper diction and manners. Considering the condescending views that upper-class Europeans had of their own lower classes, the assumption that Oceanians would effortlessly adopt their customs is at best amusing. For their part, Ahutoru, Omai, and Nayti raised their status by manipulating Europeans; Hongi and Te Pehi Kupe supplemented their status symbols; and Kalakaua discovered missionaries did not typify the Western elite.

The United States

New England shipping linked the United States to the Pacific long before its land frontier reached California. John Ledyard, an American-born British marine who served on Cook's last expedition, reported the profits that Northwest American furs made in China. In 1784, one year after U.S. independence from England, the *Empress of China* sailed to Canton to exchange New England ginseng for tea. New England vessels soon controlled much of the fur and sandalwood trade to China, and they so dominated whaling that even French and British ships relied on captains from Nantucket.[41] Growing numbers of Oceanians circulated in New England seaports, and Melville wrote of the New Bedford docks, "actual cannibals stand chatting at street corners; savages outright; many of whom yet carry on their bones unholy flesh . . . Feegeeans, Tongatabooarrs, Erromangoans, Pannangians, and Brighggians." He portrayed Queequeg as an idol-worshiper and preserved-head salesman, who brought his harpoon to breakfast.[42]

In fact, Nantucket newspapers accused South Sea sailors of performing pagan rites on the docks in the light of the full moon, but more sympathetic observers attributed such scenes to "innocent frolics." In the whaling port of Cold Spring Harbor on Long Island, "Bedlam Street" was known for its many *kanaka* residents. They whittled bone ornaments on the front porch of the Stone Jug, where the proprietress got along well with them. But they suffered from the damp, cold climate, and a victim of tuberculosis was buried in a nearby wood by his friends. Joining the crew of a New England ship was a form of initiation, as we have seen. On one whaler, Amo the Kanaka explained that he wanted to go on to "Merick" because, "I like see all; and get my sister three fathom (six yards) red ribbon!" His shipmates laughed at such a long distance to travel for ribbon, but he said, "plenty time." Amo had second thoughts at Cape Horn, where it was so cold that he put on as many clothes as he could fit. He tried to join the crew in a snowball fight, but it was too icy for his fingers.[43]

The first Pacific Islanders in New England may have been Atu and Opai, two young Hawaiian sailors who arrived at Boston on the fur trader *Columbia* in 1790. Their captain, Robert Gray, exchanged cannon salutes with the harbor fort, and a crowd gathered on the dock. Like Ka'iana in Canton, Atu dressed in a chiefly feathered helmet and cloak, "like a living flame." Billed as a crown prince, he walked through the streets arm in arm with Gray to meet with the governor, whose oratory foretold a friendly intercourse between the Commonwealth of Massachusetts and Hawai'i. "The prince," reminisced a local newspaper, "was an Apollo in personal symmetry and beauty." Yet both Hawaiians quickly tired of Boston and shipped out again for the Pacific.[44] Delano's Hawaiian cabin boy "Bill" arrived in Boston in 1803 and "performed on the Boston stage several times, in the tragedy of Captain Cook, and was much admired by the audience and the publick in general." Did Bill play a patriotic killer or a Lono-worshiper? One clue may be that when Delano took him back to Hawai'i, Bill chose not to disembark. He went on to Canton and was paid off there.[45]

A true Hawaiian "prince," Humehume (George Kaumuali'i of Kaua'i), came to Providence, Rhode Island, in 1805 at the age of eight. His chiefly father gave the captain of the *Hazard* seven thousand dollars to finance his education, but George wound up working as a servant in Connecticut. After four years, the money was gone, along with the health of the captain, who moved with George to Massachusetts. George survived as a carpenter and farmhand until the War of 1812, when he enlisted in the United States Navy at Boston as landsman "George Prince." In 1813, his ship, the USS *Enterprise,* fought against HMS *Boxer.* George later claimed to have been wounded in the side by a boarding pike, but in fact, he did not join that ship until 1815. He also claimed to have fought in 1815 on Stephen Decatur's flagship, the USS *Guerrière,* against Barbary pirates at Algiers and Tripoli. Yet in actuality, he served on the *Enterprise* in the Mediterranean—after Decatur's victories—and then transferred to the *Guerrière* in New York.[46] Like most sailors, he had learned to embellish his autobiography.

As in Europe, most *kanaka*s voyaged through others' texts. In 1819, the *Lion* brought three tattooed Marquesans to Providence from Nuku Hiva, which had been claimed as a U.S. possession during the War of 1812. "They appear to be inoffensive youths," a newspaper said, "and as they are American citizens, having been adopted by the great American family, we trust they will be treated with kindness and hospitality."[47] That same year, another Marquesan, Thomas Patu, arrived in Boston via Canton, after escaping from service as a royal bodyguard in Hawai'i. He found work as a house servant for a sea captain, attended a Sabbath school, and quickly learned the English alphabet. But his studies suffered when he took up with "vicious boys" who lured him back to sea. After barely surviving a frigid sealing cruise in the South Shetland Islands, he returned to school under the care of his latest captain. Patu fell ill in Boston, however, and moved to Coventry, Connecticut, where he lived with a benevolent Christian family. Before he relocated, he was said to have attended Boston theater performances until he decided, "too much negro there."[48] This quotation from Hiram Bingham begs the question, did Patu acquire prejudice toward U.S. blacks in the company of fellow seamen—what "theaters" were these?—or was he perhaps put off by the era's racist minstrel shows? Like Temoteitei in London or Maoris in Sydney, Patu may simply have wanted to distance himself from people whose low status was a local tradition.

The theatricality of Oceanians in America persisted. In 1831, Benjamin Morrell brought two kidnap victims, Sunday and Monday, to New York as "objects of much curiosity." Like Maitey in Berlin, they were displayed among bows and arrows, spears, paddles, fishing lines, bark cloth, and other artifacts. A newspaper reported, "They have been visited by thousands . . . with wonder and gratification." The money that Sunday and Monday raised was supposedly to defray "the expense, of a voyage by which they may return to their own country, somewhat enlightened and improved." Morrell wrote that after two years in his care, the tattooed "cannibals" became "civilized, intelligent men, well fitted for becoming proper agents, or interpreters and missionaries to open an intercourse with their native isles, which cannot fail of resulting in immense commercial advantages to the United States." Sunday, "who was a chief in his native country, has a great taste for the mechanic arts," Morrell said, "particularly such as require the use of machinery and edge tools. He visits, of his own accord, the different factories and workshops, with the inquisitive eye of a philosopher, and is never satisfied until the use and principle of every operation have been explained to him."

Yet Monday, a Micronesian, "was suspicious, moody, and difficult of restraint. He could not be made to understand that, in taking him from his native land, the whites could have had other than hostile intentions. No kindness could win his confidence." Monday hated American food, clothing, and the cold climate; he often wept and soon died,[49] like so many other *kanaka*s outside the Pacific. In 1836, a sea captain displayed a Fijian at the Baltimore Museum. Later, deported Chief Vedovi of Fiji arrived in New York dying of tuberculosis and was sent straight to the Naval Hospital. Wilkes had arrested him for killing Americans and wanted to show off U.S. power. At sea en route, Vedovi had attended the crew's Fourth of July celebration "dressed out after the Fijian fashion." When he died in New York, his skull was added to a scientific collection.[50]

The link between New England seaports and churches led to the first Christian mission to Hawai'i in 1820. In 1809, Henry Opukahaia and Thomas Hopu arrived in New York on a China trader. They attended a theater with their captain but were surprised to see men and women eating together in restaurants—a *kapu* in their own country that foreign contact would end before either of them got home again. The ship continued on to New Haven, Connecticut, where the two Hawaiians were taken into the homes of local families. In his sailor suit, Opukahaia (or "Obookiah") amused people by mimicking their peculiarities and asking, "who dis?" Then a friend demonstrated Henry's own awkward walking style, and the young Hawaiian fell laughing to the floor. Mission accounts claim that he wept at Yale when he confronted his ignorance. Opukahaia began his education as a Christian and often walked miles to proselytize among other Hawaiians. George Sandwich had been in New England so long that he barely remembered his own language, but Opukahaia recruited him as a student for the Foreign Mission School in Cornwall. Opukahaia worked as a farmhand until his health failed one winter. He died without ever seeing home again, but his martyred death became the motivating cause for the mission.

Hopu went to sea again during the War of 1812, but he came back to New England after his misadventures in the West Indies. He lived long enough to leave for Hawai'i with the first missionaries on the *Thaddeus* in 1819 and later went to California in the gold rush. So did William Kanui, who arrived at Boston in 1809 with his brother and four other Hawaiians, all of whom were taken in by local families as servants and farmhands. With only "haphazard schooling" and limited prospects, Kanui and his brother enlisted on American privateers during the War of 1812, perhaps crossing paths with Hopu and Kaumuali'i. After their discharges, Kanui and his brother sailed for New York, but the brother died in Providence en route. Kanui soon joined Opukahaia and company in New Haven. John Honori'i arrived in Boston in 1815 and became the third ex-seaman that the missionary vessel *Thaddeus* would take to Hawai'i as interpreters and assistants.[51] New England churches thus helped *kanaka*s to find secure homes and farmwork in a harsh climate and, like the English in Polynesia, used them as native teachers.

Yarn-spinning George Kaumuali'i worked as a servant to the purser of Charlestown Navy Yard before he found his way to the Hawaiian colony in Connecticut. He was one of the founding students of the Foreign Mission School at Cornwall. The missionaries taught him to play the bass viol and sing hymns, and his self-esteem rose after so many years of hard struggle. Yet he was never as inspired by Christianity as his Hawaiian shipmates on the *Thaddeus*.[52] The Marquesan Thomas Patu at first resisted Christianity because he felt "my heart good enough," but he began praying with John Paru, a Hawaiian, and in 1823 he too entered the school. Patu visited the grave of Opukahaia, but his own health had been declining and he died of a sore throat later that year. Not all Hawaiians converted or died in New England. In 1826, *kanaka* seamen Homimano and George Naua returned to Honolulu from Boston on the schooner *Missionary Packet,* which was destined for sale to Princess Nahi'ena'ena as a yacht.[53]

Oceanian diplomats also visited the United States. On behalf of King Kamehameha III, Timothy Ha'alilio visited Washington, D.C., in 1842 with missionary William Richards to win support for Hawaiian sovereignty. At first put off by Ha'alilio's "dark complexion," Secretary of State Daniel Webster finally gave in to Richards's persistence and, in effect, extended the Monroe Doctrine to Hawai'i. A more formal diplomatic treaty was signed in 1849, but did this agreement protect the independence of Pacific Islands, or compromise it? The American press was talking "manifest destiny" and celebrating the annexation of half of Mexico. In 1853, the same year that the U.S. Navy bought land on North Bonin Island and forced Japan to sign an unequal trade treaty, the *Emma Parker* brought to Boston some missionized Tahitians. A typical newspaper said they served "as proofs of the advanced state of civilization to which they have attained. They are light hearted, merry, affable; fond of music and social enjoyment, and . . . partial to Americans."[54]

Whether exploited or ennobled, Oceanian voyagers helped their region to explore the world economy before colonialism engulfed the Pacific. Like Haʻalilio, King Kalakaua hoped to use political alliances against imperialism. In 1874, he negotiated a reciprocity treaty with the U.S. government in Washington, D.C. The elimination of trade duties stimulated a sugar plantation boom in Hawaiʻi. Seven years later, he passed through New York, Philadelphia, and Washington on his way around the globe promoting the Hawaiian monarchy. But Kalakaua died in San Francisco in 1891, spiritually broken by the growing power of American residents in Hawaiʻi. His sister Liliʻuokalani, who as queen was overthrown in 1893, said of Kalakaua, "He sacrificed himself in the interests of the very people who had done him so much wrong."[55]

Such an epitaph might apply to any number of *kanaka*s whose lives were expanded or expended in the global game of "progress," whether they were museum exhibits, saved souls, or proletarians. Yet those who went beyond Oceania did not all suffer tragic consequences. Some managed to snatch ironic moments of personal glory from the maritime frontier. Kalakaua, for example, sent four young Hawaiian students to American private schools in the 1880s. Three entered a military academy in California, but the fourth, Henry Grube Marchant, studied engraving in Boston—a century after "prince" Atu had paraded through the town in full regalia. Marchant's prints became part of the Hawaiian exhibit at the Paris Exposition of 1889.[56] What would Ahutoru, the first Pacific diplomat in Europe, have thought of that success? We can only guess. Wrapped in French canvas, his body was commended to the deep off Madagascar, halfway home.

~ 8 ~

Prodigal Ghosts

Bill's home again.
Now he's an ice skater.
Back from his seafaring,
when Bill opens his mouth
the words come a-tumbling—
you never heard such jargon!
"Mi no hao!" says Bill.
Everything jibber-jabber,
jabber-jibber, pell mell!

—Hawaiian chant[1]

After a long cross-cultural voyage, returning travelers are likely to feel another kind of shock, because they are different. The beach they left behind might itself have changed, or at least look strange from a fresh perspective. Yet the concept of liminality implies, after the successful rite of passage, ultimate reintegration into society in a new role, with enhanced insight.[2] Many Oceanian returnees made an effort to fit back in, but some gave up and shipped out again. Those who stayed, like beachcombers, had new ideas and skills and could serve as war leaders, pilots, missionaries, or interpreters. If they had low rank before, they might well improve their status, unless perhaps they overplayed the Prince-in-London game. Despite the deaths from voyaging, returnees kept washing ashore, and young recruits pursued their tall tales along global sea lanes. Kanaka seamen, like modern outmigrants, created a "user-friendly" network between their homelands and a wider world.

Rites of Reentry

In Rotuma, travelers coming home were welcomed by the *mamasa* or "dry-ing" ceremony, since their feet symbolically were "still wet." If a chief, the voyager sat on fine mats in a special shelter and received a flower lei, musical and oratorical greetings, soothing *kava* to drink, and local food. Commoners underwent a simpler welcome from their own relatives. In both cases, there was no delay in expressing thanks that the voyager had sur-vived a dangerous journey. The most important gesture was being rubbed with coconut oil, to remove the sea salt, followed by a change from "wet" travel clothes into a native *sulu*.[3] In Hawai'i, important returnees would be welcomed with chants, and Vancouver noted "a prevailing custom after being some time at sea" that native mariners washed in fresh water right after landing. At Ulithi, in the Carolines, returnees gained reentry by bring-ing "news" of their travels to the local men's house.[4]

In 1851, Timarare left the *Wanderer* at his home island of Banaba in Kiribati, after an absence of three years. On the beach, an elderly priestess passed a handful of leaves over his face and body, chanting, "May your days be long! May your coconuts yield abundantly, and your friends be numerous!" Timarare's father had died, so in addition to his trade box of exotic treasures, the voyager now owned coconut plantations. A happy crowd followed him to his family home, where another priestess sprinkled water from a coconut shell onto his head and face and chanted vehemently to drive away any evil lurking in the house. Timarare's sea chest was full of tobacco, clothing, and metalware, and for extra effect he fired a musket at intervals to announce his success overseas. Soon local chiefs came to his welcome feast and began to divest him of a few gifts. Yet the ex-sailor still had enough property left to be a very eligible bachelor. At Timarare's request, his captain shot off a double-barreled gun.[5]

Such receptions could be affected by the presence of Euroamericans. The return of three Palauan women after four tragic years in Bombay was over-shadowed by Amasa Delano's presenting their chief with firearms. In 1774, when Pautu of Tahiti returned from Peru in Spanish clothes, he was so overwhelmed by his relatives' "weeping bitterly, kissing him, and lavishing their caresses on him in such profusion that they left him no chance to utter a word." His female kin cut themselves with sharks' teeth to show their love. But Pautu obeyed Spanish padres and asked them to stop.[6] Two young Maori chiefs, after visiting Australia, vowed to their shipmates to act like stiff-upper-lipped Englishmen and not weep when they returned home, but the customary nose-rubbing, hugging, crying, joyful exclamations, and rit-ual scarring by their families brought grateful tears to their eyes. In 1825, black-clad Boki and other chiefs in Liholiho's entourage returned with the royal coffins to Honolulu, amid wailing from the beach and cannon salutes between HMS *Blonde* and the harbor fort. Returnees also expressed sad farewells to white shipmates. Leaving a longtime Hawaiian shipmate at Honolulu, a seaman wrote, "I shall never forget the feelings manifested towards me by this native and his relatives as I took the parting hand."[7]

Some *kanaka*s, however, did not succeed at reentry and stayed in the *limen*. Both Atu and Opai, whom Gray had taken to the Northwest as cabin boys and paraded through Boston, found it difficult to readjust to Hawai'i. In 1791, Opai came home on the *Hope*, but after a two-year absence, he was said to have difficulty understanding the language—or since he was from Kaua'i, perhaps it was the dialect of the big island of Hawai'i that was strange? Fellow Kauaians told him about the current interisland war, so Opai stayed with Kamehameha instead of going home to Kaua'i. Yet ten months later, he joined the crew of Vancouver's *Discovery*, calling himself Kalehua or Jack Ingraham. "Jack" helped the ship provision at Kaua'i and Ni'ihau and went twice more to the American Northwest.[8] In 1792 Atu returned to Ni'ihau, where his family came off in canoes and greeted him warmly. But he refused to go ashore, and with Gray's permission, he continued to Canton and out of historical view. Similarly, Delano's cabin boy Bill, who had performed on the Boston stage, returned to Hawai'i in 1804, "but not wishing to remain there, he went to Canton in the *Pilgrim*, where he was paid off, and I have heard nothing of him since."[9]

Not only Hawaiians might find home unappealing after a long career of voyaging. Maui, or Tommy Drummond, returned to New Zealand with Samuel Marsden on the *Active* in 1814, after eight years in Australia. He was entranced by the old songs and tales he heard from Maori chiefs on board, but after trying to settle at Bay of Islands, he shipped out on the whaler *Jefferson* and died in England. John Nicholas speculated, "the restless spirit of curiosity was too powerful in his mind, and induced him to give up his ease and a fixed abode, for hardship and precarious adventure."[10] Changes on the beach could also make homecoming difficult. In 1807, a chiefly Tongan couple returned home after several years in Fiji and Australia, only to find Tongatapu in civil war, so they went back to Sydney. Jo Bob of Rarotonga had been looking forward to getting home, but after discovering that everyone he knew was busy building a Christian church, he returned to his ship.[11]

Tuati, or John Sac, had long served on American ships, and he was very nostalgic and enthusiastic, having bragged to his shipmates about how great a place Aotearoa was. But he arrived in Bay of Islands in 1840, just when Britain was annexing New Zealand. First, local Maoris charged a high price for his canoe ride to shore, and then his family was dismayed by rising English immigration. Proud Tuati wound up "sitting on a log, greatly mortified, depressed, and incensed at such treatment." He returned on board and remained, in effect, in voluntary exile. In some cases, the same urge that sent Oceanians to sea in the first place, perhaps dissatisfaction at their situation, might explain their continuing to voyage. Phebe, a Fijian girl, revisited Nadi in 1849, but her mother, a chief's captive, told her to stay with the American captain's wife she had been serving. Otherwise, she might be harmed. Reluctantly, Phebe chose to go back to Salem, Massachusetts, a virtual prisoner of the *limen*.[12]

Foreign *Mana*

In 1788, Chief Ka'iana disembarked at Hawai'i with four swivel cannons, six muskets, three barrels of gunpowder, and five double canoes loaded with metal tools and iron bars. This arsenal added to Kamehameha's prestige and power just as he was expanding his conquests to the rest of the island chain. Ka'iana had voyaged to China and to the American Northwest with fur traders, and he was so impatient to get home that he got violently angry. At Kaua'i, however, he found himself a political exile in Kamehameha's war, so he decided to join his relatives on Hawai'i. Kamehameha gave Ka'iana land and security as rewards. Before parting from the *Iphigenia*, Ka'iana helped it provision, found divers to recover a cable and anchor, and probably sold the captain sandalwood. He aroused suspicion by inquiring about the defenses of visiting vessels, but when shipmasters blamed Ka'iana for the seizure of the schooner *Fair American* and a white beachcomber in 1790, he presented written testimonials from captains who had traded safely with him.

Ka'iana was most respected for his military skills. He taunted enemy chiefs in battle and exhorted his own warriors to fight more bravely. In fact, his success as a war leader for Kamehameha aroused the jealousy even of the king. When Ka'iana was discovered having an affair with the king's favorite wife, Ka'ahumanu, he had to switch sides and fight against Kamehameha. He apparently died fighting against the invasion of O'ahu in 1795. Vancouver claimed that Ka'iana's use of firearms had "produced in every chief of consequence an inordinate thirst for power; and a spirit of enterprise and ambition." But Ka'iana certainly had no monopoly over guns in Hawai'i, since Kahekili also used beachcombers and firearms against Kamehameha. Moreover, military competition had always helped Hawaiian chiefs to increase their *mana,* so Ka'iana was actually playing a traditional role with new weapons. He also helped to recruit other returnees like Kalehua and Kualelo into Kamehameha's retinue.[13]

As we have seen, King Kamehameha deliberately sent young Hawaiians overseas to train seamen for his new war fleet. Returnees might receive land, horses, and status as interpreters or ship pilots. Kalehua (or Opai, or Jack Ingram) of Kaua'i, served Kamehameha's ally, Ke'eaumoku of Kona. He joined the chief's entourage after returning from Boston, and then, like a roving Hawaiian trade envoy, sailed with Vancouver to the northwest coast and came back with his favorite captain, Ingraham. Kalehua helped to negotiate the exchange of provisions for cattle and firearms, despite Vancouver's reluctance to give guns to Ke'eaumoku, who had masterminded that schooner seizure in 1790. Kalehua also translated for Vancouver's inquiry into the murders of two men from HMS *Daedalus* in 1793, and when Kamehameha offered Hawai'i to Vancouver as a British "protectorate" in 1794. Another returnee witnessed the murders of the men from the *Daedalus* and testified, but he was understandably afraid to lead Vancouver to the killers.[14]

Oceanian voyagers were opportunists seeking the best of both worlds, but sometimes they had to choose sides. When Kualelo came back from London in 1792, he had already given away most of his treasures playing chief in Tahiti. In Hawai'i, he disembarked with only a shirt, two pairs of trousers, and a few trinkets, "like a convict," a shipmate wrote, "to his place of transportation." He soon lost even those meager souvenirs and had to beg for gifts from passing ship captains. But when he entered Kamehameha's entourage, he received land, a house, and high rank in exchange for serving Ka'iana.[15] The story could also go from riches to rags. Humehume, or George Kaumuali'i, was heir to the kingdom of Kaua'i and signed onto American ships as "George Prince." He came home with the first New England preachers and persuaded his father to welcome them. Yet Bingham said George quickly showed "downward tendencies" and became "a professed skeptic." Kamehameha II soon kidnapped the elder Kaumuali'i to O'ahu and forced him to marry the widowed Ka'ahumanu, so George lived in poverty with his wife and a handful of followers near the beach. When his father died while the king was in England, George raised an army and attacked the royal fort at Waimea, Kaua'i. His cannons, however, missed their targets, his men panicked, and, like his father, George went to O'ahu as a prisoner.[16]

Choosing foreign allies could be just as hazardous. In 1825, High Chief Boki returned from London with Liholiho's casket, having negotiated a treaty with England. But Queen Ka'ahumanu dominated the government, and she sided with American missionaries. In his struggle for power, Boki even welcomed French Catholics, but he lost the *no'a* pebble in his hand, as John Papa I'i put it. His secret plotting failed against Ka'ahumanu loyalists. In addition, Boki's business ventures failed, so he embarked, debt-driven and politically isolated, to his doom in Vanuatu in 1829. Nor did his wife Liliha, who had accompanied him to London, succeed in her coup plans in 1831.[17] Factions of U.S. or British supporters also competed in the 1874 royal election. Dowager Queen Emma, a longtime Anglophile who had visited Queen Victoria, lost an unpopular legislative vote to David Kalakaua. Kalakaua went to Washington, D.C., to negotiate the reciprocity treaty he had promised to American backers. But when he visited other monarchs around the world, built Iolani Palace, and proposed a confederation with Samoa, the American residents turned on him, stripped him of his power with a "bayonet" constitution, and overthrew his sister in 1893. The new government even met in Iolani Palace while the queen was confined in her apartments upstairs,[18] making Kalakaua's homecoming chant of 1881 more poignant:

> I have traveled over many lands and distant seas,
> to India afar and China renowned.
> I have touched the shores of Africa
> and the boundaries of Europe,
> and I have met the great ones of all the lands.
>
> As I stood at the side of heads of governments,
> next to leaders proud of their rule,
> their authority over their own,
> I realized how small and weak is the power I hold.
> For mine is a throne established upon a heap of lava.
> They rule where millions obey their commands.
> Only a few thousands can I count under my care.
> Yet one thought came to me of which I may boast,
> that of all beauties locked within the embrace of
> these shores, one is a jewel more precious than any
> owned by my fellow monarchs.
> I have nothing in my Kingdom to dread.
>
> I mingle with my people without fear.
> My safety is no concern, I require no bodyguards.
> Mine is the boast that a pearl of great price
> has fallen to me from above.
> Mine is the loyalty of my people.[19]

A British protégé, Hitihiti, had a colorful career in the Society Islands. In 1774, Hitihiti arrived at Tahiti, after seven months with Cook's second expedition around the South Pacific. Pomare I welcomed the young Boraboran and offered him land, status, and a high-born beauty to marry. But Cook preferred to return Hitihiti to Ra'iatea, where he had begun his voyage. Having learned to shoot, he helped the British pursue gun-thieves on Huahine, but he arrived at Ra'iatea with only one servant boy. His brother had taken over his "estate" and would allow Hitihiti only two small pigs to offer Cook as gifts. Overindulging in *kava* only temporarily softened the pain of Hitihiti's abandonment on the beach, so Cook wrote a letter of reference and allowed the traveler to fire cannons on King George's birthday. But he was saddened by Hitihiti's tearful desire to remain with the ship: "At Otaheite he might have had any thing that was in their power to bestow, whereas here he was not the least noticed." By 1777, however, Hitihiti was back at Tahiti, where he lived with a pretty wife at Matavai Bay, spoke better English than the returning Omai, and invited Cook to dine with him ashore. He often came out drunk to ships and asked for gifts from old friends, but as adviser to Pomare I, he greeted Bligh on the *Bounty* in 1788.[20]

In fact, after the famous mutiny, Hitihiti willingly accompanied Fletcher Christian's men to Tubuai, where he used his musket in battle against native enemies. He only returned to Tahiti when the mutineers split up. Hitihiti wisely rejoined Pomare and fought successfully against his rivals, often in company with mutineers who chose to stay at Tahiti. He reportedly told his sentries to call out "all's well" (in English) every half hour to show the enemy that they were prepared for night attacks. He also warned the mutineers when HMS *Pandora* arrived in 1791 and expressed horror at the idea of helping the warship hunt down his fugitive friends. Although he traveled with the *Pandora* as far as Huahine, he was back at Tahiti again in 1792, when Bligh arrived in HMS *Providence* to complete his breadfruit mission. Hitihiti even helped Bligh to catch a native thief by chasing him in his own canoe. In 1824, when Kotzebue visited Tahiti, a seventy-year-old man calling himself "Cook" boasted of traveling with his namesake around the Pacific. He drew a world map for the Russians and mimed the use of a sextant. Since Hitihiti was about seventeen in 1773, this old man might well have been the peripatetic Boraboran, living out the remnants of his glory.[21]

Other Polynesian voyagers also tried to parlay their foreign *mana* into local power. Another Tahitian, Tapiru, had gone with Hitihiti and the mutineers to Tubuai in 1789, but he returned to offer his skill with firearms to Pomare's rivals. Using guns and powder from the shipwrecked whaler *Matilda,* Tapiru became "a Person of some power," in Bligh's estimation. In 1792, he kept his five muskets (compared to Pomare's eight) under his sleeping mat. Bligh demanded the return of the weapons, but Tapiru only returned some cash from the *Matilda.*[22] In the Marquesas, Temoana had fled Nukuhiva on a British vessel when support from a passing U.S. warship had not secured his "kingship." After bitter experiences in England and Samoa, he returned home in 1839 to lead a thousand warriors on a war of conquest, hoping to imitate the achievements of Tahitian and Hawaiian monarchs. Yet lacking the power to win, and rejected by British warships, Temoana turned to the French after 1842. They established him as "King Charles of the Marquesas," with a small, well-furnished cottage near the beach under the protection of a fort. Temoana mediated during a civil war on Ua Pou, but Nukuhivans continued to resist his authority. In 1852, he criticized misbehavior by whaling crews and French soldiers alike, so the French arrested him and locked him up on Tahiti for ten days. Temoana then began to go barefoot, drink to excess, and ridicule the whites, but he finally converted to French Catholicism and died, in Jacques Arago's words, "a trinket king."[23]

With Sydney so nearby, Maori voyagers had major impact on local power struggles. Tuki and Huru brought potatoes from Australia and Ruatara brought wheat, both key export crops that enabled Maoris to sell ship provisions and get firearms and other manufactures. Moehanga regretted getting tools from King George instead of firearms, but Te Pahi brought home a white beachcomber from Australia, married him to his daughter, and made him a war chief.[24] Maori chiefs also brought their own weapons expertise back to Aotearoa. On Marsden's *Active,* they spent hours cleaning their guns, making cartridge boxes, or safeguarding their gunpowder. In New Zealand, they disembarked in full redcoat uniform with swords and shot off muskets to impress their kin and rivals. Ruatara intimidated George of Whangaroa, the cause of the *Boyd* massacre, to reconcile with both the English and Bay of Islands Maoris, saying to Marsden, "as soon as New Zealand man see musket presented at him, he run away." Tuhi, who visited England, argued that fighting interested Maoris more than farming. He used guns from whalers to kill two hundred enemies in war and bragged of personally taking twenty-two lives—though he assured Marsden he never fought on Sundays.[25]

But the best-known Maori returnee was Hongi Hika. On a visit to Parramatta in 1814, he so charmed Marsden that the missionary became Hongi's main apologist, despite the Maori chief's bloody wars. Hongi sold the mission land for forty-eight axes and always welcomed Marsden hospitably, styling himself "the friend of the English." Hence, Marsden wrote, "Shunghee is a man of the mildest manners and disposition and appears to possess a very superior mind." After his voyage to England in 1820, Hongi traded most of his presents in Sydney for three hundred muskets and gunpowder and composed a chant about his planned wars of revenge. At Bay of Islands, he drank cow's milk to symbolize the *mana* he had obtained from the *pakeha* (whites) and lined up his muskets in rows, giving each the name of a Ngapuhi defeat it would avenge. In his battles, Hongi wore a red coat, armor, a helmet, and sword, and spied on enemies with a telescope. He bowed and saluted Te Hinaki, in military fashion, before killing the chief in combat and drinking his blood.

A Quaker commentator wrote that once Hongi threw aside "the mask of Christian meekness which he had worn in this country, he appeared in his true character of an ambitious and bloodthirsty warrior." Yet even Hongi's descriptions of killings and his displays of dead enemy heads on poles did not prevent Marsden from defending him. The Anglican missionary even compared the Maori desire for *utu* (revenge) to the Old Testament's "eye for an eye" dictum, and he explained away a Ngapuhi attack on the Wesleyan mission at Whangaroa, arguing that the choice of location had been unfortunate, because Hongi's father had originally owned that land before losing it in warfare. Like a modern defense lawyer, Marsden wrote, "Shunghee has lately suffered very great personal as well as family afflictions." In fact, Marsden proposed to Maori chiefs that they make Hongi their king. When he first came back from England, "Shunghee had impressed the natives with a very great idea of the power of King George—he used to tell the chiefs that if king George was to go to war with them there would be only one battle, and New Zealand would be conquered." Yet other Maori chiefs complained that Hongi was trying to monopolize trade, and that he made profits selling preserved, tattooed heads to passing ships.

Hongi's warriors would camp on beaches alongside their ornamented canoes, stacking their muskets "in regular good order," and they used military engineering to get at enemies they devoured or enslaved. His "musket wars" temporarily upset the balance of power on the North Island, killed thousands of other Maoris, and caused hundreds of refugees to migrate southward. Eventually, however, his rivals acquired their own guns from the ship trade, and Hongi was wounded in the chest. At first, he showed off a whistling bullet hole through his lung with good humor, but he died in 1828 on a bed surrounded by weapons. His allies divided up his armor as trophies, and his relatives exhumed his bones after a year, painted them with red ochre, and hid them to safeguard their *mana*. Hongi's Maori neighbors dreaded him, but the English who met him described him as mild-mannered. New Zealand historian Arthur Thomson treated him as a hero: "He had a high sense of honor and a tender heart . . . and no insult ever provoked him to take the life of a European."[26] Hongi obviously knew which face to show his audiences.

In hierarchical Polynesia, it was generally difficult for a returnee without traditional status to translate his foreign wealth and connections into lasting prestige. The best-documented example of this kind of failure is Omai, who returned to Tahiti with Cook in 1777. When leaving the Society Islands three years earlier, Cook had regarded Omai as "dark, ugly and a downright blackguard [commoner]." Now, however, a sailor said of Omai that Cook "played him off as a prodigy of genius, in honour of Pretanee, where, it was given out, his talents had been much improved."[27] A veteran actor on English and other beaches, Omai was also very jealous of being upstaged. Instead of befriending another Society Islander who had been to Peru, he quickly hustled the competitor off Cook's ship, "being displeased there was a traveler upon the island besides himself." Omai stayed in an abandoned Spanish padres' house while on Tahiti, adding another layer of cross-cultural theatricality to the place. He at first pretended not to recognize his sister, but his mother struck her own face and arms with shark's teeth and gave provisions to the British, who rewarded her with red bird feathers from Tonga. Omai gave some of the prestigious feathers (used in cloaks) to his brother and to chiefs.

Cook observed ruefully, "it was evident to everyone that it was not the Man but his property they were in love with." Omai's reputation ashore grew as he bragged about his travels and gave away his wealth. He passed out more red feathers as he walked to Pomare I's residence, even though his British mentors advised him to save them for the king himself. Omai wore a British captain's uniform, but he was not formally recognized until he uncovered in deference to Pomare. In response to questions, he so magnified what he had seen in England that, according to John Rickman, "The king seemed more astonished than delighted . . . and suddenly left Omai" to talk with Cook and the other officers. Cook and Omai conspired in improvised dramatics for the sake of their intertwined images. In a suit of armor, Omai galloped about on a horse, a creature the Tahitians had never seen before. The crowd gathered too near and impeded his ride, so he shot pistols in the air and waved his sword like a medieval knight. After a fireworks display, Cook and Omai together led a fleet of war canoes against Pomare in a mock sea battle. Omai taunted his opponents to throw their spears at him, but his armor protected him from injury. He paraded triumphantly in his canoe along the shore, but Cook wrote disappointedly, "it did not draw their attention so much as might be expected."

After giving Pomare "various ironware articles," Omai received a double canoe and sixteen paddlers from the chief. When Mo'oreans stole one of Cook's goats, Omai and three of his paddlers joined a British expedition that marched over the hills burning houses. He himself volunteered to kill the first man they met and advised Cook to "shoot every Soul." Mo'orean canoes were actually broken into pieces to use in building Omai a house on Huahine. On the way there, however, mist separated Omai's canoe from Cook's ship. As if to rescue himself from oblivion, Omai fired off a cannon on his canoe, which the *Resolution* answered through the fog. He also hoisted a British flag on his mast as he reached Huahine. Cook "purchased" an acre and a half of land around the beach for Omai, his two Maori boys, and a handful of Tahitian servants. The British built him a house (without ironwork that might be stolen), dug a powder magazine for his firearms, planted an English garden, and provided him with a menagerie of livestock, all surrounded by a moat-like ditch. Omai's "noble" fantasy seemed complete.

As King would do for Tuki and Huru in Aotearoa and Kotzebue for Kadu in the Marshalls, Cook warned the people of Huahine that he would return and punish anyone who dared to tamper with Omai's fine estate. Yet British marine John Ledyard commented, "Omai had ever since our arrival among these isles been declining not only in our estimation but in the opinions of the natives, among whom he was envied for undeserved riches and despised for his obscure birth and impudent pretentions to rule and command, in short his ignorance and vanity were insupportable." Cook had already complained on Tahiti that Omai "associated with none but refugees and strangers whose sole views were to plunder him." Even the chiefs resented it when Omai passed out quality goods to marginal "rascals" who misled him and betrayed his naive friendship. On Huahine, Omai protested that his new house had only one story, as an English pigsty would, but Cook only laughed. A Boraboran, whom Cook had punished severely for stealing a sextant, uprooted many of Omai's plants, tore down his fence, and set loose several animals, vowing to kill the upstart as soon as Cook left. Although caught again, the man escaped overboard at night and cast a gloomy shadow over Omai's future.

Omai became more dejected as Cook's departure neared, but the two charlatans rode horseback together daily, and Cook supplied his protégé with prodigious wealth. Omai displayed his treasures in public, shot off fireworks, and, with Cook's help, held several feasts at which he eagerly gave out nails, red feathers, white shirts, glassware, and chinaware, to local chiefs. It was obvious that his status would last only as long as his possessions did. Both Omai and his Maoris begged not to be left behind, but finally Cook fired a salute of five cannons and sailed away. Later visitors heard that Omai enjoyed "every fine woman on the island" and rode his horse so often that Huahineans tattooed its image on their legs. But he expended all his gunpowder in a victorious war against Ra'iatea and Borabora, and he died only four years after Cook left—of "natural" causes, either a viral fever or syphilis.[28] Twenty years later, Tahitians told James Wilson a strange story about a big monkey left behind by Cook that became a chief with a wife and thirty servants. One day, the "great man dog" disgusted his spouse by eating flies, so she fled to the hills, where a jealous suitor killed the pursuing monkey. Such an odd tale might be an appropriate epitaph for Omai, whose exotic souvenirs and surviving animals were divided up by those who would once have sacrificed him for blasphemy. Even the boards of his house disappeared behind the beach.[29]

Like Ka'iana or Hitihiti, high-ranking Polynesians were more likely to remain celebrities when they came home. In 1794, Lieutenant Governor King personally returned his Maori captives Tuki and Huru, who both claimed to have traditional status. He estimated that one hundred fifty people paddled out to the ship in canoes: "Tookee was instantly recognised by most of the natives . . . and most of the natives came on board, embracing and shedding tears of joy over Tookee, whose first and earnest enquiry was after his parents, family, and chief." A female relative said they were all well, but "His father and chief were still inconsolable for his loss." King gave out presents to the informants and went on to Bay of Islands, where Huru wept at hearing that his chief's son had died in battle. King took the two travelers and a chief into his cabin and emphasized how important it was for them to get home safely. He gave the chief and his paddlers presents, and Tuki told onlookers about the wonders of Norfolk Island. King demonstrated his musket and cannon firepower, sent the two travelers ashore to a cheer from the crew, and vowed to return to see that his flax teachers faired well. Huru became a war chief under Korokoro, who would visit Marsden in Australia.[30]

In 1839, however, a Maori commoner who had passed himself off as a chief in England, returned to Aotearoa with a shipload of English settlers. Wakefield wrote, "Nayti seemed much pleased at our kind treatment of his countrymen. He was at first ashamed of their rude appearance, and often apologized for it. He seemed, too, suspicious and afraid of them, and inclined to cling to us in consequence." In fact, his compatriots ridiculed his pretensions and soon divested him of all his possessions, leaving him only a blanket and mat. Nayti died in poverty of tuberculosis.[31] Similarly, Moehanga, a "slave" who had presented himself in England as "a man of some consequence," arrived home on a whaleship with little fanfare in 1807. A few years later, his supply of hardware had been exhausted, as he predicted, by his social obligations. Yet Moehanga was a more persistent voyager than Nayti. In 1814, he boarded Marsden's *Active* asking for gifts. Not only had his superiors dispossessed him, he said, but after he stole an ax from the visiting *Ferret* in desperation, his chief had had him flogged and banished. Now Moehanga was working as an interpreter for a different chief, who lived a bit south of Bay of Islands.

Like a true cross-cultural actor, he led his British guests arm-in-arm from the beach through the crowd, "Europee fashion," as he called it. He talked constantly, but his English had so deteriorated that neither side could really communicate effectively. Moehanga was living like a Maori again, but he wanted to revisit England. In 1819, he still lived south of Bay of Islands but visited ships to tell travel stories and again guided Marsden. In 1827, twenty years after his liminal voyage to London, Moehanga was serving as interpreter for "King George" (Te Uruti) of Bay of Islands, whose "uncle" he said he had become. He also claimed to have been to England again, and to India, which Peter Dillon later learned was a lie. He asked Dillon to take him and "King George" to India so they could obtain firearms. Instead, Dillon dubbed Moehanga "King Charley" and took him and his son, along with several other Maoris, on his search for La Pérouse. They sailed to Tonga, Rotuma, Vanikoro, and back to Bay of Islands.[32]

Perhaps the most colorful, and factually questionable, return by an Oceanian to a position of power was that of Morrell's Sunday, or Darco, who reportedly became "king" of his island of Witu near New Britain in 1834. According to Thomas Jacobs, who claimed to have learned Darco's language aboard ship, "Prince Tellum-by-by" was a chief's son whose father had died during his four-year absence. At "Riger," Darco's mother's island—whose "red" chiefs were said to be descended from a French surgeon named Laveaux of the La Pérouse expedition—Morrell's ship was mistaken for Pongo, a monster who had supposedly attacked in "ancient" times with fiery mouths that shot a now-sacred cannon ball. Like Omai in Tahiti, Darco took off his foreign clothes. He then shouted, in Jacobs' words, "Me hab been to America . . . Me no white!" After telling his stories and hearing about the political situation on "Nyappa," the island his father had ruled, Darco told Morrell to stay at Riger that day. The crew had to remove their shirts, "to conform to their style of dress, and thus gain their confidence and friendship."

Even a kidnapper like Morrell had to rely to some extent on his guide, so he demonstrated his cannon power to see that Darco was "crowned King" of Nyappa. The new chief then confirmed the worst fears of rival hill people that he was in league with Pongo, by conquering them with firearms. Darco soon reverted to native dress, complete with feathers in his hair, but like a smart beachcomber, he kept the knowledge of how to load a gun to himself. He seemed quite content with both his inherited status and his wealth of foreign hardware, and he told wondrous tales of what he had seen in America. Darco traded a considerable cargo of shell to Morrell, but he declined an offer to return to the United States, saying, "No; me more happy here!" Such a sailor's tale is reminiscent of *Typee,* also set in the mid-1800s. Melville wanted to escape from the Marquesan valley where he was held prisoner, and his only hope was Marnoo, a "tabooed kannaka" who had sailed as far as Sydney and spoke pidgin English. Marnoo arranged a rescue by Karakoee of O'ahu, a beachcomber who offered trade goods from a whaleboat manned by five other "tabooed natives" from Nukuhiva harbor.[33] Dependency on the maritime frontier could thus be two-way.

New *Atua*

As we have already seen in the cases of Moac and Digal in the Carolines, efforts by foreign missionaries to use indigenous agents were not always successful. In 1774, two Tahitians returned from a year in Spanish Peru accompanied by two Franciscan padres, an interpreter, a servant, and a portable house. Two compatriots had died in Valparaiso and Lima, but Thomas Pautu and Manuel Tetuanui were expected to help start a Catholic mission at Tahiti. Pautu went ashore well-clothed, received a warm welcome from his family, and negotiated a site for the padres' hospice with Pomare I. Tetuanui's father, who had given the Spaniards permission to take his boy to Peru, stayed on the *Aguila* for several days, reportedly "lost in contemplation at again seeing his son, and marveling at the stories he related about Lima." But the strategic mission failed. Fathers Gerónimo and Narciso felt insecure and rarely left their hospice, complaining that the Tahitians openly mocked their celibacy. The servant boy, Francisco, showed disrespect to the padres, mistreated young Tetuanui, and alienated other Tahitians in disputes over property. Finally, Máximo Rodriguez, the interpreter, rejected the padres' demands that he cook for them. Even the viceroy of Peru criticized the padres for lacking "such personal qualities as the apostles enjoyed" and at their request removed them to Peru after only a year.

A closer look reveals that Pautu and Tetuanui found the cultural ambiguities of their roles impossible to resolve. When he first arrived, Pautu did what the Spanish expected, explaining to Pomare that he had earned the cross around his neck by learning the catechism and being baptized. But property became an issue, as fights broke out between white sailors and Tahitians over clothes. The Spanish threatened to withdraw the padres, and Rodriguez noted, "The two natives Pautu and [Tetuanui] now became very morose and said they would cast themselves ashore naked, that they wanted no clothes nor anything else from us, but only to stay in their own country." Pautu tried to remove his clothing and offer it to Pomare, but the Spanish padres stopped him. He still wanted to give young Chief Vehiatua clothing of a compatriot who had died in Lima, and a show of respect was necessary, so Pautu cleverly improvised. He uncovered both shoulders for Vehiatua, then pulled his shirt up over the shoulder *closest* to Rodriguez, thus embodying his liminal frontier.

Vehiatua started toward the ship, but Pautu warned his chief and Pomare as well, not to board the *Aguila*. He said they might be taken to Lima just as he had been, Rodriguez wrote, because the Spanish wanted to be "masters of the island" and reduce the Tahitians to "slavery." But the chiefs listened to Rodriguez instead and actually shooed Pautu away, treating him as "no more than a humbug whom, as such and also as a thief, they had held in poor esteem even before he went to Lima." Like Omai, Pautu may thus have been marginal even before he shipped out. All accounts agree that he now stripped himself of his Spanish clothes and went about only in a loincloth, claiming, "he wished to be free and follow his own bent." Somewhat later, he asked forgiveness and offered to return to Peru, but he seemed more interested in getting clothes from his treasure chest to give Vehiatua. Just before the padres left for Peru, the "apostate" Pautu paid them a friendly visit with his wife.

Young Manuel Tetuanui suffered ostracism even harsher than Pautu's. At first kept on board the *Aguila* because he had caught smallpox returning from Peru, he proved useless to the padres as a house servant, "because of his tender age." Chief Vehiatua, himself only about eight years old, came with his mother to claim all of Tetuanui's clothes and stripped him in front of the padres. The missionaries took back everything but a red sash, which Vehiatua wore as a loincloth. Tetuanui found himself in the awkward position of having to translate to the padres when his compatriots ridiculed their sexlessness. Finally, the Spanish servant boy abused him, and his father stole some cloth. Afraid of being beaten again, Tetuanui refused to stay at the mission anymore and insulted Rodriguez, who hit him and afterwards wrestled with his father. Vehiatua tried to rectify matters by threatening to burn Tetuanui's family home, banish his father, and take away their lands. The father returned some cloth to save the house, but even so they became poverty-stricken wanderers. After a halfhearted offer to go back to Lima, Tetuanui disappeared.[34]

In the tradition of Moac and Digal, natives helping missionaries had to play a delicate diplomatic game in the *limen* between power structures. In the beginning, it was often not so much the Christian message as material cargo that interested Oceanians. Hence, Pautu and Tetuanui's difficulty in getting the possessive padres to pass tribute on to their chiefs. In contrast, a Makatean navigator taken to Peru by the *Aguila* in 1774 seems to have come back to be like Hitihiti. Of high rank to begin with, Puhoro parlayed his plentiful stock of Spanish ironware into a respected post in a chief's entourage. It was most likely Puhoro who blew a conch shell to announce himself before entering Cook's cabin in 1777. He intimidated prodigal Omai, who refused to share the stage with him. A second Peru veteran who visited Cook's ship was described as "a low fellow and a little out of his senses, and this opinion was confirmed by his countrymen." The latter may have been Pautu, who apparently was a commoner. In 1789, one of them, probably Puhoro, boarded the *Mercury* at Matavai Bay. George Mortimer wrote, "He seemed very partial to the Spaniards, and spoke much of the favourable reception he had met with at Lima."[35]

In Hawai'i, Queen Ka'ahumanu allowed the first New England missionaries to stay because an English-speaking returnee from the fur and sandalwood trades insisted that the intentions of the *haole* (whites) were good. "Sir Joseph Banks," as he called himself, had been to China, so he had the clout to contradict suspicious chiefs who warned that the Americans wanted to take the land. Joe pointed out that the missionaries came peacefully—and with their women, unlike earlier visitors. He set an example, at first, by attending the religious services and literacy classes. But, according to Bingham, the chiefs made so many demands on Joe's services as an interpreter in ship trading that he fell prey to "the lovers of rum-selling and dram-drinking . . . from whose influence he never escaped." Still, in 1825 Ka'ahumanu appointed Joe as official guide for Lord Byron, who had brought back Liholiho's body from London, so Joe hiked with his tourists to see Kilauea Volcano. On the way they came upon a mullet-filled fishpond, and he joked, "O dis noting, sir—noting—I see him before now;—he so full fish, I see one man, he fall backwards in him, he no sink at all!" In 1831, affable Joe Banks set sail for Tahiti on his own schooner, explaining, "I like take the sun, sail out o' sight o' land, and go to any part o' the world."[36]

The 1820 mission had been inspired by the "martyrdom" of Opukahaia in New England, and four Hawaiian ex-seamen came along to assist the *haole* preachers. George Kaumuali'i turned rebel on Kaua'i, as we have seen, but Opukahaia's old shipmate Thomas Hopu and John Honori'i translated sermons "with peculiar freedom and force." Nevertheless, Bingham would not allow native teachers to be ordained as ministers. The fourth ex-sailor, William Kanui, was soon expelled from the church for excessive drinking and reportedly "became a wanderer for many years."[37] Hopu, too, was suspended from his teaching job more than once for "irregular conduct," and Honori'i died. Mission historian Sheldon Dibble criticized Hawaiian teachers for spiritual flaws and egotism: "To have visited a foreign land, to be better clad than their fellow countrymen, to receive some attention from chiefs and foreigners, were distinctions which their weak brains and unstable minds could not endure." Charles Stewart, however, praised their preaching skill, and even Bingham slowly warmed to the idea of ordaining a few:

> Native Christians engage in prayer with great propriety, both as to matter and manner, but rarely, or never, by a committed form. They often use Scripture

phraseology, not in a stereotyped order, but adapt their thanksgivings, confessions, and petitions to the circumstances in which they are placed, uttering them in a natural, slow, distinct, and reverential manner.[38]

By the mid-1800s, when thousands of Hawaiians were shipping out yearly, the Honolulu Seaman's Chapel attracted *kanaka*s as well as other sailors; Dr. Rufus Anderson found an ex-voyager attending church in Waimea, Kaua'i. Old Jonah had "a governing mind" and had been "an agent of the old chiefs in every species of service." Anderson wrote that with a glowing face and a knowing twinkle in his eye, Old Jonah listened to his sermon, which referred to "Jerusalem and other places." After church, when he was asked about the accomplishments of the Christian mission in Hawai'i, Jonah "replied that the first period was one of luxuriant growth, but the time of sifting had now come, and it was seen what was good."[39] That sifting included rivalry between politico-religious factions. A Hawaiian woman named Louisa, or Rika, had traveled with a sea captain to Guam and returned to preach her own version of Catholicism as a self-styled priestess. At first, she lived with the family of Spaniard Don Francisco de Paula y Marín and converted his household servants and a few other Hawaiians. In 1827, her little congregation greeted the first French priests to arrive in Hawai'i. Perhaps desperate for support, they did not overtly object to her unorthodoxy. Bingham asked to examine Louisa's catechism book, but she refused to show it to him, saying, "you don't believe it is true."

Queen Ka'ahumanu had already allied herself with the New England Protestants, so she banned Catholic worship in 1831. She also took Louisa into her household as a servant, hoping to control her, but she found her to be "haughty and disrespectful." Louisa was then locked in irons and sent to Maui for banishment on Kaho'olawe. William Richards of the Lahaina Mission then intervened, so Louisa was brought back to Honolulu and forced to labor in the bullrush swamps of Waikiki with other unrepentent Catholics. Nevertheless, she persisted in her faith and baptized, among others, elderly chiefess Kalola. In 1839, the French warship *L'Artemise* forced the kingdom to tolerate Catholic missionaries.[40] One convert was Kepelino Keauokalani, a descendant of the priest Pa'ao, who was baptized Zepherin and went briefly to Tahiti to assist Father Ernest Heurtel in 1847. Kepelino became an important Hawaiian historian. In 1862, royal official and legislator William Hoapili also left the New England fold, became an Anglican priest and visited England with Dowager Queen Emma. In 1874, however, he would oppose her candidacy in the royal election and support David Kalakaua. Kepelino backed Emma, but as we have seen, she lost the legislative vote to her American-backed rival.[41]

As in Europe itself, religion could not be separated from local power struggles. Te Morenga lived with Marsden at Parramatta in 1815–16, and in New Zealand he served the missionary as an interpreter and informant. Yet Te Morenga seems to have had his own agenda in mind. He was a rival of Hongi Hika, Marsden's favorite, and complained that Hongi monopolized both mission stations and their trade. Te Morenga tried to represent Marsden's teachings to other Maoris, but he argued that settlers would be more convincing and even built a road to give the mission easier access to his own people. Te Morenga told Marsden that he respected Christ, who "was good and over Whom the atua of New Zealand had no power," but "their [Maori] god was always angry."[42] By the 1850s, missionary-educated Maori pupils of Octavius Hadfield were organizing an alliance against land sales and mobilized armed resistance to British settlement. Tamihana Te Rauparaha went to England to meet Queen Victoria in 1851 and returned to promote the creation of a Maori monarchy. Hoping for the kingship himself, he traveled around North Island preaching unity, the protection of native land rights, and the creation of a new lawmaking system. As the King Movement grew, more traditional leaders emerged, and in 1858 Te Wherowhero was elected Potatau I. But it was too late to stem the tide of *pakeha* settlement. Chief Wharepori sold land to the New Zealand Company in 1839, but he later said, "They will be too strong for us; my heart is dark."[43]

In the central Pacific, simply being a Christian soon invited the slang label "missionary." Langi returned to Tonga from Tahiti and Sydney to preach the gospel five years before white missionaries arrived. John Williams went to Samoa on the *Messenger of Peace* with Chief Fauea, who had converted in Tonga along with his wife. They told people about the steel axes and saws the white preachers had. Yet they also advised the native teachers with Williams not to ban all amusements immediately but to win the hearts of the people by preaching the gospel and teaching literacy.[44] The mission had to compete, however, with "sailor" cults founded by beachcombers. This opposition included a Samoan returnee called Sio, or Joe. Aboard ship, he had been skilled with a drill, or *vili* in Samoan, hence his nickname Joe Gimlet, or Siovili. In the 1820s, he traveled with his chief from Samoa to Tonga by canoe, then to Tahiti by tradeship and possibly on to Sydney, returning home on a whaler. A Samoan hymn credited the two with reaching Britain, and a "Land of Compassion" beyond. His travels gave Siovili prestige, and he wrapped an English book in *tapa* cloth and prayed. He said Jesus, by taking possession of an old priestess, could heal the sick during nighttime ceremonies. Like the Mamaia prophets he had met in Tahiti, Siovili permitted polygamy, dancing, and traditional feasts; he had guns shot off in celebrations. He told his flock to harvest their crops and slaughter their animals for huge feasts, because Jesus was going to walk across the waves, bring riches from the sky, and punish the wicked. Siovili converted Chief Mata'afa, but by the late 1850s only a few elderly believers continued to wait on the beach, watching the waves, in vain.[45]

On Pohnpei and Rotuma, *kanaka* returnees openly flouted their rowdy sailor manners to undermine missionary morality, because like Kalakaua they knew firsthand that white men were not so pious at home.[46] "English Jim," the Tahitian harbor pilot at Papeete for two decades, built himself a career on his sound knowledge of seamanship from being "a travelled man." Jim was piloting at Tahiti in 1826, after working on whalers, and by 1834, he charged fifteen Spanish dollars for his services, half of which went to Queen Pomare IV. He dressed in European fashions and ran a laundry business on the side. Considered eccentric, he reportedly claimed that thunder and lightning warned of ships of war, unusually clear weather meant a merchant vessel approached, and whale spouts in the harbor foretold the arrival of a whaleship. Jim also said that a sacred bird could predict invasions and that palm fronds in a grove where men had been hanged spoke to him with dead souls' voices in the breeze. Melville met Jim at Tahiti in 1842 and, in *Omoo,* dressed the old pilot in a naval frock coat. Jim came out in a canoe, hit a paddler for poor steering, and offered his services to the mate: "You sabbee me? You know me, ah? Well: me Jim, me pilot—been pilot now long time." He claimed the *Julia* was under his authority until the anchor dropped; he guided the helmsman with an air of "immense importance."[47]

On Pukapuka, in the Cook Islands, trader Robert Frisbie described an old returnee in his stories named Uiliamu, or William. The leather-skinned voyager was said to wear the brim of a European straw hat and a grass skirt. He shared his tobacco with Frisbie and insisted, "Me no Puka-Puka Kanaka! Whaler-man!" William called himself a *tutae-auri* (heathen) and said he had nothing to do with Christians. Expecting to find a kindred soul in Frisbie, "he accompanied me to the village, going before me with an air of possessorship, for he told me that he meant to adopt me as his son, exhibiting me to all the Christians as the white man whose Godlessness was equal to his own." They became neighbors, and William's wife cooked for Frisbie, whom the ex-whaler nicknamed Ropati (Robert) "Cowboy." To show his contempt for the Sabbath, William chopped wood on Sunday and then drank rum with his white man. He said he preferred fat women and loved to tell stories of his liaisons with *wahine* from other islands in his whaling days. He also told Frisbie the legend of Big Stomach, a monstrous invader who was finally killed by local warriors. William asked Frisbie if he believed the story, and when the American said yes, the old salt complained, "the damn fool missionaries say all our Puka-Puka stories are lies." William explained that seabirds were the souls of dead Tema Islanders, and he improvised the life stories of his ancestors based on the condition of their headstones in the graveyard. Frisbie pointed out that there were no names on the headstones, but William growled,

> Hell and damnation! You got no eyes? What they teach you in the white man's school? . . . When you are an old lubber like me, you'll know all these old Puka-Pukans. Yes, and you'll see them too. Many's the night I have.[48]

～9～

Legacies

There's beauty here on Pua-ka-'ilima
that island in the sea,
but the Kona wind blowing inland
breaks every leaf and tree.
Along the ridge a frigate bird soars
in quiet contentment,
alone with my diamond ring.

—Chant of a Hawaiian guano-digger
on Howland atoll[1]

From early contact, many Oceanians saw foreign ships as a new opportunity. Kapupuʻu is remembered in Hawaiian tradition for going aboard Cook's ship to "scoop up" iron, though he paid with his life. Chiefs attempted to harness Euroamerican *mana* by adopting strange armaments, attire, and protocols and even by converting their interisland shipping to Western-style vessels. On the decks of visiting ships, local people traded for exotic tools, clothing, and vanities. They normally had to leave the vessel before it sailed away, but as time passed both chiefs and commoners began shipping out, a rather logical extension of their seafaring heritage. The earliest travelers were kidnapped, as we have seen, but in 1767 "Joseph Freewill" started a trend toward rising voluntarism. As the quotation above shows, even *kanaka* guano-diggers on lonely atolls had dreams of what their hard-earned wages would buy—and enable them to do when they got home (i.e., marry). The voyaging continues today on jet aircraft to the industrial countries of the Anglophone Pacific rim, the latest frontier of Oceanian exploration.

Gains and Losses

Kanaka seamen who appropriated the new shipping could be portrayed, collectively, either as actors who helped to shape their own history or as exploited pawns, depending on one's emphasis. Yet subjective human realities do not often fit into tidy categories, and the data on such voyagers suggest that they experienced varying combinations of choice and coercion. The penetration of Western capitalism into island societies generated new relationships over time and prepared the way for colonization, but within that liminal zone of entanglements, Oceanians often extracted their own meanings from a "dialectic of international inequalities and local appropriations."[2] To begin with, Oceanians on "foreign" ships were by definition in a dependent role, since others controlled the capital, technology, planning, and chain of command. This structural disadvantage left them open to victimization in both pay and treatment and caused *kanaka* mutinies. Yet the hardships of the work environment did not deter Oceanians from shipping out and struggling to "scoop up" what they could. Given their assigned roles, they showed courage, strength, and persistence and made the cross-cultural encounters two-way.

Kanaka "waisters," for example, became the backbone of Pacific whaling. That unskilled category was boot camp for greenhands, and regionally a pool of local seamen circulated through it, perhaps rising to ordinary seaman or boatsteerer with experience. In 1857–58, the American whaler *Addison* hired fourteen Hawaiians as "seamen" and paid each a 1/140 lay (percentage of gross profits); two other Hawaiians were hired as cabin boys at smaller 1/150 lays. Yet eight more Hawaiian recruits lacked ranking or lays and were described as "servants" to the crew, that is, "waisters" without job descriptions who did whatever dirty work was required. The lays paid to the Hawaiian seamen were actually better than what white Ordinary or Able-Bodied Seamen received, 1/175 and 1/150, respectively, and quite a bit better than the wages of American greenhands on board, 1/200 to 1/225 lay. But Hawaiians were often hired only for a summer of whaling off Japan, less than a year, so their ultimate pay was far less than that of crew members who worked the full voyage from New England and back. The eight "servant" *kanaka*s reveal the proletarian underbelly of the Pacific maritime workforce: those who did the worst jobs and were rewarded so poorly that they often escaped mention. Meanwhile, in Micronesia, *kanaka*s shipped out for tobacco, a consumable kind of currency that also suggests addiction.[3]

Yet with experience, and rising Euroamerican dependency on local labor pools, wages slowly improved over time. In 1797, the sealer *Nautilus* hired six Hawaiians as "landsmen," its next-to-lowest wage category, and two other Hawaiians as servants, its lowest rank. Paid as greenhands, the landsmen received only 60 percent of an Ordinary Seaman's wages, and half an Able-Bodied Seaman's. This pay scale was not out of line with common practice, except that the men recruited for such low-paying jobs as boat handling were only seasonally employed. Their payment in "slops" (goods from the ship's store) probably suited their own goals as much as their employer's, because their home economy was not monetized. But contractual agreements required of foreign captains by the Hawaiian kingdom after 1841 helped to raise the wages of *kanakas*. By 1844, Foreign Minister Robert Wyllie boasted that three-fourths of native seamen earned equal pay.[4] In the South Pacific, British regulation and market demand also improved the treatment of Oceanian seamen in the nineteenth century. Even before the British annexation of New Zealand, the whaler *Australian* hired seven Maoris in 1836–37 as Ordinary Seamen at 1/170 lay, compared to 1/160–1/180 for white Ordinaries. Another Maori was hired at 1/160 lay and, after his promotion to boatsteerer (harpooner), at 1/100 lay, the standard wage for that rank. A Tahitian boatsteerer on the same ship also received 1/100 lay.[5]

The following table summarizes selected data on the 250 best-documented voyagers, who constitute a focus group for this study. Thousands of Oceanians shipped out on foreign ships, so this summary is obviously only a small sampling statistically, but textually these individuals are overrepresented in the historical records, which are primarily Euroamerican journals and ship logs. It is not surprising, then, that a large proportion, 41 percent of the total, consists of "ennobled tourists" who traveled with relatively high status, though not all did so voluntarily, especially in the early days of contact. There is far more information on Omai, for example, than on the average *kanaka* ship worker. Polynesian representation in these records clearly outweighs that of Micronesians or Melanesians, which is consistent with the high levels of participation by native seamen from Hawai'i, what is now French Polynesia, and Aotearoa (New Zealand). Although the figures are only suggestive, the 90 percent voluntarism rate among Polynesians, including ordinary *kanakas,* is striking, particularly when contrasted with Micronesian and Melanesian examples, in which frank accounts of kidnapping by the early Spanish explorers raise the coercion rate. The high overall rate of voluntary recruitment, 72 percent even with Spanish abductions in Micronesia and Melanesia allowed for, also contrasts with the death rate abroad of 23 percent.

In fact, the death rate approximates the mortality rate among white seamen involved in the trans-Atlantic slave trade between Africa and America,

The 250 Best-Documented Oceanian Voyagers

Origin	Status		Voluntary?		Voyage[a]			Fate[b]		
	High	Low	Yes	No	O	R	B	D	R	U
Polynesia (168)	74 44%	94 56%	152 90%	16 10%	45 27%	53 32%	70 41%	40 24%	87 52%	41 24%
Hawaiian (63)	20	43	56	7	3	1	16	4	14	2
Tahitian[c] (45)	22	23	40	5	9	13	21	7	15	14
Maori (NZ) (38)	20	18	35	3	8	9	5	2	18	3
Other (22)	12	10	21	1	7	9	7	2	7	9
Micronesia (46)[d]	18 39%	28 61%	17 37%	29 63%	10 22%	22 48%	14 30%	13 28%	15 33%	18 39%
Chamorro (15)	3	12	1	14	2	11	1	—	2	1
Palauan (17)	8	9	8	9	—	4	1	—	1	11
Other (14)	7	7	8	6	3	3	8	4	3	1
Melanesia (37)[d]	12 32%	25 68%	11 30%	26 70%	3 8%	28 76%	6 16%	4 11%	10 27%	23 62%
Totals (251)	104 41%	147 59%	180 72%	71 28%	58 23%	103 41%	90 36%	57 23%	112 45%	82 33%

[a] Categories: Oceania (only), Rim (of Pacific), Beyond.
[b] Categories: Death (overseas), Return (to stay), Unknown (including those who shipped out again).
[c] "Tahitian," for convenience, includes all French Polynesia.
[d] Reflects early Spanish exploration more than later trade or whaling era.

where Euroamericans were as vulnerable to tropical diseases as Oceanians were to Eurasian microbes.[6] When the death rate is added to the 33 percent whose ultimate destinies were unknown because they journeyed out of the records, it seems clear that most *kanakas* literally cast their fates to the winds when they sailed off on foreign ships. Even if we consider the woeful lack of documentation on the vast majority of voyagers, the 45 percent known return rate is still low, because Euroamerican accounts would generally try to represent their recruits' experiences in a favorable light. It is also worth noting that two-thirds (64 percent) of the seamen journeyed only within the Pacific basin, either to the rim or inside Oceania, which is probably a fair assessment. The proportion who sailed beyond the Pacific is higher among Polynesians, especially Hawaiians who were likely to see New England on whaleships. The focus group sampling indicates that Oceanian voyaging on foreign ships tended to be risky, mostly regional in scope, and, as contact intensified in strategic ports, increasingly voluntary—despite the fact that the majority were common seamen, not privileged passengers.

Within the unknown fate category is a hidden statistic: almost one-fifth of these individuals shipped out again, instead of settling back into their home society for good. Some Oceanian seamen were already marginals, like many of their international counterparts. Tupaia and Omai were refugees, and Ahutoru and Lee Boo were expendable envoys. Princes George Kaumuali'i and Temoana were fleeing power struggles, and Pedro and Kokako were escaping captivity. Harry Maitey and Henry Opukahaia were reputedly "orphans," while Moac, Digal, and Kadu were castaways. Yet even if we add all the nameless "natives" who were blackbirded and perished without a trace, voyaging was not monopolized by lost souls. Charles de Varigny complained that young Hawaiian men, if they needed money, preferred shipping out to working long hours on plantations. They displayed a "strong emotional attachment to the whaling industry [and] a taste for far-flung adventures." In fact, young men who went overseas were often acting out a rite-of-passage of their gender and age-group. By the mid-1800s, the large numbers involved—20 percent of young adult Hawaiian males—suggest that even "mainstreamers" found the lure of adventure and profit too strong to reject.[7]

There was racism on Euroamerican ships, as we have seen. It could take many forms, from harsh treatment that caused some Oceanians to desert, go crazy, or mutiny, to sarcastic representations. Few Pacific Islanders rose above the rank of boatsteerer on foreign ships, though they could command their own schooners in the so-called mosquito fleets of coastal New Zealand and Hawai'i. British laws in the early 1800s required that nonwhite seamen be speedily repatriated instead of being left in Sydney or London—supposedly in the name of humanitarian concern. By the 1870s, Australian maritime unions were pressuring shipping companies not to hire Asian or Oceanian seamen who competed with whites, and the post–1901 "White Australia" policy further restricted access to Sydney's shipping. Similarly, Hawaiians working in California or Oregon felt increasing resentment from white workers once the border of the United States reached the Pacific coast. As Oregon's delegate to Congress said in 1850, "Canakers or Sandwich Islanders . . . are a race of men as black as your negroes of the South, and a race, too, that we do not desire to settle in Oregon." Hawaiians were denied citizenship in Oregon, and after the decline of the Hudson's Bay Company south of the forty-ninth latitude, they lost their main employer in the Northwest.[8]

There is also evidence that the drastic depopulation experienced on many Pacific Islands as a result of foreign contact was sometimes worsened by ship recruitment. In the Cook Islands, for example, the same foreign vessels that brought devastating epidemics also took away healthy young men for labor. By the 1840s, so many Rarotongan sailors had never come back again—95 percent, according to one missionary—that local chiefs required their young men to get permission before shipping out. Still, the south coast often escaped regulation. Rotuman chiefs also required authorization, and guarantees to support sailors' wives, because disease and emigration were undermining the local population. Females increasingly outnumbered males, and the total number of residents continued to decline.[9] Maoris too suffered from alien diseases, and about half of those who stayed at the "safe haven" of Marsden's Parramatta farm died there or en route home again. His mission finally had to stop sending Maoris out of the country. Hawaiian newspapers debated the issue in the 1840s, when at least five hundred young Hawaiians left on ships every year. While the indigenous population declined, three thousand young *kanaka*s were at sea.[10]

Available statistics are too incomplete to measure accurately the loss from seafaring, because no record was kept of what proportion of recruits returned, but the anecdotal evidence is rather grim. George Simpson, whose fur company took hundreds of Hawaiian men to the Northwest yearly, blamed the steady decline of indigenous numbers partly on recruitment for ship crews: "About a thousand males in the very prime of life are estimated annually to leave the islands [and] a considerable portion of them are said to be permanently lost to their country, either dying during their engagements, or settling in other parts of the world." Cabinet minister Varigny argued that tempting pay advances lured "the very finest flower of . . . hale and hearty male natives" into unhealthy or cold climates where they died. He called ship recruitment "a system of conscription, profitable to none but the foreigner; and the population continued to decrease at an alarming rate." Varigny blamed rising female prostitution (and consequent infertility from venereal disease) on wives' being abandoned by their sailor husbands. In 1847, the Hawaiian kingdom passed a law that required ship recruits to post a bond as support for their wives and families, just as ship captains had to post bonds to return the sailors.[11]

Interior Minister Keoni Ana wrote of Hawaiian sailors, "All these are in the prime of life, and many who go never again return to this country. . . . Look at this ye who are astonished at the depopulation of these islands." Yet he continued, "we must not forget that there is much of good connected with this evil . . . the whaling ships lay the foundation for nearly all our foreign commerce, and it is from them we receive our money." Both Varigny and Ana were afraid that if Hawai'i stopped supplying sailors, it might lose precious wages and trade. Foreign Minister Wyllie actually disputed the notion that seafaring decreased the population and added, "many of them returned [with] a degree of knowledge and civilization, useful to their countrymen, and more than compensating for the loss of those who never came back." "All these travelled kanakas are readily distinguishable amongst the population," he said, "by their superior cleanliness, dress and assimilation to foreigners in their manners and habits." It could be argued that many Oceanians had been lost at sea in ancient voyages, and the death rate among seamen in the British navy could reach 50 percent, mainly due to disease or accidents, not combat. Considering the choices of premature death available, one is reminded of the Tikopian voyaging chant: "If we stay on land we shall die; if we go to sea we shall die; let us go then."[12]

Foreign travel itself might render mainstream migrants marginal and produce uprooted malcontents, like the *kanaka*s who came home to ridicule their chiefs. Oceania's growing integration into a world economy was proto-colonial, as capitalists conscripted African slaves, Chinese coolies, Indian indentured laborers and lascars, Manila-men, and now *kanaka*s into their tropical enterprises. By the mid-1800s, one out of every five sailors in the American whaling fleet was Oceanian, suggesting a certain degree of acquiescence, even complicity. The only way to survive, even to succeed, on an alien deck was to learn the rules of an unequal system and then explore the boundaries of the roles open. Given the power hierarchy of the deck, *kanaka*s had to do what was expected, and they did so with skillful mimicry. Many earned the chance to travel by observing and helping crews in port with energy and enthusiasm. Coming from societies that respected elders and chiefs, Pacific Islanders also pleaded their case, using simple gestures or a few common words, with someone who might grant them permission to ship out. If necessary, they even stowed away and then depended on the mercy of the captain.

Once inside the cabin, forecastle, or hold, they had to adjust quickly, learning the ship's jargon and enduring initiations from shipmates. From crow's nest to whaleboat, they had a new maritime system to learn and pass on to those who followed them. Nicknames like Jim Crow or Tellum-by-by Darco were, in a sense, theatrical disguises tolerated by cross-cultural voyagers who had their own agendas. The experienced Maori sailor E Ware joked, took the wheel, and showed off his skill to win jobs on ships. Some *kanakas* donned their new clothes and words with such determination that they came to identify themselves culturally as foreign. Their strategic self-identification as "others" was typified by the *kanaka* crewmen on the *Wanderer* in 1851, who insisted that Solomon Islanders in canoes were untrustworthy and backward—though their prejudiced captain failed to see the distinction. A Pohnpeian who visited Hawai'i later told visitors, "Me no black man. Me go Hawaii." Similarly, a Tannese nicknamed Dick sold yams from his canoe in exchange for tobacco, saying, "me too much like-em smoke." He said that he had worked in Australia, and even though his white master mistreated him, he was "all the same white man."[13]

Even indigenous leaders set an example for copying the foreigners. A Fijian chief who returned from Sydney wore English-style clothes to show that he was as "civilized" as resident Oceanian missionaries. Chief Basset of New Caledonia visited Sydney with his brother, learned English, and wore cotton shirts. An English captain said, "The white people gave him the credit of having been a greater tyrant and cannibal, until his intercourse with a somewhat better class of English and his visit to Sydney." Basset would offer his coconuts to thirsty whites, but he decapitated a local woman who took one and displayed her head as a warning. Hawaiian chiefs looted their islands for sandalwood to trade for status symbols. They wore Euroamerican fashions and had servants push them around in four-wheeled carts. Yet overworked commoners suffered from illness and lack of time for food production, thus worsening depopulation.[14]

Many native leaders were simply being pragmatic in an age of growing pressure and temptations from outside powers. The Hawaiian chiefs who survived Liholiho's tragic journey to London spoke often of England's deadly diseases, yet they also made a point of praising the country to sea captains whose trade they desired. Despite Lauri's tales of the harsh winters in St. Petersburg, Hawaiian chiefess Namahana told Kotzebue she had heard such positive things about the kindness, wisdom, and accomplishments of the Russians that she wished she could make the same journey.[15] A Hawaiian sailor asked King Kamehameha III to forgive him for leaving Honolulu without permission, but the king scolded him only mildly and expressed thanks he had returned alive from the Arctic—where another

Hawaiian on the same ship had died. The first Kamehameha and Pomare quickly saw the need to get people trained in foreign nautical and military technology, and later kings like Kalakaua and Tupou regarded the world economy as a source of innovations to protect their islands' sovereignty. The intensifying scramble for colonies in the late 1800s ruined Kalakaua's Polynesian confederation, but Tupou's royal constitution survived British hegemony.[16]

Kanaka loyalty, clowning, and tractability drew frequent compliments from foreign mariners, unsurprisingly, while recalcitrant behavior or physical resistance incurred just the opposite. In 1837, a Boston paper condescendingly wrote of Pitcairn Islanders, "In intellect and habits, they form a link between the civilized European and unsophisticated Polynesian." Well-traveled Rotumans reportedly showed shrewdness in business and were more cosmopolitan in their worldview. Litton Forbes wrote, "It is no rare thing to find men who have visited Havre, or New York, or Calcutta, men who can discuss the relative merits of a sailors' home in London or Liverpool, and dilate on the advantages of steam over sailing vessels. Thus the native of Rotumah is more than usually capable and intelligent." Such comments showed considerable Eurocentrism, but they also revealed the emerging power structures that Oceanians had to cope with. Today, Rotuman migrants are among the most successful people in urban Fiji, and they retain their Rotuman identity.[17]

Third-party beaches highlighted the cross-cultural nature of the voyage: how many layers of identity clothed a *kanaka* on shore liberty? In their dependent roles, far from home, they often sided with their white shipmates against other natives. Maoris, as we have seen, looked down on Australian Aborigines, and Ka'iana of Hawai'i was said to disdain both Chinese and Native Americans. Hawaiians in the American Northwest even helped fur companies to colonize the Nez Percé with forts and unfair treaties. Yet Atu seemed truly tempted to desert the *Columbia* and join the Indians, and later Hawaiian fur company employees intermarried with Native American women. In 1809, Tahitian sailors dealing with Fijians were said to "despise them and say they are truly savages."[18] Yet they were caught in between: a ship had fired on a canoe, causing vengeful Fijians to mistreat two Tahitians. At times, it may have been an act of self-esteem or survival for Oceanians to set themselves apart from marginalized—or competitive— nonwhites. Phebe, a Fijian girl traveling with Lady Wallis, was blamed for theft and called a cannibal by a jealous African American servant woman. Hami Patu distanced himself from African Americans in New England theaters, and Omai hurried Puhoro right off Cook's ship. A degree of "otherness" was perhaps precious.

In fact, mimicry, which helped Oceanians so well in their role-playing, was a double-edged stratagem. "In the ambivalent world of the 'not quite/not white,' on the margins of metropolitan desire,"[19] mimicry could empower *kanaka*s to criticize their hosts. Satire has threatened elites since ancient times, and Ra'iatea, the spiritual center of eastern Polynesia, was noted for its roving *arioi,* or proselytizing "comedians," to which Tupaia and Hitihiti belonged. Both E Ware's calculated imitation of shipmates' quirks and "King Manini's" humorous singing about his coworkers revealed subtle resistance to domination. Desertion was another form of protest, what Marcus Redicker calls "an affirmation of the sailor's own power." It could take cultural form when Oceanian ex-sailors went conspicuously "native" once home again. The Maori chief Titore became a Christian in Australia and visited England, but when he returned to Aotearoa, he had himself tattooed to avoid being taken for "a woman." In Melanesia, William Giles wrote, "It is usual for all the Kanakas to resume their old savage customs again as soon as they return to the Islands and their first proceeding is to discard all their clothes."[20]

Many Oceanians retained noticeable pride in their own heritage. Tupaia, Atu, Ka'iana, and various Maoris wore traditional dress on foreign shores, and their reactions to what they saw—even secondhand, in Euroamerican texts—comment on "enlightened" Western civilization. Te Pahi argued with Governor King in Sydney that no Maori would punish anyone for taking food, and Palu Mata Moina and his wife could not understand why Sydney residents did not invite them to eat when they were hungry. Both Ka'iana and Lee Boo were more generous toward Chinese sampan beggars than their white companions were. The Hawaiian high chief Manui'a, as Kamehameha's envoy between islands, had already experienced foreign ships before going to London. On his return, he took issue with an Englishman on HMS *Blonde* who complained about Hawaiians' eating fish raw on the deck. Manui'a said that "he saw plenty of poor people in England, but we see none here, that they got plenty of poi, taro and fish and none want for anything like many a man at home."[21] Lee Boo said Londoners lived in stacks of strangely isolated "boxes," and Tupou of Tonga learned a constitutional lesson from the number of beggars in Sydney. Returnees argued that some white men were less pious at home than in the Pacific, and they foresaw the imperial conquest of their islands.

Around the world, seaports tended to harbor more than ships. Their need for labor attracted a distinctive, semiskilled working class whose motivations included both sheer necessity and a thirst for adventure. The individual's act of boarding a ship became part of a collective process that drew rural people toward active ports, into the arms of economic demand

and perhaps back again, according to the fluctuations of profit.[22] Sadly, *kanakas* rarely escaped a menial function on ships, and when Oceanians acquired their own Western-style vessels, obligations to family and chiefs often made it hard to accumulate capital and compete with expatriate traders. The Siassi of New Guinea, so active as middlemen in precolonial days, found it hard to adapt to changes in trade patterns and to demands that they produce copra or work on distant plantations. In 1964, a Siassi told anthropologist Marshall Sahlins, "We are a trading people, all we need is a ship."[23]

Nevertheless, Oceanian voyagers played a significant role in Euroamerican shipping and, as beachcombers and returnees, in the acculturations between their islands and other worlds. They are credited with introducing outrigger canoes and island drumming to the Bonin (Ogasawara) Islands of Japan, where their genes live on in some local families. They introduced *lomilomi* salmon to Hawai'i from the Northwest American coast, wheat and potatoes from Australia to New Zealand, and liquor distilling from Hawai'i to Tahiti and Fiji. Like jet-setting island elites of today, Hitihiti, Ka'iana, Jem, and Ruatara were pan-Pacific personalities who converted their voyaging into prestige. Enterprising Hongi Hika went to Australia to meet Marsden, sold him land for a mission, and sailed to London, all to equip his conquering warriors with muskets. Travel offered a peculiar chance to improvise, to test the odds. Like big men in Vanuatu or *kula* traders, the new voyagers were on a quest for liminal souvenirs, talismans of exotic difference, and strange power. Distance had *mana*.

In fact, Oceanians today continue to find a role in global seafaring. In Honolulu harbor, Hawaiians can still be found on the docks, operating tugboats and commanding larger ships. One-fifth of Rotuman men work on ships, and several are pilots or captains. Sometimes relatives sign on to a ship together, creating floating kin networks on their favorite vessels. Fijians and ni-Vanuatu work on Asian-operated fishing vessels but complain about long hours and unsanitary working conditions. In age-old fashion, a boat owner responded, "They wouldn't be coming back for more if they weren't satisfied." In 1967, a Marine Training Center, one of several in the south Pacific, opened on Tarawa in Kiribati. Every year, a hundred young men study seafaring skills in classrooms and model ships; two thousand i-Kiribati currently work at sea, half of them on German ships that go as far as Bremen. Despite concerns about working conditions on Korean fishing boats and the danger of being exposed to drugs overseas, the sailors send home more than two million Australian dollars annually to their families. Such remittances are significant in a small, resource-poor nation, and some wives actually say they enjoy having their men stay away for extended periods! Tarawans joke about what sailors bring home, such as large radios, tape decks, and video recorders. They say a young man in long pants on a motor scooter must be a sailor, and if there is a young woman on the back seat, she must be a nurse.[24]

Ghostly Voices

Maritime frontiers produce storytelling, as when the ancient Phoenicians invented sea monster tales to keep rivals from following their trade routes. Seamen, after all, travel for a living, and accounts of exotic or risky adventures entertain as well as inform. My own experience has taught me to accept sailor "history" as generically embellished, containing negotiable amounts of "truth." Yet most Oceanians on foreign ships left no written memoirs, so the historian has to seek their feelings indirectly, through the selective, biased accounts of white shipmates. Another solution would be to visit every island to collect oral traditions and thus attempt to recreate the viewpoints of the Islanders who participated or remember those who did. The story of Lojeik's being kidnapped from Ebon and changed at sea (see preface) shows how rewarding such a search could prove. With the help of the Alele Museum in Majuro, I heard it from Namar Milne in 1989. That tale, still alive after 150 years, emphasizes the sense of loss that Oceanians felt when their young men were abducted, and it also presents the liminal puzzle of Jake's new sailor identity. Most attacks on foreign ships by Pacific Islanders were, in fact, acts of revenge for exactly the kind of kidnapping in Lojeik's tale. Yet the story also shows remarkable forgiveness for that crime, once Lojeik came back with positive things to say.

This indigenous testimony reminds us of other captures of Oceanians with intent to treat them "well" and create ambassadors. Cook did it in Aotearoa and Williams at Niue, like the conquistadores before them. Outsiders used their lack of a common language to rationalize ruthless behavior, but the tactic obviously risked failure. When the Spanish sent a New Guinean ashore in 1528, they witnessed his murder before he reached the beach—his voiceless homecoming. The unhappy tradition of Mesiol of Pohnpei showed that a great deal of kidnapping in the Pacific was not followed by good treatment. Nor were receptions abroad for volunteers always pleasant, as the tale of Palu Mata Moina of Tonga in Sydney demonstrated. Yet Palu and his wife eventually chose to return to money-hungry Sydney, despite their harsh visit, and other coerced voyagers even presented written letters of recommendation from their captors. Lojeik's transformation is exemplified by his not being recognized at first: like Omai and Darco, he had to strip off his foreign clothes to show his hidden tattoo— perhaps an apt metaphor for the inner *kanaka* identity. I asked Namar Milne questions for more details—a violation of procedure when collecting a received tradition—and he was happy to improvise, so Lojeik's "voyage" continued.

Recollections by actual participants are very hard to recover, because of the early time frame of this book, but they resonate, as partial texts,[25] through intermediaries. José Taitano was kidnapped from Guam, but he chose to spend the next twenty years sailing on ships. According to his descendant Carlos, José returned home with a pocket full of Mexican pesos, married, and loved to tell his offspring how, as "Joe Guam," he had seen King Kalakaua of Hawai'i and U.S. President Abraham Lincoln. Epeli of Rotuma told his story in mixed English and Rotuman to an anthropologist in 1913. Epeli said he had shipped out to escape a religious civil war in 1878, at the age of fifteen. "Went looking for money," he said, "then I got a fever." He survived and traveled for thirteen years, visiting New Zealand, New York, London, South Africa, India, and half a dozen Pacific Islands from New Guinea to Samoa. He once disembarked in Sydney and "played around." After presumably spending all his money in typical sailor fashion, he went to work in the Torres Strait as a pearl diver, as many Rotumans did in the nineteenth century. Years later, he bought passage to Fiji, whose British rulers had annexed Rotuma. Epeli was broke, having spent his wages on women and rum. He finally came home because "white man's lands are good but if no money no food. Here a man has no money, but there's plenty to eat." [26]

In fact, Rotuman ex-sailors like Epeli often served as informants to anthropologists, because they spoke English and could translate. Considering the accuracy of most sea stories, one wonders how much their help affected portrayals of their cultures! In 1880, a British administrator on Rotuma complained, "nine tenths of the men under thirty have left their homes and bear one another out in their stories. Many of them have come back with most mischievous ideas which are for the most part unfortunately quite true." He blamed the missionaries for starting "a general exodus" by banning "all harmless amusements" and called returnees "too much civilized for the public good." They were said to despise people who lived the traditional way, especially their chiefs. Kava-drinking stories incorporated foreign nautical terms and place names into their imagery, and songs accompanied by ukeleles referred to *forau* (foreign) travels:

> Be careful not to get lost out there,
> You've lingered long in the cold of the rain,
> Your relatives are awaiting you in Rotuma.[27]

Euroamerican journals often describe returnees who presented themselves as special repositories of wisdom on the wonders overseas. In Hawai'i, where so many young men traveled to the American Northwest,

John Turnbull wrote that part of being respected was "describing with great emphasis and extravagance the singular events of their voyage." Thomas Jacobs, rather hypocritically, mocked exaggerations in his Melanesian shipmate's tales: "Darco indulged in the traveller's license to an almost unpardonable degree" and gave his fellow New Guineans the impression that America was "situated in the moon." Darco also told them of six-story houses, steam-propelled ships, horse-drawn carriages, stone pavements, and water "as solid as stone." Moehanga said that other Maoris listened but did not take him seriously when he talked about what he had seen in his travels, such as water being piped into people's houses. But he also told Dillon that he had been to India, which turned out to be untrue.[28]

Oceanian audiences could be skeptical, as we have seen. When Ruatara told his Maori friends about seeing horses, which he described as large dogs that could "carry men and women about in land canoes," his listeners plugged their ears in disbelief. A few tried to ride their pigs around but fell off laughing into the dirt. People laughed at a Fijian who claimed, over a bowl of kava, to have seen sawmills run by water power. But then, he had already bragged that when he tried to measure the size of an Australian building with his arms, he had to give up after three months because it was too large. Similarly, Lauri said he had seen a house in Russia so large, he walked for three days without coming to the end of it. How must it have sounded when he claimed that in winter he covered his entire body in fur clothing to avoid losing a nose or ear? Or that "cold changed water into a solid substance, resembling glass in appearance, but of so much strength that it was used for a high road, people passing over it in huge chests drawn by horses, without breaking it?"[29]

Exaggerated tales could, of course, boost the interests of foreigners as well as amuse them. Omai, for example, was said to have told Tongans and Tahitians about British power, which was the basis of his own new status. In the Cook Islands, he said Britain "had ships as large as their island, that carried guns so large that several people might sit within them and that one of these guns was sufficient to destroy the whole island at one shot." English chroniclers also say he told Pomare I that King George had a court as brilliant as "the stars in the firmament," dominions as vast as "heaven," and power as great as "the thunder that shakes the earth." Britain, he claimed, had three hundred thousand warriors and twice that number of sailors, "who traversed the globe, from the rising of the sun to his setting" in warships that made Tahitian war canoes look like mere outriggers. London alone had more people than all the Society Islands and over one hundred kinds of four-footed animals that would overrun the land if some were not killed for food. Pomare I seemed to know that Omai was lying, to some extent, and quickly lost interest.[30]

McCluer said his Palauan voyagers to Canton told their families that British warships were as big as islands and that Chinese were "effeminate and crafty," not "brave and warlike" like the English. Vancouver noted that Jack Ingraham, or Opai, who had already been to Boston with Gray, magnified the powers of Britain as the *Discovery* sailed among the Hawaiian islands: "It would not be his fault, if we were not in high repute amongst the islanders." Even Siovili's voyaging hymn about "dashing through the waves" praised the governor of Australia as "a great king."[31] Such tales excited curiosity and helped to recruit new *kanaka*s, who appropriated in their turn portions of the liminal deck. Across Oceania, voyagers' news of the outer world filtered through native voices before it refracted through written texts. After Te Pahi's return from Australia, his daughter composed a chant, which Maoris could still recite for visitors seven years later. The stories told by Kadu of Woleai helped earn him a safe haven among the Marshallese, who sang for years about him and Kotzebue.[32] Yet poor Sam Kanaka of Nauru, as we saw, had no one to communicate with and was shot as he leaped from bunk to bunk in the bowels of a whaleship.

Even death could be survived by a few heroes. In 1772, Cook said that people from Aotearoa to Tahiti asked about his deceased navigator, Tupaia, and "like true Philosophers [they] were perfectly satisfied with the answers we gave them." A mission historian wrote that Hawaiians "had no more thought of Opukahaia and his companions than Americans would have of some wandering sailors." But the martyred "Obookiah" lived on. Hiram Bingham claimed that reading and interpreting Opukahaia's memoir in Sunday school caused Hawaiian students to weep over his death scene.[33] Soon after, the fatal journey of King Liholiho and his wife to England would be immortalized in a hula chant. Winee, Lee Boo, and Tapeooe all sent home gifts—the first migrant remittances—from their deathbeds. Lee Boo's father was said to have counted the moons since his son's departure by tying knots in a rope, which he finally buried when he gave up hope. But after eight years, McCluer arrived with livestock, weapons, cloth, and perhaps Lee Boo's precious blue glass vases.[34]

It is possible that a society accustomed to paying compensation for injury might accept a substitute. A Maori chief whose son had died in Australia sat the family in a circle on the deck of the *Dromedary,* where he mourned over the boy's mat, "the only relic of him." Then he accepted a musket and powder, as he said, "to salute the memory of his child." In Tahiti, Máximo Rodriguez told Tipitipia's family that their son had died in Lima, but he assured them that the Spaniards had made every effort to save his life: "With that they embraced me and sat me down between them; and then some conversation ensued about my staying in the island, at which they were highly gratified."[35] Yet Lojeik's story reminds us of the loss to their families when Oceanians shipped out. George Paniani, the national archivist of the Cook Islands, told me that in the land title cases he often researches, descendants of sailors who worked on whaleships often complained that the men did not provide well for their families and left a meager inheritance.[36]

This legacy lives on in modern Pacific novels, such as John Pule's *The Shark That Ate the Sun.* Pule juxtaposes two diasporas: recent Niuean migration to New Zealand, and work overseas in the nineteenth century. In 1870, Makatahi wrote to his brother from Tahiti, "I wear good clothes and maybe you wouldn't recognize me, eh. The years have carved time onto my face." After two years of hard work on the guano atolls, Makatahi was waiting to sail on a copra vessel to Hawai'i: "I am free to travel and see places I have heard of from some of the men who work on the ships." He wrote of Tahiti, "the women are hard to hold, their hips are muscles and their arms speak another lingo. All we do is smoke and drink." Makatahi reached England and South America, but his letters said that he was homesick. His brother wrote back, "We are proud of you making it to England. . . . The old man who remembers the arrival of Captain Cook died last week at a great age." He urged Makatahi to come home, because his gardens were overgrown, adding:

> I myself want to go away from here, be like you, and see the world, but the old folks do not want to see me go, as most of the young men have already gone to find work on the phosphate fields. . . . We are all waiting for you at the wharf.[37]

Unfortunately, Makatahi never returned, any more than Siovili's Christ came walking across the waves. There was, as Pule suggests, continuity between shipping out and modern outmigration, reinforced by the plantation labor trade that circulated 120,000 Oceanians around the region. From the mid-nineteenth century into the early 1900s, ships hired both native seamen and labor recruits. In the 1970s, Peter Corris interviewed Solomon Islanders who had once worked in Queensland and found that several had done more than one job. "Tommy" Taeova had been a "horse boy" in Australia, a diver on Thursday Island, and, at different times, a sailor and plantation worker. Another returnee had been a cook on land and sea, and some had married women from the countries where they had worked. Egita came home to Malaita, after forty years abroad, with a Tongan wife. Women, too, could bring men home to be beachcombers. In the 1980s, a Fijian named Kava married a Rotuman woman and moved to her island, where he is credited with reviving the arts of boat-building and deep-sea fishing. Half a million Oceanians are now voyaging to the rim of their holistic "sea of islands."[38]

Beyond the Beach

In all three Pacific diasporas, whether sending double-hulled canoes to colonize newly discovered islands, shipping out on foreign vessels, or flying to Auckland or Los Angeles, Oceanians have built human networks across borders. In the circuitry of old "kanakadom," ships picked up seamen and discharged them wherever convenient. In 1854, the whaler *Miantonomi* hired "a native" at Pohnpei to replace "Sam Kanaka," who had deserted. Melville hinted at this matrix in *Typee,* when a network of "tabooed kannakas" rescued him. Not all native voyagers were helpful diplomats. In 1851, a whaler at Hilo wrote, "Our Kanakas also left us here, and this, we were not sorry for; they are not the most agreeable ship mates in the world." In fact, white seamen did not always appreciate returnees who might compete with their version of the world. In Fiji in 1875, Commodore Goodenough wrote, "A regular traveled ape came up . . . and talked a good bit of English. He had been to Sydney." The Hawaiian word *kanaka* traveled around the region in shipboard pidgin, onto plantations and into modern national symbolism. Today native Hawaiians call themselves *kanaka maoli* (true people), and indigenous groups in New Caledonia use the collective label Kanak (from the French *canaque*) and hope to call their independent country Kanaky. A pan-Pacific identity that had menial connotations has thus become a sign of liberation.[39]

Oceanians, like many other peoples, had a tradition of seeking what was over the horizon, as Mary Helms suggests, to "acquire symbolically potent material goods or knowledge from a geographically distant, supernaturally charged realm." Captain François Péron wrote of Hawaiians in the 1820s, "Un-grateful children of nature . . . they cast unhappy looks beyond the seas; they hope to brave the vast space which separates them from another world; almost all ask to be admitted among us."[40] Those who took passage on foreign ships garnered firsthand experience in strange lands and cultures, and prestigious souvenirs. Even the kidnapped Maori flax-dressers, Tuki and Huru, spoke so highly of Norfolk Island that Te Pahi and Maui shipped out to see the place. Oceanians knew that the sea was a road map, not a barrier, and that sailing routes, like highways, connected worlds. They and foreign mariners met in a common frontier zone, and like the white seamen who came to explore their islands, Pacific voyagers combed distant beaches. Sailors normally see only limited aspects of the countries they visit, but in the maritime networks of the eighteenth and nineteenth centuries, seamen played a crucial role in cross-cultural interaction. Global shipping routes gave Oceanians unprecedented mobility that made every sailor a "man of the world" capable of creative survival.[41]

While aboard alien vessels, both ennobled tourists and *kanaka*s became what Victor Turner would call "structurally invisible." Like other neophytes undergoing initiations, they obeyed their mentors as long as they represented the "common good," developed camaraderie with their shipmates, and explored "a realm of pure possibility." After being reshaped, survivors tried to apply their "enhanced knowledge of how things work" to their own societies.[42] Most Oceanian voyagers endured the tests of the deck and the dark dungeons below only for a while, relinquishing control to foreigners but keeping in their hearts a sense of self and attachment to home. Some *kanaka*s revolted openly against abuse, lost hope because of physical or cultural kidnapping, or escaped to another beach. All too many died of surprise fates. For true seafarers, perhaps marginal to begin with, the journey itself became home, and they kept shipping out, chasing a star into other mysteries. Their *terra incognita* was always in their soul, beckoning. Those who returned home struggled to communicate what they had discovered, perhaps even to profit by it, if people would only listen. Like microcosms of Oceania itself, they tried to adapt the maritime frontier to the heritage of their birth, but sometimes they had to settle for being colorful oracles by the sea.

In 1989, I interviewed a Marshall Islander named Biliet Lokonwa who was over one hundred years old. Through an interpreter from the Alele Museum in Majuro, Biliet told me of travels on German, Japanese, and English trading vessels in the late nineteenth and early twentieth centuries. His little room in a house by the Yacht Club was festooned with memorabilia, like a shrine to the glory days of his youth. He showed me the list on his door of those Marshallese who had sailed with him to San Francisco in 1913. Like Lojeik in reverse, he unbuttoned his shirt to reveal an American eagle he had had tattooed on his chest to prove where he had been. Seventy-six years had wrinkled the eagle, but that did not diminish the glee with which neighbor children still listened to his tales. For Biliet, like many people who refer back to some bigger-than-life adventure in their past, memories of his traveling days made him feel special, worthy of ongoing respect. He vowed that if he could, he would return to San Francisco, find an old woman there who had once been "kind" to him, and settle down for good. Above all, he wanted to walk on the new bridge people said had been built across the entrance to the bay since his visit: the Golden Gate.[43] Who, I wondered, was whose noble savage?

～ 10 ～

Reflections

I will search upwind only.
—Voyaging Chief Matai-welu[1]

Given the anecdotal nature of most of the evidence, this account has essentially been a sea story, an impressionistic bridge between the legendary voyages that first peopled the Pacific Islands and today's better-documented outmigration to the anglophone Pacific rim. It is tempting to emphasize continuities among those three diasporas, as if a voyaging dynamic might explain the revival of long-distance travel in Oceania and its redirection outward. Yet the differences among ancient canoe epics, liminal seafaring on foreign vessels, and transnational circulation on modern aircraft offer an opportunity to reflect on the significance of our sea story in Pacific and world history.

The early voyages of discovery and settlement were undertaken by small groups over millennia. Ben Finney, an anthropologist and veteran of the *Hokule'a* reenactments since 1976, posits an ongoing process whereby overpopulation, defeat in war, or the ambitions of younger sons of chiefs stimulated journeys eastward, that is, upwind. Fishermen like Hawai'i Loa could thus find new islands and safely return on the prevailing trade winds for women and supplies. Frontier outposts could also nurture contacts with their points of origin, and unsuccessful explorers relied on the environmental escape route home. Colonization became a cultural tradition: "After all, their ancestors had been rewarded with landfalls on island after island as they sailed farther and farther into the Pacific."[2] The peopling of Oceania amazed even a world traveler like Cook, and it ranks with the migrations of Native Americans across the Bering Strait and of Bantus across the Congo forest as one of the great epics of human history. Yet in the fourteenth century A.D., when Europe's population was being devastated by the Black Death, climatic change increased the frequency of tropical storms in the Pacific and effectively ended long-distance voyaging.[3]

By the time Magellan crossed their region in 1521, most Oceanians had settled into relatively localized exchange networks. The alien intrusion did not immediately alter the course of Pacific history, but it represented a structural transformation, sporadic at first and intensifying after Cook's eighteenth-century explorations. European efforts to appropriate data from around the world into their own intellectual frameworks, coupled with mercantile desires to gain direct access to the booming economies of Asia, inaugurated a process of "peripheralization" in Oceania. Gradually, foreign ships would attract increasing numbers of Pacific Islanders away from subsistence production toward long-distance trade. In exchange for metal tools and exotic status symbols, they sold sandalwood and bêche-de-mer to China, provisions to whalers, and plantation products farther afield. This new international division of labor between Euroamerican cores of capitalism and overseas peripheries providing cheap labor and raw materials was the broad context for Oceanian's shipping out, first as captives and later for wages. The strangers' need to replenish ship crews thus stimulated a revival of Oceanian voyaging, albeit within unequal power structures. As the Pacific, like the Atlantic and Indian oceans, was integrated into an emerging global economy, *kanaka*s joined lascars, Kru, Manila-men, and slave or indentured plantation workers in mobile tropical labor pools.[4]

Meanwhile, the information that Europeans gathered overseas caused new debates among their intellectuals about the nature of the world, to the point where the pope had to decree that Native Americans were indeed human beings, not products of a separate creation. Europeans tried to fit Oceanians into their own notion of a "chain of being" in which some peoples had remained "noble savages" (or ignoble heathens) untainted by "civilization." European imaginations also imposed new geographic labels of convenience: Pacific (a misnomer), Polynesia, Melanesia and Micronesia (all Greek words), Solomon Islands and New Guinea (transfers from Israel and Africa), Marquesas and Marianas (homage to mentors). The representations of Oceanians in written records, as we have seen, were often encoded in condescending language that assumed inequality. Edward Said has called "orientalism" an invented category of study that enabled Europeans to distinguish the West from the rest. Imperialism in the Pacific would reinforce such "otherness," even when it claimed to be uplifting native peoples into Christianity or capitalism—or to be salvaging their "primitive" cultures in anthropological studies.[5]

Yet as Michel Foucault said, wherever there is power, in language or in practice, there is also resistance,[6] however overt (mutiny) or subtle (mimicry). Even Omai, tragically appropriated specimen that he was, tried in his own way to use the *limen* to advantage; and returnees Ka'iana and Hongi died of war wounds in a blaze of embellished glory. On the local level, many chiefs adopted outsider technologies of war and navigation and status symbols, and Euroamerican vessels came to depend on island provisions, exports and seamen. Despite the introduction of alien diseases and the growing indebtedness and dependency on imports that paved the way for colonialism, there was a period from the late eighteenth century to the late nineteenth century when shipping out was counterexploratory, even opportunistic. Oceanian monarchs created new forms of sovereignty, and thousands of individuals circulated in pan-Pacific "*kanaka*dom." In short, the reawakened and globalized maritime frontier was an arena of mutual interaction, where people tested their customs against novel experiences and responded creatively to differences.[7]

This dialectical encounter, as we have seen, was liminal, especially when *kanaka* voyagers boarded Euroamerican ships and explored their routes of commerce. The transformative nature of the experiment had a feedback effect on island societies, as indigenous beachcombers and returnees passed on intelligence data to their constituencies that accelerated yet also mediated the changes taking place. *Kanaka*s were not the majority of the population, but their travel experience helped to shape the thinking of chiefs and commoners alike about the wider world—its temptations as well as its dangers. Some voyagers became permanent exiles by choice, because they had seen more than they could ever explain—or abandon. Despite the structural disadvantages they often experienced as workers in someone else's enterprise, they could still extract a measure of control over their own destiny as agents in the process of globalization. They had no monopoly over cross-cultural mediation, but their seafaring helped to make the modern Pacific what it is.[8]

Today a third diaspora is flying back and forth between their islands and the Pacific rim economies of New Zealand, Australia, and the United States. It too is part of a global process, since World Bank estimates suggest that 100 million people, mainly from poor countries, are now crossing borders legally or otherwise. Like Asians and Africans in London or Algerians in France, Pacific Island migrants since World War II have often followed quasi-colonial paths, such as enlisting in the U.S. Navy, pursuing higher education in California, or being recruited for factory labor in Auckland. Many analysts regard such emigration as a sign of neo-colonial dependency, as uprooted refugees from commercialized but underdeveloped economies move powerlessly through transnational circuits leading from one exploitative sweatshop to another. In the Pacific, some observers argue that self-sustaining island development is actually discouraged by foreign aid grants (to create markets) and by remittances sent home by relatives living abroad—which often create more consumerism, not local production. Even the level of remittances tends to decline over time as migrants acculturate to their host environments, unless the diaspora is continually replenished with fresh bodies (thereby causing a "brain drain").[9]

Yet the participants themselves are not always so pessimistic. In fact, like the adventurers of old, they display active agency, using family networks and traditional notions of reciprocity as survival strategies. Epeli Hauʻofa of Tonga, himself a citizen of "Oceania" because of his own migratory background, has traced the genealogy of contemporary outmigration back to the shipping out of *kanaka* seamen, plantation workers, and Polynesian missionaries (like his family)—and beyond to the epic voyaging of the first diaspora. Despite the proletarian roles many modern migrants assume overseas and their struggle with pressures to assimilate into their host societies, he describes them as independent decision makers who fly far above the gloomy discourses of scholars: "Oceania is vast, Oceania is expanding. . . . We must not allow anyone to belittle us again, and take away our freedom."[10] Ultimately, *kanaka* voyagers and their transnational heirs reveal the complex interplay in modern history between global process and local initiative. They still dare to sail upwind.

~ *Notes* ~

Preface

1. Greg Dening, *Islands and Beaches,* 32.
2. For an overview, see K.R. Howe, preface to *Where the Waves Fall.*
3. The best is E.H. McCormick, *Omai: Pacific Envoy.* Thomas Clark's *Omai* seems to borrow from George Keate's account of Lee Boo of Palau, on 26–27. For appendices on Moyhanger (Moehanga), Kadu, and Lauri, see John Savage, *Some Account of New Zealand;* Adelbert von Chamisso, *A Voyage Around the World;* and V.M. Golovnin, *Around the World,* respectively.
4. Raymond Davis, *Reminiscences,* 230–32.
5. Namar Milne, interviews by author, Majuro, Marshall Islands, July 1989.
6. Victor Turner, *The Forest of Symbols,* 93–111. Greg Dening has extended the idea of liminality to the "ambivalent space" represented by the decks of foreign ships in Pacific ports. See *The Bounty: An Ethnographic History,* 31.
7. Joseph Conrad, closing sentence in *Heart of Darkness and The Secret Sharer.*
8. C.F. Wood, *A Yachting Cruise in the South Seas,* 6–7.
9. Herman Melville, *Moby Dick,* 60.
10. Joseph Conrad, *Lord Jim,* 275.
11. Daniel Defoe's *Robinson Crusoe* is considered the first English novel, yet it was based partly on the true adventures of Alexander Selkirk. Crusoe's obsession with creating a little England on his island includes training "Friday" in his version of "civilization." This contrasted with the romanticizing about "noble savages" by Jean-Jacques Rousseau and Denis Diderot during the French Enlightenment. The latter bemoaned Tahiti's fate after European contact. See Bill Pearson, *Rifled Sanctuaries: Some Views of the Pacific Islands in Western Literature.*
12. Clive Moore, *Kanaka,* 47.
13. See introduction, in Brij Lal, Doug Munro, and Edward Beechert, eds., *Plantation Workers.*

Chapter 1: A Second Diaspora

1. Quoted in Robert Frisbie, *The Book of Puka-Puka,* 128.
2. Epeli Hau'ofa, "Our Sea of Islands," 153. The term *diaspora* is Greek, originally denoting dispersions of exiles from their homelands. See Gérard Chaliand and Jean-Pierre Rageau, *The Penguin Atlas of Diasporas,* xiii.
3. Martha Beckwith, *Hawaiian Mythology,* 363–75. Tongan oral tradition also credits a voyager, Lo'au, with centralizing and stratifying their society. See Ian Campbell, *Island Kingdom: Tonga Ancient and Modern,* 8.
4. Quantification of the subjects of this study is almost impossible because of insufficient documentation; most of the data is anecdotal. Hence the thirty-thousand figure is only an informed "guesstimate," extrapolated from scant numbers and a sense

of overall patterns. Apart from cautious estimates of "hundreds" serving on whaleships in New Zealand or Kiribati (see Harry Morton, *The Whale's Wake,* 169, and Barrie MacDonald, *Cinderellas of the Empire,* 16–24), only Hawaiian newspapers and government records come close to firmer statistics. Ralph Kuykendall, in *The Hawaiian Kingdom,* 1: 312–13, suggests that from four to five hundred Hawaiians shipped out every year in the 1850s, based on treasury receipts for bonds paid by their captains (though apparently records of how many returned are lacking). Fur company manager George Simpson claimed in 1847 that "about a thousand" seamen left annually (*An Overland Journey Round the World,* 245, and the *Polynesian* of August 8, 1846 said that 651 sailed on whalers from 1845 to 1846, while another five hundred worked in the American Northwest for fur companies. The latter also estimated that three thousand Hawaiians were working abroad at any given time, mainly on ships—the equivalent of one-fifth of the young male population. A rough average of five hundred Hawaiian seamen shipping out annually during the peak of the whaling era, from the 1840s to the 1860s, would yield ten thousand recruits, probably a conservative figure, given the claim that three thousand were overseas at a time (though that includes four hundred beachcombers in Tahiti, and many recruits were at sea for more than a year or else reshipped). Hawai'i's location gave it disproportionate representation in the *kanaka* work force, so allowing for a century of all kinds of ship work—and the report by Samuel Morison in *The Maritime History of Massachusetts,* 185 and 323, that American whalers lost from three to four thousand crewmen to desertion every year in the 1850s, mainly in the Pacific—the thirty-thousand figure is not unreasonable and may well be too low. Today, Kiribati produces a hundred sailors yearly and has two thousand working at sea, out of a population of less than ten thousand. See Alaima Talu, "Towards Quality in Education," 237–49.

5. Grant McCall and John Connell, eds., *A World Perspective on Pacific Islander Migration: Australia, New Zealand and the U.S.A.,* 6–9.

6. Ales Hrdlicka, *The Aleutian and Commander Islands,* 142–43; Thomas McFeat, ed., *Indians of the North Pacific Coast,* 17–27; Vi Hilbert, *Haboo: Native American Stories,* 77.

7. Thor Heyerdahl, *American Indians in the Pacific;* John Murra, *The Economic Organization of the Inka State,* 140–41; Clements Markham, ed., *Reports on the Discovery of Peru,* 14–19, and *History of the Incas by Pedro Sarmiento de Gamboa,* 135–36.

8. Peter Buck, in *Vikings of the Pacific,* 322, speculates that Polynesian voyagers to the Peruvian coast acquired the sweet potato from Quechua Indians (whose word for the tuber, *kumar,* is like *kumara* in Maori) in exchange for coconuts.

9. Louise Levathes, *When China Ruled the Seas,* 25–32; Joseph Needham, *Science and Civilisation in China,* vol. 4, part 3: 548–53; Katherine Plummer, *The Shogun's Reluctant Ambassadors.*

10. Patrick Kirch, *The Evolution of the Polynesian Kingdoms;* Philip Curtin, *Cross-Cultural Trade in World History,* 159–72; Ian Hughes, *New Guinea Stone Age Trade,* 13–22.

11. Buck, *Vikings of the Pacific,* 42; Ben Finney, *Voyage of Rediscovery.*

12. Teuira Henry, *Ancient Tahiti,* 94, 230–41; Beckwith, *Hawaiian Mythology,* 364; Dennis Kawaharada, ed., *Voyaging Chiefs of Havai'i.*

13. Alice Pomponio, *Seagulls Don't Fly into the Bush,* 23; Douglas Oliver, *Oceania,* vol. 2, chapter 12.

14. William Alkire, *Coral Islanders,* 122–24; Tom Davis, *Vaka.*

15. William Lessa, *Ulithi,* 17–18.

16. Joel Bonnemaison, "Territorial Control and Mobility within niVanuatu Societies," 62–64; Robert McKnight, "Commas in Microcosm," 27–29; Asesela Ravuvu, *Facade of Democracy,* 58–60; Ranginui Walker, *Ka Whawhai Tonu Matou,* 44–55.

17. Paula Paige, ed., *The Voyage of Magellan*, 27–28; Clements Markham, ed., *The Voyages of Pedro Fernandez de Quiros*, 1: 16–29.

18. Greg Dening, ed., *The Marquesan Journal of Edward Robarts*, 180–81; Amasa Delano, *Narrative of Voyages*, 79–80.

19. George Mortimer, *Observations and Remarks Made during a Voyage*, 23–27; J.C. Beaglehole, ed., *The Voyage of the Endeavour*, 156–57.

20. Hugh Carrington, ed., *The Discovery of Tahiti*, 136–37; Dorothy Kahananui, ed., *Ka Mooolelo Hawaii*, 34–35, 181–82.

21. J.C. Beaglehole, ed., *The Voyage of the Resolution and Discovery*, part 1: 269–77; James Munford, ed., *John Ledyard's Journal*, 104–9; Henry Zimmermann, *Voyage Around the World*, 27–40. Marshall Sahlins' argument, in *Historical Metaphors and Mythical Realities*, that Cook was seen as Lono has been disputed by Gananath Obeyesekere, in *The Apotheosis of Captain Cook*, and rebutted in Sahlins' *How Natives Think*, ad nauseam. Samuel Kamakau, in *Ruling Chiefs of Hawai'i*, 92ff, uses oral traditions to show that Hawaiians were divided in their response to Cook's visit.

22. Anne Salmond, *Two Worlds*, 87–88.

23. Ibid., 88–89; Kamakau, *Ruling Chiefs*, 95, 101.

24. Markham, *Voyages of P.F. de Quiros*, 1: 25–29.

25. John Marra, *Journal of the Resolution's Voyage*, 45.

26. Beaglehole, *Voyage of the Resolution and Discovery*, part 1: 229–36, 265–67; John Rickman, *Journal of Captain Cook's Last Voyage*, 173–74; Kahananui, *Ka Mooolelo Hawaii*, 167–68; David Malo, *Hawaiian Antiquities*, 51–52.

27. Adelbert von Chamisso, *A Voyage Around the World*, 315; James Smith, ed., *Archibald Campbell*, 123–25; John Nicholas, *Narrative of a Voyage*, 1: 65; Greg Dening, *Islands and Beaches*, 18; Beaglehole, *The Voyage of the Endeavour*, 80–84.

28. Beaglehole, *Voyage of the Resolution and Discovery*, part 1: 265, 577; Alan Howard and Robert Borofsky, *Developments in Polynesian Ethnology*, 256–60; Sahlins, *Historical Metaphors and Mythical Realities*, 46–66.

29. Hugh Carrington, ed., *Discovery of Tahiti*, 137–66, 203–27; Louis Antoine de Bougainville, *A Voyage Around the World*, 213–17; James Wilson, *A Missionary Voyage*, 140; Otto von Kotzebue, *A New Voyage Around the World*, 2: 148; Kahananui, *Ka Mooolelo Hawaii*, 176–79; Pearson, "European Intimidation and the Myth of Tahiti," 199–217.

30. Frank Debenham, ed., *Voyage of Captain Bellingshausen*, 2: 261; Kotzebue, *A New Voyage*, 2: 147–48.

31. François Péron, *Mémoires du Capitaine Péron*, 2: 148.

32. Robert Rogers, *Destiny's Landfall*, 13, 19; Kotzebue, *A New Voyage*, 2: 187. For "bummer," see Log of the *Avola*, June 17, 1872. The term is still used today by sailors to describe salespeople who board ships, as I saw in Singapore. When my captain tried to keep the vendors and prostitutes off, a policeman said, "It is the way of life of Singapore."

33. Carrington, *Discovery of Tahiti*, 146, 185.

34. Frederick Beechey, *Narrative of a Voyage*, 1: 274; Bolton Corney, ed., *The Quest and Occupation of Tahiti*, 2: 127; Edmund Fanning, *Voyages Around the World*, 126, 147.

35. Robert Jarman, *Journal of a Voyage*, 117–18; Nicholas, *Narrative of a Voyage*, 1: 285–86; Benjamin Morrell, *Narrative of Four Voyages*, 372.

36. Charles Wilkes, *Narrative of the United States Exploring Expedition*, 3: 170, and 4: 191; Shineberg, *Trading Voyages*, 119; Bruce Cartwright Jr., "Extract from the Diary of Ebenezer Townsend Jr.," 20; Log *Seashell*, 9/3/1853, 4/28/54.

37. Nicholas Thomas, *Entangled Objects*, 110–16; Bougainville, *Voyage*, 214;

Kotzebue, *New Voyage,* 2: 189–90; Beechey, *Narrative,* 1: 271–72; Beaglehole, *Voyage of the Resolution and Adventure,* 270, 382–83, 531, 578; Francis Hezel, *Foreign Ships in Micronesia,* 266.

38. Francis Olmstead, *Incidents on a Whaling Voyage,* 210; R.G. Jameson, *New Zealand, Southern Australia and New South Wales,* 235; Beechey, *Narrative,* 1: 307–8. For an overview of trader and missionary impact, see K.R. Howe, *Where the Waves Fall,* chapters 5 and 6.

39. William Armstrong, *Around the World with a King,* 173; Kotzebue, *A New Voyage,* 2: 233, 273–74; Olmstead, *Incidents,* 190–91; Caroline Ralston, *Grass Huts and Warehouses;* David Stannard, *Before the Horror.*

40. Kotzebue, *A Voyage of Discovery,* 2: 47–48, 68–69, and *A New Voyage,* 2: 187–88; G.H. von Langsdorff, *Voyages and Travels,* 1: 186; Caroline Ralston, "Hawaii 1778–1854," 21–40

41. Howe, *Where the Waves Fall,* 127–40; Niel Gunson, "Pomare II of Tahiti and Polynesian Imperialism," 70–71; Frederick Bennett, *Narrative of a Whaling Voyage,* 132; J. Wilson, *A Missionary Voyage,* 59–61, 168.

42. J. Wilson, *Missionary Voyage,* 13–14; Niel Gunson, "Journal of a Visit to Raivavae," 201; Gunson, "Pomare II," 69; Beechey, *Narrative,* 1: 281–83; Niel Gunson, "An Account of the Mamaia or Visionary Heresy of Tahiti," 216–40.

43. Mortimer, *Observations and Remarks,* 48–49; William Bligh, *A Voyage to the South Sea,* 121–22; Douglas Oliver, ed., *Return to Tahiti,* 227; Edward Edwards, *Voyage of the H.M.S. 'Pandora,'* 119; J. Wilson, *Missionary Voyage,* 138–43; F. Bennett, *Narrative,* 71.

44. Kahananui, *Ka Mooolelo Hawaii,* 170; Kamakau, *Ruling Chiefs,* 97–98, 161–62; Gabriel Franchère, *Journal of a Voyage,* 61–64.

45. J. Smith, *Archibald Campbell,* 111–15, 153–54; Hiram Bingham, *A Residence of Twenty-One Years in the Sandwich Islands,* 44–52.

46. Peter Corney, *Voyages in the North Pacific,* 71; Sheldon Dibble, *A History of the Sandwich Islands,* 61; William Wilson, ed., *With Lord Byron at the Sandwich Islands,* 38–39

47. Kotzebue, *A New Voyage,* 2: 221–28; Bingham, *Residence,* 125–26; Simpson, *Overland Journey,* 2: 18; G.D. Gilman, "Old Time Hawaiian Coasting Service," 85–87; W. Wilson, *With Lord Byron,* 19–20.

48. Mary Kawena Pukui and Alfons Korn, eds., *The Echo of Our Song,* 83–85; Mifflin Thomas, *Schooner from Windward,* 26–61; Andrew Farrell, ed., *John Cameron's Odyssey,* 216–32; Thomas Thrum, "Hawaiian Maritime History," 72–74.

49. W.H. Dawbin, "The Maori Went A-Whaling," 19. For an overview of Maori relations with British explorers, traders, and missionaries, see Howe, *Where the Waves Fall,* 206–17.

50. Robert McNab, ed., *Historical Records of New Zealand,* 1: 257–63, 316–29, 608–64.

51. E. Dieffenbach, *Travels in New Zealand,* 2: 108; McNab, *Historical Records,* 1: 295; John Elder, ed., *Letters and Journals of Samuel Marsden,* 399; Felix Maynard and Alexandre Dumas, eds., *The Whalers,* 176; Murray Bathgate, "Maori River and Ocean Going Craft," 362–63; Marion Diamond, "Queequeg's Cremates," 135–36.

52. Morrell, *Narrative,* 372–74; Dora Head, ed., *The Journal of Charles O'Hara Booth,* 218; Frank Bullen, *The Cruise of the Cachalot,* 232–38; Jarman, *Journal,* 149; Dawbin, "Maori," 22; Dieffenbach, *Travels,* 1: 52–54.

53. Francis Hezel, *The First Taint of Civilization,* 47–48; Francis Hezel and Marjorie Driver, "From Conquest to Colonization"; Charles Le Gobien, *Histoire des Iles Marianes,* 272–73, 377; Vicente Diaz, "Simply Chamorro."

54. Kotzebue, *Voyage of Discovery,* 2: 230–43; Hezel, *Foreign Ships,* 18; Rogers, *Destiny's Landfall,* chapters 1–5.

55. Howe, *Where the Waves Fall,* 281–87.

56. Chamisso, *Voyage,* 313–14; Kotzebue, *New Voyage,* 2: 220; *The Polynesian,* August 8, 1846.

57. *Wahine* is the Hawaiian word for woman (similar to *vahine* in Tahitian), and through ship pidgin it became a palimpsest among seamen for native females, with a sexual undertone. Terms like squaws, niggers, or trollops were also used.

58. Chamisso, *Voyage,* 119; Zimmermann, *Voyage,* 28; Kahananui, *Mooolelo,* 168; Kamakau, *Ruling Chiefs,* 101; Ralston, "Changes in the Lives of Ordinary Women in Early Post-Contact Hawaii," 45–64.

59. J.F.G. de La Pérouse, *A Voyage Round the World,* 129; Marra, *Journal,* 43–44; Rickman, *Journal,* 50–51; Helen Rosenman, ed., *An Account in Two Volumes of Two Voyages,* 1: 102–6; Richard Cruise, *Journal of a Ten Months' Residence in New Zealand,* 120–21, 173; David Hanlon, *Upon a Stone Altar,* 78–80; Journal of the *Chili,* July 1856.

60. Beverley Hooper, ed., *With Captain James Cook,* 68; Debenham, *Voyage,* 2: 263; Nicholas, *Narrative,* 1: 201–10; Cruise, *Journal,* 142–79; Edward Wakefield, *Adventure in New Zealand,* 1: 46–50, 322–30; Elliott Snow, ed., *The Sea, the Ship and the Sailor,* 173.

61. Beaglehole, *Voyage of the Resolution and Adventure,* 225; Carrington, *Discovery of Tahiti,* 184–85, 208; Marra, *Journal,* 18, 102; Owen Rutter, *The Journal of James Morrison,* 31.

62. Bingham, *A Residence,* 283–88; Dibble, *History,* 190–95; Cruise, *Journal,* 178; J. Smith, *Archibald Campbell,* 135–37; Sahlins, *Historical Metaphors,* 55–66.

63. Beaglehole, *Voyage of the Resolution and Adventure,* 413–14, and *Voyage of the Resolution and Discovery,* part 2: 1218–22; John Meares, *Voyages Made,* 28; W. Kaye Lamb, ed., *A Voyage of Discovery,* 2: 688–89, and 3: 892–95.

64. J. Wilson, *Missionary Voyage,* 113–14.

65. Dening, *Marquesan Journal,* 122–35, 203–5; Edward Lucatt, *Rovings in the Pacific,* 1: 188–89.

66. Kahananui, *Mooolelo,* 245–47; Pauline King, ed., *Robert Dampier,* 50; *Ke Au Okoa,* July 31, 1865 to February 1866; Liliuokalani, *Hawaii's Story by Hawaii's Queen,* 132, 181.

67. McNab, *Historical Records,* 1: 378; R. Gerard Ward, ed., *American Activities in the Central Pacific,* 3: 231; John McCluer, *Journal of a Voyage to the Pelew Islands,* 259; Peter Dillon, *Narrative and Successful Result of a Voyage,* 1: 241–48, 296–97, and 2: 228.

68. Pukui and Korn, *Echo of Our Song,* 103–5.

Chapter 2: Shipping Out

1. Quoted in Frisbie, *Book of Puka-Puka,* 2.

2. Hughes, *New Guinea Stone Age Trade,* 17; Leonard Andaya, *The World of Maluku,* 89; Michael Smithies, "A New Guinean and the Royal Society," 365–71. *Papuan* is a Malay word for someone with curly hair, and Europeans named New Guinea for the dark-skinned inhabitants who they thought resembled the people of the Guinean coast in West Africa. For an overview of Pacific exploration, see the trilogy by O.H.K. Spate or chapter 4 in Howe, *Where the Waves Fall.*

3. Rogers, *Destiny's Landfall,* 10.

4. Clements Markham, ed., *Early Spanish Voyages to the Strait of Magellan,* 50–69. Urdaneta said in 1527 that the Spaniards had 105 surviving men at Tidore (p. 53), but in 1528 Saavedra found 120 (pp. 124–26). Did the latter count the surviving Cham-

orros in his estimate, while the former had not? Perhaps the Chamorros got no farther than the Philippines, as Hezel suggests in *First Taint,* 14. After 1565, Manila became the Spanish base for trade with Asia. See Spate, *The Spanish Lake.*

5. See George Foster, *Culture and Conquest,* who argues that only a frontier version of Spanish culture was introduced to the American colonies, one born of the seven-hundred-year *reconquista* against the Muslims who first invaded Spain in A.D. 711 and were not driven out until 1492, when Columbus was hired to find gold in Asia for another crusade to liberate Jerusalem.

6. Paige, *Voyage of Magellan,* 27–31; Hezel, *First Taint,* 11.

7. Markham, *Early Spanish Voyages,* 61–69, 126–28.

8. Rogers, *Destiny's Landfall,* 14–15; Andrew Sharp, *Adventurous Armada,* 37–56.

9. Markham, *Voyages of P.F. de Quiros,* 1: 29, 224–77, 299–311, and 2: 437–40, 490–502; Celsus Kelly, ed., *Australia de Espiritu Santo,* 1: 187–88, 230–36. Quiros's ship was the *San Pedro y San Pablo,* and he named his two voyagers to Mexico Pedro and Pablo. Because Catholics often received the name of the patron saint of their birthday, Quiros's use of his own name, Pedro, was thus a double vanity. The only Spanish legacy to Melanesia was a few place names, including the Solomon Islands, Santa Cruz Islands, and Santo.

10. Henry Stevens, ed., *New Light on the Discovery of Australia,* 145–71.

11. Dening, *Islands and Beaches,* 23; Spate, *Spanish Lake,* and *Monopolists and Freebooters.*

12. William Dampier, *A New Voyage Round the World,* 342–67.

13. Jean-Jacques Rousseau, *The First and Second Discourses,* 176–83, 228–29; Bernard Smith, *European Vision and the South Pacific,* 133–54; Spate, *Paradise Found and Lost,* 185–263.

Post-modernist critics have recently attacked the so-called Enlightenment project for suggesting that Western reason was more progressive than alternative worldviews, both in Europe and abroad. Such arguments have merit, particularly in cases of imperialistic "brainwashing," but reason has actually been a lonely voice in modern world history, as two devastating world wars and a "cold war" demonstrate.

14. Helen Wallis, ed., *Carteret's Voyage Round the World,* 200–2.

15. Carrington, *Discovery of Tahiti,* 187–89.

16. Bougainville, *Voyage,* 216–76; John Dunmore, *French Explorers in the Pacific,* 83; Maurice Thiéry, *Bougainville,* 214–15.

17. Bougainville, *Voyage,* 278–92; W. Pearson, "European Intimidation." When he published his journal, Bougainville tried to answer criticism of his taking Ahutoru on his fatal journey away from Tahiti by stressing the man's voluntarism.

18. Denis Diderot, *Rameau's Nephew and Other Works,* 186–92, 226.

19. J.C. Beaglehole, ed., *The Endeavour Journal of Joseph Banks,* 1: 270–316, and *Voyage of the Endeavour,* 117, 563–64.

20. Beaglehole, *Endeavour Journal,* 1: 368.

21. Ibid., 314–31; Beaglehole, *Voyage of the Endeavour,* 140–53, and *Voyage of Resolution and Adventure,* 235; Stanfield Parkinson, ed., *Journal of a Voyage,* 73, 88–87, 182.

22. Beaglehole, *Voyage of the Resolution and Adventure,* 211–29, 399–400; George Forster, *A Voyage Round the World,* 1: 362–64, 388, 400; Hooper, *With Captain James Cook,* 66–77; Rutter, *Journal,* 112. The "O" in Omai is really a particle that marks the subject of a sentence, especially proper names, and "mai" is a directional indicator, for toward the speaker or from a place. Hence, embedded in the name that Omai was called was the notion that he was a traveler.

23. Beaglehole, *Voyage of the Resolution and Adventure,* 399.

24. G. Forster, *Voyage,* 1: 411–48, 495, 504–29, 562–82; Michael Hoare, ed., *The*

Resolution Journal of Johann Reinhold Forster, 2: 370, and 3: 422–27, 491–92; Beaglehole, *Voyage of the Resolution and Adventure,* 230–51, 295, 356, 377; Rickman, *Journal,* 51–55, 85; Zimmermann, *Voyage,* 14–20.

25. Hoare, *Resolution Journal,* 3: 509–22; Rutter, *Journal,* 53–75; Greg Dening, *The Bounty,* 39; Oliver, *Return to Tahiti,* 227, 240.

26. B. Corney, *Quest and Occupation of Tahiti,* 1: 9–15, 254, 342; 2: 1–4, 59, 87, 148–73, 304–10; and 3: 210.

27. John Dunmore, ed., *The Expedition of the St. Jean-Baptiste,* 98–100, 154–56, 198–201; McNab, *Historical Records,* 2: 245–57, 277–315.

28. Beaglehole, *Endeavour Journal,* 1: 403–406, and *Voyage of Endeavour,* 170–72.

29. George Keate, *An Account of the Pelew Islands,* 240–54. Karen Niro, in "Linkages between Yap and Palau," suggests "Lebuu" was part-Yapese. He is not remembered in Palau.

30. Meares, *Voyages,* 9–10.

31. McNab, *Historical Records,* 1: 120–93, 289, 334–51, and 2: 539–42; Elder, *Letters and Journals,* 63–70.

32. J. Wilson, *Missionary Voyage,* 81, 120–38, 147; William Crook, "An Account of the Marquesas," 150; Thomas Hopoo, "Memoirs," 43–44; Catherine Stauder, "George, Prince of Hawaii," 32; Cruise, *Journal,* 31; John Williams, *Missionary Enterprises in the South-Sea Islands,* 31–67; Noel Rutherford, "George Tupou I and Shirley Baker," 157–58.

33. Siméon Delmas, *Essai d'histoire de la Mission des Iles Marquises,* 21–22; Mortimer, *Observations and Remarks,* 31, 48–49, 55; Frank Broeze, ed., *A Merchant's Perspective,* 71; Rosenman, *An Account,* 1: 106–7; Wakefield, *Adventure,* 1: 32–33.

34. John Savage, *Some Account of New Zealand,* 36–41, 94–95; Edwin Dwight, ed., *The Memoirs of Henry Obookiah,* 6–8; J.C. Mullett, *A Five Years' Whaling Voyage,* 44–46; Michael Roe, ed., *The Journal and Letters of Captain Charles Bishop,* 101–41; Harold Williams, ed., *One Whaling Family,* 326; Log *Cortes,* 2/16/1844; Log *Arabella,* 12/24/1834.

35. C.S. Stewart, *A Visit to the South Seas,* 52; Beechey, *Narrative,* 1: 293; Dillon, *Narrative,* 2: 119–21; Wilkes, *Narrative,* 3: 166–71, 249; V. M. Golovnin, *Around the World in the Kamchatka,* 176; John Erskine, *Journal of a Cruise among the Islands,* 398–407; Julien Laferrière, *Voyages aux Iles Tonga Tabou, Wallis et Foutouna,* 457–58.

36. John Davies, *The History of the Tahitian Mission,* 165–66; Beechey, *Narrative,* 1: 243, 281–83; Lucatt, *Rovings,* 1: 240–61; Wilkes, *Narrative,* 1: 328; Tetens, *Among the Savages of the South Seas,* 20, 67–69; W.L. Allardyce, "Rotooma and the Rotoomans," 132–33.

37. Richard Greer, "Wandering Kamaainas," 222; *The Friend,* September 4, 1844; Farrell, *John Cameron's Odyssey,* 178–79, 211; Davis, *Reminiscences,* 199; *Ka Nona Nona,* April 17,1844.

38. Ross Cox, *The Columbia River,* 44; Franchère, *Journal,* 70; Alexander Spoehr, "Fur Traders in Hawai'i," 33; Wilkes, *Narrative,* 3: 386; Delano, *Narrative,* 392.

39. McNab, *Historical Records,* 1: 257–58, and 2: 316–29; Olmstead, *Incidents,* 277; H.Williams, *One Whaling Family,* 267–68; Laferrière, *Voyages,* 469; Diamond, "Queequeg's Crewmates," 132; C. Wood, *A Yachting Cruise,* 10, 16–17.

40. C. Wood, *A Yachting Cruise,* 6–7; Melville, *Moby Dick,* 60–61; Everard Im Thurn and Leonard Wharton, eds., *The Journal of William Lockerby,* 75–76.

Chapter 3: Rites of Passage

1. Una Robertson, *Mariners' Mealtimes and Other Daily Details of Life,* 2; N.A.M. Rodger, *The Wooden World,* 60.

2. Rodger, *The Wooden World*, 345–46. For Euroamerican maritime culture, also see Marcus Rediker, *Between the Devil and the Deep Blue Sea;* Robertson, *Mariners' Mealtimes;* Knut Weibust, *Deep Sea Sailors;* Charles Kindleberger, *Mariners and Markets;* Margaret Ceighton, *Rites and Passages;* and John Masefield, *Sea Life in Nelson's Time.*

3. For nonwhite seamen, see Spate, *Spanish Lake,* 223; George Brooks, *The Kru Mariner;* Hugh Tinker, *A New System of Slavery,* 41; Rhys Richards, "The Manilla-Men and Pacific Commerce"; Olmstead, *Incidents,* 45.

4. Melville, *Moby Dick,* 186; Morison, *Maritime History,* 158.

5. This rough estimate is based on the following data: Wilkes, *Narrative,* 5: 485, describes the American whaling fleet as numbering about 16,000 sailors in 1845. Morison, *Maritime History,* 185 and 323, estimates that American whaling crews lost as many as 3,000–4,000 deserters annually in the 1850s, most of whom were replaced by *kanakas.* R. Schmitt, *Demographic Statistics,* 182, suggests that the total number of Hawaiians overseas remained at 3,500–4,000 from 1848 to 1860, the peak of whaling, and *The Polynesian,* August 8, 1846, gives a figure of 3,000 for Hawaiians then working on foreign ships. Hence the one-fifth estimate, which is probably safe considering that Hawaiians did not monopolize *kanaka* positions. It also correlates well with the known proportion of *kanakas* in crews like the *Addison's* in 1856–60, in Stanton Garner, ed., *The Captain's Best Mate,* 252–65.

6. Olmstead, *Incidents,* 327; J. Ross Browne, *Etchings of a Whaling Cruise,* 504–5.

7. Melville, *Moby Dick,* 36.

8. Rodger, *Wooden World,* 207.

9. Kindleberger, *Mariners and Markets,* xii.

10. Masefield, *Sea Life,* 57–59; Salmond, *Two Worlds,* 107–11; Rediker, *Between,* 3–5; Dening, *Bounty,* 17–18.

11. Rediker, *Between,* 31–33, 80–83; Richard Henry Dana, *Two Years Before the Mast,* 320–25; Morrell, *Narrative,* 468; Browne, *Etchings,* 191, 504; Beaglehole, *Voyage of the Resolution and Adventure,* xxxiii.

12. Masefield, *Sea Life,* 180–81.

13. Robertson, *Mariners' Mealtimes,* 9, 18; Kindleberger, *Mariners,* xv, 14; Morison, *Maritime,* 323–24.

14. Wilkes, *Narrative,* 4: 113.

15. Jacques Arago, *Narrative of a Voyage Round the World,* 1: 29–36; Charles Ferguson, *Experiences of a Forty-Niner,* 4–5; Edward Bell, *Journal of the Chatham,* 18; Creighton, *Rites and Passages,* 117.

16. Louis Kornitzer, *The Pearl Trader,* 1–2; Melville, *Moby Dick,* 11–16; Rediker, *Between,* 7–8, 80. For an extended discussion of motivations, see Kindleberger, *Mariners and Markets,* 1–24.

17. Bullen, *Cruise,* 1; Browne, *Etchings,* 373–74; Dibble, *History,* 29; Dillon, *Narrative,* 1: 207; Charles de Varigny, *Fourteen Years in the Sandwich Islands,* 133; Dana, *Two Years,* 111; Frederic Howay, "Brig Owhyhee on the Columbia," 325. Kindleberger, in *Mariners and Markets,* 56–58, reports that a common cause of death on British warships was falling off the gangway in the dark when returning to the ship after drinking. "Drunk nets" had to be rigged under the plank. In fact, naval authorities used grog to pacify their crews.

18. Keate, *Account,* 268–69; Rosenman, *Account,* 1: 97; Davis, *Reminiscences,* 204; Dibble, *History,* 55–56.

19. Beaglehole, *Endeavour Journal,* 1: 314; Mullett, *Five Years,* 46; Bougainville, *Voyage,* 275–78; J. Williams, *Missionary Enterprises,* 259–60; Rosenman, *Account* 1: 203.

20. C. Moore, *Kanaka,* 47; Hooper, *With Captain James Cook,* 80; Dunmore, *Expedition,* 201, 265–66; Kotzebue, *Voyage,* 2: 166; Williams, *Missionary Enterprises,* 260; Rosenman, *Account,* 1: 97–99.

21. Bougainville, *Voyage,* 333–35; Frederic Lutke, *Voyage autour du Monde,* 1: 293; Morrell, *Narrative,* 466.

22. Bingham, *Residence,* 464.

23. William Giles, *A Cruize in a Queensland Labour Vessel,* 43, 223–26; Snow, *The Sea,* 173; Bullen, *Cruise,* 222.

24. Dana, *Two Years,* 1; Robertson, *Mariners' Mealtimes,* 7–8; Rediker, *Between,* 11.

25. Log *Seashell,* October 2, 1854; Stewart, *Visit,* 224.

26. Davis, *Reminiscences,* 331; John Papa I'i, *Fragments of Hawaiian History,* 87.

27. Keate, *Account,* 268; Beaglehole, *Endeavour Journal,* 1: 403–4; Debenham, *Voyage,* 1: 256; Erskine, *Journal,* 28.

28. Kotzebue, *Voyage,* 2: 125–26; Rickman, *Journal,* 53–54.

29. Rosenman, *Account,* 1: 107; Dillon, *Narrative,* 1: 202, 214; McNab, *Historical Records,* 1: 635–36; Arthur Thomson, *The Story of New Zealand,* 1: 281.

30. Stewart, *Visit,* 321; Olmstead, *Incidents,* 193, 284–88; James Goodenough, *Journal of Commodore Goodenough,* 298.

31. Mark Kaplanoff, ed., *Joseph Ingraham's Journal of the Brigantine HOPE,* 47–48, 54; G. Forster, *Voyage,* 1: 354.

32. Bougainville, *Voyage,* 278–80; Nicholas, *Narrative,* 1: 79, 122; *Cruise, Journal,* 26.

33. G. Forster, *Voyage,* 1: 419–20; Dunmore, *French Explorers,* 88, 170–71; Beaglehole, *Voyage of the Resolution and Adventure,* 892. White seamen also sailed under assumed names. One mustered on the *Bounty* as Alexander Smith, then reverted to John Adams on Pitcairn. Dening, *Bounty,* 86.

34. Davis, *Reminiscences,* 198–201; Log *Petrel,* 5/3/1871; Garner, *Captain's Best Mate,* 258; Roe, *Journal,* 306–7.

35. Morrell, *Narrative,* 466; Thomas Jacobs, *Scenes, Incidents and Adventures in the Pacific Ocean,* 23; E. Bell, *Journal,* 1: 145; Lamb, *Voyage,* 2: 451; Erskine, *Journal,* 179, 291; Cartwright, "Extract," 20; Dillon, *Narrative,* 1: 248; J.W. Davidson, *Peter Dillon,* 92–93, 106, 120.

36. Broeze, *Merchant's Perspective,* 74; Golovnin, *Voyage,* 187; Tetens, *Among the Savages,* 77; *Cruise, Journal,* 64–65; Log *Two Brothers,* 9/15/1859, 9/15/1861; Dillon, *Narrative,* 1: 103; Stevens, *New Light,* 145; Farrell, *Odyssey,* 164–70.

37. Roger Keesing,"Plantation Networks, Plantation Culture," 163–64; Bougainville, *Voyage,* 264; Anne Ellis, ed., *The Early Diary of Frances Burney,* 1: 333–35; B. Corney, *Quest and Occupation,* 1: 349–55; McNab, *Historical Records,* 1: 637, and 2: 257; Nicholas, *Narrative,* 1: 74.

38. John Jones, *Life and Adventure in the South Pacific by a Roving Printer,* 36; Davidson, *Dillon,* 96; Mullett, *Five Years,* 44.

39. John Turnbull, *A Voyage Round the World,* 2: 10–12; Dwight, *Memoirs,* 10–11.

40. Dunmore, *Expedition,* 264–65. In Sam Low's film, *The Navigators,* Mau Piailug, who navigated the *Hokule'a* from Hawai'i to Tahiti in 1976, speaks of the authority of the navigator of a Pacific voyaging canoe, and archaeologist Patrick Kirch suggests that the Hawaiian chiefly hierarchy may have derived from the "society of the canoe."

41. Marra, *Journal,* 219–20; Bougainville, *Voyage,* 335.

42. Kotzebue, *Voyage,* 1: 126–30, and 3: 100–101; Rickman, *Journal,* 55–57.

43. Jacobs, *Scenes,* 24; *Cruise, Journal,* 27–28, 64–65; Elder, *Letters,* 61–67, 87.

44. Kotzebue, *Voyage*, 1: 319, and 2: 130; McNab, *Historical Records*, 1: 636.

45. Jacobs, *Scenes*, 87; Debenham, *Voyage*, 2: 309.

46. Nicholas, *Narrative*, 2: 216–17; McNab, *Historical Records*, 2: 226; Beaglehole, *Endeavour Journal*, (1962) 1: 403; Kotzebue, *Voyage*, 2: 122–30; Armstrong, *Around the World*, 9–10; Robert Young, *The Southern World*, 233; Rosenman, *Account*, 1: 203–6; Cruise, *Journal*, 23–27.

47. Wilkes, *Narrative*, 2: 17; 4: 112–13; and 5: 485; Bullen, *Cruise*, 4.

48. Erskine, *Journal*, 367; F. Bennett, *Narrative*, 71, 285; Hoare, *Resolution Journal*, 3: 371; Beaglehole, *Endeavour Journal*, 1: 403; Rosenman, *Account*, 1: 97; Nicholas, *Narrative*, 1: 67; Cruise, *Journal*, 23, 157.

49. Mullett, *Five Years*, 44–46; Bernice Judd, ed., "Native Hawaiians in London," 14.

50. Davis, *Reminiscences*, 198–207; John Webster, *The Last Cruise of 'the Wanderer,'* 2–3.

51. Kotzebue, *Voyage*, 2: 123; Rhys Richards, "Indigenous Beachcombers," 2–3; Wilson, *Missionary Voyage*, 92, 120; Roe, *Journal*, 240; McNab, *Historical Records*, 1: 664.

52. Diamond, "Queequeg's Crewmates," 127.

53. Herman Melville, *Omoo*, 72; A. Grove Day, *Mad About Islands*, 74; Thomson, *Story*, 1: 248; H. Williams, *Whaling Family*, 267–68, 298.

54. David Hanlon and Epensio Eperiam, "The Sage of Mesiol"; Samuel Morison, "Boston Traders in the Hawaiian Islands," 27; Edwin Rich, ed., *History of the Hudson's Bay Company*, 2: 615; K.R. Howe, "Tourists, Sailors and Labourers"; Wood, *Yachting Cruise*, 73; Straubel, *Whaling Journal*, 114–15.

55. Morison, *Maritime History*, 158, 323–24; Frederick Schmitt, *Mark Well the Whale*, 26.

56. Paul Gordon and Danny Reilly, "Guest Workers of the Sea," 74; Erskine, *Journal*, 345–46.

57. Frederic Howay, *Voyages of the "Columbia" to the Northwest Coast*, 150–51; Roe, *Journal*, 306–7; Langsdorff, *Voyages*, 1: 187; Edwin Rich, ed., *Simpson's 1828 Journey to the Columbia*, 1: 103; Stephen Reynolds, *The Voyage of the New Hazard*, 143–45; Cox, *Columbia River*, 45; Charles Frouin, *Journal de Bord*, 310.

58. Giles, *Cruize*, 38, note 9; Diamond, "Queequeg's Crewmates," 128; Elder, *Letters*, 63–67.

59. A.T. Yarwood, *Samuel Marsden*, 169, quoting Marsden to Pratt, 11/28/1814; Elder, *Letters*, 136, quoting Marsden to Pratt, 9/30/1814.

60. Davidson, *Peter Dillon*, 130–31; F. Bennett, *Narrative*, 66; Erskine, *Journal*, 398–407.

61. P. Corney, *Voyages*, 105; Reynolds, *Voyage*, 143–45.

62. Webster, *Last Cruise*, 42–43; Log *Josephine*, October 15, 1849; Log *Elizabeth*, February 25, 1849; McNab, *Historical Records*, 1: 668; Kotzebue, *Voyage*, 2: 140–41.

63. Varigny, *Fourteen Years*, 105, 133–34; Wilkes, *Narrative*, 4: 220.

64. *The Friend*, September 4, 1844; Garner, *Captain's Best Mate*, 255–58; F. Schmitt, *Mark Well*, 27–28, 121; Greer, "Wandering Kamaainas," 222; Log *Emerald*, May 3, 1834; Litton Forbes, *Two Years in Fiji*, 226; Straubel, *Whaling Journal*, 114–15.

65. Cox, *Columbia River*, 45; F. Schmitt, *Mark Well*, 94; Davidson, *Dillon*, 96; J.S. Polack, *Manners and Customs of the New Zealanders*, 2: 121; Jameson, *New Zealand*, 238; Jarman, *Journal*, 149; Ward, *American Activities*, 3: 33–34, and 4: 39–40; Thomas, *Schooner*, 42; Hezel, *Foreign Ships*, 86; Alastair Couper, "Islanders at Sea," 234.

66. Diamond, "Queequeg's Crewmates,"126–34; Wakefield, *Adventure*, 1: 21, 32–33; Lucatt, *Rovings*, 1: 240, 308–18; Wilkes, *Narrative*, 1: 328; Melville, *Omoo*, 28.

Chapter 4: Contested Decks

1. Witi Ihimaera, *The Whale Rider*, 5–6.
2. Lal, Munro, and Beechert, *Plantation Workers*, 1–43; Syed Alatas, *The Myth of the Lazy Native;* Lucatt, *Rovings*, 1: 325–27.
3. A. Grove Day, ed., *Louis Becke*, 44–45.
4. Davis, *Reminiscences*, 331; Giles, *Cruize*, 37; Nicholas, *Narrative*, 1: 74, 255–58.
5. Dana, *Two Years*, 117; Kotzebue, *Voyage*, 1: 250, and 3: 100; Chamisso, *Voyage*, 160.
6. F. Bennett, *Narrative*, 285; McNab, *Historical Records*, 2: 226–27; Wakefield, *Adventure*, 1: 33; Cruise, *Journal*, 26.
7. James Munger, *Two Years in the Pacific*, 64–70; Kotzebue, *Voyage*, 2: 132, and 3: 104; Bullen, *Cruise*, 211; Wilkes, *Narrative*, 3: 27; Dana, *Two Years*, 10–13, 117; Bingham, *Residence*, 67; P. Corney, *Voyages*, 105–106.
8. Arago, *Narrative*, 1: 26–29; Weibust, *Deep Sea*, 135–46.
9. J.A. Carnes, *Journal of a Voyage*, 18.
10. Quoted in Wilkes, *Narrative*, 3: 76; Epeli Hau'ofa, "The Future of Our Past," 157–58.
11. Wakefield, *Adventure*, 1: 75. "Jim Crow" was a hapless nineteenth-century minstrel caricature. See Wilkes, *Narrative*, 2: 55, and 3: 130, and Ward, *American Activities*, 5: 179. Later, the same stereotype was applied to racial segregation laws in the post–Civil War American South.
12. Kotzebue, *Voyage*, 2: 126–27, 141; Chamisso, *Voyage*, 160.
13. Wood, *Yachting Cruise*, 25; Beaglehole, *Voyage of the Resolution and Adventure*, 839.
14. Nicholas, *Narrative*, 1: 255–58; Kotzebue, *Voyage*, 3: 102; Chamisso, *Voyage*, 160.
15. Cruise, *Journal*, 117; Tetens, *Among*, 69; H. Williams, *Whaling Family*, 267–68.
16. F. Bennett, *Narrative*, 285; Dillon, *Narrative*, 1: 275–79; Davidson, *Peter Dillon*, 92–93, 119–22.
17. Lucatt, *Rovings*, 1: 99; Stewart, *Visit*, 1: 220, and 2: 13; Beaglehole, *Voyage of the Resolution and Adventure*, 401; Bingham, *Residence*, 89; Farrell, *Odyssey*, 216.
18. Kotzebue, *Voyage*, 3: 101; Beaglehole, *Endeavour Journal*, 1: 314, 389, and *Voyage of the Endeavour*, 111.
19. Dillon, *Narrative*, 1: 107, 252; McNab, *Historical Records*, 2: 217–18; F. Bennett, *Narrative*, 285–86; Ward, *American Activities*, 5: 179; Bougainville, *Voyage*, 267, 276.
20. Hoare, *Resolution Journal*, 3: 393; Wakefield, *Adventure*, 1: 21; Hopoo, "Memoirs," 44; Dwight, *Memoirs*, 9; *The Friend*, September 14, 1844.
21. Webster, *Last Cruise*, 23.
22. Morison, *Maritime History*, 7.
23. Markham, *Voyages of Quiros*, no. 14: 311; B. Corney, *Quest and Occupation*, 3: 210; H.E. Maude, *Slavers in Paradise;* Dillon, *Narrative*, 1: 102–12; Robertson, *Mealtimes*, 50.
24. Jean Randier, *Men and Ships around Cape Horn*, 129; Wilson, *Missionary Voyages*, 113–14; Mullett, *Five Years*, 47; Dening, *Marquesan Journal*, 170; Log *Roman II*, January 11, 1852.
25. Garner, *Captain's Best Mate*, 130–31; Ward, *American Activities*, 3: 360.
26. Alexander Ross, *Adventures of the First Settlers on the Oregon*, 59–66, 74; Franchère, *Journal*, 72–74.

27. Delano, *Narrative*, 393; Meares, *Voyages*, 27.

28. A.M. Hocart, "Fiji and Rotuma"; Nicholas, *Narrative*, 1: 119; Dillon, *Narrative*, 2: 324–25.

29. Wakefield, *Adventure*, 1: 67; F. Bennett, *Narrative*, 156.

30. Farrell, *Odyssey*, 206; Cruise, *Journal*, 27, 208; Elder, *Letters*, 64.

31. I'i, *Fragments*, 157; Mary Kawena Pukui and Samuel Elbert, *Hawaiian Dictionary*, 36.

32. P. Corney, *Voyages*, 15; Broeze, *Merchant's Perspective*, 74–75; Wilkes, *Narrative*, 4: 112, 206; Ward, *American Activities*, 2: 74–75, 161–63.

33. Saul Riesenberg, ed., *A Residence of Eleven Years in New Holland and Caroline Islands by James F. O'Connell*, 87; Elmo Hohman, *The American Whaleman*, 185–89.

34. Browne, *Etchings*, 24, 191, 308; Creighton, *Rites*, 122.

35. Davis, *Reminiscences*, 203–5; Kindleberger, *Mariners*, 44.

36. Nicholas, *Narrative*, 1: 49–50, 64, 255–58.

37. Cruise, *Journal*, 24–36, 119–20, 207; Dana, *Two Years*, 117.

38. Melville, *Omoo*, 13, 70–94; Davis, *Reminiscences*, 215–43, 284–88; Reynolds, *Voyage*, 39–40.

39. Dillon, *Narrative*, 1: 277–78, 289–93; Hanlon and Eperiam, "Saga of Mesiol."

40. H. Williams, *Whaling Family*, 292–96; F. Schmitt, *Mark Well*, 58.

41. Charles Darwin, *Journal and Remarks*, 481–82; Lars Hellgren, *Tattooing*, 11; Riesenberg, *Residence*, 113–18; H. Williams, *Whaling Family*, 270.

42. Jacobs, *Scenes*, 24; Davis, *Reminiscences*, 263–65; F. Schmitt, *Mark Well*, 28; Munford, *Ledyard's Journal*, 34.

43. Elder, *Letters*, 63–67; Jarman, *Journal*, 166; Tetens, *Among*, 77.

44. Edouard Stackpole, *The Sea-Hunters*, 387; Erskine, *Journal*, 341–42, 366; Straubel, *Whaling Journal*, 19; Dillon, *Narrative*, 2: 325.

45. Tetens, *Among*, 70; Davies, *History*, 165–66.

46. F. Bennett, *Narrative*, 279; Bingham, *Residence*, 454; Ward, *American Activities*, 3: 39–41; 4: 360–62; and 5: 36–37.

47. Ward, *American Activities*, 6: 141–51, and 7: 209–11; Log *Sharon*, November 4, 1842.

48. Ward, *American Activities*, 4: 582; 5: 47, 192–98; and 6: 147–51; Dunmore, *Expedition*, 115–16; McNab, *Historical Records*, 1: 691–94; F. Schmitt, *Mark Well*, 66–67.

49. Golovnin, *Around the World*, 200–1; Wilkes, *Narrative*, 2: 17; Frederic Howay, "The Ship Pearl in Hawaii," 28–33.

50. Mullett, *Five Years*, 45–46.

51. Dillon, *Narrative*, 1: 92; McNab, *Historical Records*, 1: 636.

52. Stewart, *Visit*, 232; Beaglehole, *Voyage of Resolution and Adventure*, 251, 393–98; Rickman, *Journal*, 55.

53. *Archivo General de Indias* (1710), Legajo 215, no. 5, 65–77; Francisco Barras y de Aragon, "Las Islas Palaos," 1076–85; Hezel, *First Taint*, 36–47.

54. Antonio Cantova, "Letter of 10 January 1731," and "The Discovery and Description of the Islands of the Garbanzos."

55. Beaglehole, *Endeavour Journal*, 1: 318, 368, 402–63, and 2: 33–34, 91–92, *Voyage of the Endeavour*, 117, 170–91, 240, 282, 325, 566–80, *Voyage of the Resolution and Adventure*, 171–72; Hooper, *With Captain James Cook*, 49.

56. Dillon, *Narrative*, 1: 25–31, 270–96, and 2: 92–98, 114–62, 324–44; Davidson, *Peter Dillon*, 40–49.

57. Wilson, *Missionary Voyage*, 115–16; Beechey, *Narrative*, 1: 228; Lucatt, *Rovings*, 1: 250–52; Shineberg, *Trading Voyages*, 241–44; Tetens, *Among*, 67–78.

58. Webster, *Last Cruise*, 26; Jacobs, *Scenes*, 74, 94.

59. Log *Triton*, July 26, 1863; Ward, *American Activities*, 2: 61–64; Im Thurn, *Journal*, 16–19; Erskine, *Journal*, 327–45, 390–91.

60. Wilkes, *Narrative*, 1: 312–13, and 3: 267–75.

Chapter 5: Crosscurrents in Oceania

1. W.T. Pritchard, *Polynesian Reminiscences*, 232.

2. Dening, *Islands and Beaches*, 129; I.C. Campbell, "European Transculturists in Polynesia," 252–56; Thomas Bargatzky, "Beachcombers and Castaways as Innovators," 93–102; Howe, *Where the Waves Fall*, 102–7; Ralston, *Grass Huts*, 66.

3. H.E. Maude, *Of Islands and Men*, 135; Joseph Conrad, *The Secret Sharer*, closing sentence.

4. Richards, "Indigenous Beachcombers," 1; Dening, *Islands and Beaches*, 34.

5. Turnbull, *Voyage*, 2: 67; E. Bell, *Journal*, 1: 93–97.

6. William Broughton, *A Voyage of Discovery to the North Pacific Ocean*, 42; William Ellis, *Narrative of a Tour of Hawaii*, 54; Turnbull, *Voyage*, 2: 32–33, 76.

7. Richards, "Indigenous Beachcombers," 2–11.

8. Dening, *Marquesan Journal*, 4–6, 46–55, 94; Temoteitei, "Biography," 9–10; Crook, "Account," 1: 150–58. Fanning, in *Voyages*, 133–38, calls Tama an Italian, for some reason.

9. Herman Melville, *Typee*, 328–29.

10. Dorothy Barrère and Marshall Sahlins, "Tahitians in the Early History of Hawaiian Christianity," 20–23; Dorothy Barrère, "A Tahitian Journal in the History of Hawai'i," 75–77; H.E. Maude, "The Raiatean Chief Auna and the Conversion of Hawaii," 188–91; Bingham, *Residence*, 161, 181, 251, 447–55; C.S. Stewart, *Journal of a Residence in the Sandwich Islands*, 205–14, 276.

11. W.F. Wilson, *With Lord Byron*, 26, 44.

12. Stewart, *Visit*, 2: 20–21, 43; Bingham, *Residence*, 411; *The Polynesian*, August 8, 1846; Frouin, *Journal*, 310.

13. Dillon, *Narrative*, 2: 102; Pukui and Elbert, *Hawaiian Dictionary*, 317.

14. Lucatt, *Rovings*, 1: 325–27.

15. John Dominis Holt, ed., *The Hawaiian Journal of John B. Whitman*, 17; Harlan Page, *A Memoir of Thomas H. Patoo*, 6–7.

16. Nancy Morris, "Hawaiian Missionaries in the Marquesas," 46–49; Garner, *Captain's Best Mate*, 74.

17. Beaglehole, *Voyage of the Resolution and Discovery*, part 1: 70–73, 239–42, 1062–63, 1470–71, and part 2: 801, 955; Munford, *John Ledyard's Journal*; Zimmermann, *Voyage*, 14; Rickman, *Journal*, 54, 184–85; Bligh, *Voyage*, 62.

18. Ward, *American Activities*, 7: 15; Henry Byam Martin, *The Polynesian Journal*, 116, 171.

19. Richards, "Indigenous Beachcombers," 6; Augustus Earle, *Narrative of a Residence in New Zealand*, 110; Nicholas, *Narrative*, 1: 36–38, 92–96, 240–41, and 2: 209–20; Elder, *Letters*, 81–82, 125–27; Dillon, *Narrative*, 1: 213, 327.

20. John Martin, *Tonga Islands: William Mariner's Account*, 55–67, 91–92, 284; Im Thurn and Wharton, *Journal*, 201.

21. Wilkes, *Narrative*, 2: 88–91, 157, and 3: 445–48; Goodenough, *Journal*, 193–94, 233.

22. Kamakau, *Ruling Chiefs*, 284; Ralph Kuykendall, "Some Early Commercial Adventurers of Hawaii," 20–32; Charles Denison, *Old Slade*, 49–69; Edwin Burrows, "George Manini in Uvea (Wallis Island)," 48–51; Agnes Conrad, ed., *Don Francisco*

de Paula Marin, 193; Williams, *Missionary Enterprises,* 180; Ward, *American Activities,* 7: 401.

23. Andrew Muir, "William Hoapili Kaauwai," 5–9; R.W. Robson, *Queen Emma,* 59.

24. Jacob Adler and Gwynn Barret, eds., *The Diaries of Walter Murray Gibson,* 114–17, 147, 235; Jacob Adler, "The Hawaiian Navy under King Kalakaua," 7–17; Kuykendall, *The Hawaiian Kingdom,* 3: 325–39; William Kikuchi, "A Legend of Kaimiloa Hawaiians in American Samoa," 268–69; interviews by the author on Aunu'u in June 1995.

25. John Hockin, *A Supplement to the Account of the Pelew Islands,* 15–55; Golovnin, *Around the World,* 234.

26. Carlos Taitano, Letter to author about his grandfather, August 1, 1990; Ward, *American Activities,* 4: 436; Shineberg, *Trading Voyages,* 241–65, 321–24; Tetens, *Among,* 62–78.

27. Kotzebue, *Voyage,* 2: 106–220, and 3: 97–106, *New Voyage,* 1: 306–16; Chamisso, *Voyage,* 129, 157–98, 263–82.

28. Hanlon and Eperiam, "Saga of Mesiol"; H. Williams, *One Whaling Family,* 326; W.H. Wilson, Journal *Cavalier,* March 3, 1850.

29. J. Williams, *Missionary Enterprises,* 126–44, 253–68; Richard Moyle, ed., *The Samoan Journals of John Williams,* 116–18; Howe, *Where the Waves Fall,* 286–87.

30. Katherine Luomala, "A Gilbertese Tradition of a Religious Massacre," 19–25; *Ke Alaula,* March-April 1870. See Nancy Morris, "Hawaiian Missionaries Abroad," for context.

31. Erskine, *Journal,* 359, 401–2; Sione Latukefu, "The Impact of South Sea Islands Missionaries on Melanesia," 101–5; R.G. and Marjorie Crocombe, eds., *Works of Ta'unga,* and *Polynesian Missions in Melanesia;* Niel Gunson, *Messengers of Grace,* 357–64.

32. Dorothy Shineberg, *They Came for Sandalwood,* 17–22; R. Young, *Southern World,* 179–81; David Routledge, *Matanitu,* 76–87.

33. Howe, *Where the Waves Fall,* 256–59; Dillon, *Narrative,* 1: 24–25, 270–75; Wilkes, *Narrative,* 3: 25–57, 143–81; J. Martin, *Tonga Islands,* 153–54; R. Gerard Ward, "The Pacific Bêche-de-Mer Trade with Special Reference to Fiji."

34. Kuykendall, "Early Commercial Adventurers," 23–24; Gavin Daws, "High Chief Boki," 80–81; Denison, *Old Slade,* 40–41; Kamakau, *Ruling Chiefs,* 294–96; Jarman, *Journal,* 186; Shineberg, *They Came for Sandalwood,* 17–22.

35. George Turner, *Nineteen Years in Polynesia,* 490; Erskine, *Journal,* 143–46, 326–27; Shineberg, *They Came for Sandalwood,* 135–41, Pritchard, *Reminiscences,* 225–32; Goodenough, *Journal,* 222.

36. Erskine, *Journal,* 341–67; Ulysse de la Hautière, *Souvenirs de la Nouvelle-Calédonie,* 88–92; John Inglis, *In the New Hebrides,* 201–2; G. Turner, *Nineteen Years,* 397, 512; K.R. Howe, "The Fortunes of the Naisselines."

37. Allardyce, "Rotooma," 133; George Bennett, "A Recent Visit to Several of the Polynesian Islands," 477–80; Forbes, *Two Years in Fiji,* 246–48.

38. Wood, *Yachting Cruise,* 15; Goodenough, *Journal,* 317; Webster, *Last Cruise,* 3, 90; Ward, *American Activities,* 5: 61–73; Jones, *Life and Adventure,* 132, 153.

39. Inglis, *New Hebrides,* 198–207.

40. Maude, *Slavers in Paradise;* Peter Corris, *Passage, Port and Plantation;* C. Moore, *Kanaka;* Goodenough, *Journal,* 196.

41. Hezel, *Foreign Ships,* 61,109; Ward, *American Activities,* 5: 32, and 6: 193–200; *Ke Au Oka,* August 14, 1865; Tetens, *Among,* 67–98.

42. John Moresby, *Discoveries and Surveys,* 69–70; Inglis, *New Hebrides,* 212–14; Giles, *Cruize,* 38–39; Farrell, *Odyssey,* 196–97; Wood, *Yachting Cruise,* 42–43, 55–56; Wilkes, *Narrative,* 4: 106–7; Shineberg, *Sandalwood.*

43. Hezel, *Foreign Ships,* 42.

44. Dillon, *Narrative,* 1: 275–282, and 2: 114, 325; Hoare, *Resolution Journal,* 3: 427; Williams, *Missionary Enterprises,* 235; G. Turner, *Nineteen Years,* 358; Beechey, *Narrative,* 1: 303; Wilkes, *Narrative,* 3: 190.

45. Straubel, *Whaling Journal,* 27–29, 115.

46. Dening, *Islands and Beaches,* 216; Ralston, *Grass Huts,* 66; Campbell, "European Transculturists," 454.

47. Kotzebue, *Voyage,* 2: 247–48, and 3: 86–88; Golovnin, *Voyage,* 232–35; Ward, *American Activities,* 1: 80–86; 2: 16–30; 3: 311, 391, 432–48; 4: 88–95; 5: 277; and 6: 399–400; Bingham, *Residence,* 118; Kuykendall, "Early Commercial Adventurers," 32.

48. J. Bennett, "Immigration, 'Blackbirding,' Labour Recruiting?" See Farrell, *Odyssey,* 199–206, for kidnapping.

49. Straubel, *Whaling Journal,* 34–41; Wilkes, *Narrative,* 3: 370, and 4: 264–65; Elder, *Letters,* 63–64; Ward, *American Activities,* 2: 338, and 6: 237–39, 254; Munger, *Two Years,* 41, 63; Kalani English, interview 1/23/1991; Garner, *Captain's Best Mate,* 213; Lucatt, *Rovings,* 1: 151.

50. Grant McCall, *Rapanui,* 139–40; Lin Poyer, "The Ngatik Massacre"; Rhys Richards, *Whaling and Sealing at the Chatham Islands,* 43–50.

51. Shineberg, *Trading Voyages,* 286–90.

52. Dillon, *Narrative,* 2: 341–44; Rosenman, *Account,* 1: 228, 266; Log *Charles W. Morgan,* 3/2/1858; Log *Elizabeth Swift,* 1/3/1867.

53. H. Martin, *Polynesian Journal,* 57, 116, 126–27; Wilkes, *Narrative,* 3: 227–28.

54. Beechey, *Narrative,* I: 76–88, 82–106; Dening, *Bounty,* 81–89; Ward, *American Activities,* 6: 57–68; Christopher Russo, "Outmigration by Pitcairn Islanders."

55. Dening, *Islands and Beaches,* 133; Nicholas Thomas, " 'Le Roi de Tahuata,' " 8, and *Entangled Objects,* 110–16; Ward, "Bêche-de-Mer," 113–18; P.Corney, *Voyages,* 106–7; Davies, *History,* 230–31; Erskine, *Journal,* 461–62.

56. Wood, *Yachting Cruise,* 188–90; Connell, *New Caledonia or Kanaky?*

Chapter 6: From Rim to Shining Rim

1. Meares, *Voyages,* 6–7.

2. For the impact of silver, see Dennis Flynn and Arturo Giraldez, "Born with a 'Silver' Spoon." For overviews, see Howe, *Where the Waves Fall,* chapter 4; Hezel, *First Taint,* chapter 1; and Spate's trilogy.

3. Carl Sauer, *The Early Spanish Main;* Golovnin, *Around the World,* 113–67; Dana, *Two Years,* 132–36; Spate, *Spanish Lake,* 223, and *Paradise Found and Lost,* 309–21; P.A. Tikhmenev, *A History of the Russian American Company;* William Schurz, *The Manila Galleon,* 210–12.

4. Markham, *Voyages of Quiros,* no. 14: 308–11, no. 15: 490–502; B. Corney, *Quest and Occupation of Tahiti,* 1: 9–15, and 2: 1–4.

5. King, *Robert Dampier,* 13; Bingham, *Residence,* 260–61; Maude, *Slavers in Paradise,* 188–91.

6. McNab, *Historical Records,* 1: 636, and 2: 257; Davidson, *Peter Dillon,* 75–98; Lucatt, *Rovings,* 2: 53, 188–89.

7. Stevens, *New Light,* 145–71; Richards, "Manilla-Men"; Morrell, *Narrative,* 417–34; Shineberg, *Trading Voyages,* 333–37; Log *Peru,* May 16, 1831; Meares, *Voyages,* 36, 393; Delano, *Narrative,* 44–54; Mary Wallis, *Life in Feejee,* 292–300, 416–17.

8. Meares, *Voyages,* 4–7, 207–21; Nathaniel Portlock, *A Voyage Round the World,* 360–63.

9. Frederic Howay, "Early Relations between the Hawaiian Islands and the Northwest Coast," 15–17, and *Voyages of the Columbia,* 150–51; E. Bell, *Journal,* 1: 145.

10. Howay, "Early Relations," 17–19; Howay, ed., *The Journal of Captain James Colnett,* 103–98; Ralph Kuykendall, "An Hawaiian in Mexico in 1789–1790," 38–40.

11. Roe, *Journal,* 101, 140–41; Hopoo, "Memoirs," 43–44.

12. Alexander Ross, *Fur Hunters,* 194, and *Adventures,* 54–66; *The Polynesian,* August 8, 1846.

13. James Gibson, *Imperial Russia in Frontier America,* 48, 209–10; Janice Duncan, *Minority without a Champion,* 13; Basil Dmytryshyn et al., eds., *To Siberia and Russian America,* 337.

14. Tikhmenev, *History,* 150; Dmytryshyn et al., *Russian America,* 331–32; P. Corney, *Voyages,* 121–27.

15. John Cochrane, *Narrative of a Pedestrian Journey through Russia,* 263; W.F. Wilson, *With Lord Byron,* 38–39.

16. Greer, "Wandering Kamaainas," 222–23; Rich, *Simpson's Journey,* 107; Cox, *Columbia River,* 84–85, 145, 206; Momilani Naughton, "Hawaiians in the Fur Trade," 29–46; Franchère, *Journal,* 90; Gustavus Hines, *A Voyage Round the World,* 412–13; John Minto, "From Youth to Age as an American," 128; George Blue, "Early Relations Between Hawaii and the Northwest Coast," 21–22; Duncan, *Minority,* 7–19.

17. David Kittelson, "John Coxe"; J. Barry, "An Interesting Hawaiian in Old Oregon"; Ross, *Adventures,* 114

18. Franchère, *Journal,* 92–98; Malo, *Hawaiian Antiquities,* 97–98.

19. Cox, *Columbia River,* 82; Ross, *Adventures,* 103–14, and *Fur Hunters,* 117–21.

20. Cox, *Columbia River,* 145, 198, 204, 249; Simpson, *Overland Journey,* 101–2.

21. Ross, *Adventures,* 200, and *Fur Hunters,* 61–91, 173–93; Frederick Young, *The Correspondence and Journals of Captain Nathaniel Wyeth,* 237–50.

22. Dana, *Two Years,* 90–97, 195–220.

23. Greer, "Wandering Kamaainas," 223–24, and "California Gold," 159; Dana, *Two Years,* 179; Richard Dillon, "Kanaka Colonies in California," 17–23; Duncan, *Minority,* 14; *The Friend,* July 1, 1866; Charles Kenn, "A Visit to the California Gold Fields by Reverend Lowell Smith," 12–14.

24. *The Friend,* August 1, 1868; Greer, "California Gold," 167–68; Susan Bell, "Owhyhee's Prodigal," 28–29.

25. James Hunnewell, "Honolulu in 1817 and 1818," 6–7; B. Judd, "Native Hawaiians in London, 1820," 13–17.

26. Kamakau, *Ruling Chiefs,* 367; Greer, "Wandering Kamaainas," 223; *The Polynesian,* August 8, 1846.

27. Jarman, *Journal,* 220; Ward, *American Activities,* 2: 16–30, and 6: 399–400; Duncan, *Minority,* 14; Lionel Cholmondeley, *The History of the Bonin Islands,* 148–69; "Today's Japan," Hawai'i Public Television, August 31, 1992.

28. Fanning, *Voyages,* 263–66; Keate, *Account,* 272–74; McCluer, *Journal,* 159–62. Kakawaki is my rendering of what may only have been a nickname. McCluer called him Cockywack and Delano Cockawocky. Palauans do not recognize the word.

29. Keate, *Account,* 268–85; McCluer, *Journal,* 142–64; Tetens, *Among,* 73–74; Delano, *Narrative,* 393–94; Meares, *Voyages,* 7; Portlock, *Voyage,* 360; Mortimer, *Observations,* 51–52.

30. Hopoo, "Memoirs," 45; Dwight, *Memoir,* 8–9; Dibble, *History,* 61; P.Corney, *Voyages,* 71; Kuykendall, "Commercial Adventurers," 19–23; Kamakau, *Ruling Chiefs,* 279–84.

31. Tetens, *Among,* 73–74.

32. Armstrong, *Around the World,* 41–63, 126–44; Richard Greer, "The Royal Tourist," 75–84; Agnes Quigg, "Kalakaua's Hawaiian Studies Abroad Program," 171–98.

33. Bougainville, *Voyage*, 376–77, 419–47; Parkinson, *Journal*, 175–82; Beaglehole, *Endeavour Journal*, 2: 186–91, and *Voyage of the Endeavour*, 441; McCluer, *Journal*, 280–83, 418–35; Hockin, *Supplement*, 46–48.

34. Beaglehole, *Endeavour Journal*, 2: 54–55; Scott, *Remarks on a Passage to Botany Bay*, 34–61; Riesenberg, *Residence*, 86–99; Henry Reynolds, *The Other Side of the Frontier*, 121–27.

35. Wilkes, *Narrative*, 2: 163–65; McNab, *Historical Records*, 1: 257–63, 329–30.

36. Turnbull, *Voyage*, 1: 62–63, 130–31, and 3: 372–75; Im Thurn and Wharton, *Journal*, 71, 191; McNab, *Historical Records*, 1: 120–93, 258–68, and 2: 539–44; Nicholas, *Narrative*, 1: 8–11, and 2: 369–71.

37. Nicholas, *Narrative*, 2: 222–24; McNab, *Historical Records*, 1: 405–6.

38. Beaglehole, *Endeavour Journal*, 2: 54–95, and *Voyage of the Endeavour*, 305–58; Zimmermann, *Voyage*, 13; Turnbull, *Voyage*, 1: 132; R. Young, *Southern World*, 234; Rutherford, "George Tupou I," 157–58.

39. Elder, *Letters*, 61–88, 125; McNab, *Historical Records*, 1: 262–289, 293–313, 334–51; Nicholas, *Narrative*, 1: 255–58.

40. Elder, *Letters*, 35–71, 150–59, 231, 253; McNab, *Historical Records*, 1: 391–93; Nicholas, *Narrative*, 1: 183–85; Cruise, *Journal*, 31.

41. Turnbull, *Voyage*, 1: 133, and 2: 123–26; Richards, "Indigenous Beachcombers," 2, 11.

42. J. Martin, *Tonga Islands*, 67, 153–54; George Angas, *Savage Life and Scenes in Australia and New Zealand*, 206–7; Hocart, "Fiji and Rotooma," 4753.

43. McNab, *Historical Records*, 1: 363; Earle, *Narrative*, 197–99; R. Young, *Southern World*, 177.

44. Davidson, *Peter Dillon*, 92–93, 278; Wilkes, *Narrative*, 3: 143.

45. Earle, *Narrative*, 199; Turnbull, *Voyage*, 2: 125–30; Dening, *Marquesan Journal*, 199; James Backhouse, *A Narrative of a Visit to the Australian Colonies*, 454–58; Ward, *American Activities*, 6: 141–43; Webster, *Last Cruise*, 8.

46. Erskine, *Journal*, 288–89, 341–66, 474; Inglis, *New Hebrides*, 198–204; C. Moore, *Kanaka*, 274–336.

Chapter 7: In the Belly of the Beast

1. Greer, "The Royal Tourist," 105.

2. K.N. Chaudhuri, *Trade and Civilisation in the Indian Ocean*; Mervyn Brown, *Madagascar Rediscovered*, 12–21; Brooks, *Kru Mariner*; Tinker, *A New System*, 41.

3. Dampier, *New Voyage*, 342–48, 367.

4. Dening, *Marquesan Journal*, 198–236; Nicholas, *Narrative*, 2: 377–79.

5. Hockin, *Supplement*, 54–58; Delano, *Narrative*, 74–75.

6. Dillon, *Narrative*, 1: 102–12; Davidson, *Peter Dillon*, 115–32.

7. Davis, *Reminiscences*, 215–19, 284–89.

8. Armstrong, *Around the World*, 149–69; Greer, "Royal Tourist," 85–91.

9. Bougainville, *Voyage*, 454–58; Dunmore, *French Explorers*, 170–71; Dillon, *Narrative*, 1: 199; Jacobs, *Scenes*, 37–39.

10. G. Forster, *Voyage*, 1: 388; McCormick, *Omai*, 122, 193–94; E. Bell, *Journal*, 1: 94.

11. Dampier, *New Voyage*, 366; Keate, *Account*, 342–43.

12. Savage, *Some Account*, 97–100; Dening, *Islands and Beaches*, 216.

13. Bougainville, *Voyage*, 464; Angas, *Savage Life*, 247; Kaplanoff, *Ingraham's Journal*, 2–6, 49; Jacobs, *Scenes*, 24.

14. Oliver, *Return to Tahiti*, 259; Spate, *Paradise*, 173; Hopoo, *Memoir*, 46–48.

15. Page, *Memoir*, 8–11; Golovnin, *Around the World*, 264, 324.

16. Bougainville, *Voyage*, 263–75; McCormick, *Omai*, 138; Dunmore, *French Explorers*, 83, 182; Spate, *Paradise*, 245–55.

17. Diderot, *Rameau's Nephew*, 184–92; Bougainville, *Voyage*, 249.

18. Thomson, *Story*, 1: 280–82; Wakefield, *Adventure*, 1: 221–22; Frouin, *Journal*, 311; Jacob Adler, ed., *The Journal of Prince Alexander Liholiho*, 55.

19. Dampier, *New Voyage*, 345, 367.

20. McCormick, *Omai*, 73–103, 138–61, 295–336; James Boswell, *The Life of Samuel Johnson*, 2: 608; Beaglehole, *Voyage of the Resolution and Adventure*, 950–51; A. Ellis, *Early Diary of Frances Burney*, 1: 332–34, and 2: 130–39.

21. Keate, *Account*, 341–61; Daniel Peacock, *Lee Boo of Belau;* Oliver, *Return to Tahiti*, 259.

22. Temoteĩtei, "Biography," 4–13. By August 1800, a supplement to *Evangelical Magazine* claimed on p. 552 that Temoteitei was praying to Jesus Christ, not his *atua*.

23. Savage, *Some Account*, 39, 101–110; Thomson, *Story*, 1: 246; Dillon, *Narrative*, 1: 200–2.

24. Cruise, *Journal*, 27; Elder, *Letters*, 63–78, 144–45.

25. Richards, "Indigenous Beachcombers," 3–4; Smithies, "A New Guinean"; Thomson, *Story*, 1: 282; Dening, *Islands and Beaches*, 215–16; Arago, *Narrative*, 16.

26. John Elder, ed., *Marsden's Lieutenants*, 161–66; Wakefield, *Adventure*, 1: 4–6; Elder, *Letters*, 356–57.

27. McNab, *Historical Records*, 1: 635–44; Thomson, *Story*, 1: 281.

28. Wakefield, *Adventure*, 1: 221–22; Thomson, *Story*, 1: 282.

29. *Evangelical Magazine*, August 1800, 338; Ward, *American Activities*, 2: 230; W. F. Wilson, *With Lord Byron*, 26; Dillon, *Narrative*, 1: 293.

30. Edward Tagart, ed., *A Memoir of the Late Captain Peter Heywood*, 284–90.

31. E. Bell, *Journal*, 1: 9–10, 96; Delano, *Narrative*, 391–94

32. Kittelson, "John Coxe," 214–15; B. Judd, "Native Hawaiians in London," 13–17.

33. Kuykendall, *Hawaiian Kingdom*, 1: 78–81; James Jarves, *History of the Hawaiian or Sandwich Islands*, 252–55; Kahananui, *Mooolelo*, 184, 244–47.

34. Harold Bradley, *The American Frontier in Hawaii*, 412–54; Kuykendall, *Hawaiian Kingdom*, 1: 196–226; Adler, *Journal*, 27–33, 56.

35. Rhoda Hackler, "My Dear Friend," 102; Alfons Korn, *The Victorian Visitors*, 202–78; Muir, "William Hoapili," 6–7; Quigg, "Kalakaua's Hawaiian Studies Abroad Program," 170–95; Niklaus Schweizer, *By Royal Command*, 59.

36. Greer, "Royal Tourist," 93–102; Armstrong, *Around the World*, 214–47; Liliʻuokalani, *Hawaii's Story*, 132–73.

37. Golovnin, *Around the World*, 187, 201, 323–26; Broeze, *Merchant's Perspective*, 74–75.

38. Anneliese Moore, "Harry Maitey," 125–61.

39. A. Moore, "Harry Maitey," 130–41; Bougainville, *Voyage*, 264; Richards, "Indigenous Beachcombers," 4.

40. A. Ellis, *Early Diary*, 1: 337; Keate, *Account*, 349. It was during the Enlightenment that the word "civilization" itself was invented to describe polite society.

41. Foster Dulles, *China and America*, 1–3; Ernest Dodge, *New England and the South Seas*, 20–63; Edouard Stackpole, *Whales and Destiny*.

42. Melville, *Moby Dick*, 26–39.

43. Stackpole, *Sea-Hunters*, 387; F. Schmitt, *Mark Well*, 120; Jones, *Life and Adventure*, 849–52.

44. Ward, *American Activities*, 3: 142–43; Howay, "Early Relations," 14; Morison, *Maritime History*, 43; Kaplanoff, *Ingraham's Journal*, 2.

45. Delano, *Narrative*, 394.

46. Ann Spoehr, "George Prince Tamoree," 32–33; Stauder, "George, Prince of Hawaii," 28–38.

47. Ward, *American Activities*, 5: 244.

48. Page, *Memoir*, 7–11; Bingham, *Residence*, 461.

49. Ward, *American Activities*, 6: 241–54; Morrell, *Narrative*, 466; Jacobs, *Scenes*, 13–14.

50. Ward, "Pacific Bêche-de-Mer Trade," 113, and *American Activities*, 3: 467; Wilkes, *Narrative*, 4: 412, and 5: 453; Anne Clean and E. Jeffrey Stann, eds., *Voyage to the Southern* Ocean, 287. Vedovi's actual name was probably "Vidovi" in Fijian.

51. Dwight, *Memoir;* Hopoo, *Memoirs;* S. Bell, "Owhyhee's Prodigal," 26–30; Bingham, *Residence*, 57–58.

52. A. Spoehr, "George Prince Tamoree," 33–39; Stauder, "George, Prince of Hawaii," 32.

53. Page, *Memoir*, 12–39; Ralph Kuykendall, "The Schooner Missionary Packet," 82–83.

54. Ward, *American Activities*, 3: 336; Bradley, *American Frontier*, 441–46; Kuykendall, *Hawaiian Kingdom*, 1: 191–203, 374–80.

55. Kuykendall, *Hawaiian Kingdom*, 3: 17–46; Armstrong, *Around the World*, 274–75; Liliuokalani, *Hawaii's Story*, 206–9.

56. Quigg, "Kalakaua's Hawaiian Studies Abroad Program," 171, 198–201.

Chapter 8: Prodigal Ghosts

1. Pukui and Korn, *Echo of Our Song*, 109–11.

2. Turner, *Forest of Symbols*, 106.

3. Aileen Nilsen, "The Mamasa Ceremony"; Fesaitu Marseu, "The Rotuman Mamasa Ceremony"; Alan Howard, "Seamanship on Rotuma," 35.

4. Meares, *Voyages*, 338; Lamb, *Voyage*, 3: 876; Lessa, *Ulithi*, 17.

5. Webster, *Last Cruise*, 40–50.

6. Delano, *Narrative*, 74–75; B. Corney, *Quest and Occupation of Tahiti*, 2: 118, and 3: 14.

7. Elder, *Letters*, 84; W.F. Wilson, *With Lord Byron*, 33–41; Mullett, *Five Years*, 54.

8. Kaplanoff, *Ingraham's Journal*, 67–76; Lamb, *Voyage*, 2: 449–61.

9. Howay, *Voyages*, 418–19; Delano, *Narrative*, 394–420.

10. Nicholas, *Narrative*, 1: 255–58.

11. J. Martin, *Tonga Islands*, 153–54; Jones, *Life and Adventure*, 98.

12. Wilkes, *Narrative*, 2: 378; M. Wallis, *Life in Feejee*, 413.

13. Bell, *Journal*, 1: 118–22, and 2: 37–38; Kaplanoff, *Joseph Ingraham's Journal*, 69–76; Lamb, *Voyage*, 2: 476; Kamakau, *Ruling Chiefs*, 153–54; David Kalakaua, *The Legends and Myths of Hawaii*, 382–408; David Miller, "Ka'iana," 1–19; Edmund Hayes, *Log of the Union*, 76; Roe, *Journal*, 141–43.

14. Reynolds, *Voyage*, 6–7; Lamb, *Voyage*, 2: 449–51, and 3: 799–807, 878; Bell, *Journal*, 2: 238–39; Dibble, *History*, 36.

15. Lamb, *Voyage*, 2: 448–49, and 3: 875–78; Bell, *Journal*, 2: 38–62.

16. Bingham, *Residence*, 97–114; 228–39; Dibble, *History*, 172–73.

17. King, *Robert Dampier*, 29–34; Ii, *Fragments*, 154–57; Kamakau, *Ruling Chiefs*, 270.

18. Kuykendall, *Hawaiian Kingdom*, 3: 3–16, 259–65, 322–72; Liliuokalani, *Hawaii's Story*, 173–82, 226–94.

19. Pukui and Korn, *Echo of Our Song*, 150–55.

20. Beaglehole, *Voyage of the Resolution and Adventure*, 393–428, *Voyage of the Resolution and Discovery*, part 2: 1058–59; Bligh, *Voyage*, 91.

21. Rutter, *Journal*, 53ff.; Edwards, *Voyage*, 38–39, 110; Oliver, *Return*, 61–64, 154; Kotzebue, *New Voyage*, 1: 191–92.

22. Kotzebue, *New Voyage*, 1: 53–70, 133–79.

23. Stewart, *Visit*, 1: 303–21; Arago, *Narrative*, 1–16; Delmas, *Essai*, 33ff; Edward Belcher, *Narrative of a Voyage Round the World*, 1: 356.

24. Dillon, *Narrative*, 1: 200; Nicholas, *Narrative*, 2: 372–75.

25. Cruise, *Journal*, 23–41; Elder, *Letters*, 86–93.

26. Earle, *Narrative*, 87–91; S. Percy Smith, *Maori Wars of the Nineteenth Century*, 181–89, 226–28, 369–99, 422; Elder, *Letters*, 356, 388; Wakefield, *Adventure*, 1: 6; McNab, *Historical Records*, 1: 628, 668; Wilkes, *Narrative*, 2: 399; Dillon, *Narrative*, 1: 331–32; Thomson, *Story*, 1: 256–57.

27. Beaglehole, *Voyage of the Resolution and Adventure*, 428; Rickman, *Journal*, 151.

28. Beaglehole, *Voyage of the Resolution and Discovery*, part 1: 186–240; Rickman, *Journal*, 133–44, 173–82; Munford, *John Ledyard's Journal*, 46, 59; Zimmermann, *Voyage*, 22–24; Edwards, *Voyage*, 121–22; Bligh, *Voyage*, 62, 92, 144; Mortimer, *Observations*, 25.

29. Wilson, *Missionary Voyage*, 173; Beaglehole, *Voyage of the Resolution and Adventure*, 949–50; Bligh, *Voyage*, 144.

30. McNab, *Historical Records*, 1: 170–85, 254–56.

31. Wakefield, *Adventure*, 1: 26ff.

32. Savage, *Some Account*, 39, 102; Dillon, *Narrative*, 1: 202, 248–50; Nicholas, *Narrative*, 1: 426–31, and 2: 3–4; Elder, *Letters*, 202.

33. Jacobs, *Scenes*, 77ff; Herman Melville, *Typee*, 120, 193–202, 328–33.

34. B. Corney, *Quest and Occupation*, 1: 11–19, 2: 92–169, and 3: 6–89.

35. Ibid., 1: 15, and 2: 304–85; Beaglehole, *Voyage of the Resolution and Discovery*, part 1: 224; Mortimer, *Observations*, 46.

36. Bingham, *Residence*, 107, 411; Stewart, *Journal*, 355–68; W.F. Wilson, *With Lord Byron*, 44, 47.

37. Bingham, *Residence*, 103–67.

38. Dibble, *History*, 148; Stewart, *Journal*, 277–78; Bingham, *Residence*, 441, 477.

39. Rufus Anderson, *The Hawaiian Islands*, 224; Hines, *Voyage*, 216–17.

40. Bingham, *Residence*, 373, 421; Kamakau, *Ruling Chiefs*, 326–33.

41. Martha Beckwith, ed., *Kepelino's Traditions of Hawaii*, introduction; Muir, "William Hoapili," 61.

42. Elder, *Letters*, 127ff.

43. Wakefield, *Adventure*, 1: 202–3; Pei Te Hurinui, *King Potatau;* M.P.K. Sorrenson, "The Maori King Movement," 44, and "Maori and Pakeha," 179.

44. Dillon, *Narrative*, 1: 270–96; M. Wallis, *Life in Feejee*, 21; Williams, *Missionary Enterprises*, 267ff.

45. J.D. Freeman, "The Joe Gimlet or Siovili Cult"; Pritchard, *Polynesian Reminiscences*, 205.

46. Hanlon, *Stone Altar*, 101–24; Latukefu, "Impact of South Sea Islands Missionaries."

47. Beechey, *Narrative*, 1: 293–94; Wilkes, *Narrative*, 2: 4, 39; F. Bennett, *Narrative*, 66; Melville, *Omoo*, 99–100.

48. Frisbie, *Book of Puka-Puka*, 27–53, 144–78, 270–89, 347–56. Considering the fact that Frisbie met William in the 1920s, and that Pacific whaling had declined in the

1860s, it may be that William's chosen identity was a product of his own (or Frisbie's?) imaginative storytelling.

Chapter 9: Legacies

1. Pukui and Korn, *Echo of Our Song*, 80–82.
2. Thomas, *Entangled Objects*, 31–33.
3. Garner, *Captain's Best Mate*, 255–58; Log *Josephine*, August 8, 1849; Log *Elizabeth*, February 25, 1849.
4. Roe, *Journal*, 306–7; *The Friend*, September 4, 1844.
5. Straubel, *Whaling Journal*, 114–15.
6. Kindleberger, *Mariners and Markets*, 40.
7. Varigny, *Fourteen Years*, 105, 133–34; C. Moore, *Kanaka*, 48–50; *The Polynesian*, August 8, 1846. This large number of recruits also predates the Mahele, or land division, that would deprive two-thirds of Hawaiian commoners of land. See Kuykendall, *Hawaiian Kingdom*, vol. 1.
8. Duncan, *Minority*, 15–18, "Kanaka World Travelers," 107; Diamond, "Queequeg's Crewmates," 133–34.
9. R.P. Gilson, *Samoa 1830 to 1900*, 37–40; Howard, "Seamanship on Rotuma," 25–27; William Allen, "Rotuma," 579.
10. Elder, *Letters*, 234; Alfred Crosby, *Ecological Imperialism*, 241; *The Friend*, September 4, 1844; *The Polynesian*, August 8, 1846.
11. Simpson, *Overland Journey*, 245; Varigny, *Fourteen Years*, 133–34; Greer, "Wandering Kamaainas," 224; Kuykendall, *Hawaiian Kingdom*, 1: 312.
12. *Polynesian*, August 8, 1846; *Friend*, September 4, 1844; Ben Finney, "Voyaging," 350; Redicker, *Between the Devil and the Deep Blue Sea*, 33; Robertson, *Mariners' Mealtimes*, 50; Raymond Firth, *History and Traditions of Tikopia*, 139.
13. Ward, *American Activities*, 6: 130; Giles, *Cruize*, 37; Webster, *Last Cruise*, 90.
14. R. Young, *Southern World*, 177; Erskine, *Journal*, 354–57; Marshall Sahlins, *Anahulu*, vol. 2; Ralston, "Hawaii, 1778–1854."
15. Kotzebue, *New Voyage*, 2: 239–41; Beechey, *Voyage*, 1: 318–19.
16. Mullet, *Five Years*, 53; Peter Hempenstall and Noel Rutherford, *Protest and Dissent in the Colonial Pacific*, 49ff.
17. Ward, *American Activities*, 6: 67–68; Forbes, *Two Years*, 226; Alan Howard, "Rotuma as a Hinterland Community."
18. Im Thurn and Wharton, *Journal*, 137; Naughton, "Hawaiians in the Fur Trade."
19. Homi Bhabha, *The Location of Culture*, 92.
20. J.B. Bury, *A History of Greece*, 384; Teuira Henry, *Ancient Tahiti*, 95; Beaglehole, *Voyage of the Resolution and Adventure*, 415; Rediker, *Between*, 105; *Cruise*, *Journal*, 38; Giles, *Cruize*, 54.
21. W.F. Wilson, *With Lord Byron*, 44, 47.
22. Redicker, *Between*, 10–17.
23. Pomponio, *Seagulls*, 169; Couper, "Islanders at Sea," 232–36.
24. "Island Style," KHON Television, August 18, 1991; Howard, "Seamanship on Rotuma," 28; Talu, "Towards Quality in Education," 247; interview with Teresia Teaiwa, April 7, 1991; other interviews conducted on Tarawa, July 5–10, 1994; "Asia Now," Hawai'i Public Television, March 17, 1995.
25. Nicholas Thomas, in "Partial Texts," says that all our representations of the past are incomplete and biased.
26. Taitano, letter to author; Hocart, "Fiji and Rotuma," 4753.

27. Howard, "Seamanship in Rotuma," 23–39; Gordon MacGregor, "Field Notes."

28. Turnbull, *Voyage*, 1: 71; Jacobs, *Scenes*, 81–88; Dillon, *Narrative*, 1: 202.

29. Nicholas, *Narrative*, 1: 172–73; Erskine, *Journal*, 475; Kotzebue, *New Voyage*, 2: 239–40.

30. Beaglehole, *Voyage of the Resolution and Discovery*, part 1: 86, 188; Rickman, *Journal*, 139–41.

31. Hockin, *Supplement*, 36; Lamb, *Voyage*, 2: 454; Freeman, "Joe Gimlet," 188.

32. Nicholas, *Narrative*, 1: 53; Chamisso, *Voyage*, 195–98.

33. Beaglehole, *Voyage of the Resolution and Adventure*, 202–23; Dibble, *History*, 122; Bingham, *Residence*, 117.

34. Beechey, *Voyage*, 2: 105–6; Hockin, *Supplement*, 9–18; Keate, *Account*, 357.

35. Cruise, *Journal*, 31; B. Corney, *Quest and Occupation*, 3: 4–15.

36. Paniani, interview, July 21, 1993.

37. John Pule, *The Shark That Ate the Sun*, 205–7.

38. Corris, *Passage*, 151–54; Howard, "Seamanship," 31; Hau'ofa, "Our Sea of Islands."

39. Log *Miantonomi*, October 3–6, 1854; Munger, *Two Years*, 39; Goodenough, *Journal*, 299; John Connell, *New Caledonia or Kanaky?*

40. Mary Helms, *Ulysses' Sail*, 115; Péron, *Mémoires*, 2: 152–53.

41. Redicker, *Between the Devil and the Deep Blue Sea*, 7–9.

42. V. Turner, *The Forest of Symbols*, 95–106.

43. Biliet Lokonwa, interview, Majuro, July 27, 1989.

Chapter 10: Reflections

1. Finney, *Voyage of Rediscovery*, 260.

2. Ibid., 259–68.

3. Patrick Nunn, "Facts, Fallacies and the Future of the Island Pacific," in *A New Oceania: Rediscovering Our Sea of Islands*, ed. Eric Waddell, Vijay Naidu, and Epeli Hau'ofa, 114.

4. The creation of dependent "peripheries" by powerful cores of European merchant capital is described in Alan Smith, *Creating a World Economy: Merchant Capital, Colonialism and World Trade, 1400–1825*, chapter 6. For a concise discussion of the incorporation of rural and overseas labor into the post-1500 world economy, see Eric Wolf, *Europe and the Peoples without History*, chapter 12. Both works draw on the hierarchical center-periphery model developed in Immanuel Wallerstein, *The Modern World System I: Capitalist Agriculture and the Origins of the European World-Economy in the Sixteenth Century*.

5. For a discussion of European intellectual responses to the exotica they encountered overseas, see Stephen Greenblatt, *Marvelous Possessions: The Wonder of the New World*. Also see Edward Said, *Orientalism*, and, for Pacific-centered analyses, Nicholas Thomas, *Colonialism's Culture*, B. Smith, *European Vision and the South Pacific*, and Spate, *Paradise Found and Lost*.

6. Michel Foucault, *The History of Sexuality*, vol. 1, *An Introduction*, trans. Robert Hurley, 95.

7. For examples of this ethnographic approach, see Dening, *Islands and Beaches;* and Sahlins, *Historical Metaphors and Mythical Realities*. For comparison, see the excellent study of an interactive, adaptive frontier situation in Richard White, *The Middle Ground*.

8. "Modern" here refers to the framework created by global capitalism, which promotes change on many levels (for better or for worse) according to a Western-derived

ideology of continual "progress." See Jonathan Friedman, *Cultural Identity and Global Process,* chapter 11.

9. For a global analysis, see Saskia Sassen, *The Mobility of Labor and Capital: A Study in International Investment and Labor Flow.* For Pacific-centered discussions, see Geoffrey Hayes, "Migration, Metascience and Development Policy in Island Polynesia," *The Contemporary Pacific,* 3:1 (1991): 1–58; and James Fawcett and Benjamin Cariño, eds., *Pacific Bridges,* chapters 8, 9, and 16.

10. Epeli Hau'ofa, "Our Sea of Islands," and "A Beginning," in *A New Oceania: Rediscovering Our Sea of Islands,* ed. Waddell, Naidu, and Hau'ofa, 16 and 133, respectively. A similar degree of agency has been attributed to other "transmigrants" across international borders. See Linda Basch, Nina Glick Schiller, and Cristina Szanton Blanc, *Nations Unbound.*

～ *Bibliography* ～

Abbreviations:

ANU Australia National University Press
HHS Hawaiian Historical Society
HJH Hawaiian Journal of History
JPH Journal of Pacific History
JPS Journal of the Polynesian Society
UH University of Hawai'i [Press]
USP University of the South Pacific

Adler, Jacob. "The Hawaiian Navy under King Kalakaua." *HHS 73rd Annual Report 1964* (1965): 7–21.
———, ed. *The Journal of Prince Alexander Liholiho: The Voyages Made to the United States, England and France in 1849–50.* Honolulu: HHS, 1967.
Adler, Jacob, and Barret, Gwynn, eds. *The Diaries of Walter Murray Gibson 1886, 1887.* Honolulu: UH Press, 1973.
Alatas, Syed. *The Myth of the Lazy Native.* London: Frank Cass, 1977.
Alkire, William H. *Coral Islanders.* Arlington Heights, IL: AHM, 1978.
Allardyce, W.L. "Rotooma and the Rotoomans." In *Proceedings of the Queensland Branch of the Geographical Society of Australasia,* 130–44. Brisbane: Geographical Society of Australia, 1885–86.
Allen, William. "Rotuma." *Report of the Australian Association for the Advancement of Science* (January 1895): 556–579.
Andaya, Leonard. *The World of Maluku.* Honolulu: UH Press, 1993.
Anderson, Rufus. *The Hawaiian Islands: Their Progress and Condition under Missionary Labors.* Boston: Gould and Lincoln, 1864.
Angas, George French. *Savage Life and Scenes in Australia and New Zealand.* 2 vols. London: Smith, Elder, 1847.
Arago, Jacques. *Narrative of a Voyage Round the World in the Uranie and Physicienne Corvettes, Commanded by Captain Freycinet, during the Years 1817–1820.* London: Treuttel and Wurtz, 1823.
———. *Deux Océans.* 2 vols. Paris: Théatrale, 1854.
Archivo General de Indias, Seville, Spain. Ultramar, Filipinas, 1710, legajo 215, no. 5, 65–77.
Armstrong, William N. *Around the World with a King.* Rutland, VT: Tuttle, 1986.
"Asia Now." Hawai'i Public Television, March 17, 1995.
Backhouse, James. *A Narrative of a Visit to the Australian Colonies.* London: Hamilton and Adams, 1843.
Bargatzky, Thomas. "Beachcombers and Castaways as Innovators." *JPH* 15, no. 1 (1980): 93–102.

Barras y de Aragon, Francisco. "Las Islas Palaos." *Anuario de Estudios Americanos* (March 1949): 1062–95.

Barrère, Dorothy. "A Tahitian Journal in the History of Hawai'i: The Journal of Kahikona." *HJH* 23 (1989): 75–107.

Barrère, Dorothy, and Sahlins, Marshall. "Tahitians in the Early History of Hawaiian Christianity: The Journal of Toketa." *HJH* 13 (1979): 17–35.

Barry, J. Neilson. "An Interesting Hawaiian in Old Oregon." *HHS 38th Annual Report 1929* (1930): 20–24.

Basch, Linda; Schiller, Nina Glick; and Blanc, Christina Szanton. *Nations Unbound: Transnational Projects, Postcolonial Predicaments and Deterritorialized Nation-States.* New York: Gordon and Breach, 1994.

Bathgate, Murray A. "Maori River and Ocean Going Craft in South New Zealand," *JPS* 78, no. 3 (1969): 344–77.

Beaglehole, J.C., ed. *The Endeavour Journal of Joseph Banks, 1768–1771.* 2 vols. Sydney: Angus and Robertson, 1962.

———, ed. *The Journals of Captain James Cook on His Voyages of Discovery.* Vol. 1, *The Voyage of the Endeavor, 1768–1771.* Cambridge: Cambridge University Press, 1968.

———, ed. *The Journals of Captain James Cook on His Voyages of Discovery.* Vol. 2, *The Voyage of the Resolution and Adventure, 1772–1775.* Cambridge: Cambridge University Press, 1969.

———, ed. *The Journals of Captain James Cook on His Voyages of Discovery.* Vol. 3, 2 parts, *The Voyage of the Resolution and Discovery, 1776–1780.* Cambridge: Cambridge University Press, 1967.

Beckwith, Martha. *Hawaiian Mythology.* Honolulu: UH, 1970.

Beckwith, Martha Warren, ed. *Kepelino's Traditions of Hawaii.* Bishop Museum Bulletin, no. 95. Honolulu: Bishop Museum, 1932.

Beechey, Frederick W. *Narrative of a Voyage to the Pacific and Beering's Strait.* 2 vols. London: Colburn and Bentley, 1831.

Belcher, Edward. *Narrative of a Voyage Round the World Performed in the HMS Sulphur, 1836–1842.* Vol. 1. London: Smith and Elder, 1843. Reprint, London: Dawsons, 1970.

Bell, Edward. Journal of the Chatham 1791–94. 2 vols. Manuscript section, Alexander Turnbull Library, Wellington, NZ (microfilm 2356, reel 2, UH Library).

Bell, Susan N. "Owhyhee's Prodigal." *HJH* 10 (1976): 25–32.

Bennett, Frederick Debell. *Narrative of a Whaling Voyage Round the Globe from the Years 1833 to 1836.* 2 vols. London: Bentley, 1840.

Bennett, George. "A Recent Visit to Several of the Polynesian Islands." *United Service Journal* 33 (1831): 473–82.

Bennett, J.A. "Immigration, 'Blackbirding,' Labour Recruiting? The Hawaiian Experience, 1877–1887." *JPH* 11, no. 1 (1976): 3–27.

Bhabha, Homi. *The Location of Culture.* New York: Routledge, 1994.

Biliet Lokonwa. Interview by author with Carol Curtis of the Alele Museum, as translator. Majuro, Marshall Islands, July 27, 1989.

Bingham, Hiram. *A Residence of Twenty-One Years in the Sandwich Islands; or the Civil, Religious, and Political History of Those Islands.* Hartford: Hezekiah Huntington, 1849.

Bligh, William. *A Voyage to the South Sea in HMS Bounty.* London: George Nicol, 1792.

Blue, George Verne. "Early Relations Between Hawaii and the Northwest Coast, 1778–1849," *HHS 33rd Annual Report 1924* (1925): 16–22.

Bonnemaison, Joel. "Territorial Control and Mobility within niVanuatu Societies." In *Circulation in Population Movement: Substance and Concepts from the Melanesian Case,* ed. Murray Chapman and Mansell Prothero, 57–79. Boston: Routledge, Keagan and Paul, 1985.

Boswell, James. *The Life of Samuel Johnson.* Ed. Roger Ingpen. Bath: George Bayntun, 1925.

Bougainville, Louis Antoine de. *A Voyage Around the World in the Years 1766–69.* Trans. J.R. Foster. London: J. Nourse, 1772. Reprint, New York: Da Capo, 1967.

Bradley, Harold Whitman. *The American Frontier in Hawaii: The Pioneers, 1789–1843.* Gloucester, MA: Peter Smith, 1968.

Broeze, Frank J.A., ed. *A Merchant's Perspective: Captain Jacobus Boelen's Narrative of His Visit to Hawai'i in 1828.* Honolulu: HHS, 1988.

Brooks, George. *The Kru Mariner in the Nineteenth Century.* Newark, DE: University of Delaware Press, 1972.

Broughton, William. *A Voyage of Discovery to the North Pacific Ocean.* London: Cadell and Davies, 1804.

Brown, Mervyn. *Madagascar Rediscovered: A History from Early Times to Independence.* Hamden, CT: Archon, 1979.

Browne, J. Ross. *Etchings of a Whaling Cruise.* New York: Harper, 1846. Reprint, Cambridge, MA: Harvard University Press, 1968.

Buck, Peter [Te Rangi Hiroa]. *Vikings of the Pacific.* Chicago: University of Chicago Press, 1959.

Bullen, Frank T. *The Cruise of the Cachalot.* New York: Dover, 1962.

Burrows, Edwin G. "George Manini in Uvea (Wallis Island)." *HHS 45th Annual Report 1936* (1937): 47–52.

Bury, J.B. *A History of Greece to the Death of Alexander the Great.* London: Macmillan, 1963.

Campbell, Ian C. "European Transculturists in Polynesia, 1780–1840." Ph.D. dissertation, University of Adelaide, 1976.

———. *Island Kingdom: Tonga Ancient and Modern.* Christchurch, NZ: University of Canterbury Press, 1992.

Cantova, J. Antonio. "Letter of 10 January 1731." In *Historia de la Provincia de la Compañia de Jesus,* by Pedro Murillo-Velarde, 2: 381–82. Manila, 1749.

———. "The Discovery and Description of the Islands of the Garbanzos." Transcribed by Francisco Carrasco. *Boletin de la Sociedad Geográfica de Madrid* 10 (1881): 263–79.

Carnes, J.A. *Journal of a Voyage from Boston to the West Coast of Africa.* New York: Negro Universities Press, 1969.

Carrington, Hugh, ed. *The Discovery of Tahiti, A Journal of the Second Voyage of the H.M.S. Dolphin Round the World by George Robertson, 1766–68.* Hakluyt Society Series 2, no. 98. London: Hakluyt Society, 1948.

Cartwright Jr., Bruce. *Extract from the Diary of Ebenezer Townsend Jr. in Hawaii from August 12, 1798, to August 31, 1798.* HHS Reprints, no. 4. Honolulu: HHS, 1978.

Chaliand, Gérard, and Rageau, Jean-Pierre. *The Penguin Atlas of Diasporas.* New York: Viking, 1995.

Chamisso, Adelbert von. *A Voyage Around the World with the Romanov Exploring Expedition in the Years 1815–1818, in the Brig Rurik, Captain Otto von Kotzebue.* Honolulu: UH, 1986.

Chaudhuri, K.N. *Trade and Civilisation in the Indian Ocean: An Economic History from the Rise of Islam to 1750.* New York: Cambridge University Press, 1985.

Cholmondeley, Lionel Berners. *The History of the Bonin Islands from the Year 1827 to the Year 1876.* London: Constable, 1915.

Clark, Thomas Blake. *Omai: First Polynesian Ambassador to England.* Honolulu: UH, 1969.

Clean, Anne, and Stann, E. Jeffrey, eds. *Voyage to the Southern Ocean: The Letters of Lieutenant William Reynolds from the U.S. Exploring Expedition, 1838–1842.* Annapolis: Naval Institute, 1988.

Cochrane, John Dundas. *Narrative of a Pedestrian Journey through Russia and Siberian Tartary, from the Frontiers of China to the Frozen Sea and Kamchatka.* Philadelphia: Carey, Lea, 1821.

Connell, John. *New Caledonia or Kanaky? The Political History of a French Colony.* Canberra: National Development Studies Center, 1987.

Conrad, Agnes C., ed. *Don Francisco de Paula Marin: The Letters and Journal of Francisco de Paula Marin.* Honolulu: UH, 1973.

Conrad, Joseph. *Heart of Darkness and The Secret Sharer.* New York: New American Library, 1961.

———. *Lord Jim.* New York: New American Library, 1981.

Corney, Bolton G., ed. *The Quest and Occupation of Tahiti by Emissaries of Spain during the Years 1772–1776. Told in Despatches and Other Contemporary Documents.* Hakluyt Society Series 2, nos. 32, 36, and 43. London: Hakluyt Society, 1913, 1915, and 1919.

Corney, Peter. *Voyages in the Northern Pacific: Narrative of Several Trading Voyages from 1813 to 1818, between the Northwest Coast of America, the Hawaiian Islands and China, with a Description of the Russian Establishments on the Northwest Coast.* Honolulu: Thrum, 1896.

Corris, Peter. *Passage, Port and Plantation: A History of the Solomon Islands Labour Migration, 1870–1914.* Melbourne: Oxford University Press, 1973.

Couper, Alastair. "Islanders at Sea: Change, and the Maritime Economies of the Pacific." In *The Pacific in Transition,* ed. Harold Brookfield, 229–47. London: Arnold, 1973.

Cox, Ross. *The Columbia River.* Norman, OK: University of Oklahoma Press, 1957.

Creighton, Margaret S. *Rites and Passages: The Experiences of American Whaling, 1830–1870.* New York: Cambridge University Press, 1995.

Crocombe, R.G. and Marjorie, eds. *Polynesian Missions in Melanesia.* Suva, Fiji: USP, 1982.

———, eds. *The Works of Ta'unga: Records of a Polynesian Traveller in the South Seas, 1833–1896.* Suva, Fiji: USP, 1984.

Crook, William Pascoe. "Account of the Marquesas." In *Marquesan Source Materials,* ed. George Sheehan, part I: 114–83. Honolulu: Bishop Museum, 1963.

Crosby, Alfred W. *Ecological Imperialism: The Biological Expansion of Europe, 900–1900.* New York: Cambridge University Press, 1986.

Cruise, Richard A. *Journal of a Ten Months' Residence in New Zealand.* London: Longman, 1823. Reprint, Christchurch NZ: Pegasus, 1957.

Curtin, Philip D. *Cross-Cultural Trade in World History.* New York: Cambridge University Press, 1984.

Dampier, William. *A New Voyage Round the World.* London: Argonaut Press, 1927. Reprint, New York: Dover, 1968.

Dana, Richard Henry. *Two Years Before the Mast.* New York: Bantam, 1963.

Darwin, Charles. *Journal and Remarks, 1832–1836.* Vol. 3, *Narrative of the Surveying Voyages of His Majesty's Ships Adventure and Beagle between the Years 1826 and 1836.* London: Colburn, 1839. Reprint, New York: AMS, 1966.

Davidson, J.W. *Peter Dillon: Chevalier of the South Seas,* ed. O.H.K. Spate. New York: Oxford University Press, 1975.

Davies, John. *The History of the Tahitian Mission 1799–1830,* ed. C.W. Newbury. Hakluyt Society Series 2, no. 116. London Hakluyt Society, 1961.

Davis, Raymond C. *Reminiscences of a Voyage Around the World.* Ann Arbor: Chase, 1869.

Davis, Tom [Pa Tuterangi Ariki]. *Vaka: Saga of a Polynesian Canoe.* Suva, Fiji: USP, 1992.

Dawbin, W.H. "The Maori Went A-Whaling—and Became One of the World's Best Whalemen." *Pacific Discovery* 7, no. 4 (1954): 18–22.

Daws, Gavin. "High Chief Boki: A Biographical Study in Early Nineteenth-Century Hawaiian History." *JPS* 75 (1966): 65–83.

Day, A. Grove. *Mad About Islands: Novelists of a Vanished Pacific.* Honolulu: Mutual, 1987.

———, ed. *Louis Becke: South Sea Supercargo.* Honolulu: UH, 1967.

Debenham, Frank, ed. *The Voyage of Captain Bellingshausen to the Antarctic Seas, 1819–1821.* Hakluyt Society Series 2, vol. 1, no. 91, and vol. 2, no. 92. London: Hakluyt Society, 1945.

Delano, Amasa. *Narrative of Voyages and Travels in the Northern and Southern Hemispheres: Comprising Three Voyages Round the World; Together with a Voyage of Survey and Discovery, in the Pacific Ocean and Oriental Islands.* New York: Praeger, 1970.

Delmas, Siméon. *Essai d'histoire de la Mission des Iles Marquises depuis les origines jusqu'en 1881.* Paris: Annales des Sacres-Coeurs, 1929.

Dening, Greg. *The Bounty: An Ethnographic History.* Melbourne: Melbourne University Press, 1988.

———. *Islands and Beaches: Discourse on a Silent Land, Marquesas 1774–1880.* Honolulu: UH, 1980.

———, ed. *The Marquesan Journal of Edward Robarts, 1797–1824.* Canberra: ANU, 1974.

Denison, Charles W., ed. *Old Slade, or Fifteen Years Adventures of a Sailor.* Boston: Putnam, 1876.

Diamond, Marion. "Queequeg's Crewmates: Pacific Islanders in the European Shipping Industry," *International Journal of Maritime History* 1, no. 2 (December 1989): 123–42.

Diaz, Vicente. "Simply Chamorro: Telling Tales of Demise and Survival on Guam." *The Contemporary Pacific* 6, no. 1 (Spring 1994): 29–58.

Dibble, Sheldon. *A History of the Sandwich Islands.* Honolulu: Thrum, 1909.

Diderot, Denis. *Rameau's Nephew and Other Works.* Ed. Ralph H. Bowen and trans. Jacques Barzun. Indianapolis: Bobbs-Merrill, 1964.

Dieffenbach, E. *Travels in New Zealand.* 2 vols. London: John Murray, 1843.

Dillon, Peter. *Narrative and Successful Result of a Voyage in the South Seas.* 2 vols. London: Hurst, Chance, 1829.

Dillon, Richard H. "Kanaka Colonies in California." *Pacific Historical Review,* 24 (February 1955): 17–23.

Dmytryshyn, Basil; Crownhart-Vaughn, E.A.P.; and Vaghan, Thomas, eds. *To Siberia and Russian America: Three Centuries of Russian Eastward Expansion: The Russian American Colonies 1798–1867, A Documentary Record.* Vol. 3. Portland: Oregon Historical Society, 1989.

Dodge, Ernest S. *New England and the South Seas.* Cambridge, MA: Harvard University Press, 1965.

Dulles, Foster Rhea. *China and America: The Story of Their Relations Since 1784.* Port Washington, NY: Kennikat Press, 1967.

Duncan, Janice K. "Kanaka World Travelers and Fur Company Employees, 1785–1860." *HJH* 7 (1973): 93–111.

――――. *Minority without a Champion: Kanakas on the Pacific Coast, 1788–1850.* Portland: Oregon Historical Society, 1972.

Dunmore, John. *French Explorers in the Pacific.* Vol. 1, *The Eighteenth Century.* New York: Oxford University Press, 1965.

――――, ed. *The Expedition of the St. Jean-Baptiste to the Pacific 1769–70, from the Journals of Jean de Surville and Guillaume Labé.* London: Hakluyt Society, 1981.

Dwight, Edwin, ed. *The Memoirs of Henry Obookiah, A Native of Owhyhee, and a Member of the Foreign Mission School.* Honolulu: United Church of Christ, 1968.

Earle, Augustus. *Narrative of a Residence in New Zealand.* Ed. E.H. McCormick. New York: Oxford University Press, 1966.

Edwards, Edward, and Hamilton, George. *Voyage of the H.M.S. 'Pandora,' Despatched to Arrest the Mutineers of the 'Bounty' in the South Seas, 1790–91.* London: Francis Edwards, 1915.

Elder, John Rawson, ed. *The Letters and Journals of Samuel Marsden.* Dunedin, NZ: Wilkie, 1932.

――――, ed. *Marsden's Lieutenants.* Dunedin, NZ: Wilkie, 1934.

Ellis, Anne Raine, ed. *The Early Diary of Frances Burney.* 2 vols. London: Bell, 1913.

Ellis, William. *Narrative of a Tour of Hawaii, or Owhyhee.* Rutland, VT: Tuttle, 1979.

English, Kalani. Interview with author, January 23, 1991.

Erskine, John E. *Journal of a Cruise Among the Islands of the Western Pacific.* London: Dawsons, 1967.

Evangelical Magazine (London), 1800.

Fanning, Edmund. *Voyages Round the World.* Upper Saddle River, NJ: Gregg, 1970.

Farrell, Andrew, ed. *John Cameron's Odyssey.* New York: Macmillan,1928.

Fawcett, James, and Cariño, Benjamin, eds. *Pacific Bridges: The New Immigration from Asia and the Pacific Islands.* New York: Center for Migration Studies, 1987.

Ferguson, Charles D. *Experiences of a Forty-Niner in Australia and New Zealand.* Melbourne: Renard, 1979.

Finney, Ben R. *Voyage of Rediscovery.* Berkeley: University of California Press, 1994.

――――. "Voyaging." In *The Prehistory of Polynesia,* ed. J.D. Dennings, 323–51. Cambridge, MA: Harvard University Press, 1979

Firth, Raymond. *History and Traditions of Tikopia.* Wellington, NZ: The Polynesian Society, 1961.

Foucault, Michel. *The History of Sexuality.* Vol. 1: *An Introduction,* trans. Robert Hurley. New York: Vintage, 1980.

Flynn, Dennis O., and Gonzalez, Arturo. "Born with a 'Silver Spoon': The Origin of World Trade." *Journal of World History* 6, no. 2 (Fall 1995): 175–221.

Forbes, Litton. *Two Years in Fiji.* London: Longmans, Green, 1875.

Forster, George. *A Voyage Round the World.* 2 vols. London: White, 1777.

Foster, George M. *Culture and Conquest: America's Spanish Heritage.* Viking Fund Publications in Anthropology, no. 27. New York: Wenner-Gren Foundation for Anthropological Research, 1960.

Franchère, Gabriel. *Journal of a Voyage on the North West Coast of North America during the Years 1811, 1812, 1813 & 1814.* Toronto: Champlain Society, 1969.

Freeman, J.D. "The Joe Gimlet or Siovili Cult." In *Anthropology in the South Seas,* ed. J.D. Freeman and W.R. Geddes, 185–99. New Plymouth, NZ: Avery, 1959.

Friedman, Jonathan. *Cultural Identity and Global Process.* Thousand Oaks, CA: Sage, 1994.

Friend, The (Honolulu newspaper). Various issues, 1843–1954.

Frisbie, Robert. *The Book of Puka-Puka*. Honolulu: Mutual, 1957.

Frouin, Charles. *Journal de Bord 1852–1856, Chirurgien du Baleinier "L'Espadon."* Paris: France-Empire, 1978.

Garner, Stanton, ed. *The Captain's Best Mate: The Journal of Mary Chipman Lawrence on the Whaler Addison, 1856–1860*. Providence, RI: Brown University Press, 1966.

Gibson, James R. *Imperial Russia in Frontier America: The Changing Geography of Supply of Russian America, 1784–1867*. New York: Oxford University Press, 1976.

Giles, William E. *A Cruize in a Queensland Labour Vessel to the South Seas*. Ed. Deryck Scarr. Canberra: ANU, 1968.

Gilman, G.D. "Old Time Hawaiian Coasting Service." In *Hawaiian Annual and Almanac*, ed. Thomas Thrum, 85–90. Honolulu: Thrum, 1894.

Gilson, R.P. *Samoa 1830 to 1900: The Politics of a Multi-Cultural Community*. Melbourne: Oxford University Press, 1970.

Golovnin, V.M. *Around the World in the Kamchatka, 1817–1819*. Honolulu: UH, 1979.

Goodenough, James Graham. *Journal of Commodore Goodenough, during His Last Command as Senior Officer on the Australian Station, 1873–1875*. London: King, 1876.

Gordon, Paul, and Reilly, Danny. "Guest Workers of the Sea: Racism in British Shipping." *Race and Class* 28, no. 2 (Autumn 1986): 73–82.

Greenblatt, Stephen. *Marvelous Possessions: The Wonder of the New World*. Chicago: University of Chicago Press, 1991.

Greer, Richard A. "Wandering Kamaainas: Notes on Hawaiian Emigration Before 1848." *Journal of the West* 6, no. 2 (April 1967): 221–25.

———, ed. "California Gold: Some Reports to Hawaii." *HJH* 4 (1970): 157–73.

———, ed. "The Royal Tourist: Kalakaua's Letters Home from Tokio to London." *HJH* 5 (1971): 75–109.

Gunson, Niel. "An Account of the Mamaia or Visionary Heresy of Tahiti, 1826–1841." *JPS* 71, no. 2 (June 1962), 208–43.

———. "Journal of a Visit to Raivavae in October 1819 by Pomare II, King of Tahiti." *JPH* 1 (1966): 199–203.

———. *Messengers of Grace: Evangelical Missionaries in the South Seas, 1797–1860*. Melbourne: Oxford University Press, 1978.

———. "Pomare II of Tahiti and Polynesian Imperialism." *JPH* 4 (1969): 65–82.

Hackler, Rhoda E.A. "'My Dear Friend': Letters of Queen Victoria and Queen Emma." *HJH* 22 (1988): 101–30.

Hanlon, David. *Upon a Stone Altar: A History of the Island of Pohnpei to 1890*. Honolulu: UH, 1988.

Hanlon, David, and Eperiam, Epensio. "The Saga of Mesiol." *Islander Resurrection* (Guam daily), August 20, 1978, 12–14.

Hau'ofa, Epeli. "The Future of Our Past." In *The Pacific Islands in the Year 2000*, ed. Robert Kiste and Richard Herr, 151–69. Honolulu: UH Pacific Islands Studies Program, 1985.

———. "Our Sea of Islands." *The Contemporary Pacific* 6, no. 1 (Spring 1994): 148–61.

Hautière, Ulysse de la. *Souvenirs de la Nouvelle-Calédonie*. Paris: Challamel, 1869.

Hayes, Edmund, ed. *Log of the Union: John Boit's Remarkable Voyage to the Northwest Coast and Around the World 1794–96*. Portland: Oregon Historical Society, 1981.

Hayes, Geoffrey, "Migration, Metascience and Development Policy in Island Polynesia," *The Contemporary Pacific* 3, no. 1 (1991): 1–58.

Head, Dora, ed. *The Journal of Charles O'Hara Booth, Commandant of the Port Arthur Penal Settlement*. Hobart, Australia: Tasmanian Historical Restoration Association, 1981.

Hellgren, Lars. *Tattooing: The Prevalence of Tattooed Persons in Total Populations.* Stockholm: Almqvist and Wiksell, 1967.

Helms, Mary W. *Ulysses' Sail: An Ethnographic Odyssey of Power, Knowledge, and Geographical Distance.* Princeton: Princeton University Press, 1988.

Hempenstall, Peter, and Rutherford, Noel. *Protest and Dissent in the Colonial Pacific.* Suva, Fiji: USP, 1984.

Henry, Teuira. *Ancient Tahiti.* Bishop Museum Bulletin, no. 48. Honolulu: Bishop Museum, 1928.

Heyerdahl, Thor. *American Indians in the Pacific: The Theory Behind the Kon-Tiki Expedition.* London: Allen and Unwin, 1952.

Hezel, Francis X. *The First Taint of Civilization: A History of the Caroline and Marshall Islands in Pre-Colonial Days, 1521–1885.* Honolulu: UH, 1983.

———. *Foreign Ships in Micronesia: A Compendium of Ship Contacts with the Caroline and Marshall Islands 1521–1885.* Saipan: U.S. Trust Territory Historic Preservation Office, 1979.

Hezel, Francis X., and Driver, Marjorie C. "From Conquest to Colonisation: Spain in the Mariana Islands 1690–1740." *JPH* 23, no. 2 (1988): 137–55.

Hilbert, Vi, ed. *Haboo: Native American Stories from Puget Sound.* Seattle: University of Washington Press, 1985.

Hines, Gustavus. *A Voyage Round the World: With a History of the Oregon Mission.* Buffalo: Derby, 1850.

Hoare, Michael E., ed. *The Resolution Journal of Johann Reinhold Forster, 1772–1775.* Hakluyt Society Series 2, nos. 152–55. London: Hakluyt Society, 1982.

Hocart, A.M. "Fiji and Rotuma [ca. 1913]." MS 60, file no. 4753. Alexander Turnbull Library, Wellington, NZ.

Hockin, John Pearce. *A Supplement to the Account of the Pelew Islands, Compiled from the Journals of the Panther and Endeavour, 1790.* London: W. Bulmer, 1803.

Hohman, Elmo P. *The American Whaleman: A Study of Life and Lore in the Whaling Industry.* New York: Longman's, Green, 1928.

Holt, John Dominis, ed. *The Hawaiian Journal of John B. Whitman, 1813–1815, An Account of the Sandwich Islands.* Honolulu: Top-Gallant, 1979.

Hooper, Beverley, ed. *With Captain James Cook in the Antarctic and Pacific, The Private Journal of James Burney, Second Lieutenant of the Adventure on Cook's Second Voyage, 1772–1773.* Canberra: National Library of Australia, 1975.

Hopoo, Thomas. "Memoirs of Thomas Hopoo." *HJH* 2 (1968): 42–54.

Howard, Alan. "Rotuma as a Hinterland Community." *JPS* 70, no. 3 (September 1961): 272–99.

———. "Seamanship on Rotuma." Paper presented at the annual meeting of the Association for Social Anthropology in Oceania, Victoria, B.C., Canada, March 27–30, 1991.

Howard, Alan, and Borofsky, Robert. *Developments in Polynesian Ethnology.* Honolulu: UH, 1989.

Howay, Frederic W. "Brig Owhyhee on the Columbia, 1827." *Oregon Historical Quarterly* 34, no. 3 (September 1933): 324–29.

———. "Early Relations between the Hawaiian Islands and the Northwest Coast." In *The Hawaiian Islands,* ed. Albert P. Taylor and Ralph S. Kuykendall, 11–38. Honolulu: Cook Commission, 1930.

———. "The Ship Pearl in Hawaii in 1805 and 1806." *HHS 46th Annual Report 1937* (1938): 27–38.

———, ed. *The Journal of Captain James Colnett Aboard the Argonaut from April 26, 1789 to November 3, 1791.* Toronto: Champlain Society, 1940.

————, ed. *Voyages of the "Columbia" to the Northwest Coast, 1787–1790 and 1790–1793.* Boston: Massachusetts Historical Society, 1941.

Howe, K.R. "The Fortunes of the Naisilines: Portrait of a Chieftainship." In *More Pacific Islands Portraits,* ed. Deryck Scarr, 1–17. Canberra: ANU, 1979.

————. "Tourists, Sailors and Labourers: A Survey of Early Labour Recruiting in Southern Melanesia." *JPH* 13 (1978): 22–35.

————. *Where the Waves Fall: A New South Sea Islands History from First Settlement to Colonial Rule.* Honolulu: UH, 1984.

Hrdlicka, Ales. *The Aleutian and Commander Islands and Their Inhabitants.* Philadelphia: Wistar, 1945.

Hughes, Ian. *New Guinea Stone Age Trade: The Geography and Ecology of Traffic in the Interior.* Canberra: ANU, 1977.

Hunnewell, James. "Honolulu in 1817 and 1818: Voyage in the Brig Bordeaux Packet." *HHS Papers,* no. 8 (1909).

Ihimaera, Witi. *The Whale Rider.* Auckland, NZ: Heinemann, 1987.

Ii, John Papa. *Fragments of Hawaiian History.* Ed. Dorothy B. Barrère, trans. Mary Kawena Pukui. Special Publication, no. 70. Honolulu: Bishop Museum, 1983.

Im Thurn, Everard, and Wharton, Leonard C., eds. *The Journal of William Lockerby, Sandalwood Trader in the Fijian Islands during the Years 1808–1809.* Hakluyt Society Series 2, no. 52. London: Hakluyt Society, 1925.

Inglis, John. *In the New Hebrides: Reminiscences of Missionary Life and Work.* London: T. Nelson, 1887.

"Island Style." KHON Television, Honolulu, August 18, 1991.

Jacobs, Thomas Jefferson. *Scenes, Incidents, and Adventures in the Pacific Ocean, or the Islands of the Australasian Seas, during the Cruise of the Clipper Margaret Oakley, under Capt. Benjamin Morrell.* New York: Harper, 1844.

Jameson, R.G. *New Zealand, Southern Australia and New South South Wales: A Record of Recent Travels.* London: Smith, 1842.

Jarman, Robert. *Journal of a Voyage to the South Seas in the "Japan."* London: Longman, 1838.

Jarves, James J. *History of the Hawaiian or Sandwich Islands.* Boston: Tappan and Dennet, 1843.

[Jones, John D.] *Life and Adventure in the South Pacific by a Roving Printer.* New York: Harper, 1861.

Judd, Bernice, ed. "Native Hawaiians in London, 1820." *HHS 55th Annual Report 1946* (1947): 13–17.

Ka Nona Nona (Hawaiian-language newspaper, Honolulu). Various issues, 1841–45.

Kahananui, Dorothy M., ed. *Ka Mooolelo Hawaii.* Honolulu: UH, 1984.

Kalakaua, David. *The Legends and Myths of Hawaii: The Fables and Folk-lore of a Strange People,* ed. R.M. Daggett. Rutland, VT: Tuttle, 1972.

Kamakau, Samuel M. *Ruling Chiefs of Hawaii.* Honolulu: Kamehameha Schools, 1961.

Kaplanoff, Mark D., ed. *Joseph Ingraham's Journal of the Brigantine HOPE on a Voyage to the Northwest Coast of North America, 1790–92.* Barre, MA: Imprint Society, 1971.

Kawarahada, Dennis, ed. *Voyaging Chiefs of Havai'i.* Honolulu: Kalamaku Press, 1995.

Ke Alaula (Hawaiian-language newspaper, Honolulu). Various issues, 1866–73.

Ke Au Okoa (Hawaiian-language newspaper, Honolulu). Various issues, 1856–73.

Keate, George. *An Account of the Pelew Islands, Situated in the Western Part of the Pacific Ocean. Composed from the Journals and Communications of Captain Henry Wilson, and Some of His Officers. . . .* London: G. Nicol, 1789.

Keesing, Roger. "Plantation Networks, Plantation Culture: The Hidden Side of Colonial Melanesia." *Journal de la Société des Océanistes* 42, nos. 82–83 (1986): 163–70.

Kelly, Celsus, ed. *La Australia del Espiritu Santo, The Journal of Fray Martin de Munilla and Other Documents Relating to The Voyage of Pedro Fernandez de Quiros to the South Sea (1605–1606).* Hakluyt Society Series 2, nos. 126–27. London: Hakluyt Society, 1966.

Kenn, Charles. "A Visit to the California Gold Fields by Rev. Lowell Smith, 1858–59." *HHS 74th Annual Report 1965* (1966): 7–16.

Kikuchi, William Pila. "A Legend of Kaimiloa Hawaiians in American Samoa." In *Hawaiian Historical Review: Selected Readings,* ed. Richard A. Greer, 268–69. Honolulu: HHS, 1969.

Kindleberger, Charles P. *Mariners and Markets.* New York: New York University Press, 1992.

King, Pauline, ed. *Robert Dampier: To the Sandwich Islands on H.M.S. Blonde.* Honolulu: UH, 1971.

Kirch, Patrick Vinton. *The Evolution of the Polynesian Kingdoms.* Cambridge: Cambridge University Press, 1989.

Kittelson, David. "John Coxe: Hawaii's First Soldier of Fortune." In *Hawaiian Historical Review: Selected Readings,* ed. Richard A. Greer, 213–18. Honolulu: HHS, 1969.

Korn, Alfons L. *The Victorian Visitors.* Honolulu: UH, 1938.

Kornitzer, Louis. *The Pearl Trader.* New York: Sheridan House, 1937

Kotzebue, Otto von. *A New Voyage Around the World in the Years 1823, 24, 25, and 26.* 2 vols. London: Colburn and Bentley, 1830. Reprint, New York: DaCapo, 1967.

———. *A Voyage of Discovery into the South Sea and Beering's Straits, for the Purpose of Exploring a North-East Passage, Undertaken in the Years 1815–1818.* 3 vols. London: Longman, 1821. Reprint, New York: Da Capo, 1967.

Kuykendall, Ralph S. "An Hawaiian in Mexico in 1789–1790." *HHS 32nd Annual Report 1923* (1924): 37–49.

———. *The Hawaiian Kingdom.* 3 vols. Honolulu: UH, 1938–67.

———. "The Schooner Missionary Packet." *HHS 43rd Annual Report 1933* (1934): 81–90.

———. "Some Early Commercial Adventurers of Hawaii." *HHS 37th Annual Report 1928* (1929): 15–33.

Laferrière, Julien. *Voyages aux Isles Tonga Tabou, Wallis et Foutouna, à la Nouvelle-Calédonie et à la Nouvelle-Zélande, Révue Coloniale.* Vol. 3, section 2, no. 19. Paris: Annales Maritimes et Coloniales, Tome 92, 1845.

Lal, Brij; Munro, Doug; and Beechert, Edward, eds. *Plantation Workers: Resistance and Accommodation.* Honolulu: UH,1993.

Lamb, W. Kaye, ed. *A Voyage of Discovery to the North Pacific Ocean and Round the World, 1791–1795.* Hakluyt Society Series 2, nos. 163–66. London: Hakluyt Society, 1984.

Langsdorff, G.H. von. *Voyages and Travels in Various Parts of the World during the Years 1803–1807.* 2 vols. Ridgewood, NJ: Gregg, 1968.

La Pérouse, J.F.G. de. *A Voyage Round the World, 1785–88.* London: Hamilton, 1799.

Latukefu, Sione. "The Impact of South Sea Islands Missionaries on Melanesia." In *Mission, Church, and Sect in Oceania,* eds. James A. Boutilier, Daniel T. Hughes, and Sharon W. Tiffany, 91–108. ASAO Monograph, no. 6. New York: University Press of America, 1978.

Le Gobien, Charles. *Histoire des Isles Marianes.* Paris: Pepie, 1700.

Lessa, William A. *Ulithi: A Micronesian Design for Living.* New York: Holt, Rinehart and Winston, 1966.

Levathes, Louise. *When China Ruled the Seas.* New York: Simon and Schuster, 1994.
Liliuokalani. *Hawaii's Story By Hawaii's Queen.* Rutland, VT: Tuttle, 1964.
Logs of Nineteenth-Century U.S. Whaling and Trading Vessels:
  Arabella, Sag Harbor, James Pierson, 1830–34.
  Avola, Sharon, Zenas A. Bourne, 1870–77.
  California, New Bedford, Charles H. Adams, 1849–51.
  Charles W. Morgan, New Bedford, Thomas C. Landers, 1863–67.
  Chili, New Bedford, Journal Albert F. Peck, 1856–63.
  Cortes, New Bedford, John W. Hammond, 1842–46.
  Elizabeth, New Bedford, Journal Thomas Bryant, 1847–51.
  Elizabeth Swift, New Bedford, Reuben Pontius, 1863–67.
  Emerald, Salem, John H. Eagleston, 1833–36.
  Josephine, Sag Harbor, Reminiscences, H.H. Frary, 1846–49.
  Miantonomi, New Bedford, William W. Clement, 1853–54.
  Ocean, New Bedford, William C. Fuller, 1853–56.
  Peru, Salem, John H. Eagleston, 1830–33.
  Petrel, New Bedford, Edwin J. Reed, 1871–74.
  Roman II, New Bedford, Pardon Tripp, 1850–52.
  Sea Shell, Warren, Log George Wheldon, 1853–56.
  Sharon, Fairhaven, Howes S. Norris and Thomas Smith, 1841–45.
  Triton, New Bedford, Roland Packard, 1860–65.
  Two Brothers, New Bedford, Joshua B. Davis, 1858–63.
Low, Sam. "The Navigators: Pathfinders of the Pacific." Hawaii Public Television, 1983.
Lucatt, Edward. *Rovings in the Pacific, from 1837 to 1849.* 2 vols. London: Longman, Brown, Green and Longmans, 1851.
Luomala, Katharine. "A Gilbertese Tradition of a Religious Massacre." *HHS 62nd Annual Report 1953* (1954): 19–25.
Lutke, Frederic. *Voyage Autour du Monde, 1826–1829.* 3 vols. Paris: Didot, 1835. Reprint, New York: Da Capo, 1970.
McCall, Grant. *Rapanui: Tradition and Survival on Easter Island.* Honolulu: UH, 1981.
McCall, Grant, and Connell, John, eds. *A World Perspective on Pacific Islander Migration: Australia, New Zealand and the U.S.A.* Kensington, Australia: University of New South Wales, 1993.
McCluer, John. Journal of a Voyage to the Pelew Islands in the H.C. Snow Panther, 1790–92. Manuscript section, British Museum, London.
McCormick, E.H. *Omai: Pacific Envoy.* Auckland, NZ: Auckland University Press, 1977.
MacDonald, Barrie. *Cinderellas of the Empire: Towards a History of Kiribati and Tuvalu.* Canberra: ANU, 1982.
McFeat, Thomas, ed. *Indians of the North Pacific Coast.* Seattle: University of Washington, 1966.
MacGregor, Gordon. "Field Notes, Legends, Songs, History, and Notes on Physical Anthropology from Rotuma [ca. 1932]." Manuscript section, Bishop Museum, Honolulu.
McKnight, Robert. "Commas in Microcosm: The Movement of Southwest Islanders to Palau, Micronesia." In *Exiles and Migrants in Oceania,* ed. Michael Lieber, 10–33. Honolulu: UH, 1977.
McNab, Robert, ed. *Historical Records of New Zealand.* 2 vols. Wellington, NZ: McKay, 1908 and 1914.
Malo, David. *Hawaiian Antiquities.* Special Publication, no. 2. Honolulu: Bishop Museum, 1951.
Markham, Clements R., ed. *Early Spanish Voyages to the Strait of Magellan.* Hakluyt Society Series 2, no. 28. London: Hakluyt Society, 1911.

————, ed. *History of the Incas by Pedro Sarmiento de Gamboa and The Execution of the Inca Tupac Amaru by Captain Baltasar de Ocampo.* Hakluyt Society Series 2, no. 22. London: Hakluyt Society, 1907.

————, ed. *Reports on the Discovery of Peru.* Hakluyt Society Series 1, no. 47. London: Hakluyt Society, 1872.

————, ed. *The Voyages of Pedro Fernandez de Quiros, 1595–1606.* Hakluyt Society Series 2, nos. 14–15. London: Hakluyt Society, 1904.

Marra, John. *Journal of the Resolution's Voyage in 1771–75.* Reprint, New York: Da Capo, 1967.

Marseu, Fesaitu. "The Rotuman Mamasa Ceremony." In *Pacific Rituals: Living or Dying?* ed. Gweneth and Bruce Deverell, 3–22. Suva, Fiji: USP, 1986.

Martin, Henry Byam. *The Polynesian Journal of Captain Henry Byam Martin, R.N., In Command of the H.M.S. Grampus-50 Guns at Hawaii and on Station in Tahiti and the Society Islands, August 1846 to August 1847.* Salem, MA: Peabody Museum, 1981.

Martin, John. *Tonga Islands: William Mariner's Account.* Tonga: Vava'u Press, 1981.

Masefield, John. *Sea Life in Nelson's Time.* New York: Macmillan, 1925.

Maude, H.E. *Of Islands and Men: Studies in Pacific History.* Melbourne: Melbourne University Press, 1968.

————. "The Raiatean Chief Auna and the Conversion of Hawaii." *JPH* 8 (1973): 188–91.

————. *Slavers in Paradise: The Peruvian Labour Trade in Polynesia.* Canberra: ANU, 1981.

Maynard, Felix, and Dumas, Alexandre, eds. *The Whalers.* New York: Hillman-Curl, 1937.

Meares, John. *Voyages Made in the Years 1788 and 1789, from China to the North West Coast of America.* London: Walter, 1790.

Melville, Herman. *Moby Dick.* New York: Bantam, 1981.

————. *Omoo: A Narrative of Adventures in the South Seas.* Vol. 2. Evanston, IL: Northwestern University Press, 1968.

————. *Typee: A Peep at Polynesian Life.* New York: Penguin, 1983.

Miller, David G. "Ka'iana, the Once Famous 'Prince of Kaua'i'." *HJH* 22 (1988): 1–19.

Milne, Namar. Interviews by author with assistance from translators Lenn Lenja and Carol Curtis, as well as from Reverend Kaniki of the Alele Museum. Majuro, Marshall Islands, July 11 and 21, 1989.

Minto, John. "From Youth to Age as an American." *Oregon Historical Quarterly* 9, no. 2 (June 1908): 127–72.

Moore, Anneliese. "Harry Maitey: From Polynesia to Prussia." *HJH* 11 (1977): 125–61.

Moore, Clive. *Kanaka: A History of Melanesian Mackay.* Port Moresby: University of Papua New Guinea Press, 1985.

Moresby, John. *Discoveries and Surveys in New Guinea and the D'Entrecasteaux Islands.* London: John Murray, 1876.

Morison, Samuel Eliot. "Boston Traders in the Hawaiian Islands, 1789–1823." In *Proceedings of the Massachusetts Historical Society.* Vol. 54. Boston: Massachusetts Historical Society, 1920.

————. *The Maritime History of Massachusetts, 1783–1860.* Boston: Houghton Mifflin, 1921.

Morrell, Benjamin. *A Narrative of Four Voyages to the South Sea, North and South Pacific Ocean. . . .* New York: Harper, 1832. Reprint, Upper Saddle River, NJ: Gregg, 1970.

Morris, Nancy J. "Hawaiian Missionaries Abroad, 1852–1909." Ph.D. dissertation, University of Hawai'i, 1987.

————. "Hawaiian Missionaries in the Marquesas." *HJH* 13 (1979): 46–58.

Mortimer, George. *Observations and Remarks Made during a Voyage to the Islands of Teneriffe, Amsterdam, Maria's Islands Near Van Diemen's Land, Otaheite, Sandwich Islands; Owhyhee, the Fox Islands on the North West Coast of America, Tinian, and from Thence to Canton, in the Brig Mercury, Commanded by John Henry Fox, Esquire.* London: T. Cadell, 1791. Reprint, New York: Da Capo, 1975.

Morton, Harry. *The Whale's Wake.* Honolulu: UH, 1982.

Moyle, Richard M., ed. *The Samoan Journals of John Williams, 1830 and 1832.* Canberra: ANU, 1984.

Muir, Andrew Forest. "William Hoapili Kaauwai: A Hawaiian in Holy Orders." *HHS 61st Annual Report 1952,* (1953): 5–13.

Mullett, J.C. *A Five Years' Whaling Voyage, 1848–1853.* Fairfield, WA: Galleon, 1977.

Munford, James Kenneth, ed. *John Ledyard's Journal of Captain Cook's Last Voyage.* Corvallis, OR: Oregon State University Press, 1963.

Munger, James F. *Two Years in the Pacific and Arctic Oceans and China.* Vernon, Canada: Howlett, 1852.

Murra, John Victor. *The Economic Organization of the Inka State.* Greenwich, CT: JAI Press, 1980.

Naughton, E. Momilani. "Hawaiians in the Fur Trade: Cultural Influence on the Northwest Coast, 1811–1875." M.A. thesis, Western Washington University, 1983.

Needham, Joseph. *Science and Civilisation in China.* Vol. 4, part 3. Cambridge: Cambridge University Press, 1971.

Nicholas, John L. *Narrative of a Voyage to New Zealand, Performed in the Years 1814 and 1815, in Company with the Rev. Samuel Marsden.* 2 vols. Auckland, NZ: Wilson and Horton, 1971.

Nilsen, Aileen. "The Mamasa Ceremony." In *Rotuma: Split Island,* ed. Chris Plant, 79–86. Suva, Fiji: USP, 1977.

Niro, Karen. "Linkages between Yap and Palau: Towards Regional Histories." Paper presented at the Pacific History Association Conference, University of Guam, 1990.

Nunn, Patrick. "Facts, Fallacies and the Future of the Island Pacific." In *A New Oceania: Rediscovering Our Sea of Islands,* ed. Eric Waddell, Vijay Naidu, and Epeli Hau'ofa, 112–15.

Obeyesekere, Gananath. *The Apotheosis of Captain Cook.* Princeton: Princeton University Press, 1992.

Oliver, Douglas. *Oceania.* 2 vols. Honolulu: UH Press, 1989.

————, ed. *Return to Tahiti: Bligh's Second Breadfruit Voyage.* Honolulu: UH, 1988.

Olmstead, Francis. *Incidents on a Whaling Voyage.* London: Neale, 1844.

Page, Harlan. *A Memoir of Thomas H. Patoo of the Marquesan Islands.* Andover, MA: American Tract Society, 1825.

Paige, Paula Spurlin, ed. *The Voyage of Magellan: The Journal of Antonio Pigafetta.* Englewood Cliffs, NJ: Prentice-Hall, 1969.

Paniani, George. Interview by author. Rarotonga, July 21, 1993.

Parkinson, Stanfield, ed. *A Journal of a Voyage to the South Seas in His Majesty's Ship, Endeavor. Faithfully Transcribed from the Papers of the Late Sydney Parkinson, Draughtsman to Joseph Banks.* Richardson and Urguhart, 1773. London: Facsimile, Libraries Board of South Australia, Adelaide, 1972.

Peacock, Daniel J. *Lee Boo of Belau: A Prince in London.* Honolulu: UH, 1987.

Pearson, Bill. *Rifled Sanctuaries: Some Views of the Pacific Islands in Western Literature.* Auckland, NZ: Auckland University Press, 1984.

Pearson, W.H. "European Intimidation and the Myth of Tahiti." *JPH* 4 (1969): 199–217.

Pei Te Hurinui. *King Potatau: An Account of the Life of Potatau Te Wherowhero, the First Maori King.* Wellington, NZ: The Polynesian Society, 1959.

Péron, François. *Mémoires du Capitaine Péron sur les Voyages aux Côtes d'Afrique, en Arabie, à L'Ile d'Amsterdam, aux Iles d'Anjouan et de Mayotte, aux Côtes Nord– Ouest de L'Amérique, aux Iles Sandwich, à la Chine, etc.* 2 vols. Paris: BrissotThivars, 1824. Reprint, New York: Da Capo, 1971.

Plummer, Katherine. *The Shogun's Reluctant Ambassadors: Sea Drifters.* Tokyo: Lotus, 1985.

Polack, J.S. *Manners and Customs of the New Zealanders.* Vol. 2. London: Hatchard, 1840.

Polynesian, The (Honolulu newspaper). Various issues, 1840–64.

Pomponio, Alice. *Seagulls Don't Fly into the Bush.* Belmont, CA: Wadsworth, 1992.

Portlock, Nathaniel. *A Voyage Round the World; but More Particularly to the North-West Coast of America: Performed in 1785, 1786, 1787, and 1788.* London: Stockdale, 1789.

Poyer, Lin. "The Ngatik Massacre: Documentary and Oral Traditional Accounts." *JPH* 20, no. 1 (1985): 4–22.

Pritchard, W.T. *Polynesian Reminiscences, or Life in the South Pacific Islands.* London, 1866. Reprint, London: Dawsons, 968.

Pukui, Mary Kawena, and Elbert, Samuel H. *Hawaiian Dictionary.* Honolulu: UH, 1986.

Pukui, Mary Kawena, and Korn, Alfons L., eds. *The Echo of Our Song: Chants and Poems of the Hawaiians.* Honolulu: UH, 1973.

Pule, John Puhiatau. *The Shark That Ate the Sun.* New York: Penguin Books, 1992.

Quigg, Agnes. "Kalakaua's Hawaiian Studies Abroad Program." *HJH* 22 (1988): 170–208.

Ralston, Caroline. "Changes in the Lives of Ordinary Women in Early Post-Contact Hawaii." In *Family and Gender in the Pacific,* eds. Margaret Jolly and Martha Macintyre, 45–64. Cambridge: Cambridge University Press, 1989.

———. *Grass Huts and Warehouses: Pacific Beach Communities of the Nineteenth Century.* Honolulu: UH, 1978

———. "Hawaii, 1778–1854: Some Aspects of Maka'ainana Response to Rapid Cultural Change." *JPH* 19, no. 1 (January 1984): 21–40.

Randier, Jean. *Men and Ships around Cape Horn, 1616–1939.* London: Barker, 1968.

Ravuvu, Asesela. *Facade of Democracy.* Suva, Fiji: Reader, 1991.

Rediker, Marcus. *Between the Devil and the Deep Blue Sea: Merchant Seamen, Pirates, and the Anglo-American Maritime World, 1700–1750.* New York: Cambridge University Press, 1987.

Reynolds, Henry. *The Other Side of the Frontier: Aboriginal Resistance to the European Invasion of Australia.* New York: Penguin, 1982.

Reynolds, Stephen. *The Voyage of the New Hazard to the Northwest Coast, Hawaii and China, 1810–1813,* ed. F.W. Howay. Salem, MA: Peabody Museum, 1938.

Rich, Edwin E. *History of the Hudson's Bay Company, 1670–1870.* London: Hudson's Bay Record Society, 1959.

———, ed. *Simpson's 1828 Journey to the Columbia.* Vol. 10. Toronto: Champlain Society for Hudson's Bay Record Society, 1947.

Richards, Rhys. "Indigenous Beachcombers: The Case of Tapeooe, a Tahitian Traveller from 1798 to 1812." *The Great Circle* 12, no. 1 (1990): 1–14.

———. "The Manilla-Men and Pacific Commerce." *Solidarity* 95 (1983): 44–57.

———. *Whaling and Sealing at the Chatham Islands.* Roebuck Society Publication, no. 21. Canberra: Roebuck Society, 1982.

Rickman, John. *Journal of Captain Cook's Last Voyage to the Pacific Ocean.* London: E. Newbery, 1781. Reprint, New York: Da Capo, 1967.

Riesenberg, Saul H., ed. *A Residence of Eleven Years in New Holland and the Caroline Islands by James F. O'Connell.* Honolulu: UH, 1972.

Robertson, Una. *Mariners' Mealtimes and Other Daily Details of Life on Board a Sailing Warship.* Dundee, Scotland: Unicorn Preservation Society, 1979.

Robson, R.W. *Queen Emma: The Samoan-American Girl Who Founded an Empire in 19th Century New Guinea.* Sydney: Pacific, 1973.

Rodger, N.A.M. *The Wooden World: An Anatomy of the Georgian Navy.* London: Collins, 1986.

Roe, Michael, ed. *The Journal and Letters of Captain Charles Bishop on the North-West Coast of America, in the Pacific and in New South Wales 1794–1799.* Hakluyt Society Series 2, no. 131. Cambridge: Hakluyt Society, 1967.

Rogers, Robert F. *Destiny's Landfall: A History of Guam.* Honolulu: UH, 1995.

Rosenman, Helen, ed. *An Account in Two Volumes of Two Voyages to the South Seas by Captain Jules Sebastian-Cesar Dumont d'Urville.* Honolulu: UH, 1987.

Ross, Alexander. *Adventures of the First Settlers on the Oregon or Columbia River.* Ann Arbor: University Microfilms, 1966.

———. *The Fur Hunters of the Far West.* Ed. Kenneth A. Spaulding. Norman, OK: University of Oklahoma Press, 1956.

Rousseau, Jean-Jacques. *The First and Second Discourses.* Ed. Victor Gourevitch. New York: Perennial, 1986.

Routledge, David. *Matanitu: The Struggle for Power in Early Fiji.* Suva, Fiji: USP, 1985.

Russo, Christopher. "Outmigration by Pitcairn Islanders." Seminar paper, History 675E, University of Hawai'i, 1993.

Rutherford, Noel. "George Tupou I and Shirley Baker." In *Friendly Islands: A History of Tonga,* ed. Noel Rutherford, 154–72. New York: Oxford University Press, 1977.

Rutter, Owen. *The Journal of James Morrison, Boatswain's Mate of the Bounty, Describing the Mutiny and Subsequent Misfortunes of the Mutineers Together with an Account of the Island of Tahiti.* London: Golden Cockerel Press, 1935.

Sahlins, Marshall. *Anahulu.* Vol. 2. Chicago: University of Chicago Press,1992.

———. *Historical Metaphors and Mythical Realities: Structure in the Early Sandwich Islands Kingdom.* Ann Arbor: University of Michigan Press, 1981.

———. *How Natives Think.* Chicago: Univiversity of Chicago Press, 1995.

Said, Edward. *Orientalism.* New York: Vintage, 1979.

Salmond, Anne. *Two Worlds: First Meetings between Maori and Europeans, 1642– 1772.* Honolulu: UH, 1991.

Sassen, Saskia. *The Mobility of Labor and Capital: A Study in International Investment and Labor Flow.* New York: Cambridge University Press, 1990.

Sauer, Carl O. *The Early Spanish Main.* Berkeley: University of California Press, 1966.

Savage, John. *Some Account of New Zealand.* Reprint, Christchurch, NZ: Capper Press, 1973.

Schmitt, Frederick P. *Mark Well the Whale! Long Island Ships to Distant Seas.* Port Washington, New York: Kennikat Press, 1971

Schmitt, Robert C. *Demographic Statistics of Hawaii, 1778–1965.* Honolulu: UH, 1968.

Schurz, William. *The Manila Galleon.* New York: Dutton, 1939.

Schweizer, Niklaus R., ed. *By Royal Command: The Official Life and Personal Reminiscences of Colonel Curtis Pi'ehu Iaukea at the Court of Hawaii's Rulers.* Honolulu: Hui Hanai, 1988.

Scott, James. *Remarks on a Passage to Botany Bay, 1787–1792, A First Fleet Journal.* Sydney: Angus and Robertson, 1963.

Sharp, Andrew. *Adventurous Armada: The Story of Legazpi's Expedition.* Christchurch, NZ: Whitcombe and Tombs, 1960.

Shineberg, Dorothy. *They Came for Sandalwood: A Study of Sandalwood Trade in the South West Pacific, 1830–1865.* Melbourne: University of Melbourne Press, 1967.

———, ed. *The Trading Voyages of Andrew Cheyne, 1841–1844.* Honolulu: UH, 1971.

Simpson, George. *An Overland Journey Round the World, during the Years 1841 and 1842.* Philadelphia: Lea and Blanchard, 1847.

Smith, Alan. *Creating a World Economy: Merchant Capital, Colonialism and World Trade, 1400–1825.* Boulder: Westview Press, 1991.

Smith, Bernard. *European Vision and the South Pacific, 1768–1850.* Oxford: Oxford University Press, 1960.

Smith, James, ed. *Archibald Campbell: A Voyage Around the World from 1806 to 1812.* Honolulu: UH, 1967.

Smith, S. Percy. *Maori Wars of the Nineteenth Century.* Reprint, Christchurch, NZ: Capper, 1984.

Smithies, Michael. "A New Guinean and the Royal Society, 1816–1817." *Hemisphere* 4 (1983): 365–71.

Snow, Elliot, ed. *The Sea, the Ship and the Sailor.* Salem, MA: Marine Resource Society, 1925.

Sorrenson, M.P.K. "Maori and Pakeha." In *The Oxford History of New Zealand,* ed. W.H. Oliver and B.R. Williams, 168–93. Wellington, NZ: Oxford University Press, 1981.

———. "The Maori King Movement, 1858–1885." In *Studies of a Small Democracy: Essays in Honour of Willis Airey,* ed. Robert Chapman and Keith Sinclair, 33–55. Auckland, NZ: Blackwood and Janet Paul, 1963.

Spate, O.H.K. *Monopolists and Freebooters.* Canberra: ANU, 1983.

———. *Paradise Found and Lost.* Minneapolis: University of Minnesota, 1988.

———. *The Spanish Lake.* Canberra: ANU, 1979.

Spoehr, Alexander. "Fur Traders in Hawai'i: The Hudson's Bay Company in Hawai'i, 1829–1861." *HJH* 20 (1986): 27–66.

Spoehr, Ann Harding. "George Prince Tamoree: Heir Apparent of Kauai and Niihau." *HJH* 25 (1981): 31–49.

Stackpole, Edouard A. *The Sea-Hunters: The New England Whalemen during Two Centuries, 1635–1835.* New York: J.B. Lippincott, 1953.

———. *Whales and Destiny: The Rivalry Between America, France, and Britain for Control of the Southern Whale Fishery, 1785–1825.* Amherst: University of Massachusetts, 1972.

Stannard, David E. *Before the Horror: The Population of Hawai'i on the Eve of Western Contact.* Honolulu: UH, 1989.

Stauder, Catherine. "George, Prince of Hawaii." *HJH* 6 (1972): 28–44.

Stevens, Henry N., ed. *New Light on the Discovery of Australia, as Revealed by the Journal of Captain Don Diego de Prado y Tovar.* Trans. George F. Barwick. Hakluyt Society Series 2, no. 64. London: Hakluyt Society, 1930.

Stewart, C.S. *Journal of a Residence in the Sandwich Islands during the Years 1823, 1824, and 1825.* Honolulu: UH, 1970

———. *A Visit to the South Seas in the U.S. Ship Vincennes, During the Years 1829 and 1830.* New York: Praeger, 1970.

Straubel, C.R., ed. *The Whaling Journal of Captain W.B. Rhodes, Barque Australian of Sydney, 1836–1838.* Christchurch, NZ: Whitcombe and Tombs, 1954.

Tagart, Edward, ed. *A Memoir of the Late Captain Peter Heywood.* London: E. Wilson, 1832.

Taitano, Carlos. Letter to author about his grandfather José, August 1, 1990.

Talu, Sister Alaima. "Towards Quality in Education." In *Atoll Politics: The Republic of Kiribati,* ed. Howard van Trease, 237–49. Suva, Fiji: USP, 1993.

Teaiwa, Teresia. Interview by author. Honolulu, April 7, 1991.

"Temoteitei: Biography." Evangelical Magazine, January 1800, 3–14.

Tetens, Alfred. *Among the Savages of the South Seas, Memoirs of Micronesia, 1862–1868.* Trans. Florence M. Spoehr. Stanford: Stanford University Press, 1958.

Thiéry, Maurice. *Bougainville: Soldier and Sailor.* London: Grayson, 1932.

Thomas, Mifflin. *Schooner from Windward: Two Centuries of Hawaiian Interisland Shipping.* Honolulu: UH, 1983.

Thomas, Nicholas. *Colonialism's Culture: Anthropology, Travel and Government.* Princeton: Princeton University Press, 1994.

———. *Entangled Objects: Exchange, Material Culture and Colonialism in the Pacific.* Cambridge, MA: Harvard University Press, 1991.

———. " 'Le Roi de Tahuata': Iotete and the Transformation of South Marquesan Politics, 1826–1842." *JPH* 21, no. 1 (1986): 3–20.

———. "Partial Texts: Representation, Colonialism and Agency in Pacific History." *JPH* 25, no. 2 (1990): 139–75.

Thomson, Arthur S. *The Story of New Zealand.* New York: Praeger, 1970.

Thrum. Thomas G. "Hawaiian Maritime History: A Brief Sketch of Noted Vessels and Commanders in the Development of the Coasting Service of the Hawaiian Islands." In *Hawaiian Annual and Almanac for 1890,* ed. Thomas Thrum, 66–79. Honolulu: Thrum, 1889.

Tikmenev, P.A. *A History of the Russian-American Company.* Trans. and ed. Richard A. Pierce and Alton S. Donnelly. Seattle: University of Washington Press, 1978.

Tinker, Hugh. *A New System of Slavery: The Export of Indian Labour Overseas, 1830–1920.* New York: Oxford University Press, 1974.

"Today's Japan." Hawai'i Public Television, August 31, 1992.

Turnbull, John. *A Voyage Round the World, in the Years 1800, 1801, 1802, 1803, and 1804 . . . .* 3 vols. London: Phillips, 1805.

Turner, George. *Nineteen Years in Polynesia: Missionary Life, Travels, and Researches in the Islands of the Pacific.* London: John Snow, 1861. Reprint, Papakura, NZ: McMillan, 1984.

Turner, Victor. *The Forest of Symbols: Aspects of Ndembe Ritual.* Ithaca: Cornell University Press, 1967.

Varigny, Charles de. *Fourteen Years in the Sandwich Islands 1855–1868.* Trans. Alfons L. Korn. Honolulu: UH, 1981.

Waddell, Eric; Naidu, Vijay; and Hau'ofa, Epeli, eds. *A New Oceania: Rediscovering Our Sea of Islands.* Suva, Fiji: University of the South Pacific, 1993.

Wakefield, Edward Jerningham. *Adventure in New Zealand, from 1839 to 1844.* 2 vols. Reprint, New York: Da Capo, 1971.

Wallerstein, Immanuel. *The Modern World-System I: Capitalist Agriculture and the Origins of the European World-Economy in the Sixteenth Century.* New York: Academic Press, 1974.

Wallis, Helen, ed. *Carteret's Voyage Round the World, 1766–1769.* Hakluyt Society Series 2, no. 124. Cambridge: Hakluyt Society, 1965.

Wallis, Mary. *Life in Feejee, or Five Years Among the Cannibals by a Lady.* Suva, Fiji: Fiji Museum, 1983.

Walker, Ranginui. *Ka Whawhai Tonu Matou: Struggle Without End.* Auckland, NZ: Penguin Books, 1990.

Ward, R. Gerard, "The Pacific Bêche-de-Mer Trade with Special Reference to Fiji." In

Man in the Pacific Islands: Essays on Geographical Change in the Pacific Islands, ed. R. Gerard Ward, 91–123. Oxford: Clarendon Press, 1972.

———, ed. *American Activities in the Central Pacific, 1790–1870.* 8 vols. Ridgewood, NJ: Gregg Press, 1966.

Webster, John. *The Last Cruise of "the Wanderer."* Sydney: Cunninghame, 1863.

Weibust, Knut. *Deep Sea Sailors: A Study in Maritime Ethnology.* Stockholm: Norstedt and Soner, 1969.

White, Richard. *The Middle Ground: Indians, Empires, and Republics in the Great Lakes Region, 1650–1815.* New York: Cambirdge University Press, 1991.

Wilkes, Charles. *Narrative of the United States Exploring Expedition, 1838–1842.* 5 vols. Philadelphia: Lea and Blanchard, 1845. Reprint, Upper Saddle River, NJ: Gregg Press, 1970.

Williams, Harold, ed. *One Whaling Family.* Boston: Houghton-Mifflin, 1964.

Williams, John. *Missionary Enterprises in the South-Sea Islands.* Philadelphia: Presbyterian Board, 1907.

Wilson, James. *A Missionary Voyage to the Southern Pacific Ocean, 1796–98.* New York: Praeger, 1968.

Wilson, William F., ed. *With Lord Byron at the Sandwich Islands in 1825, Being Extracts from the MS Diary of James Macrae, Scottish Botanist.* Pamphlet. Honolulu, 1922.

Wilson, William H. Journal, *Cavalier,* Stonington, CT, 1848–1850. MR 110, Blunt White Library, Mystic, CT.

Wolf, Eric. *Europe and the People Without History.* Berkeley: University of California Press, 1982.

Wood, C.F. *A Yachting Cruise in the South Seas.* London: Henry King, 1875.

Yarwood, A.T. *Samuel Marsden: The Great Survivor.* Melbourne: Melbourne University Press, 1977.

Young, Frederick G., ed. *The Correspondence and Journals of Captain Nathaniel J. Wyeth, 1831–36.* New York: Arno Press, 1973.

Young, Robert. *The Southern World: Journal of a Deputation from the Wesleyan Conference to New Zealand and Polynesia.* London: John Mason, 1858.

Zimmermann, Henry. *Voyage Around the World with Captain Cook, 1776–1780.* Trans. U. Tewsley. Wellington, NZ: Alexander Turnbull Library, 1926.

~ *Index* ~

⌁ *About the Author* ⌁

David A. Chappell received his Ph.D. in Pacific history from the University of Hawaiʻi, where he teaches Pacific and world history. He has lived in and around the Pacific for twenty years, worked on ships, and written for local magazines and newspapers as well as scholarly journals.